GLOBAL WARRIOR

GLOBAL WARRIOR

AVERTING WWIII

ILLUSTRATED

H. JOHN POOLE
FOREWORD BY
GEN. ANTHONY C. ZINNI USMC (RET.)

POSTERITY
PRESS

Published by Posterity Press
P.O. Box 5360, Emerald Isle, NC 28594
(www.posteritypress.org)

Cataloging-in-Publication Data
Poole, H. John, 1943-
Global Warrior.
    Includes bibliography and index.
    1. Infantry drill and tactics.
    2. Military art and science.
    3. Military history.
I. Title.   ISBN: 978-0-9818659-3-5   2011   355'.42
Library of Congress Control Number: 2011927404

Cover art © 2011 by Stefan Verstappen
Edited by Dr. Mary Beth Poole
Proofread by William E. Harris

First printing, United States of America, July 2011

To all U.S. military leaders who feel personally responsible for their combat losses.

One Global Competitor's Version of Progress

Contents

Illustrations

Figures

Chapter 21: *Policeman Tactics*

Tables

Foreword

Over the last two decades, since the collapse of the Soviet Union, we have struggled to cope with a rapidly changing world that has produced a series of strange new threats. These threats have defied the ability of our superb conventional military forces to effectively deal with them. The chronic nature of these threats has led many national security strategists to believe that we are in an era of persisting conflict. Although these threats may not be existential in their challenges, they do present a debilitating series of blows that collectively can diminish our power, prestige, and resources,

The "New World Order" optimistically foreseen by our leaders in the early 90's has turned into a confusing state of disorder. We have not been able to craft a set of strategies and policies to deal with the dynamics of this changed world order. No-state entities have challenged the supremacy of sovereign states; globalization has shrunk the planet; information technology and social media have altered the way we interact; and vast migrations have challenged group identities. Add to these factors global urbanization, environmental degradation, economic crises, and many other elements of change and you have a very different, restless world. This has been the breeding ground for terrorists, insurgents, and criminal organizations that thrive in this set of conditions. We have thrown our conventional power at these threats with unsatisfactory results.

Only a few strategic thinkers have examined these growing challenges with fresh, new thinking. John Poole is one of them. His series of works have provided innovative and intelligent approaches to this problem. *GLOBAL WARRIOR* is the latest book to offer a new and insightful way to take on the threats. In an era of economic constraints, he proposes emphasis on highly trained and expertly led forces that are not just a composition of a few elite units, but an expanded capability that takes advantage of the hallmark of the U.S. military—superb small-unit leadership. This approach would be a revolution in tactical thinking and is an example of Poole's creative emphasis on a "bottom up" approach to meeting the current challenges to our security.

We have too few innovative and creative thinkers taking on the complex threats we face. John Poole is clearly one of the few. We need to pay greater attention to his concepts so articulately offered in this book and his other works.

GEN. ANTHONY C. ZINNI USMC (RET.)
FORMER HEAD OF CENTCOM

Preface

The World's Best Hope

More of the earth seems in "flux" than at any other time in its recent history. While a belated rush toward democratic reform may be the reason, no one knows for sue. Some of the planet's most nefarious elements have regularly expanded their empires through lofty promises. With December 2012 so quickly approaching, Americans want answers. While few believe the Mayan calendar will end with a massive cataclysm, most still expect an increase to the turmoil. Why would the next global conflict have to start with a nuclear exchange? Both previous world wars (WWI and WWII) were initiated by conventional attacks, but the third need not be. If the United States (U.S.) security establishment learned anything from Iraq, it is that wars can now be waged in non-martial arenas. In fact, the initial stages of WWIII may already be in progress. As negative as this idea may sound, it carries with it great assurance. For, with the right kind of U.S. involvement, any further escalation can be averted.

This research has been primarily done to assist America with her sacred quest for worldwide freedom. With as many lives as have been already invested, she can't stop now. It is also for any U.S. officers (whether commissioned or noncommissioned) who have yet to discover the value to their mission of Posterity Press books and training. Many honestly believe U.S. intelligence gathering and squad tactics to be so refined as to need no supplement. But, what if there were a worldwide takeover attempt in progress that was so subtle as to be barely noticeable? Would those perpetual optimists still be as comfortable? Or would they—as loyal and dedicated Americans—be looking for new ways to handle a nontraditional threat? As with 4th-Generation Warfare (4GW), this takeover might be mostly manifested in political, economic, and psychological arenas. Its details would not be readily apparent from the public news media or electronic intelligence. And the martial portion of its remedy might require minimal force—something that only more proficiency at small-unit tactics can produce.

Global Warrior is about how the Pentagon might successfully counter a widespread yet largely subliminal threat from the East. While Asians are no smarter than Westerners individually, neither are they as trusting of one person's opinion nor as encumbered by European organizational structure. As such, their governmental agencies are better at handling grassroots problems, and their armies better at subliminally attacking "like a thousand razor cuts." This has nothing to do with Communism or Islam *per se,* but with a much earlier predisposition toward "collective opinions" and "bottom-up problem solving."

Instead of taking offense at the suggestion of societal oversight, all U.S. security personnel should now try to improve each department's efficiency. Most easy is removing outmoded procedures and shortening chains of command.

If most U.S. governmental extensions are "top heavy," then the Director of National Intelligence (DNI) and Pentagon have another good way to protect America. More completely to forestall another 9/11, the intelligence agencies have only to streamline their organizational structures. To preclude any more battlefield stalemates, the military service branches have only to do likewise. However, Western-style bureaucracy has become so ingrained into American society, that an agency's top leader can have trouble changing the most mundane of procedures over a period of years. He may manage a "policy change," but its application (however progressive) will almost certainly mirror tradition. As such, he would never even consider eliminating an intermediate headquarters.

There is only one way an already overstretched U.S. military can handle any more theaters of war. With a limited manpower pool, the Pentagon would have to spread thousands of tiny detachments across several continents. Until more special operators were trained, its building block would be the U.S. rifle squad. Such widely dispersed infantry squads would only require more training. While serving as force multipliers for local security units, they would need more surprise-oriented (vice firepower-dependent) movement technique and a better way of training indigenous personnel. The former would be to compensate for any lack of heavy weaponry, and the latter to exploit all cultural propensities.

America's war planners have correctly surmised that squad tactics evolve with technology. Yet, they conveniently forget that rich nations don't require much small-unit finesse. What their armies don't need, they don't develop.

If the most sophisticated small-unit maneuvers have instead occurred where firepower was lacking, then U.S. infantrymen may have some serious catching up to do. As their Eastern adversaries develop technologically, those GIs (Government Issues) will have even more reason to close this tactical gap. Just to counter the most recent developments in surveillance technology, American maneuver elements will have either to get much smaller or to forfeit all semblance of surprise. With modern man-portable weaponry, they could still adequately defend themselves. (The Russians now have a shoulder-fired thermobaric round with the killing radius of a 155-mm howitzer.[1])

Within the highly stratified U.S. military, it is difficult to emphasize squads without appearing to "under-regard" platoons, companies, and battalions. That, in turn, impugns the value of all staff noncommissioned officers (SNCOs), Lieutenants, Captains, Majors, and Lieutenant Colonels. There is no slight intended, only an offer to assist. Others have walked in those same lonely shoes. It's to these self-sacrificing middle managers this book has been specifically dedicated. They bear an awesome responsibility. While entrusted with the lives of America's youth, they must somehow acquire more tactical insight than their organizations have to offer. Most are well versed in American combat procedure, but warfare—as an overall concept—is more complicated than that. Ever since the first world war, Eastern armies have formed their defensive strongpoints around lone squads, and preceded every offensive push with a single squad. All the while, American infantry officers have been lucky to spend six months with a rifle platoon, before having to move on to some exceedingly boring staff assignment.

Since Officer Candidate or SNCO School, most U.S. leaders have been continually told how superior they are at all things. As improbable as this may seem, many see no reason to doubt it. There is a good reason for all this optimism, of course. No fault of their own, it has more to do with organizational heritage. Officially acknowledging any shortfall in the preparation of leaders might cause subordinates to more often question their orders. As with any Western-style bureaucracy, degree of control is the overriding concern. Over the many years, this state of organizational bliss has been only occasionally interrupted by the loss of enlistees "who had yet to learn the system" or of a war "due to extenuating circumstances."

As all U.S. military leaders belong to an "elite organization that never loses in combat," most assume victory will somehow be theirs as well. Many a young officer or SNCO has fallen victim to this all-too-cozy expectation. Overwhelming firepower will not always suffice, and even the most talented of America's warrior elite will occasionally lose an engagement. That's where he might have most easily learned something. But, when one never admits failure, one has no reason to improve.

For America's wartime units, firepower has been and still is the name of the game. This game has some less-than-ideal ramifications. Since WWI, far too many U.S. units have not matched up well—tactically—with their Eastern counterparts. As unlikely as this may seem to today's active-duty community, it is nevertheless well documented. Over the years, Generals Patton,[2] Collins,[3] Simmons,[4] and Scales,[5] have all admitted to it. And far too many company commanders have failed to mention it on their after-action reports (this author included [6]). Only after separation from the service and with some outside reading, is one likely to discover what a few "world-class" squad maneuvers might have meant to his mission. Chronic disregard for any foe's strengths can result in too many casualties and then a serious guilt trip.[7] Yet, this is just one of the many challenges of being a U.S. military officer.

All "top-down" organizations unwittingly suffer from this same problem. It primarily comes from placing too much emphasis on rank. As opposed to "defending one's country" or "learning how better to accomplish one's mission," career-oriented U.S. service personnel must inordinately focus on promotion. If they take too long reaching the next rank, they are unceremoniously sacked. As might be expected, most spend more time meeting their reporting senior's responsibilities than their own. Instead of tactics, company grade officers study operations. And, instead of operations, field grade officers study strategy. All the while, too little attention is paid to how most effectively run a platoon or squad.

While theoretically being prepared to take a fallen superior's place, everyone is also becoming easier to control. Add to this "help-the-boss syndrome" a steady diet of transfers, and one's sanity soon takes precedence over any extracurricular learning. Though better able to follow orders, the fledging U.S. leaders don't get the chance to explore their own jobs, much less those of subordinates. Among WWII and Korea veterans, this little organizational quirk has been good for many a laugh at Happy Hour. It's all part of the infamous *Peter Principle:* "In a hierarchy, every employee tends to rise to his level of incompetence." Take heart, however, for there are ways to tactically compensate for the debilitating effect of Western bureaucracy. This book offers a quick and enjoyable refresher for those who—through no fault of their own—have too quickly risen through the ranks.

Global Warrior has several parts. The first features some of the world's least publicized hot spots. Most are in Asia or along its underdeveloped periphery. As such, all residents are "bottom-up" thinkers from "bottom-up" organizations. Most of America's past foes have also shared this thought process. That's why they've been so hard to outsmart. Lacking the wherewithal to fight any other way, even Western Hemisphere guerrillas prefer grassroots-type tactics. Within the U.S. military, only the lowest ranks perceive the world in this manner. Their "take on things" seldom reaches any commander.

The second part deals with how best to approach such a widespread challenge. U.S. forces cannot help with every foreign crisis, but neither can they ignore them. Historians generally agree that America's isolationism may have helped to precipitate both world wars. As Pope John Paul II so aptly attested before his death, the United States is still the world's best hope.[8] Adequately to fulfill this hope, American troops must now be present in more places at once.

Finally, the third part provides U.S. riflemen with more of the movement techniques they will need to operate alone. Without advanced maneuvers, the tiny and often-isolated U.S. contingents would be in too much danger to even be allowed. Yet, most U.S. military leaders still see their riflemen as world-class warriors. How could they not be—with all of the millions of man-hours dedicated to their training? To admit to any bottom-echelon deficiency would be disloyal to the overall organization. However, if asked, the troops would almost certainly opt for more independent action and the skill to accomplish it. Which group is right? The fate of the world may well rest on the answer. To further complicate matters, the role of rifleman and policeman are merging. As such, the last chapter has been devoted to police tactics. May God continue to bless this wonderful nation and all of its fine security personnel.

The Book's Possible Shortcomings

To achieve adequate detail, this research has been restricted to some of the more subtle evidential threads worldwide. Those threads encompass every 4GW arena (martial, economic, political, and psychological/religious), but they may or may not adequately depict the whole. While assessing an Eastern threat, this researcher also makes little attempt to conform with "conventional Western wisdom."

The Book's Overriding Utility

Historically, "Far Eastern" perspectives have played little role in U.S. security planning. With the world situation quickly deteriorating, another look at this alternative way of doing things may be in order. Having drawn from the Asians much longer experience with battle, *Global Warrior* should constitute a useful supplement for U.S. intelligence gatherers and troop trainers. However, no amount of new information will do U.S. forces much good until they have the "foreign-tactics" authorities to sort it. In Eastern wars of national liberation, most strategic goals are realized "from the bottom up." At the Pakistani border, this is called "death by a thousand razor cuts."[18] In difficult terrain, such an effort must also be countered from the bottom up. This researcher provides enough advanced tactical technique to make this possible. To prevent any further escalation to—and then finally win—the ongoing global conflict, read further.

LT.COL. H. JOHN POOLE USMC (RET.)
FORMER GY.SGT. FMCR

Acknowledgments

To the Holy Spirit belongs the credit for everything useful herein. Thanks be to God for an opportunity to help the world's best hope—America.

Part One

The World's Ongoing Crises

"I regard myself as a soldier, though a soldier of peace."
— Mahatma Gandhi

(Source: Attributed to the father of modern India, Mahatma Gandhi)

1 _____ Introduction

● How can the Pentagon best help this country?
● Can defense contracts alone get the job done?

Those to whom more loyalty is owed.

(Source: Credited to Edward Molina, © 1999, but may be slightly modified "public-domain" material)

The New Twist on an Old Problem

The greatest threat to the global community is now economic followed by political takeover. The purveyors of such expansion can be loosely grouped into three categories: (1) Islamist; (2) Communist (or formerly Communist); and (3) criminal. While all can violently attack, they prefer to so quietly subvert each nation as to be barely noticeable to its leaders. That's because the "expansionists" are mostly Eastern and working from the "bottom up," whereas their quarries are mostly Western and watching from the "top down." Having inherited the hierarchical mind-set of European monarchs, the latter regularly have trouble seeing the trees for the forest. Around them, an expansionist "pine beetle" would be perfectly safe.

Because these three categories of aggressors are so similar in purpose and method, one is tempted to look for collusion between them. Of particular note would be whether the Communists have been using Islamic extremism as a screen and criminal activity as a local source of nontraceable funding. This researcher is no exception. Thus, all links between categories will be thoroughly investigated. Yet, because of the very real "personification of evil" all humans endure, there may be no cooperation between categories or "worldly" coordinator.

Why the Culprits Are So Hard to Contest

If there are any hard links between Islamists, Communists, and criminals, Washington appears to be unaware of it. That may be because of the "Administration" perspective. Most such offenders work up from the bottom so as to make sister cells and parent factions nearly impossible to trace. Only through a similar *modus operandi* can one usually identify an affiliate. For each incursion, so much evidence has been intentionally hidden that just piecemeal hints remain. Such hints are often too tiny to be recorded. Then, the problem becomes one of a "dot picture" with too few dots. All the proof—of whatever size—would have to be assessed at once. In other words, all circumstantial evidence worldwide would have to be somehow compared. While computer searches come immediately to mind, they are only as useful as their data bank size. For this type of research, the human mind may be more appropriate. Through a lifetime of experience, it automatically knows which minutia to save. U.S. intelligence analysts also gather details, but many go to waste. The picture they might have collectively painted never rises to the top of any single agency or emerges from the national network—as was painfully obvious during 9/11.

Because of how U.S. intelligence is gathered, neither has it been all that helpful to police and military units over the years. Most American agencies so compartmentalize their efforts (limit their specialists to specific regions and topics) that even *modus operandi* trends are hard to assemble. Part of the problem is in too much electronic versus human intelligence. Yet, from a military standpoint, it goes much deeper than that. Company commanders from the Vietnam era remember very little help from their S-2's in closing with the enemy.[1] Normally, this section could only provide locations of past contacts and suspected weaponry. During that era, there must have been too few U.S. intelligence analysts who realized the marked differences in the East Asians' thought process and maneuvers.

Whereas Washington is generally oblivious to what individual agency workers might discover about threats to the nation, Communist regimes seem fully aware of any encroachment—however small—to their operations. This "bottom-echelon awareness" allows them to better control the ebb and flow (momentum) of every battlefield initiative. One of the best—albeit painful—examples of this Western "blind spot" involves 9/11.

The Best Known Example of Organizational Oversight

The word from Washington is that *al-Qaeda* ran 9/11 and that the Afghan War is to deprive *al-Qaeda* of safe haven. While both are true, the overall story is more complicated. And, the often-repeated claim that 9/11 was planned in Afghanistan is categorically false. Shortly after the truck bombing of the World Trade Center in 1993, Ramzi Yousef and his chief deputy were plotting in the Philippines to fly an explosive-laden airplane into the Pentagon.[2] As a New York court was later to convict Yousef and two co-conspirators of planning the 1994 operation (Opplan Bojinka), the details of its second phase are now a matter of public record. This second phase involved crashing planes into Central Intelligence Agency (CIA) headquarters and other buildings. Among those being considered were the Pentagon and World Trade Center.[3] A full report of the plot was given by the Philippine police to the Federal Bureau of Investigation (FBI) in 1995.[4]

So, 9/11 may have—at some point—been discussed in Afghanistan, but it was originally planned and then very probably coordinated from Southeast Asia. Right before it occurred, two of the hijackers attended a "terrorist summit" in Kuala Lumpur.[5] Then, one or both may have accompanied their handler to Hong Kong.[6] By this time, Yousef had already been to Hong Kong.[7] After 9/11, one of Opplan Bojinka's other designers took refuge with his Chinese-*Ma-*

laysian "wife" in pro-Chinese Cambodia.[8] So *al-Qaeda* may, or may not, have acted unilaterally, and it doesn't really need Afghanistan as a safe haven.

Curbing the Expansionists Will Take More Security at Home

Whether elected or not, most U.S. leaders think it their prerogative to base all decisions on personal experience. Only the most dedicated do enough "homework" to guarantee success. Against a clever adversary, this unfortunate habit has resulted in more than one forfeit. Still, all leadership habits aside, the main problem is in the "top-down" procedures on which all Western bureaucracies depend.

Many months prior to 9/11, an FBI informant was invited to join Mohammed Atta's *al-Qaeda* cell. Instead of being allowed to infiltrate it, he was instead assigned to an untargeted "sting."[9] The dichotomy between top-down procedure and bottom-up opportunity was almost certainly to blame. Someone senior had decided that stings were the best way to find terrorists. When two very promising prospects showed up some other way, the original policy took precedence over an exception. Or, in the vernacular of all U.S. combat veterans, "the sacrosanct plan preempted good fortune." Until the West comes to better appreciate the limitations of its favorite bureaucratic model, it will continue to have trouble with Eastern adversaries.

As do most Communist entities, the North Vietnamese Army (NVA) operated from the bottom up. Its initial identification of lucrative targets came from lone scouts. Its reconnaissance of attack objectives was done—from the inside—by sappers.[10] It then made the initial breach of each U.S. perimeter with a single squad. As such, widely disseminating every aspect of the NVA's squad tactics might have greatly helped American troops. However, the big thinkers never thought of that. No American grunt was ever told the NVA assault would copy the German Stormtroopers of 1918. The only difference was in a mortar deception instead of artillery, and shrapnel-free satchel charges instead of concussion grenades. Nor was the Asian thought process ever explained. It is so unlike that in the West as to make this little oversight almost criminal. It is holistic whereas the American way is compartmentalized. Every Asian soldier—however lowly—knows enough of the overall mission to not impede it, whereas Western subject-matter experts routinely work at cross-purposes. Every NVA private was kept apprised of all commanders' intentions in his chain of command. Should he stumble upon a target of opportunity, he was then able single-handedly to make a strategic contribution. All the while, his American counterparts were so busy following orders as to routinely ignore opportunities.

Having a widely different cultural heritage, America's governmental agencies (to include those military) operate—almost entirely—from the top down. While only occasionally capitalizing on frontline observations, they much prefer to act on laboriously staffed "big-picture" assessments. In fact, their Commander in Chief might take considerable exception to their not closely enough following his strategic instructions. As a result, threats that do not mesh well with the current Administration's foreign policy tend largely to be overlooked. Additionally, any traces of expansionist activity by supposed allies are seldom deemed important enough to ever record or report.

There is evidence that Communist-nation bureaucracies don't suffer from these same deficiencies. They may have other shortcomings, but not these. Of course, whatever they do correctly surmise will almost certainly be misused by their Communist masters. Still, the initial intelligence gathering may be well worth emulating. Within North Vietnam's military and other government agencies (as per the Maoist Chinese model), there was the *"Kiem Thao"* system.[11] Through organized sessions, each unit's "fighters" were asked constructively to criticize their "leaders." Those lowly fighters were further encouraged to check all combat after-action reports for accuracy and detail. As a result, NVA units more often learned from their mistakes in Vietnam than did their opposition. That U.S. forces have only lost a handful of battles over the last 250 years should be adequate proof of what the troops at Bataan, Kasserine Pass, the Hurtgen Forest, and Chosin Reservoir might call "the occasional exaggeration."

General Giap has supposedly said in his memoirs that North Vietnam would have surrendered if the U.S. had followed through with its Hanoi bombing or Tet response. Past military leaders of Communist nations aren't allowed many admissions of weakness. If General Giap did say this, he was just rubbing in the loss (to cause a former foe to "lose more face"). This was an adversary so skilled at light-infantry tactics as to need no artillery, tanks, or planes, and only what else it could steal from an oversupplied opponent. America could have completely flooded Hanoi and blocked Haiphong Harbor and still lost the war. For years, high ranking U.S. Army members blamed the *New York Times* for the defeat. News outlets doesn't lose wars. Tactically deficient armies lose wars. The NVA and their Viet Cong (VC) allies were simply better at small-unit maneuver than their American counterparts. There is no glory in erroneously claiming to have won some war or engagement. In fact, most Asians think it a major dishonor. Minimally, it forfeits all opportunity to correct what was wrong.

Now That the Full Truth Be Known

With the ultimate reason for so little U.S. tactical reform now out in the open, one can wholeheartedly return to combatting the expansionists. Despite news media and politicized accounts to the contrary, the world's overall welfare has now reached a pandemic stage. Its most serious threats have become so sophisticated as to be fully achievable through the targeted country's own democratic processes. Those familiar with their subtle manifestations in one place would be much more likely to spot them in another. This particular researcher has recently visited many different parts of the world. He is also aware of what tiny U.S. contingents might do locally to stop the incursion. It is along this less-trodden path that most Americans should head. Otherwise, whatever happens to the rest of the world will eventually happen to them.

The *Status Quo* Is Now Extremely Dangerous

That the U.S. constitutes the world's biggest drug market and that most of the world's heroin comes from Afghanistan are givens. The head of the U.S. Drug Enforcement Administration (DEA) personally admitted to Congress at the end of the Soviet Afghan War that over half of all heroin on U.S. streets was coming from southern Afghanistan.[12] Yet, the latest drug threat assessments from the National Drug Intelligence Center (NDIC) and United Nations Office on Drugs and Crime (UNODC) barely mention the almost certain sequel to this heroin conduit.[13] The former even attests to "little availability of Southwest Asian heroin in America."[14] Under normal circumstances, such high-level assurances would be comforting. However, some well-respected media sources beg to differ. One Texas police officer says that chemical tests have shown most of the heroin coming up from Mexico to be of Afghan origin.[15] On two separate occasions in 2010, ABC's Nightly News noted a veritable flood of 70% pure heroin into the Midwest. Bags of the stuff were selling for $5 each or free to the school kids.[16] Yet, in May 2009, the White House Drug Czar announced the traditional "War on Drugs" was over, with the new focus on how to limit prescription medicine abuse.[17] While this is also important, it in no way jeopardizes national security. With the mushrooming of methamphetamine use, a huge influx of Afghan heroin would effectively break an already overloaded U.S. criminal justice system. The resulting crime spree would almost certainly destabilize the nation.

It's now widely acknowledged that *al-Qaeda* has been trying to flood this country with narcotics. Certain "business-loving" nations may be doing likewise. The strategy of "death by a thousand razor cuts" is what defeated the Soviets in Afghanistan.[18] Why couldn't its 4GW sequel involve high profits and reach all the way back to the occupiers' homeland?

To have any chance of winning the overall conflict, this country needs to get much more serious about interdicting the Afghan drug conduit. With that much product comes a certain amount of "high-level" corruption. As in Pakistan, enough such corruption might have an influence over U.S. foreign policy. Or, as was suspected during the Vietnam War, it might result in the unwitting "transpo" of contraband by U.S. military conveyance. When possibly dealing with such a concerted effort to undermine this country, there must be complete unity of purpose between all governmental entities. Without a drastic change to the way things are done, America's intelligence community predicts dire consequences.

2 The National Intelligence Estimate

- Which entities most threaten world peace?
- Is there any "hard" evidence of collusion between them?

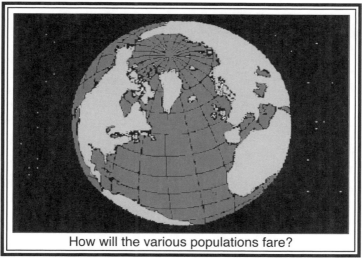
How will the various populations fare?

(Source: FMFM 0-1 [1979], p. 4-63)

Something U.S. Leaders Won't Be Able to Manage Alone

With the U.S. media now mainly focused on internal issues, many Americans have become isolationist in their attitudes. At this crucial juncture in their history, they can't afford to be. Instead, they must encourage a wider (and smarter) application of U.S. foreign assistance. If they don't, whatever happens to the rest of the world will eventually befall its most popular destination for migrants and drugs. Enough of the right kind of foreign assistance would take America's military and other security agencies more fully utilizing their lowest ranks.

11

Many nations are now experiencing as much duress (albeit subtle) as just before WWII. While more comprehensive U.S. foreign policy would help, rescuing the world this time around will now be up to a new kind of infantryman. In effect, the U.S. can no longer financially afford to deploy fully supported mechanized armies in support of freedom. Nor will a few special operators here and there be enough.

Now necessary will be a major shift in how the U.S. military projects its power. A dramatic change makes perfect sense, because today's threats are so vastly different from before. Just as predator drones are improper to law enforcement, so too are they of little use in a 4GW environment. For both settings, martial initiatives are best accomplished by tiny, highly skilled ground elements. An already oppressed population does not perceive impromptu missiles as a way to limit casualties, ground incursions, and rebel command structures—particularly in Asia, where leaders play much less of a role. Such a population sees only another terrifying explosion that may or may not have hit the right target, along with whomever was nearby. U.S. military assistance is not more widely sought by troubled nations because of fears it might entail drone-delivered munitions.

The new way will fix all this. If U.S. troops are as talented as their leaders profess, then they should have little trouble acquiring a 4GW skill set. The only real hurdle will be sufficient authority to operate alone. With too little money to deploy any other way, those leaders will have to give up some of the control they have so carefully coveted. It's all about the numbers—more insurgencies than there are task forces to handle them. For the first time since 1776, low-ranking members of America's security establishment will have to make enough of an individual contribution to collectively prevent the next holocaust. They will be necessarily manning thousands of tiny outposts that are far from any parent unit or supporting arms. After irrefutable evidence of the deteriorating situation, this book will provide those isolated troops with other ways to survive.

What Has Prompted Such a Drastic Change in Policy

Following the demise of the Soviet Union, many Americans assumed the Communist threat to be over. Yet, the CIA's *World Factbook* still describes the People's Republic of China (PRC) as a

"Communist state."[1] It is to the PRC America currently owes most of its massive debt. On 4 July 2010, Adm. Mike Mullen (Chairman of the Joint Chiefs of Staff) courageously pointed out this debt now constitutes the biggest single security threat to the nation. Its yearly cost in interest (some $600 billion) is nearly as much as the wartime defense budget.[2]

Thus, China poses every bit as much threat as *al-Qaeda*, and they are not alone in their destabilization of America. If the latest national intelligence estimate took no notice of this, there would be no reason to change how the U.S. military operates overseas. However, this is not the case. Its projection for 2025 is dire.

The Good News Is More Cooperation between Agencies

Since April 2005, some 16 U.S. intelligence community organizations have been overseen by a DNI Director. Helping him is the National Intelligence Council (NIC). Its job is to provide senior policy makers with foreign-policy analyses developed throughout the community as a whole. The below-described projection— *Global Trends 2025: The National Intelligence Council's 2025 Project*—is therefore the consensus opinion of all U.S. intelligence agencies on the state of the world in 15 years. The DNI at the time of its release has since lost his job.[3]

Then There Is the Bad News

On 21 November 2008, America's most recent intelligence projection was summarized by Tom Gjelten on National Public Radio (NPR). To comply with copyright law, his article—"Analysts: By 2025, U.S. Won't Be Top World Power"—will have to be largely paraphrased.

> U.S. intelligence agencies have concluded that the United States is likely to lose its dominant global position in the coming years, with economic and political power shifting to countries such as China and India.[4]
> — NPR's "Morning Edition" News on NIC Report

This assessment contrasts sharply with the conclusions of a

similar study by the same agencies in 2004. The earlier report projected "continued U.S. dominance" through the year 2020. The new assessment sees the United States becoming "one of a number of actors on the world stage" with the U.S. dollar being only one of several internationally acceptable currencies.

With PRC espionage and cyber activity against the U.S. now at record levels,[5] this assessment is sobering. These intelligence analysts foresee increased international conflict over food, water, energy, and other scarce resources. International institutions—from the International Monetary Fund to the United Nations (U.N.)—will become less effective, thus creating more global players. "Non-state actors," like tribal groups, religious organizations, private corporations, and organized-crime networks, will eventually come to the forefront.[6]

Among the study's more startling conclusions is that some regime in Eastern or Central Europe "could effectively be taken over and run by organized crime." The report also speculates that some states in Africa or South Asia could "wither away" as a result of their governments' failure to provide basic services to their populations. By 2025, according to the report, China and India will be leading economic players, with Turkey, Indonesia, and Iran in the "up and coming" category. Most disturbing is how well the Western political and economic models are expected to fare against their Communist and Islamist counterparts. The economic stress on many countries will be so "exacerbated" by the current international financial crisis as to lead to drastic reversals.[7]

> [S]ome countries . . . recently persuaded to follow the Western economic model . . . have since become disillusioned.
> . . . "They've made adjustments away from populist regimes, . . . socialist regimes, . . . one-party dominated systems, and they are still waiting for the payoff.[8]
> — NPR's "Morning Edition" News on NIC Report

As a result, there will be a major shift in the preferred economic model. To the extent that a country's politics follow its economic procedures, this could spell big trouble for the West. "[A] lot of young people with the normal healthy disrespect for authority . . . would be potentially mobilized for all kinds of things." Before the revolution would come more state-sanctioned repression.[9]

The economic model that has largely prevailed since World War II—Western democratic capitalism—may no longer be favored. Instead, "state capitalism" such as that practiced in Russia and China could be ascendant.[10]
— NPR's "Morning Edition" News on NIC Report

These analysts paid particular attention to the demographic factors that could lessen global stability. Many Middle Eastern countries will have far younger populations. Luckily, they and the rest of the world will be less influenced by terrorism. There will also be a "worldwide shift" from petroleum to new energy technologies. Unfortunately, the new supplies of energy will still not be enough to match the demand, thus leading to conflicts.[11] Thus, a further analysis of so "prestigious" a projection is most certainly in order. Its most shocking conclusions must be individually scrutinized.

No Longer the World's Most Dominant Power?

Whether or not America loses its position of prominence, its responsibilities to the various peoples of the world will remain the same. It must check Islamist, Communist, and criminal expansion worldwide or eventually encounter them at home. If the U.S. government were to bargain (or borrow) away any part of its economic or political stature, it might eventually be forced to accept the recipient's agenda.

While this NIC projection mentions two possible successors to America's preeminence, only one of them is a legitimate contender—the PRC. The CIA's *World Factbook* further describes the PRC as follows: (1) controlled by the Chinese Communist Party (CCP) with "no substantial political opposition groups"; (2) "officially atheist"; (3) a "major transshipment point for heroin produced in the Golden Triangle"; and (4) a "source country for methamphetamine and heroin chemical precursors."[12] The PRC will not be as human-rights oriented as America has been, for its overall goal appears to be economic and then political domination.

Increasing Conflict over Natural Resources?

This planet has only a finite supply of natural resources. (See

Figure 2.1: Every Nation Needs Enough Fuel
(Source: Corel Clipart, image designator "37C048.jpg")

Figure 2.1.) Every sovereign nation considers its resource conduits to be of strategic importance (i.e., enough reason to go to war). As international policing alliances weaken and "non-state actors" appear, there will be more active competition for those conduits. There is already instability along them. (See Map 2.1.) The U.S. can either choose to ignore this instability or get somehow involved.

The ongoing chaos may have been intentionally engineered as a portion of someone's expansionist agenda. To find its hidden instigator, one only has to see where most of the natural resources are going.

Successful Expansion by All Three Groups?

The prospect of a criminal government in Eastern Europe is

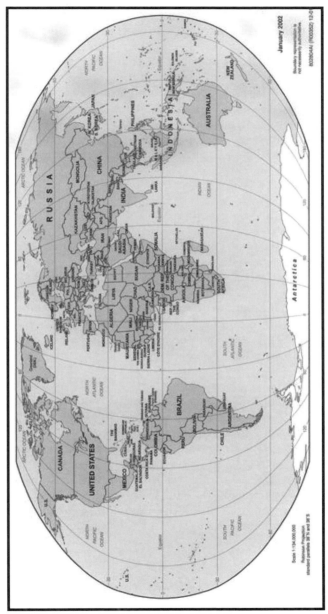

Map 2.1: An Ever-Shrinking Neighborhood
(Source: Courtesy of General Libraries, University of Texas at Austin, from their website for map designator "world_pol02.pdf")

not very encouraging. The country with the most internationally active organized-crime elements is Russia. Those elements, along with certain Chinese triads, have already been spotted in Panama.[13] While drug smuggling appears to be their aim, political expansion might more interest their governments.

"That some states in . . . South Asia could 'wither away' " does not come as particularly good news either. One doesn't have much trouble guessing which country would most benefit from their loss. If Indonesia and Iran will both be in the "up and coming" category by 2025, there will have to be considerable Islamist progress worldwide.

The Rise of State Capitalism?

Officially to suggest that something may replace "democratic capitalism" casts a definite shadow over Western-style democracy. To preserve the latter, one wouldn't want the economic system of a criminal state from Eastern Europe or atheistic government from Asia. Disillusionment within former Soviet-Bloc countries that "follow the Western economic model" might most easily arise from two sources: (1) Russian subterfuge; and/or (2) doubt in America's willingness to stand by them.

A Less Hospitable Environment for *al-Qaeda?*

The killing of fellow Muslims has now made *al-Qaeda* more of a pariah than caliphate nucleus. Much of the Afghan population has already grown to loath its heavy-handedness. Its lack of recent political involvement may also result in less strategic progress than Shiite counterparts (like Lebanese *Hezbollah)*. Still, it may be *al-Qaeda* trying to undermine the Pakistani government.[14] With more political sophistication, it could still become a formidable adversary.

Everything Points to a Different Kind of Threat

Instead of the media attention of the early 21st century, the miscreants may now be going after bigger and better things—like government takeovers. Such takeovers could occur by either coup or election.

Democracy works only as well as security at the voters' level. To prevent the expansionists from winning too many elections, the U.S. may have to start taking a bigger interest in local security throughout the Developing World.

Trends to Track

While Islamist, Communist, and criminal activity was widespread before 2010, much of its associated chaos seemed to be along natural-resource conduits to powerful nations. Petroleum was the most usual commodity in transit, but minerals were also being moved. While no nation wanted more narcotics for itself, several were helping arch rivals to obtain them.

As the conflict in one of southwest Asia's biggest oil-producers (Iraq) was winding down, others farther east were heating up. Russia had just invaded Georgia, thereby limiting Europe's access to Caspian Sea gas.[15] Western powers were trying to make southern Afghanistan safe enough for their own Caspian pipeline.[16] And the PRC was building roadways through northern Pakistan and Afghanistan,[17] with which to better access Iranian oil.[18]

In Central Africa, there was a big civil war raging between Muslim and Christian halves of petroleum-rich Nigeria. Just to the northeast, there was tension between Muslim and Christian regions of Sudan over respective oil rights. In Southeast Asia, there had been fighting near the region's two biggest deposits of natural gas—under Sulawesi and the Spratley Islands. *Al-Qaeda* was supposedly responsible for the first,[19] but only the Chinese Navy was involved in the second.[20] This worldwide interest in oil conduits was mostly visible at shipping chokepoints. There was trouble on both sides of the Red Sea approaches to the Suez Canal (Somalia and Yemen), just to the north of the Straits of Malacca (Thailand),[21] and near the Panama Canal (Colombia).

Links of mining to open warfare were less obvious. The Chinese had recently traded a thousand mile road from their Benguela railhead in Zambia to the war-torn and mineral-rich northeastern Congo.[22] They were also building a railroad from what once was an American airbase in now-leftist Ecuador to mines in the Andes.[23]

19

Finally, there was tumult around the world's biggest sources of illicit drugs (Colombia for cocaine and Afghanistan for heroin). This fighting had also spread to key countries along the drug conduits—e.g., Mexico and Pakistan.

Who Was Ultimately Responsible for all this Trouble?

In almost every case, there are religious/tribal differences in play as well as commodity trading. Which first caused the violence would depend upon local circumstances, but history attributes more armed conflict to man's quest for resources than for converts. If one were to find nearly identical incitements to chaos in every location, what would this mean? It might mean religious or tribal tensions were being exploited (or aggravated) to gain a bigger share of the wealth.

There is only one way to confirm or deny a global conspiracy. It is separately to assess the progress of all three expansionist elements.

3

The Islamist Threat

- Where is there Islamist expansion?
- Why is it on both sides of the southern entrance to Suez?

Among other things, *Hezbollah* has evolutionary way to stop armor.

(Source: Courtesy of Michael Leahy, coverart from *Tactics of the Crescent Moon*, © 2004)

Al-Qaeda's Continuing Activity

While *al-Qaeda* no longer has much organizational structure, neither has its influence been greatly lessened by ten years of bombardment. As will be shown in Part Two, *al-Qaeda* now wields almost as much power in Yemen and Somalia as it did in Pakistan and Afghanistan. In the first two locations, it seems interested in the adjacent sea-lanes. (See Map 3.1.) In the Afghan/Pakistani theater, it has supported both the drug trade and Taliban resurgence. There, it operates as more of an advisor and force multiplier than operational headquarters. If a new caliphate is its goal, then the

Map 3.1: Modern-Day Islamists Seem Interested in Suez
(Source: Courtesy of General Libraries, University of Texas at Austin, from their website for map designator "n_africa_mid_east_pol_95.jpg")

first site is more probable. While Pakistan and Afghanistan were part of the Muslim Empire for a while, they were nowhere near its center. (See Map 3.2.)

Probable Caliphate Location

The third Islamic Caliphate did not include any part of Pakistan, whereas the previous one did. (See Map 3.3.) Thus, Lebanon, Yemen, or Somalia would make a more appropriate nucleus for a modern caliphate.

There was an exceptionally advanced civilization in the Indus Valley, but it was not Muslim. While Northern Europeans groveled in caves around 2500 B.C., Indus Valley inhabitants were enjoying public baths and flowing sewers in the veritable metropolises of Mohenjo Daro and Harappa. (See Map 3.4.) However, this Indus Valley society predated the Muslim Empire by over 3,300 years. Islam does have some early roots, but they are not early enough. The *Koran* considers Ishmael, Abraham's first son with Sarah's handmaid, to be a prophet of Islam. Yet, Ishmael was not born until around 1970 B.C. in what is now Iraq.[1]

The Overall Picture

How active *al-Qaeda* currently is in Iraq is anyone's guess, because all the media hype about "al-Qaeda in Iraq" has virtually disappeared since the Baghdad Surge. *Al-Qaeda* is known to be as skilled at media manipulation as it is at terrorism. It not only welcomes the blame for every anti-Western attack worldwide, but will even seek it out. Therefore, there is no telling how many events originally attributed to "al-Qaeda in Iraq" were actually the doing of someone else—like Iran's Revolutionary Guard Corps (IRGC) or

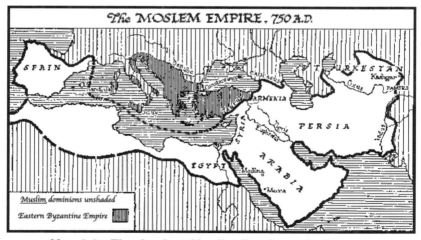

Map 3.2: The Ancient Muslim Empire at Its Largest
(Source: Courtesy of fordam.edu/halsall, at Medieval Sourcebook, from H.G. Wells, *A Short History of the World* (London: 1922), map designator "islam2map.tif")

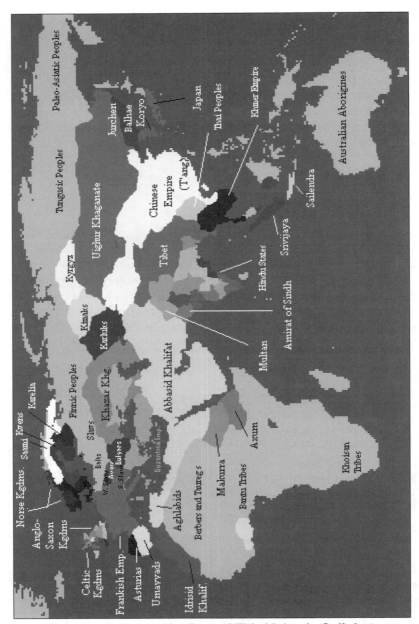

Map 3.3: Pakistan Not Part of Third Islamic Caliphate

(Source: Wikipedia.org, s.v "Gilgit-Baltistan," under provisions of GNU Free Documentation License, map designator "Old_World_820.png")

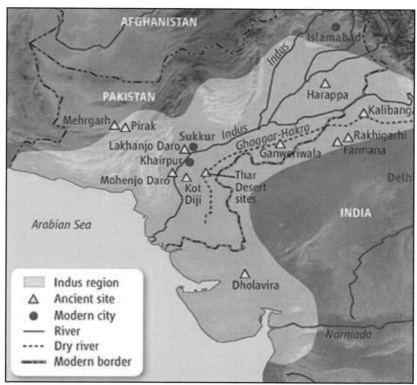

Map 3.4: The 5,000-Year-Old Indus Valley Civilization
(Source: " 'Pakistan' Existed 5000 Years Ago," *Rupee News*, 27 November 2007, appears to be locally produced, © n.d., map designator "indus-civilization-map.jpg")

its Lebanese offspring and proxy *Hezbollah*. As Salafists, Sunni and Shiite extremists easily cooperate against a common enemy. While *al-Qaeda* continues to threaten American's "domestic tranquility" and wartime fortunes, it has yet to take over any foreign government—nor will it do so in Pakistan. Until this occurs to a nuclear-armed nation, Iran will continue to pose the most serious Islamist threat to the U.S.

The Global Extent of Iranian Influence

Iran has been sending munitions directly to several guerrilla

25

movements, and indirectly to others. Not all operate in the Middle East. The incessant arms shipments to Lebanese *Hezbollah* notwithstanding, Iran has also been distributing weapons to Shiite rebels in northern Yemen,[2] Islamic rebels of indeterminate sect in Nigeria,[3] and mostly Sunni rebels in Afghanistan.[4] It has also been providing ordnance (and who knows what else) indirectly to Communist rebels in Colombia, Mexico, and Peru—through Venezuela's Bolivarian Revolution.[5] There is nothing even vaguely Islamic about Hugo Chavez's hemisphere-wide rebellion, nor do many dissatisfied Muslims live in Colombia, Mexico, or Peru. Thus, there are only a few possible explanations for Iran's interest. Either it wants to undermine the West any way it can, it has been somehow paid to support Marxist/Maoist movements, or it has a drug-trafficking interest in the region. All three countries have been instrumental in the production and shipment of narcotics to America. There is evidence to suggest that *Hezbollah's* attack on Mexican officials in October of 2001 was a paid "hit."[6]

As insinuated below, Iran's growing interest in the Western Hemisphere may have something to do with its East Asian benefactor. Either way, Iran and its various proxy armies remain a significant threat to world peace.

> The State Department report on international terrorism for 2009 released August 5, 2010, again stated (as it has for more than a decade) that Iran "remained the most active state sponsor of terrorism" in 2009, and it again attributes the terrorist activity primarily to the Qods [or Quds] Force of the Revolutionary Guard. On October 27, 2008, the deputy commander of the Basij [or Baseej] became the first top Guard leader to publicly acknowledge that Iran supplies weapons (and possibly advice) to "liberation armies."[7]
>
> — Congressional Research, 26 October 2010

How Can Iran Project So Much Power Far from Home?

Now quite adept at asymmetric warfare and covert operations, the IRGC gives Iran the capability of conducting unconventional warfare (UW) using foreign movements as proxies.[8] The IRGC's prime mover in these overseas adventures is its Quds Force. The

Quds Force has worked with Lebanese *Hezbollah,* both Shiite and Sunni militias in Iraq, and both Shiite and Sunni militias in Afghanistan.[9]

The al-Quds (Jerusalem) Force was originally created by the IRGC to organize, train, equip, and finance foreign Islamic revolutionary movements. Its most recent activity may indicate help to any anti-Western insurgency, however inspired. The Quds Force was very involved in Iraq and has also been in Afghanistan since 2001 (initially with American permission).[10] Its 15,000 members also provide advice and weaponry to pro-Iranian factions in Lebanon, the Persian Gulf States (most notably Kuwait), Israel's Gaza Strip and West Bank, Central Asia, Venezuela, and any number of other places. While some of these Quds personnel may be gathering intelligence, others are almost certainly assisting with local terrorism and revolution.[11]

There are [Quds Force] Directorates for Iraq; Lebanon, Palestine, and Jordan; Afghanistan, Pakistan, and India; Turkey and the Arabian Peninsula; Asian countries of the former Soviet Union, Western nations (Europe and North America), and North Africa (Egypt, Tunisia, Algeria, Sudan, and Morocco).[12]

— Ctr. for Strat. & Internat. Studies, August 2007

That the Quds Force is primarily about training and advising revolutionaries, vice only arming them, is not that difficult to substantiate. Quds brings its most promising candidates back to Iran for advanced instruction.

The Quds force seems to control many of Iran's training camps for unconventional warfare, extremists, and terrorists. . . . It has at least four major training facilities in Iran. The Quds force has a main training center at Imam Ali University . . . in Northern Tehran. Troops are trained to carry out military and terrorist operations, and are indoctrinated in ideology. There are other training camps in the Qom, Tabriz, and Mashhad governates, and in Lebanon and the Sudan. These include the Al Nasr camp for training Iraqi Shi'ites and Iraqi and Turkish Kurds in northwest Iran, and a camp near Mashhad for training Afghan and Tajik revolutionaries. The Quds seems to help operate the

Manzariyah training center near Qom, which recruits from foreign students in the religious seminary and which seems to have trained some Bahraini extremists. Some foreigners are reported to have received training in demolition and sabotage at an IRGC facility near Isfahan, in airport infiltration at a facility near Mashad and Shiraz, and in underwater warfare at an IRGC facility at Bandar Abbas (Venter, "Iran Still Exporting Terrorism," *Jane's Intel. Review*, Nov. 1997, 511-516).[13]
— Ctr. for Strat. & Internat. Studies, late 2004

The extent to which the Quds Force has now incorporated Lebanese *Hezbollah* (originally an IRGC creation) into its foreign escapades will be the focus of this chapter. While there is also "Party of God" (literal translation of *Hezbollah)* factions in Iran and several other nations, any further use of the term *"Hezbollah"* will infer Lebanese descent. Just as the IRGC leads the *Baseej* (Iran's massive conscript army) in Iran, so too would *Hezbollah* possibly help the Quds Force to lead, train, and recruit a foreign proxy. Having single-handedly stopped the Israeli sweep into southern Lebanon in 2006, *Hezbollah* could also deploy a foreign expeditionary force. To help Afghanistan's Taliban regime with its fight against the Northern Alliance, *al-Qaeda* once fielded its own special assault unit (Brigade 055).[14]

Hezbollah's Expanding Wartime Capabilities

While fighting heavy Israeli armor in southern Lebanon in the summer of 2006, *Hezbollah* convincingly demonstrated a new way to repel a Westernized "liberation force." This way involved the "remote-control killing of modern tanks" from a belt of belowground strongpoints (the state of the art in defensive formations since WWI).[15] With Chinese help, Iran had just developed a 333-mm rocket that could be fired remotely. In all likelihood, something much smaller—yet still remotely controlled—had already been shared with *Hezbollah*.

Industry sources said the [Iranian] effort, reportedly aided by China, was designed to turn the Fajr-3 [rocket] into a more mobile and accurate system. . . .

An earlier version . . . was supplied [by Iran] to Hizbullah in Lebanon. . . .

Each battery contains a command post vehicle, with each launcher equipped with a mission computer and capable of being fired via remote control from a distance of one kilometer.[16]
— *Geostrategy-Direct,* 31 May 2006

Since then, Israeli intelligence officers have found command and control centers, and a missile and rocket fire-control center in Lebanon, that were of Iranian design.[17]

This remotely controlled killing of sophisticated main battle tanks (some of them Merkava Mark IVs) involved no collocated human spotters or trigger-pullers. As such, it constitutes an evolutionary advance in the art of anti-armor warfare and deserves a further look. Should any other insurgent movement acquire this same equipment and its associated techniques from *Hezbollah,* it will have a much better chance of repelling any Western-assisted relief effort.

[An] epochal shift [in anti-armor warfare] had occurred . . . in the small village of Bint Jbiel . . . and . . . defile of Wadi Saluki, where Hezbollah fighters ambushed and destroyed a battalion's worth of Israel's blitzkrieg heavy tanks.[18]
— Maj.Gen. R.H. Scales U.S. Army (Ret.), 2007

The good general went on to explain the shift. The battles at Bint Jbiel and Wadi Saluki had shown how well-trained, dug-in, and camouflaged rebels could—with precision weaponry—defeat a modern mechanized force with total air superiority. He says that's why Iraqi and Afghan insurgents can only be defeated by opposing infantry. Finally, he predicts that with arms from the second precision revolution, "skilled infantrymen will make mechanized warfare a relic of the Machine Age."[19] Such a statement will not make the tank or plane manufacturers very happy.

A Detailed Description of *Hezbollah's* Method

When the defensive belt along Lebanon's southern border was

attacked by a fully supported Israeli force in the summer of 2006, *Hezbollah's* advanced tactical abilities became more abundantly clear.

In early June of 2006, *Hamas* had allowed its fighters to tunnel into one of Israel's Gaza outposts to seize a hostage. Israel soon responded by bombing and entering parts of the Palestinian enclave.[19] On 12 July, *Hezbollah* then upped the ante by crossing the Lebanese-Israeli border to capture two more Israeli soldiers.[20] As this raid had been preceded by a brief rocket barrage, the Israelis hit back with a limited-objective ground assault. Then, by all indications, things began to go wrong.

First, the Israelis' goal of raiding all the way to the Litani River (18 miles) had to be modified to creating a buffer zone 1.2 miles deep,[21] and then further reduced to bulldozing a half-mile-wide "no-man's land."[22] On 26 July, Israeli planes "mistakenly" bombed a U.N. border outpost containing a Chinese peacekeeper.[23] Both China and North Korea maintain embassies in Beirut,[24] so the inference was clear. Israel had sent her mechanized infantry against a defense line that was at least partially of Chinese or North Korean design,[25] and was in no mood for the targeting input of Asian forward observers. Just as U.S. troops had experienced trouble with the defense line just north of the 38th parallel in 1953, so did the Israelis have a hard time with this one. *Hezbollah's* first belt-like bastion was full of bunkers, caves, and tunnels.[26] On 30 July, Sheikh Naim Qassem—*Hezbollah's* second in command—boasted that *Hezbollah's* stockpiling of arms and preparation of numerous bunkers and tunnels over the past six years had been the key to its resistance. He further proclaimed, "If it was not for these preparations, Lebanon would have been defeated within hours."[27]

This sounds very much like an underground strongpoint defense—the state of the art in protective formations. Only highly skilled light infantry can deal with something like that without taking heavy casualties. Unfortunately, neither Israel nor any of its Western allies has any real light infantry.

Fully aware that *Hezbollah* could claim victory from a limited Jewish offensive, Israel sent 10,000 more troops and scores of additional tanks across the border about 1 August. Its goal this time was to create a five-mile-deep zone that U.N. peacekeepers and the Lebanese army could then successfully occupy.[28] On 8 August, Israel's deepest penetration was reported to be only 4 kilometers in the direction of Taibeh.[29] The very next day, Israel announced an all-out assault on the border region involving a much greater number of troops and tanks. It also said it needed another 30 days to achieve its objective. Whether this objective had expanded in depth was not clear. This time, Israel had wisely decided to attack the defensive formation from east to west, instead of head on. Unfortunately, *Hezbollah* defenders were still able to largely negate the effect of the Israeli air force by moving through tunnels Iran had built.[30] While the terrain in southern Lebanon is not as daunting as what was faced by U.S. forces just inside North Korea in 1953, this defense line had the advantage of modern technology. In addition to Fuel-Air-Explosive (FAE) anti-personnel missiles and infrared-detonated anti-tank mines above ground, it had an advanced command-and-control network below ground.[31] The extent of the tunneling may never be known, but *Hezbollah* fighters kept reappearing in places already under Israeli "surface control."[32] The comparisons with Iwo Jima are far from coincidental.

> [There were] bunkers housing . . . advanced eavesdropping and surveillance equipment and monitoring cameras. . . . [F]ighters [kept] constantly popping up . . . , firing, and then vanishing again.[33]
> — *The Times* (UK), 10 August 2006

Israeli armor was particularly hard pressed by *Hezbollah's* "high-tech" anti-tank-missile methodology.

> In one hidden bunker, Israeli soldiers discovered night-vision camera equipment connected to computers that fed coordinates of targets to the Sagger 2 missile.[34]
> — *The Washington Post,* 14 August 2006

Hezbollah's strongpoints were also heavily disguised. To spot an enemy bunker, the Israeli soldier had to be standing right in front of it.[35] This sounds all too familiar to veterans of Iwo Jima, Korea, and Vietnam. Many still dream of bunker apertures just noticed a few feet away. Yet, contemporary U.S. leaders continue to deny any correlation between these in Lebanon and the Asian model. Isn't it possible that the Chinese and North Koreans have been using Lebanon as a testing site for new ways to incorporate modern technology into an already formidable defensive scheme? Both Russia and Germany used the Spanish Civil War as a laboratory in which to assess their equipment.

On 14 August, a U.N.-sponsored cease fire went into effect. Resolution 1701 forbade *Hezbollah* from bearing of arms south of the Litani River. By the last day of the war, Israeli troops had only reached the Litani in places. Yet, *Hezbollah* still managed to launch it biggest daily total of rockets and missiles—some 250.[36] Since then, *Hezbollah* has built a new defense line north of the Litani.

The degree of sophistication with which an Islamist movement was able to face down 350-400 main battle tanks and their supporting fighter-bombers is quite troubling. (See Figure .1.) Through the combination of video camera and computerized missile, *Hezbollah* had managed to destroy over 50 of those tanks (by the Israelis' own count).[37] Of course, a few had been killed the old-fashioned way. Throughout Israel's long occupation of southern Lebanon, *Hezbollah* had made a veritable art form out of remotely detonating a below-surface charge wherever Israeli tanks became canalized. This charge did not have to be "shaped" to penetrate, only big enough to lift the whole tank off the ground. When it came back down, it may have looked battle-worthy, but all crew members were dead from the concussion.

Hezbollah's Expertise Is Not Just in Tank Killing

It was not *al-Qaeda* that introduced the suicide vest to the Middle East and then Southwest Asia, it was *Hezbollah*.[38] Since then, *Hezbollah's* suicide-glorifying coloring book has convinced many a destitute Palestinian pre-teenager to become a human bomb. Despite *al-Qaeda's* subsequent adoption of the adolescent bomber concept in Iraq and Afghanistan, "big picture" American war planners still worry more about *Hezbollah's* "anti-air capabilities" than its distribution of coloring books. (It is this same "top-down" perspective that makes it so hard for frontline U.S. units to make any real progress.)

Of additional note is *Hezbollah's* expertise at "human intelligence" gathering. With good enough intelligence, one's new proxy doesn't need any "high-tech" equipment. Much of his human intelligence is acquired through a "neighborhood watch" system that would put the Viet Cong counterpart to shame.[39] The best way

Figure 3.1: Israeli Armor Had a Hard Time at Bint Jbiel
(Source: U.S. Air Force Clipart Library (www.usafns.com/art.shtml), image designator "scott_et_al_long%20war%20presen copy07 copy.jpg")

to demonstrate its power is through an event that so demoralized the Israeli government as to cause it to abandon its occupation of South Lebanon. This occurred over ten years ago, but in the area of small-unit tactics, a decade means nothing to those who have yet to learn the initial lesson. The lesson is that opportunistic sense easily trumps established procedure.

When Israel Quit Running Commando Raids on Lebanon

After October 1995, Israel noticed an increase in *Hezbollah's* ability to determine the whereabouts of high-ranking personnel and commandos in South Lebanon.[40] While leaks in the Southern Lebanese Army (SLA) may have been part of the problem, a vast "neighborhood watch" had also been set up by the enemy. *Hezbollah* depended most for real-time intelligence on the local population and long-range observation (through binoculars).[41]

Then, it was an Israeli naval commando raid into South Lebanon on 5 September 1997 that ended the Israeli occupation. Days

33

beforehand, local inhabitants had been alerted to the impending raid by an increase in Israeli aircraft and boat activity.[42] However, it was how the incursion was so effectively terminated that deserves Western attention. Moshe Rudovsky, whose son was killed in this raid, says he learned from highly credible sources that his son's squad had been detected by enemy radar as they approached the beach.[43] Then, once ashore, the commandos were tracked by nonelectronic means. This can only be accomplished by a skilled stalker.

> Rudovsky claims, however, that following the Hezbollah discovery of the "Israeli" force, the enemy declared a "radio silence," refraining from using any communications equipment that might disclose its presence, all the while tracking the IDF [Israeli Defense Force] fighters.[44]
> — Hare'etz (Tel Aviv), 13 August 1998

By this time, *Hezbollah* had also become quite proficient with opportunistically installed and remotely controlled mines.[45] After 12 of 16 members of the above-mentioned commando unit were killed by a single blast,[46] one wonders how proficient. One of the following must have happened: (1) the Israeli's precise route had been leaked ahead of time; (2) their explosives had been accidentally detonated; (3) a huge charge had been tossed into their midst; (4) a preregistered artillery or mortar round had gotten them; or (5) an anti-personnel mine had been command-detonated nearby. While the overlay to a map or aerial photograph could not have pinpointed the commandos' route in enough detail to prearrange a sufficiently lethal mine, the Israeli high command still prefers the first two explanations. Both, albeit implausible, infer the commandos were simply under long-range surveillance the whole time. If they were additionally being tailed, they may have met with one of the other possibilities during (or right after) a rest stop. Only a technology-oriented Westerner would fail to expect that skilled an opponent. While admittedly difficult, it would be well within the capabilities of a skilled tracker who knew the neighborhood to somehow arrange the ambush. Luckily there exists a detailed account of what really happened.

> For 10 days, . . . the MK drone—a pilotless reconnaissance plane—had flown over the fields and orange groves at the northern end of Insariyeh. Ghalib Farhat had seen

the drones clearly from his one-story house on the edge of the village. Their presence had puzzled him. Insariyeh was far from "Israel's" occupation zone and there was little that could interest the "Israelis" in the village.

The naval commandos silently emerged from the water onto a rocky beach. . . . The team had to sneak across the road and pass through a gate in a 3-meter high concrete wall running along the east side of the highway to reach the cover of banana plantations and orange groves before continuing up the hill to Insariyeh. . . . Under the cover of a banana plantation, the team began the hard uphill march to the cliff-top village. . . .

. . . Ghalib was . . . bothered. Hezbollah fighters were operating in the area. They had arrived in the village about the same time that the drones had appeared 10 days earlier. Each night at about 10:00 P.M., a car with its lights switched off drove slowly along the lane past his home toward the village of Loubieh, 1 kilometer to the north. Four or five people would climb out of the car and disappear into the orange groves. They were there again that evening.

Kurakin and his 15 [Israeli] soldiers were struggling up the hill, fighting through dense undergrowth. He paused and beckoned to the radio operator. Kurakin wanted to take a short cut. There was a track running . . . between an orange grove and a windbreak of pine trees which would allow his team to move faster and bring him out midway along the lane between Insariyeh and Loubieh. His superior authorized the move and Kurakin led his team in the new direction. . . .

The "Israeli" [commando] team approached the lane between Insariyeh and Loubieh cautiously. Kurakin, the radio operator and one other soldier led the rest of the team by a few meters. As they reached the gate near the lane, Kurakin motioned them to halt. He and his two companions darted across the road and crouched beside a pile of garbage. Kurakin turned to order the other commandos forward. As he did so, a massive explosion engulfed the commandos, killing several of them instantly. Barely having time to recover from the shock of the blast, the team was hit by a second bomb which exploded in a huge bubble of orange flames with hundreds of steel ball bearings ripping through the "Israeli" unit. Kurakin raced back across the road to help the survivors. Then the machineguns opened up from the orange grove to the north. A bullet struck Kurakin in the head, killing him instantly. . . .

An "Israeli" Army commission of inquiry concluded that the commandos were the victims of a chance guerrilla ambush. . . . Hezbollah has maintained [virtual] silence over the affair. . . . Three years after the raid . . . , Hezbollah's southern commander, Sheikh Nabil Qaouk, is still reluctant to reveal the truth behind the battle. "It's still too early to tell the secrets of Insariyeh. The "Israelis" know that Hezbollah was aware of the operation but they don't know how. But I will say that our presence there was not a coincidence," Qaouk told The Daily Star. . . .

. . . Sayyed Hassan Nasrallah . . . perhaps gave the most accurate account of the . . . the Insariyeh battle. . . . He said groups of fighters armed with roadside bombs had deployed throughout the South . . . in anticipation of further commando raids.

"The nightwatchers are in most towns and villages, and are waiting for them using booby traps, rifles and mortar fire," Nasrallah said. . . .

. . . [N]ear the gate leading into the orange grove, beside a pair of iron water pipes, there are two small holes in the ground, marking the spot where the bombs exploded. Seared onto the iron pipes in front of each hole are the flattened remains of dozens of steel ball bearings—the shrapnel in the bombs.[47]
— *The Daily Star* (Lebanon), 9 June 2000

A high-level probe later determined that there had been no intelligence leak.[48] The commandos had probably picked up a "tail" at the hole in the wall near the beach. After watching them enter the natural lane running between orange grove and windbreak, their stalker had only to relay their route to a hilltop command post by blinking infrared light (or some other nonelectronic means). By the time the commandos reached the intersecting road, a roving claymore team was ready for them. There is one other possibility. Several claymore clusters may have been set up along the road at probable crossing points. Then, when the hilltop observer saw black shapes crossing the whitish-appearing road, he may have remotely

Figure 3.2: Preliminary Drones Had Doomed the Commandos
(Source: U.S. Air Force Clipart Library (www.usafns.com/art.shtml), image designator "1-07aa.tif")

detonated the closest cluster and told the machinegunner to fire onto this same location. The rest is history. The loss of these commandos so shook Tel Aviv's confidence in its own armed forces that they were all withdrawn from South Lebanon in May 2000.

Hezbollah's More Recent Forays Outside of Lebanon

Shiite *Hezbollah* currently supports Sunni *Hamas* in Israel's Gaza Strip and West Bank, so a few *Hezbollah* advisors should be expected at these locations. However, what if *Hezbollah* has been further honing its wartime skills through other foreign deployments?

While Lebanese *Hezbollah's* presence in Iraq during the U.S. occupation is not easy to prove, it is still widely believed throughout Lebanon.[49] Al-Sadr had announced his intention as early as 2 April 2004 to open Lebanese *Hezbollah* chapters in Iraq,[50] and an *Hezbollah* office was subsequently reported in Basra.[51] On 21 May 2004, thousands of Shiites marched in Beirut after *Hezbollah* leader Nasrallah accused the U.S. of desecrating holy shrines in Iraq. The marchers were all wearing white shrouds to symbolize their willingness to die in defense of the holy cities of Najaf and Karbala.[52] In early 2005, *Iraqi News* reported *Hezbollah* advisers serving with *Ansar al-Islam*,[53] a Sunni militia closely allied with *al-Qaeda*.[54] That Lebanese *Hezbollah* was recruiting for the Iraq War comes as no particular surprise, but whether it wanted those recruits as *Baseej* (ground troops to be led by its own personnel) is a totally other question. Within "occupied Palestine," it has preferred to arm, train, and then simply advise an independent proxy army. Still, some of the U.S. engagements near the Syrian border in 2004 looked very much like contact with a full-sized unit in transit.[55] Perhaps *Hezbollah* personnel were simply escorting aspiring *jihadists* to the war zone. Of all Iraqi militias suspected of using *Hezbollah* advisers, the Mahdi Army is at the top of the list.

> U.S. officials have long suggested that al-Sadr receives direct support from Iran's Revolutionary Guard and Lebanon's Hezbollah.[56]
> — *Christian Science Monitor,* 19 April 2004

> It [al-Sadr's rebellion] was prepared well in advance at the behest of Tehran . . . by the Shiite master terrorist Imad Mughniyeh [erstwhile director of operations for Lebanese Hezbollah]. Its purpose: to trigger Iran's Spring Offensive against the Americans in Iraq.
> Sunday night [4 April 2004], the young radical cleric al-Sadr told cheering followers in Kufa: "From now on we are the beating arm of the Hezbollah and Hamas in Iraq." The crowds, raising clenched fists, declared: "The occupation is over! Sadr is our ruler!"[57]
> — Israeli intelligence bulletin, 5 April 2004

Of course, *Hezbollah's* participation in Iraq may not have been all above board. Deception is, after all, the name of the game in Asia. This includes South Asia. One of the most interesting possibilities is that *Hezbollah* was supporting one or more Sunni proxies in Iraq, just as it had *Hamas* in Israel.[58]

In July 2004, it was reported that *Hezbollah* had been supporting al-Zarqawi [al-Qaeda in Iraq].[59] In fact, "Iran . . . [had originally] helped [to] smuggle . . . al-Zarqawi out of Afghanistan and into Lebanon where . . . [he was] linking up with *Hezbollah*."[60] Bin Laden has personally met with *Hezbollah's* operations chief Mughniyeh, and *al-Qaeda* operatives have also been trained in the Bekaa Valley on more than one occasion.[61] So the possibility of Lebanese *Hezbollah* involvement in things normally attributed to *al-Qaeda* is very real.[62]

> Though intelligence analysts differ over Zarqawi's exact relationship to Osama bin Laden, they agree . . . he has . . . links . . . with . . . Lebanese Hezbollah. . . .
> American intelligence officials have said they tracked Zarqawi to a meeting in south Lebanon in August 2002 with Hezbollah leaders.[63]
> — *Christian Science Monitor,* 23 January 2004

Where Else in the World Might *Hezbollah* Now Appear?

The next most logical place to look for *Hezbollah* is in northern Yemen. In fact, wherever the IRGC is involved with its "Islamic Revolution," there should also be *Hezbollah*. Really only of interest is *Hezbollah's* specific role in the proceedings. On 11 January 2007, Director of the Defense Intelligence Agency (DIA) testified before the American Senate that Iran's Quds Force has "the lead for its transnational terrorist activities, in conjunction with Lebanese *Hezbollah* and Iran's MOIS [Ministry of Intelligence and Security]."[64] In essence, *Hezbollah* is still an instrument of Iranian foreign policy.

Hezbollah Actually Is in Yemen

In February 2010, one of America's most respected nongovernmental intelligence sources announced that *Hezbollah* was withdrawing its 400-man contingent from Northern Yemen in response to an IRGC directive. Its purported 160 casualties implies direct involvement in combat with the Saudis, possibly as an assault battalion. Any doubt as to *Hezbollah's* presence in Yemen can be quickly eliminated by looking at its new Turkish website. Sporting Lebanese *Hezbollah's* flag on its main page, this website is full of images of *Hezbollah* personnel helping Houthi rebels.[65] Still, there is no evidence of a rebel unit being led by them. Whether or not the Yemeni *"Baseej"* are being led by *Hezbollah* personnel, they are almost certainly being trained by them.

> Yemen's state-controlled press claims Houthi rebels have been trained in an Iranian-run camp across the Red Sea in Eritrea. Yemen's president . . . says members of Lebanon's Iran-backed Hizbullah militia are teaching them.[66]
> — *The Economist,* 19 November 2009

This still leaves open the possibility of a *Hezbollah* assault battalion or special-operations unit. Deploying tiny component contingents against separate targets makes the latter more probable. During the early years in Lebanon, *Hezbollah* would occasionally conduct an exemplary attack its proxies could emulate. Only one thing is certain, *Hezbollah* people were definitely involved in the fighting.

> Hezbollah sources have told STRATFOR that they have troops actively engaged in combat in Yemen.[67]
> — *STRATFOR Weekly,* 3 February 2010

Iran's Ultimate Motive

Throughout history, powerful nations have often surrounded themselves with "buffer states"—neighboring countries that share their political perspective. Iran has been doing some of this in the Persian Gulf.

> Tehran has widened its subversive activities in the Arabian Peninsula. . . . Although the UAE [United Arab Emirates] claims the island of Abu Musa as part of its sovereign territory, Iranian forces have [nevertheless] occupied it. . . . Recent statements by Khomeinist clerics assert that Bahrain, too, is an Iranian possession under the name of Mishmahig Island. . . .

. . . Iranian intelligence has also been expanding its cells and cadres in the large Shia community of Bahrain.[68]
— *The Australian Conservative,* 12 July 2010

The riots in Bahrain following the overthrow of Mubarak in Egypt were primarily Shiite in composition.[69] Of course, Iran has also been working on bigger neighbors to the west and east. It has been guilty of "dispatching operatives, special forces and *Hezbollah* trainers throughout the Shia areas of [Iraq]."[70] It has also "infiltrated Afghanistan's Shi'ite Hazara community . . . and provided logistical support to the Taliban."[71]

However, Iran's northern and southern flanks are still relatively uncovered at its borders with pro-Western Turkey and Pakistan. This vulnerability to invasion may be the reason for her proxy armies in more distant locations. Able to strike back if Iran were ever attacked, those proxies would constitute a type of deterrent.

Iran has consistently reminded the world about the network of proxy groups that the country can call upon to cause trouble for any country that would attack its nuclear weapons program.[72]
— *STRATFOR Weekly,* 3 February 2010

Or, Iran may think PRC assistance in the U.N. well worth the price of involvement with far-flung Communist insurgencies. It would effectively draw the West's attention away from their ultimate instigator. After all, the Iranians have been helping Sunnis so radical as to consider every Shiite a heretic. Why couldn't they also consort with Socialists?

[T]he Iranians also have a pragmatic streak and will work with Marxist groups like the Kurdistan Workers' Party.[73]
— *STRATFOR Weekly,* 3 February 2010

Or, Iran may just be exporting its own brand of Islamic Revolution to build up a Shiite empire. In fact, it may have created *Hezbollah* precisely for this purpose.

The Islamist Shias are also jihadists, in the sense that they call for the establishment of a future Imamate, a Shia form of Islamic Caliphate. . . .

Hezbollah was an Iranian project designed to export its revolution globally and it fast became the single most dangerous terrorist network.[74]
— *The Australian Conservative,* 12 July 2010

Whatever the reason, Iran is on the move and generally being ignored by Washington. Its force multiplier within the various foreign proxies appears to be *Hezbollah*. More used to active combat than the Quds Force, it would also look less like an Iranian instrument.

Hezbollah a Little Farther from Home

Hezbollah is now also involved in West Africa, but possibly for reasons other than revolution. Though most of Africa's Muslim populations are Sunni, *Hezbollah* is known to run a drug conduit to Venezuela and possibly Curacao through Guinea-Bissau and some of its West African neighbors (like Cape Verde, Guinea, Mauritania, Niger, Mali, Ghana, Benin, Togo, Gambia, and Nigeria).[75]
Of course, not all of *Hezbollah's* "Dark Continent" activity is aimed at drug trafficking.

North Africa has been home almost exclusively to Salafi jihadists, it has witnessed increased activity by Tehran's Shi'ite operatives. According to Moroccan authorities, Iran has funded religious institutions whose first mission is to convert Sunnis to Shia, in what is coined as "Tashyeeh." In 2009 and 2010, the Rabat government shut down a number of these entities. . . .
Iran has also worked to penetrate West Africa since the 1980's. Taking advantage of the substantial size of the Lebanese communities in Senegal, Liberia, Sierra Leone, the Ivory Coast, Benin, and Nigeria, Hezbollah has developed financial and intelligence networks that span the entire region. . . .
. . . But [Lebanese] Hezbollah has gained valuable experience in penetrating Lebanon, Egypt, Iraq, Yemen and the countries of northern Africa, which enables Iran to do considerable damage to the U.S. in case of open conflict.[76]
— *The Australian Conservative,* 12 July 2010

While the *Al-Qaeda*-Oriented World Slept

In late January 2011, after two weeks of populist rioting in Tunisia, Egypt, and Yemen, Lebanon's coalition government collapsed after the resignation of 10 ministers representing *Hezbollah*. Then, when *Hezbollah* candidate Najib Miqati was named as Lebanon's new prime minister a few days later,[77] the dirty deed was complete. A Mediterranean country near the mouth of the Suez Canal was now being ruled by a terrorist organization. By 2 May 2011, even *Time Magazine* had confirmed that *Hezbollah's* Nasrallah was now essentially in charge of the country.[78]

One of two things had happened: (1) either Islamist or Communist factions had staged the other riots as a screen; or (2) *Hezbollah* had taken advantage of a coincidental diversion. Either way, most Americans remained oblivious to the fact that the Free World had just suffered another major setback. Both ends of the feared "Radical-Shiite Crescent" were now in place. Next included would almost certainly be Iraq.

As the "pro-democracy" demonstrations spread through North Africa and the Middle East in February and March 2011, the despotic rulers of Iran were in no way threatened by it. In fact, they welcomed it.[79] That's the nature of revolutionary government. While promoting revolution elsewhere, it has the internal security apparatus—in this case, the IRGC—to squelch it at home. The only other revolutionary government in this region is Sudan. It, in turn, has been heavily invested by the most powerful revolutionary government in the world—the PRC. As most of the separatist movements in North Africa have been supported from Sudan over the years,[80] one wonders how interested the PRC may be in Libyan oil and the Suez Canal.

Iran Finally Implicated in the 2011 Uprising

When the revolutionary zeal of February 2011 spread to Bahrain in the form of Shiite discord, Iran's involvement was almost certain but never fully confirmed. On 15 March, Iranian "destabilization" of the region was the reason given for a Saudi/UAE relief operation to bolster the Bahraini king.[81] Yet, Iran did not to meddle in the affairs of longtime allies. During the Syrian riots, it behaved as it would have at home—by supporting the establishment.

Iran's Overall Influence on Iraq

While Iran is no more "martially" proficient than any other Middle Eastern nation, it has become quite proficient in the other 4GW arenas. Few Americans now doubt its goal of a Shiite-dominated government in Iraq and Shiite "imamate" stretching all the way to the Mediterranean. Through many years of electoral engineering,[82] it has now managed a coalition of sorts between moderately pro-Iranian al-Maliki and fiercely anti-Western al-Sadr. A slim ballot-box victory by U.S. favorite Allawai in March 2010 did little to change this equation. Al-Sadr's political movement did so well in the 2010 election—capturing 40 of the available 325 parliamentary seats [83]—that it became the deciding factor. Unfortunately, al-Sadr has had the support of Iran, the IRGC, and its Quds Force since the very start of the Iraq War. This support included active-combat advisors.[84]

> The Iran-based Mr. Sadr gave his backing . . . , bringing al-Maliki almost to the parliamentary majority needed to form the next government.[85]
> — *Wall Street Journal,* 6 October 2010

In the end, the widely respected Mr. Allawi had to settle for the chairmanship of a new policy council.[86] Whether the U.S. military can finally claim victory in Iraq will now fully depend on future elections.

Ahmadinejad's Rather Cozy Relationship with Karzai

Prior to the Taliban regime's ouster from Kabul in 2001, the Northern Alliance (once called the United Front) was—for all practical purposes—an Iranian proxy.[87] As President Karzai originally came from the Northern Alliance, it should come as no particular shock that he warmly welcomed his Iranian counterpart during a state visit in March 2010,[88] or that he accepts millions of dollars in cash from him yearly.[89]

Iran has now been accused by America's erstwhile Anti-Terrorism Czar of moving its proxy war from Iraq to Afghanistan.[90] This does not seem to bother President Karzai. While the sacks of money seem a bit strange, they don't automatically infer a sellout. Drug deals regularly create large amounts of cash that must somehow be laundered. Because raw currency leaves no electronic trail, it is also used in the payoffs associated with corruption. If the Iranians are simply trying to control Afghan politics with money, they won't be alone in this endeavor. *Newsweek* reports Karzai's cabinet split between a pro-Iranian faction led by former warlord Khalili and a pro-U.S. group headed by finance minister Zakhilwal. It says the former currently has the upper hand.[91] Only left to be determined is whether a huge Communist neighbor had also been working its wiles.

The Communist Threat

● Where do Maoist revolutions rage?

● Which Communist state poses the biggest threat?

The PLA includes more than just all service branches.

Atheistic Communism Is Alive and Well

With the dismemberment of the Soviet Union and merger of global economies, many Americans now believe the Communist threat to be over. It isn't. The CIA's *World Factbook* still describes five nations—the PRC, North Korea, Vietnam, Laos, and Cuba—as being "Communist states."[1] Only at issue is how much danger they pose.

Of the five, only Vietnam and Laos seem content with their existing borders. North Korea has lately been far more menacing to its southern neighbor. In March 2010, one of its torpedoes halved a South Korean corvette, killing 46 sailors. Eight months later, its artillery pounded a South Korean island killing or injuring 23 of what were mostly Marines.[2]

North Korea's longtime patron—the PRC—has been more discreet with its aggression. Its most widely reported excesses have also involved territorial waters. This should come as no surprise—because "Chinese waters" extend far beyond the U.N. standard of 12 nautical miles and seem to include everything of strategic value. China's navy has now forcefully annexed all of the Spratley Islands from Vietnam, the Philippines, Malaysia, and Taiwan.[3] Located some 600 miles to the south of Hainan, those islands just happen to be sitting atop the second biggest oil and natural-gas deposit in the Western Pacific.[4]

Sadly, China's territorial assertiveness hasn't been limited to its Asian neighbors. In April 2001, a People's Liberation Army (PLA) fighter jet bumped a U.S. surveillance plane operating 70 miles from Hainan Island. This plane and its crew were only returned after a forced apology and exorbitant fine.[5] Then, almost eight years later, five Chinese vessels blocked and surrounded a U.S. surveillance ship—again in international waters—some 75 miles from Hainan Island.[6] Even for today's more "charm-oriented" PRC, "saving territorial face" seems ultimately to entail a military showdown. With its current generation of young officers reportedly as hawkish as the Japanese of the 1930's,[7] this does not come as particularly good news to war-weary Americans. Yet, even without any open warfare, China seems destined to inherit the world. With business extensions, peacekeeper contingents, pipeline security, and intelligence services operating in every corner, the PLA doesn't need to invade anyone. Mao Tse-Tung has provided a much safer way to project its influence, and this "way" has been greatly refined over the last 30 years.

While the PRC may not now oversee as much "revolution" as it did in the 1970's and 1980's in Africa, it still indirectly abets it in several locations. After an 18-year Maoist rebellion, neighboring Nepal now has a rebel leader for prime minister. China's new Western Hemisphere surrogate—Cuba—has been widely supporting not only guerrilla factions, but also leftist candidates (through its sub-satellite Venezuela). Meanwhile, North Korea has only been transporting drugs, providing tunneling advice, and supplying nuclear technology and site-hardening advice to radical regimes,

Islamist movements, and drug cartels.[8] As long as no Communist country actually marches into any other, America's leaders seem content to borrow more money and ignore the subversion.

For Those Who Now See the PRC As Their Friend

While totally based on fact, the above assessment of PRC intentions now clashes with "conventional U.S. wisdom." Some of America's most respected journalists believe North Korea would have become a far bigger problem if not for the calming effect of the PRC. Perhaps they have forgotten that hordes of PRC troops backed North Korea's invasion of the South in 1950. Still, those U.S. journalists are right about one thing. Any call, however hypothetical, for an American military response to such excesses will only make things worse. Both Communist armies literally feed off any suggestion of open combat. Yet, giving China whatever it wants is not the answer either. Openly appeasing a fledgling superpower with this poor a human-rights record can only lead to more worldwide instability. First will come the inexpensive trade products and low-interest loans, and then the "political" advice. As was Japan in December of 1941, China is not above a little diplomatic deception. The probability of a well-funded yet totally obscure Chinese lobby in Washington is also high.

Modern Communism As an Ideology

After Fidel Castro was heard in the summer of 2010 to off-handedly admit his system hasn't been working all that well, several well-meaning columnists again decreed that Communism was dead. In a free society where a Chinese lobby is probable, one must take such articles with a grain of salt. Communism is not dead. It has simply "morphed" into a dangerous hybrid.

More than an economic model, Communism is also a political doctrine. As with any such doctrine, its most serious problems arise from totalitarian execution. Then, all original philosophies are adapted to the regime's distorted agenda. The "people's" will becomes subservient to that of the State, and the State ends up controlling every aspect of the people's lives—to include their religion, location, and access to the truth. Communism is merely a more concerted form of Socialism. Communist theory contends that Socialism is a transitional stage on the way to Communism. The main difference between the two ideologies is that Communists' follow the revolutionary methods of Karl Marx.[9]

> In modern usage, the term Communism is applied to the movement that aims to overthrow the capitalist order by revolutionary means and to establish a classless society in which all goods will be socially owned.[10]
> — *The Columbia Encyclopedia,* Sixth Edition, 2008

In both China and Cuba, that which is state owned is already considered to be "socially owned." Both nations still widely pursue their political agenda through whatever form of "revolution" may be least visible. Such revolutions need not be martial.

Cuba's Most Recent Initiatives

Cubans now constitute a sizeable portion of Venezuela's governing cadre. While the exact number of "foreigner-filled" billets is sketchy, Caracas residents estimated the total number of Cubans in their country in 2008 to be around 100,000.[11]

> Cuba is the Chavez government's closest ally. . . . As of February 2005, Cuba reportedly had 20,000 doctors, dentists, teachers, and sports trainers in Venezuela. . . . Fidel Castro pledged in early 2005 that the number of Cubans would increase to 30,000 by the end of the year. In 2004 President Chavez reportedly posted dozens of Cuban "advisers" to the internal security and immigration agencies of the Ministry of Interior and Justice, other key ministries, and the Central Bank. . . .
> . . . [Cuba's] Military Intelligence . . . and some Cuban military advisers reportedly are engaged in training the [Venezuelan] military. In early 2005, Venezuela's National Assembly ratified a 1999 security agreement with Cuba that is intended to facilitate cooperation between security personnel in Venezuela and Cuba.[12]
> — Library of Congress Country Profile, March 2005

> Cuba is . . . providing intelligence and security officers to Venezuela. . . .
>
> Cuban military advisers are also present [in Venezuela's armed forces].[13]
> — *Armed Forces Journal,* July 2007

The extent to which Venezuela has been subverting the rest of Central and South America with its "Socialistic" agenda is considerable and would take many pages to summarize. Those interested in its details are instead referred to *Tequila Junction.*[14] Suffice it to say that Chavez has been doing more than just supporting the now-Maoist *FARC (Fuerzas Armadas Revolucionarias de Colombia).* He and his Cuban cronies have also been providing political assistance to leftist candidates throughout Latin America. That's why only six of its 20 regimes are still rightist. Of course, Chavez has other connections too. He has made several personal visits to both China and North Korea.[15]

> Chavez will first travel to close ally Cuba, and then to China, which Chavez calls a strategic ally, for the capitalization of a six-billion-dollar bilateral investment fund. He says Caracas will use it for "socialist productive projects" [wherever in South America it chooses].[16]
> — Agence France-Presse, 20 September 2008

Cuba's New "Sugar Daddy"

Russia no longer has enough money to be Cuba's mentor. That strategic opportunity has long since been inherited by the PRC. While the PRC's subsequent support of Cuba could also be closely documented, only one of its more disturbing details will be mentioned.

> An eight-member military delegation to Cuba earlier this month was led by Lt. Gen. Peng Xiaofeng, political commissar of the Second Artillery forces [the PLA's long-range missile branch].[17]
> — *Washington Times,* 15 March 2006

Thus, both Cuba and North Korea are now veritable minions

of the PRC. Neither could have survived economically without the PRC's help. The rest of this chapter is about what China has managed—on its own—closer to home.

China's Worldwide Quest

For all of the PRC's expansionist moves, see the following: (1) in Africa, *Terrorist Trail;* (2) in Southeast Asia, *Dragon Days;* (3) in Central and South America, *Tequila Junction;* and (4) in North America, *Homeland Siege.*[18] China doesn't want to militarily occupy the world, simply to control its commerce and politics. Its various "takeover" methods will be detailed later. For now, suffice it to say there are three general categories depending on the targeted nation's weaknesses. A Maoist, "narco," or other insurgency may force its rightist regime out of power. A massive influx of Chinese immigrants and money may unfairly influence its next election. Or economic favors may cause it to compromise its foreign policy and national security.

On the Asian mainland, the Chinese are not always that subtle of course. An in-depth study of their southwestward expansion might prove useful to those trying to stabilize Afghanistan.

China's Long History of Excesses along Its Southern Border

Adjoining countries will often differ as to the exact trace of shared boundaries. Within South Asia, China has more than once used this rather common issue as its excuse to grab huge chunks of territory. The rape of Tibet was only the first of many excesses. (See Map 4.1.)

> On October 1, 1949, the People's Republic of China was formally proclaimed in Beijing and the following year launched an armed invasion of Tibet. . . . Tibet was an independent state.
>
> Under the 1951 Seventeen Point Agreement between the People's Republic of China and representatives of the Tibetan Government, which incorporated Tibet into China, China guaranteed no alteration of Tibetan political, cultural, and religious systems and institutions. The failure of the

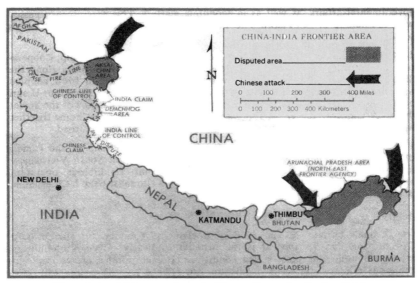

Map 4.1: Chinese Acquisitions from India in 1962
(Source: Defense Intel. Agency, "Handbook on the Chinese Forces," DDI-2680-32-76, July 1976, fig. 1, p. 1-8)

PRC to . . . uphold the Seventeen Point Agreement, and the imposition of so-called democratic reform, led to the March 1959 uprising in Lhasa. . . . The Chinese crackdown was harsh. An estimated 87,000 Tibetans were killed, arrested, or deported to labor camps. . . .

Since the revolt against Chinese rule in Tibet that began in 1956 and through the end of the Cultural Revolution in 1976, an estimated 1,200,000 Tibetans were killed and more than 6,000 religious sites were destroyed. . . . The International Commission of Jurists found that the PRC had committed "acts of genocide . . . in Tibet in an attempt to destroy the Tibetans as a religious group."[19]
— *Global Security,* 7 September 2010

At the Indian border, it was again through invasion that the Chinese got what they wanted in 1962. They had a good reason for attacking in two widely separated places at once. (Refer back to

Map 4.1.) In the below description, please note the road they had already built through Indian territory to connect Tibet with the Northern Areas of Pakistan-occupied Kashmir.

> During the mid and late 1950's, Chinese relations with India slowly deteriorated due in part to conflicting claims over nearly 40,000 square miles of territory that India regarded as its own. This territory included virtually the whole North East Frontier Agency (NEFA) of Assam and parts of Ladakh [eastern Kashmir], particularly the area of Aksai Chin through which China had constructed a highway in 1957 linking Tibet and Sinkiang. In October 1962, following mutual allegations of frontier intrusions, the Chinese launched large-scale attacks in the NEFA and Ladakh. While the Chinese forces penetrated as far down as the foothills of the Himalayas in the western sector of NEFA, they made only limited penetrations into the eastern sector and refrained from entering the plains of India, remaining within the territory claimed by China. On 21 November 1962, Peking announced a unilateral cease-fire and began withdrawing its troops back to the original line of actual control.[20]
> — U.S. Defense Intelligence Agency, July 1976

To the base of the Himalayas, China still claims most of India's Arunachal Pradesh State as its own.[21] This is the easternmost area attacked on Map 4.1. Should open warfare with the West ever come, Chinese troops will almost certainly reoccupy it—along with Assam's nearby town of Ledo. From Ledo, a road was built by the Allies during WWII that connected to the Burma Road at Lashio, which in turn went on to Kunming, China.

China's Subsequent Acquisition in Occupied Kashmir

Chinese troops never left the westernmost shaded area on Map 4.1. Though still contested by India, it became known as Aksai Chin. Then in 1963, presumably in trade for some political concession or material reward, Pakistan ceded another large slice of occupied Kashmir to the Communist Chinese. (See the crosshatched area on Map 4.2.) There was now a precedent for what would transpire in 2010.

A Slightly Different *Modus Operandi* in Nepal

In Nepal, the PRC used a more insidious strategy to bring a sovereign neighbor into its political "sphere of influence." As caretakers to a revolutionary regime, China's ruling-party believes that progress elsewhere often requires armed insurrection. So, when India's much-better-off northern neighbor began to experience a Maoist rebellion in 1990, that rebellion's source was not hard to identify. In 2008, this insurrection led to the political overthrow of an existing monarchy. That was when Nepal's young voters elected Pranchanda—an avowed Maoist—as their new prime minister on a "platform of change." For a detailed account of this nation's slide into darkness, see the annex to *Homeland Siege*.[22]

India's Ongoing Woes

For the second time in five years, the Indian government announced on 18 February 2010 that its "Naxalite" Maoist rebellion constituted its "single biggest internal security threat." In mid-April 2010, 76 Indian policemen were killed by Maoist rebels in a single incident. Whereas 55 districts in nine states had been beset by Maoists in 2004, a full third of the 636 districts in 20 of India's 28 states were by May 2010.[23]

Like all Maoist revolutions, this Naxalite rebellion has had political teeth as well. It was born near India's border with Nepal in 1967. Then, some 10 years later, the residents of the Indian state of West Bengal democratically elected a Communist government.[24] From the city of Calcutta, that government held sway over the narrow corridor of land that separated PRC-friendly Nepal from the Indian Ocean.

On a depiction of Naxalite-targeted areas produced by India's Institute of Conflict Management in 2006, one can detect Naxalite activity at unlikely places along the base of the Himalayas. (Look more closely at Map 4.2.) Throughout Assam, there has been another revolution that is more obviously Chinese supported. It is being waged by the People's Liberation Army of Northeast India.

The People's Liberation Army (PLA) was established under the leadership of N. Bisheswar Singh on September 25, 1978. . . .

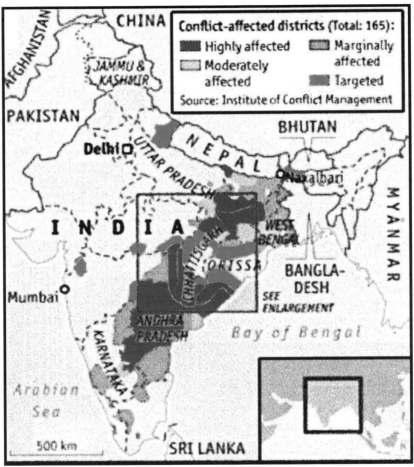

Map 4.2: Naxalite-Targeted Areas as of August 2006
(Source: Inst. of Conflict Mgt., from "A Spectre Haunting India," *The Economist*, 17 August 2006, © 2006)

It has a government-in-exile in Bangladesh where the PLA has set up a number of bases in the Sylhet district. Two camps in Myanmar and five camps in Bangladesh are currently known to exist, where about 1,000 recruits have received arms training. . . .

> July 13 [2010]: [T]he Chinese have promised to extend
> assistance only to the militant groups when the cadre
> strength reaches 30,000. . . .
> November 7 [2009]: "Sentinel" [Assam] reports that
> Chinese Army has trained cadres of the PLA outfit. . . .
> PLA militant 'sergeant' Ronny . . . stated, "China's People's
> Liberation Army remains in contact with Manipur's PLA.
> [Sixteen] 16 platoons of militants have come back to India
> after getting trained in China."[25]
> — *South Asia Intel. Review* database, Fall 2010

Just to the east of this region, Myanmar (formerly Burma) has become a close ally of the PRC. The Chinese have been building a massive oil conduit through Myanmar for many years. From the Bay of Bengal, it runs up the Irrawaddy River, then along the old Burma Road, and finally into Kunming. For its specifics, see *Dragon Days.*[26]

Bhutan May Already Have Problems

Formerly a monarchy like Nepal, Bhutan held its first election in March 2008. This momentous occasion was sadly marked by a series of terrorist bomb blasts.[27] Considering what has happened to other tiny states along the base of the Himalayas, the new government of Bhutan should be worried. (Refer back to Map 4.1.) Only its next-door neighbor to the west—Sikkim—has so far managed to avoid a Chinese incursion. (See Map 4.3.)

In 1947, Sikkim's joining of the Indian Union was rejected by a popular vote, and India's Prime Minister agreed to special protectorate status for the tiny kingdom. India would control its external affairs, defense, diplomacy, and communications, while Sikkim would otherwise be autonomous. In 1973, riots in front of the national palace led to a formal request for India's protection. Two years later, Sikkim's equivalent of prime minister appealed to the Indian Parliament for statehood. The Indian Army soon occupied Sikkim's capital city. A referendum was held in which 97.5% of those who voted elected to join the Indian Union. On 16 May 1975, Sikkim became the 22nd state of the Indian Union after its monarchy was abolished.[28]

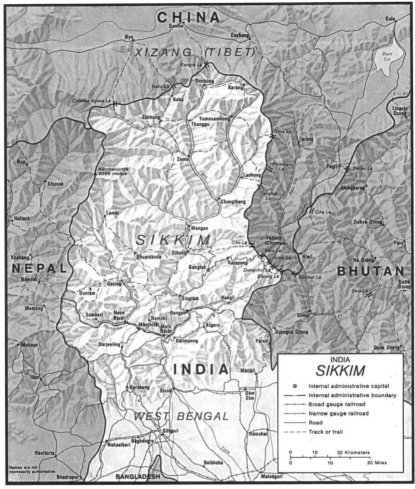

Map 4.3: India's Stopgap Measure—Sikkim
(Source: Courtesy of General Libraries, University of Texas at Austin, from their website, for map designator "sikkim.jpg")

The Latest Chinese Border Move—in Gilgit-Baltistan

In 2009, Pakistan's rulers gave a new name—Gilgit-Baltistan—to what had previously been the "Northern Areas" of occupied

Kashmir and Jammu. With a province-like legislature (though no province-like status with the Pakistani government), Gilgit-Baltistan has since been awarded many PRC-funded public-service projects. As with the Chinese-built pipelines in Sudan, some of the these "workers" are most likely PRC soldiers masquerading as security guards. Whether this can ever be proven is irrelevant, because many of the construction firms are likely to be civilian extensions of the PLA anyway—just as China Ocean Shipping Company (COSCO), Hutchison Whampoa, and others have been.[29] The real problem is that Pakistan already has a history of giving away disputed portions of Kashmir to the Chinese. As easily seen on Map 4.4, it ceded a good-sized strip along this region's eastern edge to China in 1963. Thus, the Chinese-occupied Aksai Chin may be about to get a big sister through more devious means. Sadly for India and West, this sister is in a far more important location from the standpoint of world trade.

When a *New York Times* opinion-editorial piece proclaimed on 26 August 2010 that Pakistan was handing over *de-facto* control of part of occupied Kashmir to China,[30] it made quite a stir. Though soon reprinted all over South Asia, this information never made it onto U.S. television. Its parent article indicated as many as 11,000 Chinese troops were still occupying the place.[31] A few of India's biggest newspapers quickly questioned the veracity of either claim. Then, India's *Rediff News* pointed out that it really didn't matter whether there were any uniformed Chinese troops present or not, because many of the projects had "PLA construction crews."[32] The PLA is, after all, known to still have many civilian business extensions.

When the governments of both Pakistan and China denied the *de-facto* turnover, they for the first time mentioned something about a high-altitude rail link paralleling the Karakoram Highway.[33] (See Map 4.5.) Having considerable experience with such things in Tibet, the Chinese were not only fantasizing about future possibilities. Trains can carry far more oil than trucks. As for the military presence, they finally admitted to a few PLA personnel in Gilgit-Baltistan to assist with disaster relief. " 'Chinese were working on landslide, flood-hit areas and on the destroyed Karakoram Highway with the permission of Pakistani Government,' the *Dawn* [a Pakistani newspaper] quoted Foreign Office spokesman Abdul Basit, as saying."[34]

This isn't the first time a major Western newspaper has an-

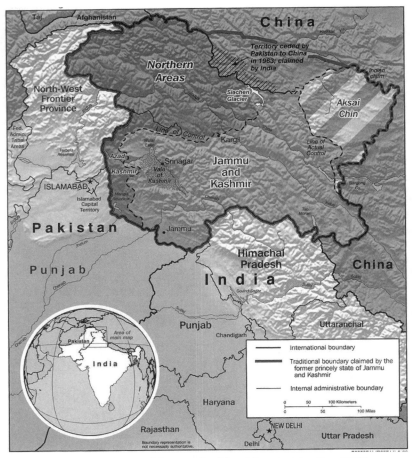

Map 4.4: Area of Strategic Significance to the PRC
(Source: Courtesy of General Libraries, University of Texas at Austin, from their website, for map designator "kashmir_region_2004.pdf")

nounced large numbers of Chinese troops in places where they shouldn't have been. In August 2000, Britain's *Sunday Telegraph* reported a "huge influx" of Chinese soldiers into Sudan to help with that nation's war in the south. Four years later, the *Washington Times* lowered the estimate to 4,000 and said that the troops were

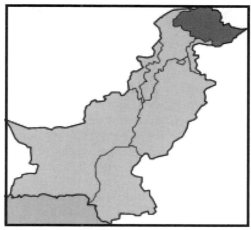

Map 4.5: Once "Northern Areas"of Pakistan-Occupied Kashmir
(Source: Wikipedia.org, s.v "Gilgit-Baltistan," under provisions of GNU Free Documentation License, map designator "PakistanNorthern.png," © n.d.)

there to protect the Chinese-built pipeline.[35] Soon, hundreds of thousands of Chinese immigrants descended on this country—enough eventually to take over much of its growing infrastructure from the bottom.[36]

Is PRC Really Getting *"de Facto"* Control of Gilgit-Baltistan?

The PRC would love to have full control over this strategic crossroads. (See Map 4.6.) Any who still doubt this need to revisit their history books. Whether that ever happens, of course, will depend on how hard the West objects to the PRC's presence. Ordinarily, the next step would be hordes of Chinese immigrants or some other way to influence the local elections. However, China does not require full political control of this area to use it as an oil conduit. It needs only a free hand with all necessary construction and security. Courtesy of Pakistan, it already has considerable leeway over the building of roads, rail lines, pipelines, and their various embellishments (like dams, bridges, tunnels, etc.). (See Map 4.7.) As in Sudan, this leeway may additionally include the positioning of Chinese troops to preclude operational disruptions.

In the future, the PRC will be quick to assume more caretaker status over Gilgit-Baltistan. Pakistan has already once ceded a disputed part of its occupied territory to China. Should it again need a financial or diplomatic favor, it could conceivably go along with gradually lessening its authority in the region. In a country where the same officials who condone drug trafficking also trade in nuclear secrets,[37] almost anything is possible.

The West will most likely ignore the extent to which the construction companies in Gilgit-Balistan represent the PLA. While their workers may not be troops in civilian clothing, they can still accomplish 4GW-like missions. As the residents of U.S. Appalachia found out the hard way in the 1930's, the only employer in an economically depressed region becomes politically powerful. In a press conference on the Gilgit-Baltistan "relief" effort, PRC Foreign Ministry spokesperson Jiang Yu said the following: "The Chinese People's Liberation Army, the Red Cross Society of China, local governments, and *Chinese enterprises* provided different forms of assistance (italics added)."[38]

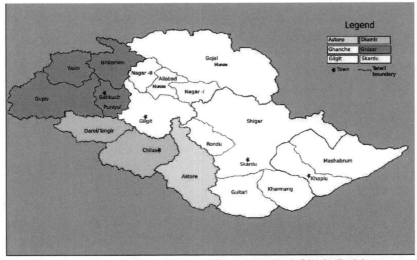

Map 4.6: Now Autonomous "Province" of Gilgit-Baltistan
(Source: Wikipedia.org, s.v "Gilgit-Baltistan," under provisions of GNU Free Documentation License, map designator "Northern_Areas_Pakistan.png," © n.d.)

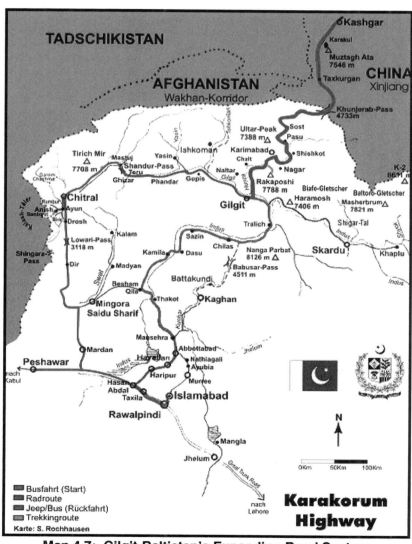

Map 4.7: Gilgit-Baltistan's Expanding Road System
(Source: "Pakistan's Newest Province 'Gilgit-Baltistan'," *Rupee News*, 29 August 2009, likely Pak. govt. produced, © n.d., map designator "karakorum-highway-chitral.jpg")

A Better Estimate on the Numbers of Troops

While at least one Indian newspaper quickly denied the presence of 11,000 Chinese troops in Gilgit-Baltistan, other media sources confirmed the presence of a few.

China has provided a soft loan of $300 million to Pakistan for reconstruction and rehabilitation . . . as follow-up on relief for the earthquake. Following the recent floods, it has taken up the task to get the Karakoram Highway back on track. Many of its military personnel are there for relief work.[39]
— *Yahoo News,* 5 September 2010

Indian military sources also . . . confirmed that a Chinese infantry battalion, or about 1,000 soldiers, has been deployed this month in Gilgit-Baltistan at the Khunjerab Pass, to provide security for Chinese workers engaged in widening the Karakoram highway and building a railroad.[40]
— *Rupee News* (Pakistan), 7 September 2010

"The Hindu" . . . reported: "On Friday (September 3) morning, Indian Ambassador to China, S. Jaishankar had conveyed New Delhi's concerns over China's recent moves in Pakistan-Occupied Kashmir in talks with Chinese Vice Foreign Minister Zhang Zhijun. . . . Zhang assured Indian officials that the troops were stationed there only for flood relief work and to provide humanitarian assistance." . . .

. . . . As regards Beijing's contention that their troops were present in the Gilgit-Baltistan region only for humanitarian relief work, the Chinese have made two humanitarian interventions in the area this year. . . . On January 4, a landslide created a huge artificial lake in the Hunza area, which subsequently burst submerging a large number of villages in the Gojal Tehsil. About 22 kms of the Karakoram Highway were submerged under water totally disrupting road communications with Xinjiang in China. . . . The Pakistan Army was . . . not able to reach the affected villages in the upstream area for want of helicopters. The Pakistan Government appealed to the Chinese for assistance. Workers of the Chinese Red Cross and engineers of the People's Liberation Army entered the Hunza area for relief. The Xinhua [news agency] reported as follows: "On January 19, at the request of the Pakistani government, the Chinese side made special arrangements to open the Kunjirap border and facilitate the purchase of relief goods. . . . The China Road and Bridge Corporation, which is conducting the project of upgradation of the Karakoram Highway, has also provided engineering consultations and equipment to help the Pakistani side to deal with the problem." The second humanitarian intervention at the request of Islamabad was made after the recent floods (B. Raman, "India Misses an Opportunity. . . ," southasiaanalysis.org).[41]

— Chennai (India) Centre for China Studies,
5 September 2010

The Extent of the Chinese-Sponsored Construction Effort

Despite all the cozy posturing, China has long wanted to bring oil and gas up the Karakoram Highway from Gwadar and Peshawar—the terminus of its new road across Afghanistan from Iran. With this initiative and others, it could successfully bypass the Straits of Malacca in time of war. As such, the PRC would be eager to help with any damage that might have recently occurred to the Karakoram Highway.

Now raising eyebrows in India is the number of Chinese construction projects already underway in the new province-like entity before the rains, landslides, and floods occurred. Some of the companies are most likely business extensions of the PLA. Though the PLA was supposedly required to divest itself of all business interests by 2000,[42] it is suspected of several major exceptions.[43] With deception so integral a part of Asia's military heritage, this should come as no surprise to any security-oriented Westerner. China still has a "revolutionary" government. Revolution (in all of its forms) most easily takes root in a volatile environment. Where Chinese peacekeepers are not allowed, Chinese enterprises get involved. Each, of course, will need its own security force. This clever way of accomplishing strategic missions without troops is most evident in Afghanistan.

Since 2004, China Railway Shisiju Group Corporation has been building a road to link Pakistan with Kabul through Jalalabad. In the late summer of 2006, this same company began an extension

65

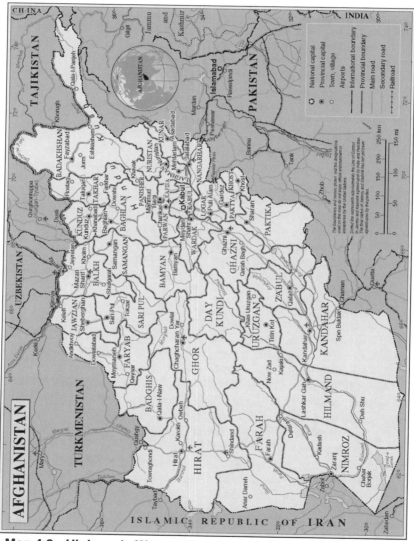

Map 4.8: Highway's Westward Extension through Afghanistan
(Source: Courtesy of the U.N., Dept. of Peacekeeping, Cartographic Section, Map No. 3958 Rev. 5, October 2005, © 2005 by the U.N.)

from Kabul westward through Wardak Province into Bamian City.[44] This road's final destination is, of course, the Iranian petroleum fields. China is also helping to build the leg to Herat.[45] (See Map 4.8.) Since January 2005, a new thoroughfare has already existed between the Dogharoun region of northeastern Iran and Herat.[46] At the other end of the above-mentioned conduit is the Karakoram Highway.

If some of the construction companies now working in Gilgit-Baltistan are indeed extensions of the PLA, then the number of uniformed troops there would be less significant. (See Figure 4.1.) Still to come under the PRC's sphere of influence, this region need not be militarily occupied. It could be somehow "purchased" from Pakistan as was the Trans-Karakoram Tract (of Indian claimed territory) in 1963.[47] (Refer back to Map 4.2.) Or its restive population could be given revolutionary and then political assistance as was done in Nepal. Or, its so-called government could be persuaded to trade full access to the area for help with its development, as was done in the Democratic Republic of the Congo's (DRC's) mineral-rich northeast in 2008.[48] At any rate, a much closer look at these construction companies is definitely in order.

According to the *Indian Express* and *Yahoo News,* there were at least 17 major Chinese projects underway in Pakistan Occupied Kashmir as of 5 September 2010. They constituted more than half all Chinese projects on Pakistani soil. All together, about 122 Chinese companies were involved. According to the article, China had suddenly increased its involvement in almost every key sector of the area's growth and taken virtual responsibility for building its basic infrastructure. The list of projects ranged from mobile connectivity services to power projects, highways, and rail links.[49] One worries about such news for two reasons. First of all, this is a sparsely populated, high-altitude region that would not normally see this much construction activity. Secondly, the Chinese provided the same kinds of support to the Taliban regime while it was still in power in Afghanistan.[50]

> In their final days, the Taliban . . . boasted that they had a strategic pact with China. Last October, . . . Jalaluddin Haqqani told reporters that China was "extending support . . . to the Taliban."[51]
> — *Christian Science Monitor,* 23 August 2002

Figure 4.1: Chinese Karakoram Highway "Guard"
(Source: Courtesy of Orion Books, from *World Army Uniforms since 1939*, © 1975, 1980, 1981, 1983 by Blandford Press Ltd., Part II, plate 81)

Confirmed Civilian Branches of the PLA

COSCO and Hutchison Whampoa have both for years been heavily referenced as continuing business extensions of the PLA. Sadly (and probably for political reasons), only the former has been definitely proven to be so.

> "Although presented as a commercial entity, COSCO is actually an arm of the Chinese military establishment. . . ," states a 1998 special report written by the House Task Force on Terrorism and Unconventional Warfare.[52]
> — *Newsmax,* 27 February 2003

There are other business appendages of the PLA, but the biggest and most active internationally is China National Electronics Import and Export Corporation (CEIEC).

> Although China officially denied that it installed the fiber-optic air defense network inside Afghanistan, the Pentagon is certain that China sold the military system to the Taliban. . . .
>
> The military command network in Afghanistan is described by Pentagon analysts as similar to the fiber-optic air defense system installed in [Saddam Hussein's] Iraq by China. . . .
>
> The fiber-optic network in Afghanistan has more than just a common thread with the Iraqi air defense system. The Chinese company CEIEC that built and installed the new system for the Taliban is also a known arms manufacturer, owned and operated by the People's Liberation Army. According to an official Defense Intelligence Agency (DIA) document, CEIEC is the prime maker of electronics for the Chinese army. The DIA documents state that virtually all CEIEC products are military in nature, including "cryptographic system," "mine detection equipment," "fiber and laser optics," "communications technology" and "radars."[53]
> — *Newsmax,* 20 October 2001

To confirm *Newsmax's* claim, one has only to visit the CEIEC website. In its introductory video, a CEIEC spokesperson clearly states the company is "state owned" and specializes in defense electronics, ship building, world trade, and overseas engineering. Among its ongoing engineering projects are hydropower dams and electric grids. Then, in what has become all-too-common PRC rhetoric, the company's president proclaims, "The process of economic globalization is inevitable." (After many decades of "hoodwinking" the West, PRC officials are often boastful.) Appearing over and over in the video is the same Chinese metaphoric cartoon—a tiny seed growing into a large tree. Its lyrics are not quite as comforting—"one seed, one world."[54] The proverbial seed is, of course, the PRC's global agenda. All Chinese Communist Party (CCP) members consider their revered nation to be the traditional center of the civilized world.

One other enterprise has been reported by several reliable

sources to be formerly "the railway arm of the People's Liberation Army." This company is China Railway Construction Corporation (CRCC). It is now the world's sixth biggest construction contractor, with projects in over 60 countries.[55] "During the 1970's (long before China had become rich), the PLA had built—at great cost—the Karakoram Highway between Xinjiang and northern Pakistan."[56] More recently, the CRCC has built the high-altitude and extremely challenging Qinghai-Tibetan railway that became operational in July 2006.[57] This may help to explain why China Railway Shisiju Group Corporation (CRSSG) is currently building the transportation corridor across Afghanistan to the Iranian oil fields. At the top of CRSSG's home page is still displayed a very distinctive CRCC logo.[58] This logo is made up of an elongated globe with CRCC inscribed across its entire width. Obviously implied is that CRSSG is a subsidiary of the once-PLA-operated CRCC.

The History of the PLA's Business Involvement

In 1949, China had only state-owned firms, and its infrastructure was in shambles. Its military was soon given economic reconstruction tasks—building railroads and factories, reclaiming wasteland, digging irrigation canals, establishing state farms, and participating in disaster relief. Having accepted this economic development role, the PLA devoted many of its structural elements—like its Engineering Corps, Railway Engineering Corps, Capital Construction Engineering Corps, Signal Corps, and Production and Construction Corps—to building up the national infrastructure. It continued with this type of work into the mid-1980's, with many of its soldiers being concurrently trained in various civilian occupations.[59]

Through a Socialist desire for military self-sufficiency, China's ruling party had allowed the PLA to create enough civilian business enterprises to financially support its own needs. The PLA soon became semi-autonomous, and this made China's civilian leaders nervous. After faring poorly in the Sino-Vietnamese War of 1979, they shrunk the military to free up more resources for economic development. This put even more pressure on the PLA to support itself.[60] It may have also given its generals the idea to use international construction as a way to further their martial strategies. Then, Deng Xiaoping began to decrease the military's participation in national-level politics. Further to streamline the PLA, he is supposed to have civilianized its Railway Engineering Corps and the Capital Construction Engineering Corps.[61] Yet, as late as the mid-1990's, the PLA still had extensive commercial holdings in non-military areas, particularly real estate. By the late 1990's, it was to have divested itself of all companies without clear military purpose. However, others may have been deemed necessary to secretly pursue global expansion. As might be expected, the management of most such operations remained unchanged, with their officers simply retiring from the PLA to run the newly formed private holding companies.[62]

[D]uring the divestment process [after 1998], the PLA's reputation suffered . . . when revelations about the involvement of military enterprises in smuggling . . . came to light. The military transferred large numbers of businesses to local governments, closed others, and, in some cases, handed them over to families of PLA officers. Thousands more . . . remained in military control.[63]
— Council on Foreign Relations, 18 September 2010

The [Chinese] People's Liberation Army must have one of the most extensive military industrial complexes in the world, employing some 700,000 employees in about 10,000 enterprises. . . . [I]n the 1980's . . . Deng Xiaoping's policy of economic reform forced the military more or less to finance its own modernization, due to a relative decline in the official budget. By conversion of part of its industries to civilian production, the [Chinese] Army was able to supplement its income. . . . In 1998, the Party demanded that the PLA withdraw from non-military commercial activities, but it remains unclear to what extent this order has been heeded.[64]
— Internat. Inst. of Social History, December 2009

Other Currently Active PLA Business Proxies

One internet encyclopedia shows about 75 Chinese corporations as still being state owned,[65] with no indication as to which may have PLA connections. While COSCO, CRCC, China Metallurgical Group Corporation (MCC), and various oil exploration companies are included on this list, notably absent are Hutchison

Whampoa, CEIEC, China State Construction Engineering Corporation (CSCEC), and China Road and Bridge Corporation (CRBC).[66]
The internet list is obviously incomplete, for three of the four omit-
ted are shown by their websites to be state owned. Like CRBC,
CSCEC appears to be formerly part of the PLA. CSCEC is now
China's biggest international general contractor—with projects
in more places than can be conveniently summarized. CRBC has
offices in 20 African nations, 10 East Asian nations, eight Central
Asian nations, and three Middle Eastern nations. Of note, almost
all are in strategically contested regions.[67]

Only Hutchison Whampoa makes no real claim to being state
owned. It does, however, build port facilities in over 54 countries
(and at both ends of the Panama Canal).[68] In the hybrid economy of
a Communist state, why couldn't a non-state-owned corporation still
support the military establishment? If neither bragged about their
relationship, who in the West would know? Hutchison Whampoa's
chairman uses the same chilling metaphor at his website as did
the chairman of CEIEC: "[Infrastructure assistance projects] are
the country's roots. And like a tree, the deeper its roots, the more
flourishing its branches and foliage."[69]

China Communications Construction Company Limited
(CCCCLTD) is also shown by its website to be an "infrastructure
construction business." More interested in "lines of communication"
than telephones, it works on ports, roads, railways, bridges, and
tunnels. Its website again shows a globe covered with CCCCLTD
projects. It further shows CRBC and China Harbor Engineering
Company (CHEC) to be subsidiaries. CRBC and CHEC were both
founded around 1979. This may indicate the previous inclusion of
both in the PLA.[70] CCCCLTD is apparently still state owned.[71]

The PLA May Even Have a Criminal Enterprise

Even a criminal enterprise is thought to be a PLA extension.
Drug trafficking is, after all, one of the world's most lucrative en-
deavors. It could pay for a lot of technological advancement. Those
who smuggle drugs and people in are also good at bringing spies
and documents out.

> People's Liberation Army owns a string of nightclubs
> with the Sun Yee On triad society. . . .

. . . One authority on triads says the "great fear" of the Hong Kong police is arms smuggling by triads in alliance with the People's Liberation Army.[72]
— *The New Republic* (Washington, D.C.), July 1997

Implications of this Hidden PLA Capability

Hopefully, this limited investigation into which construction companies might still be helping the PLA to achieve its global objectives will help to improve U.S. security. After all, the PLA is known to be an all-inclusive entity. After initially having to fix Chinese infrastructure, it seems only logical that the PLA would use foreign infrastructure building as a way to screen its expansionist activity wherever peacekeepers weren't authorized. All those new transportation corridors would also help its parent nation to fully usurp all local resources.

In true Sun-Tzu-like fashion, China appears to have effectively turned capitalism in upon itself. The long names and required acronyms for its companies simply complete the deception. If America ever wakes up to the threat, some of its past and present leaders may have some serious explaining to do. For now, only the Gilgit-Balistan example will be further expanded.

Exact Identities of the PRC Companies in Gilgit-Baltistan

Almost all the Chinese work in this remote region has to do with international transportation, as opposed to local community service (like schools, hospitals, etc.). Most notably, China Road and Bridge Corporation has taken responsibility for the upgrade of the Karakoram Highway. Two other companies will be double-laning it and the Jaglot-Skardu road.[73]

Major construction will also happen on the 500-mile rail link that parallels the Karakoram Highway between Havelian and the Khunjerab Pass. A joint venture between Pakistan Railways and Dongfang (Dongfeng) Electric Corporation will initially run only freight trains along this route.[74] (Those trains will be mostly composed of oil tanker cars.)

Naturally, more bridges will be needed. Pakistan has awarded a big contract to a Chinese state-owned company for construction of a major bridge on River Jhelum at Dhangali in Mirpur District. Further, the Xinjiang Road and Bridge Construction Company of China will be replacing five Bailey bridges on the strategically important Gilgit-Skardu road.[75]

Major transportation conduits require lots of power. China has agreed to finance the huge Diamer-Bhasha Dam project. Sinihydro may also be involved. Additionally, there will be the Magla dam-raising. This is a joint venture between China International Water and Electric Corporation and various Pakistani companies. Then, there is the Neelum-Jhelum hydropower project. China Gezhouba Water and Power Corporation has formed a consortium for this project in Muzaffarabad district. Besides these, China has taken up at least four other hydropower assignments: (1) Bhunji in Gilgit-Baltistan; (2) Kohala; (3) Naltar; and (4) smaller ones in Phendar, Harpo and Yurlbo.[76]

Transportation conduits also need communications. China Mobile (state-owned) will be providing mobile services in certain areas of Gilgit-Baltistan. The company has plans to set up more towers and expand coverage.[77]

Finally, there is a project that has nothing to do with transportation but still complies with China's main interest—natural resources. Being a mountainous region, Gilgit-Baltistan has plenty of minerals. As such, the same Chinese MCC Resources Development Company Ltd. that has been exploiting Afghanistan's massive Aynak copper reserves will be starting mineral exploration here.[78] Pakistan Surpass Mining Company, a subsidiary of China's Xinjiang Surpass Mining Company Ltd., has also submitted an investment proposal. It plans to set up a hydropower station and molybdenum processing plant in the Chupurshan Valley.[79]

Too Little Dissemination of Important Information

Possibly due to the Chinese lobby in Washington, this earth-shaking news had to be shared with the American public through an opinion editorial piece. To this researcher's knowledge, it was never repeated by a television network or wire service. Thus, both author and newspaper deserve a round of applause in what has become an environment of over-editing and "political correctness." No novice to Chinese affairs, this author is the Director of the Asia

Program at the Center for International Policy and a former South Asia bureau chief for *The Washington Post.*[80] The meat of what he had to say is this:

> Islamabad is handing over de facto control of the strategic Gilgit-Baltistan region in the northwest corner of disputed Kashmir to China.[81]
> — *New York Times,* 26 August 2010

Here's how an Indian newspaper paraphrased the rest of the *New York Times* article.

> "China wants a grip on the strategic area to assure *[sic]* unfettered road and rail access to the Gulf through Pakistan," the paper said, and for this purpose is building high-speed rail and road link. The link-up would enable Beijing to transport cargo and oil tankers from eastern China to the new Chinese built Pakistani Naval base at Gawadar, Pasni and Ormara in Balochistan . . in 48 hours.
>
> "Many of the PLA soldiers entering Gilgit-Baltistan are expected to work on the railroad. Some are extending the Karakoram Highway, built to link China's Xinjiang province with Pakistan. Others are working on dams, expressways and other projects," the paper said. It said that mystery surrounds the construction of 22 tunnels in secret locations, where even Pakistanis are barred. Tunnels would be necessary for a projected gas pipeline from Iran to China that would cross the Karakorams through Gilgit. . . .
>
> Coupled with support for Taliban, Islamabad's collusion in facilitating China's access to the Gulf makes it clear that Pakistan is not a U.S. "ally," the New York Times said.[82]
> — *Rediff News,* 28 August 2010

In response to the many denials, the author of the *New York Times* article subsequently modified the numbers and types of PLA troops present in Gilgit-Baltistan. Still, his point about "PLA construction crews . . . now . . . building big residential enclaves clearly designed for a long-term presence" should not be ignored.[83] Given the PRC's knack for strategic deception and border expansion, Mr. Harrison's warning should be taken to heart.

An American scholar . . . is insisting that Islamabad has ceded control of the area to Beijing despite denials from both sides.

Harrison . . . followed up a rebuttal of his article . . . by conceding that China had not deployed combat soldiers, but "there has been an influx of construction, engineering and communication units of the People's Liberation Army into Gilgit-Baltistan . . . totalling at least 7,000 military personnel."

In addition, several thousand PLA troops are said to be stationed in the Khunjerab Pass on the Xinjiang border to protect Karakoram Highway construction crews, with ready access to Gilgit-Baltistan," Harrison wrote, adding, "the impact of such a large foreign presence in a thinly populated, undeveloped region has been profound. To local political activists, this adds up to a creeping process of de facto Chinese control over a region where Islamabad claims nominal authority but lacks the infrastructure to exercise it."[84]

— *Times of India,* 10 September 2010

The PRC's Overall Strategy Hasn't Changed Any in Asia

Now that America needs Chinese loans so badly, its leaders may tend to see China's ruling party as gradually mellowing. With regard to expansion in Asia, they would be wrong.

In October [2010], [Chinese] authorities published a map on a state-owned Website labeling an entire Indian province as Chinese territory.[85]

— *Newsweek,* 6 December 2010

This province is most likely Arunachal Pradesh at the most distant corner of Northeast India (beyond Assam). (Refer back to Map 4.1.) Its annexation would mostly complete the Himalayan barrier that China has long sought to protect its southern flank from invasion. This province's proximity to Ledo would also create another link to the oil conduit being built up the Irrawaddy in Myanmar. One Indian academic has noted that in 2008, the Indian military had experienced 270 border violations and nearly 2,300 cases of "aggressive border patrolling" by Chinese soldiers in Arunachal Pradesh.[86]

For Those Who Still Don't See Any Danger to America

To displace local manufactures, China is known to have flooded many African nations with low-price goods. Still, Americans see no problem with huge discount chains carrying mostly Chinese-made products. After watching the Soviet Union go bankrupt, the PRC has no intention of playing by Western rules. Has it not intentionally undervalued its currency to gain an unfair trade advantage?[87] Its new economic model only simulates free enterprise. As such, a "world economy" will eventually translate into one that is Chinese controlled. Along with the Chinese loans will come political "assistance."

On 21 September 2010, NPR's "Morning Edition" News carried a story about a budding business partnership between General Motors (GM) and China's state-owned SAIC (Shanghai Automotive Industry Corporation). Apparently, GM now markets more cars in China than it does in the United States. Soon to appear in U.S. movie theaters will be another collaboration between the two firms—a film entitled "Birth of a Party." The sponsor of this glowing history of the Chinese Communist Party will be none other than Cadillac.[88] An automotive magazine has confirmed the story. The movie is to commemorate China's 90th birthday. The magazine calls it blatant "propaganda,"[89] and says only SAIC Motor's parent—SAIC Group—is state owned.[90] This would suggest certain "publicly owned" subsidiaries must still do the Party's bidding. Overseas, such bidding is much easier to accomplish through joint ventures. As for GM, one might expect quite different behavior from a firm that was at the time mostly owned by the U.S. government.[91]

The Degree of China's Internal "Progress"

As the "pro-democracy" demonstrations spread across North Africa and the Middle East in February and March 2011, some Westerners wondered if China might experience any of the same. In 2007, one U.S. tourist had watched as thousands of security troops had quickly ringed a government complex on Tiananmen Square. There was no apparent reason for the display, so he could only conclude that a foreigner among school children awaiting a tour may have triggered a little government paranoia. Those troops didn't arrive by truck, so they must have come via tunnel from nearby barracks.[92] Like all revolutionary governments, Beijing maintains a massive means to limit public discord.

> One week after police quashed small protests . . . calls on the Internet . . . proved unsuccessful. Officers in Beijing beat several [Western] journalists. . . . Observers could only marvel at the brutal swiftness of the state's response.[93]
> — *Newsweek,* 14 March 2011

5   The Criminal
                                    Threat

●   Does foreign organized crime hurt U.S. security?

●   How so?

Among the law breakers are pirates.

(Source: Corel Galley Clipart, Flags, image designator "19H009.jpg")

The World's Criminality

Of the neighborhood crimes, robbery, rape, and murder receive the most publicity. On the world stage, all happen so frequently that only genocide, enslavement, and endemic looting carry any strategic significance. That's why only foreign infringements on national security will be discussed here. They mostly fall into three categories: (1) those that restrict international commerce; (2) those that so undermine U.S. society as to make it hard to govern; and (3) those that locally fund subversion to keep its instigator hidden. The first category has Gulf of Aden piracy as an example, whereas the second and third are both abundantly illustrated by international drug smuggling. As the last two pose the greatest threat to America's safety (after her debt), they will be the primary focus of this chapter.

People trafficking is also problem, as is the illicit sale of weapons, defense secrets, and any number of other things. Yet, they all follow the same smuggling routes. It is therefore those routes that must be shut down to limit the world's most strategically detrimental criminality. Without being more heavily impeded, those that still penetrate America's border defenses could eventually lead to her demise.

Main Criminal Threat Is from Drug Trafficking

America's criminal justice system is already overloaded to the point of breaking. California's prisons are overflowing. That's why any increase in the use of illegal substances in this country could prove catastrophic. Yet, despite everyone's best efforts, the statistics are not encouraging.

> The use of illegal drugs in the United States was up 9% last year. It is now at the highest level in a decade.[1]
> — NPR's "Morning Edition" News, 16 September 2010

On this same day, ABC's Nightly News confirmed those statistics and identified their source as the U.S. government. It further indicated that there had been an 8% increase in the use of high-potency cannabis (marijuana), 37% increase in ecstasy, and a 60% increase in methamphetamines. Those methamphetamines were coming up from Mexico.[2] The first two drugs are largely distributed by Chinese syndicates, whereas the third comes from Mexican cartels.

> U.S.-based Asian DTOs [Drug Trafficking Organizations] are expanding their working relationships with other [more local] DTOs . . . to increase their wholesale- and retail-level high-potency marijuana and MDMA [ecstasy] distribution operations. . . . [S]ome Asian DTOs also trade their marijuana and MDMA [3,4-methylenedioxymethamphetamine] for cocaine supplied by Mexican DTOs.[3]
> — National Drug Threat Assessment for 2009

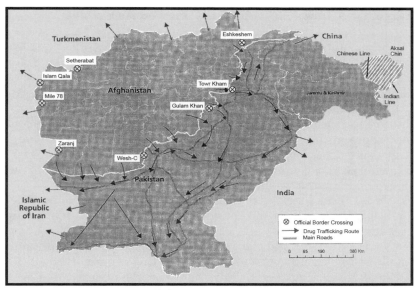

Map 5.1: Afghan and Pakistani Smuggling Routes in 2010
(Source: Courtesy of U.N. Cartographic Section and UNODC, based Maps 3, 4, and 5 of *World Drug Report 2010*, and "China_India_Pakistan_map_tmp.pdf"
[the boundaries, names,and designations shown on this map do not imply official endorsement or acceptance by the U.N.], © 2010)

The U.N.'s *World Drug Report for 2010* shows China as the traditional source of ecstasy.[4] These three drugs therefore form a lethal cocktail that may eventually lead to cocaine or heroin abuse. MDMA is often mixed with methamphetamine to make it additionally addictive.

This Puts the Afghan War into a Totally Different Light

Most members of the U.S. military have now come to realize that Afghanistan is more about narcotics than *jihad*. The routes taken by 90% of the world's heroin are now well demarcated. (See Map 5.1.)

Terrorist Attacks More Usefully Viewed As Crimes

An act of terrorism is nothing more than a sick way of attracting public attention to some cause. Only in intensity does it differ from hostage taking or serial killing. Thus, it makes no sense to blame an entire segment of some foreign population for such an act. It has been perpetrated by a tiny group of sociopaths, and it is to this group that justice must be applied. While others in the world may share in the group's overall ideology, they are not personally responsible for its misguided acts. Otherwise, every time a Christian-church goer committed an act of terrorism, all members of the same denomination would have to be put in jail.

Those tasked with U.S. security have now been forced to take a much broader look at the problem—one as alert to mundane law breakers as to suicidal malcontents. On 31 October 2010, almost ten years after 9/11 and the anthrax letters, the Muslim militants finally stumbled upon the idea to attack this country through its package delivery systems. Only then was it discovered that 90% of all air freight coming into the United States was unregulated.[5] How any nation could hope to stop a massive drug inflow without regulating its air freight, one can only wonder. The various U.S. agencies must have been conflicted as to whether to impede certain types of international trade. Until national security again takes precedence over commercial expediency, America will be under strategic threat from foreign organized crime (and any nation using it as an instrument).

6 Where Threats Combine

- Where do two out of the three threats exist?
- In which locations are all three at once?

Globally active are Communists, Islamists, and criminals.

(Source: Microsoft Office 2004 Clipart, image designator "j0234073")

Why Some Countries Are More Volatile Than Others

Areas of chronic unrest are often rich in natural resources. As was the case in colonial times, foreign elements compete for those resources. Today, many such regions suffer from Communist and Islamist influences, as well as those that are purely criminal.

"Revolutionary" Regimes Promote Insurrection Elsewhere

Along with the PRC and North Korea, Iran and Sudan also have "revolutionary" governments. This means they believe progress in other countries can best be achieved through revolution. In some places, that amounts to armed insurgency. In others, the final "politicization" phase of Mao's method is enough.

Within Asia, Insurgency and Smuggling Go Hand in Hand

Just as the North Vietnamese were able to sneak enough supplies for a takeover of Hue City through its waterways,[1] so too have the Iraqi and Afghan rebels smuggled sufficient wherewithal along public roads. That's the way insurrections are resupplied in the Eastern World. There, smuggling is as regularly practiced by guerrillas, as by criminals. (See Figure 6.1.)

Many Eastern Armies Also Consort with Smugglers

In both Pakistan and Afghanistan, governmental entities have now been irrefutably linked to drug smuggling. During the Soviet-

Figure 6.1: Communist and Islamist Rebels Both Smuggle
(Source: Courtesy of Sorman Information and Media, from Soldf: Soldaten i falt, © 2001 by Forsvarsmakten and Wolfgang Bartsch, Stockholm, p. 31)

Afghan War, much of the Afghan heroin was carried to Karachi by a Pakistani-army-run trucking company.[2] Since then, Pakistan's ISI has been partially funded through drug route protection.[3] This creates many new problems for Western "liberation" forces. With so much difficulty telling friend from foe, they first inadvertently condone some of the smuggling. (See Figure 6.2.) Then, they are unexpectedly targeted during attempts to weaken the coalition psychologically. Crime more easily occurs where authority is lacking. That's why distrust among coalition partners is so highly valued by criminal elements.

At the end of November 2010 in a remote part of Afghanistan's Nangarhar Province (possibly near where Haqqani has drug labs [4]), an Afghan policeman gunned down six U.S. soldiers. Earlier that month, an Afghan soldier had similarly killed two U.S. Marines in

Figure 6.2: With Corrupt Allies, It's Hard to Stop the Smuggling
(Source: Courtesy of Sorman Information and Media, from Soldf: Soldaten i falt, © 2001 by Forsvarsmakten and Wolfgang Bartsch, Stockholm, p. 145)

Figure 6.3: South Vietnamese Irregular with Foe-Like Footgear
(Source: Courtesy of Cassell PLC, from World Army Uniforms since 1939, © 1975, 1980, 1981, 1983 by Blandford Press Ltd., Part II)

drug-ridden Helmand Province. On 26 April 2011 inside Kabul Airport, a veteran Afghan Air Force pilot shot—execution-style—nine U.S. military personnel and a contractor "after being distressed over his personal finances." Then, just 17 days later, two U.S. Marine advisors to an Afghan police contingent were killed by one of its members.[5] All four events had the telltale indicators of drug-war violence. In another conflict many years before, there had also been rumors of heavy drug-trafficking activity. In Vietnam, U.S. troops also had trouble distinguishing the players without a score card. (See Figure 6.3.)

Many Things Are Done Differently in the East

Most Communists and Islamists are either part of, or try to

mimic, Asian culture. As a result, their thought processes are quite different from those in the West. Among other things, Asians like to solve problems from the bottom up (with a "grassroots" approach). They are also less direct during all types of transactions. Within South Asia and the Middle East (as any frequent visitor can attest), slight refinements to what has previously been promised are commonplace. Those who perform such refinements are not being "underhanded" or "disloyal," just "situationally responsive." This has created some real challenges for U.S. negotiators. Unused to this Eastern difference, they first assume that every foe has been following his commanders' instructions to the letter. Then, they try to ascertain that foe's next move from what was last said. That move will almost certainly contribute to some strategic goal, but not always directly. The goal itself will only be apparent from past actions. In essence, the Easterner can best be judged by what he has previously done.

Because of these differences in cultural orientation, Eastern military units (of whatever size) are often provided with "strategic guidance," as opposed to "specific orders." How they then comply with the guidance is up to them. With less micro-managment comes less predictability. The resulting variation in procedure so befuddles Western planners that they believe it to be asymmetric warfare. Such are the realities of dealing with an Asian unit. Whether or not the unit is an extension of a totalitarian regime, its internal functioning will still follow this bottom-up pattern.

China's Underlying Agenda

Of the world's emerging powers, China is by far the fastest growing. It has had as much trouble retrieving resources as respecting borders. Because its army was first used to rebuild homeland infrastructure, that army may now pursue its revolutionary mission through non-martial means. This type of invasion is far too subtle to evoke any response from the peace-loving and somewhat naive West.

> China's "comprehensive warfare" strategy wears down [an] enemy using non-military means. . . .
> . . . [Chinese] National Defense University Senior Col. Meng Xiansheng . . . defined the term as "the means of de-

feating enemies without waging a war through deploying a wide range of political, economic, cultural, diplomatic and military tactics."

[Col.] Meng said "comprehensive warfare" [not only] advocates the use of non-violent means in handling state-to-state disputes, . . . but also fits with China's grand strategy of "peaceful development."[6]

—*Geostrategy-Direct,* 2 August 2006

The U.S. military does not treat transnational companies which seize monopolistic profits as security threats, and in addition to their deeply rooted awareness of economic freedom, this is also related to the fact that they still limit threats to the military arena.[7]

— Concluding section of *Unrestricted Warfare*

Modern-day China has its own set of business ethics. Certain commercial products, which are not legal in the West, are still widely traded in the East and then end up in the West. Americans might view this as state-sponsored criminality.

A Relatively Foolproof Chinese Strategy Emerges

There is ample evidence that the PRC has been employing organized crime as an instrument of its foreign policy. Drug smuggling provides one of the best ways for it to secretly "hamstring" the West.

There is a well-documented history of both Russian and Chinese organized crime organizations working as tools of their governments.

In Panama, . . . there is a dangerous convergence of well-financed Chinese . . . mobs with . . . Latin American drug lords. . . . This dark partnership is a . . . direct long-term threat to . . . the United States.[8]

— American Foreign Policy Council Report, 1999

Upon assuming control of the British territory of Hong Kong in 1997, the ruling party of China was worried that Hong Kong's

Taiwan-affiliated triads would make trouble. Soon, it realized that—as criminal enterprises—those triads could be "financially influenced." And this is precisely what happened with one or more of the biggest.

> So he [Deng Xiaoping] bought them: the Sun Yee On, the largest Hong Kong triad society, no longer requires initiates to pledge allegiance to Taiwan; now it is to the People's Republic of China that they swear.[9]
> — *The New Republic,* 14-21 July 1997

Before long, the PLA was making money off the Hong Kong triad with the biggest overseas operation—Sun Yee On. It was also thinking about how to use Sun Yee On and its closest foreign competitor (14-K) against the only remaining roadblock to China's "One World" policy.[10]

The Islamists Also Traffic in Drugs to Undermine the West

Throughout South Asia, the local literature is full of partially substantiated detail. The average nonfiction book from Pakistan contains strings of poorly referenced minutia that intermittently support multiple conspiracy theories. Those books are considered legitimate research by those societies, because much of what happens in Asia is from the bottom up and intentionally hidden. While facing an Asian foe, Americans could usefully expect more conspiracies. As a way to harm the West, the Islamists have for quite some time been doing precisely what their religion forbids.

> Islam forbids the use of opium . . . but the [Afghan] militants now justify the drug production by saying it's not for domestic consumption but rather to sell abroad as part of a holy war against the West.[11]
> — McClatchy News Service, 10 May 2009

In the mid-1980's, the *Hezbollah's* use of the illicit drug trade as a funding source and a weapon against the West was sanctioned by an official *fatwa* (religious edict) issued by *Hezbollah:* We are making these drugs for Satan America

and the Jews. If we cannot kill them with guns, so we will
kill them with drugs.[12]
      — *Funding Evil,* by Rachel Ehrenfield, 2005

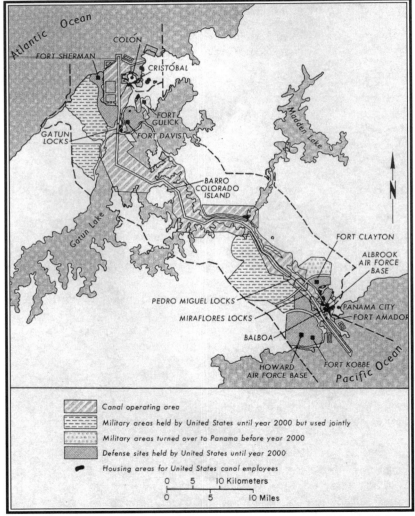

Map 6.1: Panama Is Both Trade Chokepoint and Drug Hub
(Source: DA Pamphlet 550-46 [1989])

International-Crime Factions Go After the Biggest Market

The goal of any organized-crime element is to make money. Of all the illicit activity possible, drug trafficking is by far the most lucrative. In fact, the term "organized crime" is now seldom used in any other context. As with any business enterprise, drug producers need regional consolidation centers. Among the world's best known are as follows: (1) Karachi, Pakistan, and certain U.A.E. emirates for product from "the Golden Crescent"; (2) Southern China for product from the "Golden Triangle"; and (3) Venezuela for South American cocaine bound for Europe.

The drug producers also require regional coordination centers—like Dubai in the U.A.E., Ciudad del Este in the Tri-Border Area (TBA) of Paraguay, and Panama City in Central America. Those coordination centers tend to be either centrally located or at trading hubs. (See Map 6.1.) For U.S. distribution, the drugs are now first sold to the Mexican cartels. They, in turn, have border "plazas," in-country transit centers, and final distribution points. Examples of the first are at Laredo and Juarez; of the second at San Antonio, Atlanta, and Charlotte; and of the third at Chicago, New York, and Boston.[13]

There have been Communist and Islamist elements spotted in most of these regional coordination centers: (1) *Hezbollah* at the TBA and Venezuela's Isla de Margarita;[14] (2) Hong Kong triads at the TBA and Panama City;[15] and (3) *al-Qaeda* at Karachi and Dubai. These are not just random sightings. In all but the third, the factions have set up operational headquarters. At Karachi and Dubai, Dawood Ibrahim acts on behalf of *al-Qaeda*.[16] *Al-Qaeda* does not need extra income,[17] but some of its closest affiliates—like the Islamic Movement of Uzbekistan (IMU)—may.[17] *Al-Qaeda* itself just facilitates the drug trading to undermine the West.

Guerrilla Movements Often Require External Resupply

The whole purpose of this "round robin" of issues is to show how it is through insurgency and drugs that the world's two most expansive entities extend their zones of control. While Communist and Islamist zones are not likely to overlap, they will soon so cover the earth as to limit Western influence. Most often accused of providing weapons to rebels are China, North Korea, Iran, and Russia. Two are Communist, one Islamist, and one projected by DNI to become a criminal state.[18] China and North Korea mostly send arms to Islamist rebels through Iran and Sudan.[19] Only rarely are they caught doing so directly. In separate incidents, Chinese arms have been intercepted *en route* to *Hamas* in Gaza and separatists in Yemen.[20] All the while, Russia has been indirectly arming various Western Hemisphere insurgencies through Venezuela.[21]

The World's Most Active Rebellions

Most apparent are the insurgencies in Iraq and Afghanistan. Iraq's oil has always been of immense strategic importance, and Afghanistan still produces 90% of the world's heroin. Yet, there are also uprisings in Africa, South America, and elsewhere in Asia. Among the most active on the Dark Continent are those in Sudan, the DRC, and Nigeria. There, factions of differing religious belief have been vying over regions that just happen to be rich in oil and minerals.

In the Americas, *Fuerzas Armadas Revolucionarias de Colombia (FARC)* and the Shining Path still fund their insurrections through drug involvement in two of the five countries that still have rightist regimes.[22] What's going on in Mexico can best be described as a narco-insurgency. Like Peru, Mexico narrowly escaped a leftist victory in its last election. (In June 2011, Peru must once again flirt with disaster.)

> The parallels between Pakistan and Mexico are strong enough that the U.S. military singled them out recently as the two countries where . . . the government could . . . collapse.[23]
> — *Wall Street Journal,* 21 February 2009

Al-Qaeda-supported *Jamaat i-Islami (JI)* affiliates conducted the 2009 northern envelopment of Islamabad, whereas the subsequent southern assault has been from the *al-Qaeda*-infiltrated Pakistani Taliban. Despite *al-Qaeda's* involvement, both efforts were more likely the result of internal discord. Yet, their goal was still to topple the Islamabad government. Haqqani and Hekmatyar run a lot of drugs through the Federally Administered Tribal Areas (FATA), and the Pakistani army's recent foray into their safe areas may have slightly annoyed them. As for India, the Naxalite Communist rebellion now constitutes the single greatest threat to its national security.[24] Finally, at the Isthmus of Kra in Thailand, Muslims and Buddhists have been recently at odds over territory that may someday provide a shortcut for PRC-bound oil. On the surface, all three uprisings look like religious or tribal spats, but always in the background is the issue of trade routes for scarce or extremely profitable resources. Even the spread of a Communist government from Calcutta to its surrounding states would give a certain emerging superpower more access to the Indian Ocean, and thus a safer way home for its oil.

Specifics of the Communists' Drug Involvement

That Colombian *FARC* and Peruvian Shining Path still obtain much of their funding from the protection of South America's cocaine producers needs no further proof. While both groups are Maoist, neither requires any outside assistance. This is the perfect scenario for "no-fault" Communist expansion in the region. Some of the cocaine gets transported through Central America to the United States. This has created a more consummate union of Maoist with criminal elements, for FARC may be providing the Mexican cartels with state-of-the-art tactical advice. Known to have Vietnamese short-range-infiltration experts, FARC has been showing the cartels how to safeguard their drug routes into the U.S.[25]

Of course, some of the South American cocaine is also headed for Europe. Cuba's new satellite—Venezuela—has been its primary point of debarkation. Through it all, the PRC remains cozily in the background—free of any demonstrable culpability. Yet, the CIA's *World Factbook* still describes China as a "major trans-shipment point for heroin produced in the Golden Triangle."[26] While this Asian pipeline may now run up through Mexico, it still handles most of the U.S.-bound product. America is still the world's most lucrative drug market, so this same conduit must also be carrying at least some of the Afghan heroin. However, like the PRC, Asian drug smugglers have a big advertising budget and know well the value of misinformation. That's probably why American public opinion has now swung in the wrong direction. Among the most common misbeliefs are the following: (1) that all drugs coming up from Mexico have been produced in the Western Hemisphere; and (2) that Western Hemisphere drug syndicates lack any affiliation with those from the East. The truth is quite different.

According to the UNODC, most long-distance drug trafficking involves cocaine and heroin, but some cannabis resin and ecstasy (MDMA) are also smuggled between regions. Cannabis herb (marijuana), methamphetamine, and amphetamine are generally produced locally.[27] As of September 2010, there had been a 37% increase in the use of ecstasy and 60% in the use of methamphetamines in the United States. Those methamphetamines were coming from Mexico,[28] whereas the UNODC still acknowledges China as the traditional source of ecstasy.[29] If the Chinese government could be definitively linked to either problem, it might be more often called to account. As is too often the case, it took an offhand remark from Reuters to suggest there was more to the story.

> Joaquin "Shorty" Guzman [head of Mexico's Sinaloa cartel] . . . has extended his empire from Colombia to China.[30]
> — Reuters, 19 January 2011

As of 17 January 2011, Sinaloa was the most powerful cartel in Mexico. It controlled almost all of the western half of Mexico's 2,000-mile border with the United States,[31] to include Mexicali—the traditional Chinese infiltration point.[32] Still, such a tenuous connection would never wash where PRC loans are keeping everything afloat. As luck would have it, a further look into this lackluster coincidence has produced some rather chilling results. The Reuters article goes on to explain that Guzman gets methamphetamine ingredients from China. This would make an appropriate ending to another half-baked conspiracy theory; right? Wrong. The CIA still lists China as "a source country for methamphetamine and heroin chemical precursors."[33] To prevent any U.S. resistance to its "one world" policy, China would prefer not to be the debarkation point for any fully manufactured addictives headed to the U.S. through Mexico. That would only leave a trail of possible subversion. It would instead help the Mexicans to produce their own society-ruining substances. That may also explain why Chinese chemists are currently in Pakistan's Khyber tribal agency handling the rather delicate conversion of opium brick into pure heroin.[34] Mexico and Pakistan are very much alike—both now verging on "narco-state" status. Both serve, whether by design or not, as a means through which America will be further destabilized. In March of 2007, the first evidence of drug-related Chinese intrigue surfaced in Mexico. For those who still doubt of China's capacity to "subliminally" bury its only remaining opposition to global domination, one can only suggest another look at Sun Tzu. Washington has been dangerously flirting with some of the same freedoms for which hundreds of thousands of young U.S. service personnel have already died. There should be enough smoke evident from the following string of well-substantiated facts.

In late July 2007, a Chinese national turned Mexican citizen was arrested in Maryland four months after huge amounts of drug cash were seized at his mansion in Mexico City. It seems Zhenli Ye Gon had been running the Western Hemisphere's biggest importer of pseudoephedrine, the principal ingredient of methamphetamine.[35] Upon arrest, Zhenli should have kept his mouth shut, for he may have unintentionally divulged one of China's more closely guarded strategic secrets. The Hong Kong taxation records clearly show an emigrant by the name of Zhenli Ye Gon.[36] Hong Kong is the home of China's most notorious triads. What Zhenli said is almost as mundane as the Guzman reference. Suffice it to say even highly dictatorial Oriental governments quite often work from the bottom up.

> [Zhenli] Ye Gon has said the chemicals imported by his company, Unimed Pharm Chem de Mexico SA, were legitimate and intended for use in prescription drugs to be made at a factory he was building in Toluca.[37]
> — *Washington Times,* 24 July 2007

Unfortunately, Unimed Pharm Chem de Mexico SA is actually the Mexican subsidiary of UNIMED Pharmaceutical in Hong Kong.

> Mexican law enforcement officers on March 15th seized these funds from the Mexico City home of an individual connected to the UNIMED pharmaceutical corporation of Hong Kong, China. . . .
> U.S. authorities believe UNIMED is connected with attempts, in December 2006 and February 2007, to smuggle

large amounts of the toxic chemicals used to produce methamphetamine through ports in Colima and Michoacan.[38]
   — U.S. Embassy Press Release, 20 March 2007

After Zhenli's arrest, the Mexican media was full of speculation
as to what he had been up to. One article concluded his methamphetamine precursors had been destined for Guzman. Several others
referred to some of Zhenli's e-mails as "Chinogate letters."[39] Though
never substantiated, those letters must have implied some nefarious
link to the Chinese government. There's no way of telling whether
the Mexican journalists ever realized that international triads like
to work through expatriate members. What was to be produced at
Zhenli's factory in Toluca may never be known. Most prevalent is
the belief that he was selling his smuggled ingredient to a cartel,
and that the cartel was then turning it into finished product for
the U.S. market. Either way, no links of this Hong Kong corporation to a collocated triad would ever be at issue. With the help of
the North American Free Trade Agreement (NAFTA), democracy's
sworn enemy might turn Western-style capitalism in on itself—in
true Sun Tzu fashion. At least one Hong Kong triad would be very
interested.

[The triads'] powerful influence is felt worldwide in coun-
terfeiting, arms dealing, alien smuggling and money laun-
dering. Hong Kong is a key transit point for the Southeast
Asian heroin and methamphetamine that pour into the
United States, and triads play a key role in the drugs' trans-
shipment.[40]
   — *The New Republic,* 14 & 27 July 1997

The triad most responsible for this infusion of Asian heroin and
methamphetamines is Sun Yee On. It is the only triad known to be
one of the PLA's business extensions.[41]

Members of the Sun Yee On triad have settled in Toronto,
Edmonton, and Vancouver . . . ("Asian Organized Crime,"
International Crime Threat Assessment 2000). They are
involved in the trafficking of heroin and methamphetamines
. . . to the United States.[42]
   — Report for the Library of Congress, July 2003

Since 2003, U.S. and Canadian authorities have greatly impeded the traditional Asian drug conduit through Vancouver. As a result, the Asian pipeline has largely shifted to Mexico.[43] If the PRC were now to encourage the production of methamphetamines and heroin in Mexico, who could tell which methamphetamines and heroin were actually coming from Asia? The trail of evidence would be permanently muddied. China is not like its more loosely governed neighbors. Its ruling Communist party has its totalitarian finger on everything that happens there. Those Hong Kong triads could not be feeding off America without Beijing's permission.

This methamphetamine onslaught is far from the PRC's only narcotics initiative. COSCO—a PLA-owned shipping enterprise—has for years been accused of the massive smuggling of weapons, drugs, and illegal aliens.[44] Another of the PLA's business extensions is Hutchison Whampoa. In addition to port facilities at both ends of the Panama Canal, it controls those at Freeport in the Bahamas and Veracruz, Manzanillo, Lazaro Cardenas, and Ensenada in Mexico.[45] Together will PLA affiliate Sun Yee On,[46] COSCO and Hutchison Whampoa have significant business access to the Western World. Chinese triads are known to be smuggling human contraband into Panama.[47]

By 2001, the city of Ciudad del Este, Paraguay, in the infamous TBA was home to 30,000 Chinese residents (of whom only 9,000 were registered) and many Koreans.[48] Several Chinese organized-crime families—to include Sun Ye On—have also been operating from Ciudad del Este.[49]

China's involvement in all this should come as no surprise to U.S. military and intelligence communities. The PLA's new *Unrestricted Warfare* manifesto has—since 1999—included "Drug Warfare" and "Smuggling Warfare." These terms are not used in the Western sense of "anti-drug" and "anti-smuggling" projects. Instead, they are intended in all their literal glory.[50] Within this context, events at the Mexican border look far more ominous.

China is not alone in this Communist drug effort. North Korea has also been implicated in the international trade of illicit narcotics. Heavily dependent on drug trafficking to bolster its sputtering Marxist economy, North Korea deals openly with the Hong Kong syndicates.[51] The U.S. State Department cites "credible reports of North Korean boats . . . transporting heroin and uniformed North Korean personnel transferring drugs from North Korean vessels to traffickers' boats."[52]

Specifics of *Al-Qaeda's* Drug Involvement

According to NPR, there has been an increase in *al-Qaeda* activity all across the southern Sahara from Somalia to West Africa. Specifically affected have been Niger, Algeria, Mali, and Mauritania.[53] In Mauritania and Sudan, Muslims constitute the majority population. In Somalia, Chad, Niger, Mali, Senegal, and Guinea, they practice the majority religion. While this belt is most definitely a target for more *sharia,* it may also play host to the drug pipeline from Dubai, via Yemen, to *Hezbollah's* West African outlet to South America.[54] This outlet now includes not only Guinea-Bissau, but several of its neighbors.[55] That such a route would initially cross Sudan and Chad presents no affront to common logic, as both are awash with Muslim militants. The only relatively stable area in its path is Ethiopia, and it could easily be bridged by aircraft.

Specifics of *Hezbollah's* Drug Involvement

Hezbollah has been openly acquiring funding through drug sales since the mid-1980's.[56] That's when Lebanon emerged as the Middle East's main source of narcotics, producing up to 1,000 tons of cannabis resin and 30-50 tons of opium per year. While the Lebanese government has worked hard to eradicate the Bekaa Valley poppy and marijuana crops, its restrictions on their growth have been greatly relaxed since 2007.[57] *Hezbollah* is still thought to have shifted much of its emphasis to the transport of Colombian cocaine up from South America to Europe. Its operatives frequent both Paraguay's TBA and Venezuela's Margarita Island.[58] An interagency operation in Colombia netted dozens of people associated with a *Hezbollah*-connected drug ring.[59]

> Hezbollah uses these operations [in South America] to generate millions of dollars to finance Hezbollah operations in Lebanon and other areas of the world.[60]
> — *Washington Times,* 27 March 2009

This is why *Hezbollah* depends so much on the drug conduit that runs from Venezuela to the general vicinity of Guinea-Bissau, West Africa.

Places Where Islamism, Communism, and Drugs Combine

Several areas of the world are now experiencing all three threats at once. Their most obscure malady is Communism, and least obscure drugs. In fact, many sit astride major drug routes. One such route starts in Afghanistan and then runs through Dubai, Yemen, Somalia, and the lower Sahara to West Africa. (See Map 6.2.) From there, it heads south to Venezuela and then up through Central America to the world's most lucrative narcotics market—the United States. Only two areas along this route will be discussed here—Yemen and the West African debarkation hub.

As a later chapter will show, Yemen is now a hotbed of Islamist and drug-smuggling activity. In 2002 (some 12 years after Marxist South Yemen was absorbed by North Yemen), a North-Korean-owned freighter was stopped by a Spanish warship. Purportedly carrying cement to Yemen, it instead had 15 "Scud" tactical ballistic missiles on board.[61] Those missiles were most likely destined for the Marxist separatists in Yemen's southern part. That part just happens to abut the coastal smuggling lane.

At least some of the Afghan heroin moves on from Yemen to Venezuela across the lower Sahara. A U.S. military contingent recently helped Mauritanian forces to raid an *al-Qaeda* camp in Mali. One member of this contingent noticed more Chinese in Mauritania than he had expected.[62] Below are excerpts from the UNODC. Together they help to delineate the drug conduit's path through West Africa.

> [S]hipments to . . . West Africa gained in importance between 2004 and 2007, resulting in the emergence of two key trans-shipment hubs: one centered on Guinea-Bissau and Guinea, stretching to Cape Verde, Gambia and Senegal, and one centered in the Bight of Benin, which spans from Ghana to Nigeria. Colombian traffickers often transport the cocaine by 'mother ships' towards the West African coast before off-loading it to smaller vessels. . . . Shipments are also sent in modified small aircraft from the Bolivarian Republic of Venezuela or Brazil to various West African destinations (U.K. Home Affairs Committee, "The Cocaine Trade"; "U.K. Threat Assessment of Organized Crime 2009/10").[63]
> — U.N., *World Drug Report (for) 2010*

[B]oth maritime seizures and airport seizures on flights originating in West Africa virtually disappeared at the end of 2008. Some [incoming] trans-Atlantic traffic may have shifted to private aircraft, however. In November 2009, a Boeing 727 jet was found alight in Central Mali. It is believed that the plane departed from the Bolivarian Republic of Venezuela and that it was carrying cocaine. . . . [C]ocaine trafficking via West Africa may have started to increase again in late 2009.[64]

— U.N., *World Drug Report (for) 2010*

[A]s of April 2010, the armed forces of Guinea-Bissau are controlled by people designated as drug traffickers . . . by the U.S. Government. . . . Guinea-Bissau is not unique in this respect. In Guinea, the presidential guard . . . appears to have been involved in drug trafficking. . . . After the disruptions in Guinea-Bissau and Guinea, it appears this hub relocated to the Gambia. . . . [W]ith state authorities dominating the trade in some countries, . . . there is little evidence of insurgents dealing in the drug. There have been allegations that rebels in the north of Mali and Niger, as well as political militants in Algeria, have been involved in trans-Saharan trafficking.[65]

— U.N., *World Drug Report (for) 2010*

Major drug conduits tend to transit unstable countries. This unfortunate fact leads to an important question. Did the narcotics themselves make those countries unstable, or did the narcotics smugglers do it to make their routes more impervious to attack? According to the UNODC, the countries of West Africa will need help resisting transnational organized crime. It says the region will continue to face serious threats to governance and stability as long as there are transnational smuggling markets to be served.[66]

Of the 25 countries with the highest risks of instability globally, nine were in West Africa: Niger, Mali, Sierra Leone, Liberia, Mauritania, Guinea-Bissau, Côte d'Ivoire and Benin (Hewitt et al, "Peace and Conflict 2010," Ctr. for Internat. Development and Conflict Mgt.) [67]

— U.N., *World Drug Report (for) 2010*

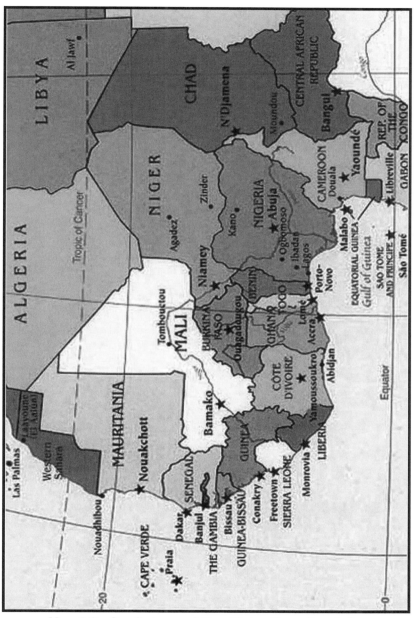

Map 6.2: Confluence of Two Major Drug Conduits
(Source: Courtesy of General Libraries, University of Texas at Austin, from their website, for map designator "africa_pol_2003.pdf")

If Asian-harvested narcotics have become such a threat to the Free World, then shouldn't trade with Communist and Islamist nations be more carefully undertaken. One of the nonmartial arenas of 4GW is, after all, economic. Because of advertising, economics and politics will always be bedfellows. Isn't the whole objective of war to replace the opposing nation's government? Americans must make doubly sure theirs isn't in play.

7 If Current Trends Continue

- Can U.S. voters be lured into state capitalism?
- Will China become the most dominant power?

Can America help the world with all three threats?

(Source: Microsoft Office 2004 Clipart, image designator "j0289947")

The Leftists Have Learned How to Win Elections

While democracy is—by far—the most equitable way to govern a freedom-loving people, it still has vulnerabilities. With enough campaign cash, someone willing to make big enough promises can often get elected. Then, as incumbent, he or she is virtually guaranteed another term in office. That's how political parties of Communist origin have managed to control much of Southern Africa since the early 1990's. Most regimes in the Western Hemisphere are now "leftist" as well. This too happened by election, with much of the campaign cash and political advice coming from nearly destitute Cuba. Because the Soviet Union had already been dissolved and Venezuela was yet to grow rich, the source of the money was most probably China. Yet, it was not only the Communists making headway.

In late January 2011, *Hezbollah*—the most militarily capable of all the Muslim extremist factions—finally took over the government of Lebanon. Yet, for most Americans, this momentous loss in the War on both Terror and Drugs was barely noticed. The U.S. news media had instead focused on populist revolts in Tunisia and Egypt.

Though clearly capable of defeating Lebanon's fledgling army for years, *Hezbollah* had preferred to use this nation's sovereignty as a hedge against attack. Allowed to defend Lebanon's southern border, it had militarily supported insurgent proxies in both Israel and Iraq.[1] Then, *Hezbollah* began to seek increasing political influence. In 2008, it achieved "veto status" over the Lebanese Parliament.[2] And on 24 January 2011, Lebanon's coalition government collapsed when 10 *Hezbollah*-affiliated ministers resigned.[3] As something similar had just occurred in Pakistan, no one in the West paid much attention. (There, Pakistan Army-affiliated *Muttahida Qaumi Movement [MQM]* had momentarily quit the coalition government over a fuel price hike.[4]) Then, on 27 January 2011, it was announced that Lebanon's new prime minister was from *Hezbollah*.[5] Again, no one in America really noticed because of concurrent news from North Africa. Populist demonstrations had forced the autocratic and U.S.-friendly leader of Tunisia from power, and similar pressures were being applied to Hosni Mubarak in Egypt. All were unfortunate coincidences, of course. Everyone knows that Sunni and Shiite extremists can't cooperate, and that national entities will never intentionally destabilize a region.

Yet, the bottom line was still the same. Another important member of the Free World community had slipped beneath the waves. Its death had come from within, after nary a shot had been fired. Yet, all who monitor terrorist activity knew a new plateau had been reached. Lebanon's new ruling party had been one of the world's most notorious non-state actors.

This is the same *Hezbollah* that had blown up 241 U.S. Marines in October 1983,[6] forced Israel to abandon Southern Lebanon in 2000,[7] and repelled a fully supported Israeli incursion in July 2006.[8] It is the same *Hezbollah* with traditional drug route involvement—(1) having made the Bekaa poppy fields into the biggest source of Middle Eastern heroin in 1985;[9] (2) having fought along the Afghan heroin's conduit to America in Yemen;[10] and (3) having run the South American cocaine's conduit to Europe.[11] This is the same *Hezbollah* that—even after the 2006 Israeli incursion—still had over 10,000 rockets and missiles (many of Chinese design) pointed at Israel.[12] The suicide bomber and advanced Improvised Explosive Device (IED) were not *al-Qaeda* inventions. *Hezbollah* had used both in Lebanon before *al-Qaeda* existed.[13]

Lebanon's arrival at radical-Shiite-state status will do much to complete the Iranian Crescent. Next for inclusion is almost certainly Iraq, where al-Sadr has been carefully following *Hezbollah's* formula.[14] Hello. How much more do Americans have to hear before they'll acknowledge a global takeover attempt? It is not just the Islamists doing it. The jewel of South Asia—Nepal—recently fell to the Communists in much the same fashion.[15]

A Question As to Timing and Coordination

Lebanon's government collapsed on 12 January 2011,[16] whereas Tunisia's riots had begun about 8 January.[17] When the *Hezbollah*-backed prime minister was installed in Lebanon on 25 January,[18] it appears not to have warranted any U.S. State Department press release. Five days later, this agency did however advise Egypt's Mubarak to cooperate with the protestors.[19] The very next day, the autocratic leader of Syria was asked if he was worried about local unrest. He said, "No, because only the pro-Western regimes were being targeted."[20]

While Mubarak has strictly controlled his country for many years, he did have the Muslim Brotherhood with which to contend. About 40% of the Egyptian demonstrators had been from the Muslim Brotherhood.[21] Formed near Cairo in 1928, this pro-Wahhabi faction has been active throughout Africa and the Levant since before WWII. An avowed enemy of "Western decadence," it has been trying for quite some time to consolidate anti-Western sentiment.[22] Yet, throughout the Cairo demonstrations, the White House had urged Mubarak to step down. On 11 February, his just-appointed Vice President announced that Mubarak was turning over the interim running of the country to its "armed forces council."[23] While America's diplomatic position is well beyond the scope of this book, it does raise a peripheral concern. In a Western-style government

105

that intentionally separates foreign-policy from military execution, is it possible that the State Department has not been talking enough with the Pentagon? The world has turned over many times since 1945. WWIII need no longer look like WWII. For several years now, wars have been largely fought in their non-martial arenas. While there may be less gore this way, individual freedoms are still forfeited.

Since the 1990's elections in Southern Africa, the West has attempted to turn all open combat into political debate. This is a noble and fairly reasonable way to further world stability. Yet, with the ongoing evolution of warfare, it is now a little naive. What if the enemy can manipulate the election process? The West was asleep at the switch when *Hamas* won the Gaza Strip elections in early 2006, and it appears to have been asleep again in Lebanon. Even the U.S. State Department has long admitted a major plank in the *Hezbollah's* political platform is to fight "all Western imperialism."[24] Yet, since March of 2005, America's elected leaders have been encouraging *Hezbollah* to enter the political arena.[25] The war in Iraq was greatly complicated when civilian administrators rushed the initial election, failing to account for a massive influx of both voters and ballots from Iran.[26] Not surprisingly, a pro-Iranian regime took over in Iraq and is still in power today. After four years of exile in Iran, the radically anti-Western Muqtada al-Sadr made a "triumphal return" to Baghdad in January 2011 to join Prime Minister al-Maliki's coalition government.[27] Considering Lebanon's fate, this did not come as particularly good news to U.S. military personnel. Born of the Tehran-supported Northern Alliance,[28] the government of Afghanistan is also pro-Iranian. That's too many pro-Iranian regimes in a corridor where an "Iranian Crescent" is thought to be forming.

With Iran now so close to being nuclear armed and its expeditionary proxy *(Hezbollah)* so proficient at modern ground warfare, somebody in Washington needs to be a bit less conciliatory. There are worse things than military confrontation. With regard to China, the threat may be closer to home. Must a targeted nation always be occupied by enemy troops, or could enough indebtedness and immigration accomplish almost as much? Ask the people of Tibet, Zimbabwe, or Venezuela. (Half of Lhasa's population is now transplaced Han Chinese.[29]) Either way, that nation's independence is compromised.

Prioritizing the Threats

America has more than one enemy. Some are more dangerous than others. Of concern lately has been the possibility of Muslim Brotherhood activities inside the U.S. The Muslim Brotherhood is, after all, the real power in Sudan. After declaring war on the West in October 2010,[30] this long-time sect was almost certainly responsible for the populist revolt in Egypt in January 2011. However, with all the counter-terrorist focus, the Muslim Brotherhood poses very little threat to America's governing fabric. Dangers of this magnitude come from a different direction and quite often masquerade as assistance.

As of January 2011, China had replaced the World Bank as primary global lender. With over two trillion dollars in reserve cash, it not only owns much of the U.S. debt, but also lends with abandon throughout the Developing World. In the latter location, it expects three things in return: (1) free access to natural resources; (2) a big market for Chinese goods; and (3) full support of Chinese policies (as in the U.N.).[31] The Head of the Joint Chiefs of Staff has already designated America's debt as its biggest security threat.[32] Nevertheless, most of her security apparatus was still aimed at Islamic radicals.

Neither is too much anti-Muslim sentiment helping to win the drug war in Afghanistan. *Al-Qaeda* is not the only international entity undermining America with narcotics. The PRC is as well. Thus, one becomes forced to consider several disturbing coincidences. The first *al-Qaeda* website was developed in Southern China.[33] The big-building attacks of 9/11 were not hatched in Afghanistan as is commonly thought, but rather in the Philippines in 1995.[34] Some of the hijackers attended a coordination "summit" in Kuala Lumpur right before the event.[35] Two U.S. tourists experienced the PRC's extreme anger after its Belgrade embassy was bombed in 1999—through a Chinese guide's cell phone tirade and subsequent kidnapping attempts.[36] The Chinese Communists don't get mad; they get even. And when Sun-Tzu-like thinkers get even, they like to push the blame off on someone else.

To be sure, Muslim extremism still poses a terroristic threat to the U.S. populace. Still, this threat is more sensationalistic than strategic. Based mostly on fear, it has only occasional substance. Whereas, the Chinese threat is almost all substance (albeit subtle and well screened by America's *jihadist* paranoia). Any number of radical Islamist infiltrators could not measurably alter the U.S. way of life. Meanwhile, all the ruling party of China now has to do to gain control over America's economy, politics, and foreign policy is to avoid an all-out war. There is a way for America to counter so pervasive an intrusion without active combat, but it must wait for Part Three. First, the extent of the same problem worldwide must be established.

Part Two

A Closer Look at Peripheral Hot Spots

"The spirit of democracy cannot be imposed from without. It has to come from within." — Mahatma Gandhi

(Source: Attributed to the father of modern India, Mahatma Gandhi)

Latest Developments in Yemen

- How badly is *al-Qaeda now* entrenched in Yemen?
- Do any other revolutionary movements exist there?

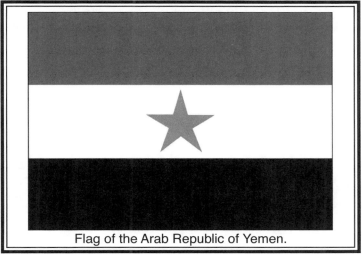

Flag of the Arab Republic of Yemen.

(Source: Corel Galley Clipart, Flags, image designator "19G015.jpg")

Old Trade Routes and the Suez Canal

As the spring of 2010 turned into summer, there was considerable *al-Qaeda* activity on both sides of the Red Sea approaches to the Suez Canal. Djibouti (with its resident U.S. Marine base) was relatively calm on one side, but Yemen was in turmoil across the straits of *Bab el Mandeb*. This country's southernmost part was beset by the same *al-Qaeda* faction that had blown up the U.S.S. Cole in 2000, and its northernmost region was still in the throes of an Iranian-sponsored rebellion.[1] Still, only the most naive of Americans believed all the trouble to be Muslim inspired. That's

111

because 3.5 million barrels of oil pass through those straits daily.[2] Wherever that much oil is involved, the world powers in most need of oil get interested. There had once been a Marxist State in South Yemen, and its secessionists were still active.

Across the Gulf of Aden (some 200 miles to Yemen's south) lay Somalia. At its northwestern extremity, independence-minded Somaliland was relatively peaceful. However, Puntland (at the "Horn of Africa") and the rest of Somalia had fallen increasingly under *al-Qaeda's* influence.[3] After a rash of piracy, this influence was now disrupting Mediterranean trade. That sea's eastern end would make the perfect home for a new caliphate. Still, controlling the southern approaches to such a caliphate may not be the Islamists' goal. It is

Map 8.1: Most Convenient Smuggling Lane to Africa
(Source: Courtesy of General Libraries, University of Texas at Austin, from their website, for map designator "somalia_rel_2002.pdf")

also here that the Middle East most discreetly abuts Africa. As such, the area is of great interest to those who smuggle Afghan heroin to America. (See Map 8.1.)

The Traditional Trade Route between Yemen and Somalia

The western extension of the ancient "Silk Route" ran offshore between Yemen and Somalia. (See Map 8.2.) Now, through these waters, pass some 20,000 vessels headed to and from the Suez Canal each year.[4] As such, the ancient trade route has become a modern-day smuggling conduit. By the Yemeni Coast Guard's own admission, major segments of Yemen's jagged 1,500-mile coastline remain unpatrolled. Along them, pirates, human traffickers, and drug smugglers continue to operate.[5]

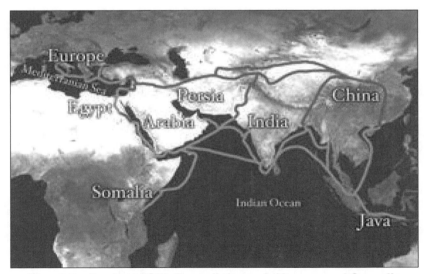

Map 8.2: Ancient "Silk Route" through Yemen and Somalia
(Source: Wikipedia.org, s.v. "Somalia," under provisions of GNU Free Documentation License, map designator "Silk_route.jpg," from NASA/Goddard Space Flight Center)

> Other experts point to [the] ties forged between Somali
> pirates . . . and criminal networks in Yemen during years
> of people-smuggling.[6]
> — Reuters, 29 August 2008

Yemen's Recent History

The modern Republic of Yemen was born in 1990, when tradi-
tionalist North Yemen and Marxist South Yemen (Aden plus all
points east) merged after years of border wars and skirmishes. The
peace broke down in 1994, and a short civil war ended in defeat for
the separatist southerners. However, the long-term prospects for a
successful coalition were poor, because of the differences in ethnic
make-up between regions. (See Map 8.3.)

At the other end of the country, there was more trouble. Since
mid-2009, hundreds have been killed and many more displaced by
clashes between government troops and northern Houthi rebels
belonging to the minority Shia Zaidi sect. The regime declared a
cease-fire with these rebels in February 2010,[7] after long accusing
Iran of supporting them.[8]

Of course, *al-Qaeda* was also at work. According to BBC News,
"Al-Qaeda in the Arabian Peninsula (AQAP) established itself in
Yemen after it was forced out of Saudi Arabia, taking advantage
of the fact that large swaths of Yemeni territory are [actually] controlled by . . . tribes, not by a government." AQAP is the merger of
"al-Qaeda in Saudi Arabia" and "al-Qaeda in Yemen." The former
came to prominence with the simultaneous suicide bombings of three
Western housing compounds in Riyadh, Saudi Arabia, in 2003. Then,
several Western workers were killed in separate incidents, and the
U.S. consulate in Jeddah was stormed in 2004. Sometime during
2006, Al-Qaeda in Yemen—was formed next-door. It has since
killed Western tourists and run an assault on the U.S. embassy in
Sanaa in September 2008. Subsequently, the two groups merged
in Yemen.

AQAP's first operation outside Yemen was carried out against
Saudi Arabia's security chief in August 2009. Most interesting
is its stated objective. Again according to BBC News, "Led by a
former aide to Osama Bin Laden, the [now-combined] group has
vowed to attack oil facilities, foreigners, and security forces as it

seeks to topple the Saudi monarchy and Yemeni government, and establish an Islamic caliphate." After the AQAP was implicated in (and implicitly took credit for) a failed attack on a U.S. airliner on Christmas Day 2009, the Yemeni government stepped up its efforts against all Islamic militants. A subsequent truce with the northern rebels then allowed it to better focus on *al-Qaeda* and the southern separatists.[9]

From Yemen's history, one might expect all of those southern separatists to be of Marxist persuasion. However, among their most prominent new leaders is Tariq Fadhli, a former ally of Osama bin Laden.[10] This apparent mixture of Islamism and Socialism is quite ominous. Despite the spatial overlap of the southern separatist movement and *al-Qaeda* network, as late as January 2010 there had been no known operational coordination between them.[11] (See Map 8.4.) Such a wedding of widely divergent ideologies suggests their overall sponsorship by a powerful third party with strategic interests in the region.

More about the Northern Rebels

In the early 1960's, Egyptian-backed Yemeni army officers ended that country's 1,000-year Shia Imamate to establish the modern Yemeni republic. When Republican troops seized Sanaa, the Imam fled to Yemen's northern mountains to conduct a counteroffensive. It is in this same region (around Saada this time) that fighting still occurs. Shia Iran stands accused of supporting the Saada rebels, though Yemen's Zaydi Shias are doctrinally different from Iran's Twelver Shias. At times, the Saada rebels may have also accepted support from *Hezbollah* and *al-Qaeda*. This region has long played host to drug smuggling and people trafficking.[12] Several foreigners have been kidnapped here over the last 15 years, but—until just recently—most were released unharmed.

In August 2009, the Yemeni army launched a fresh offensive against Shia rebels in the northern Sa'ada Province. Hundreds of thousands of people were displaced by the fighting. The conflict took on an international tone on 4 November 2009 as clashes broke out between the northern rebels and Saudi security forces along the Yemeni-Saudi border. Houthi leaders subsequently claimed there had been U.S. air strikes launched against them, but this claim was

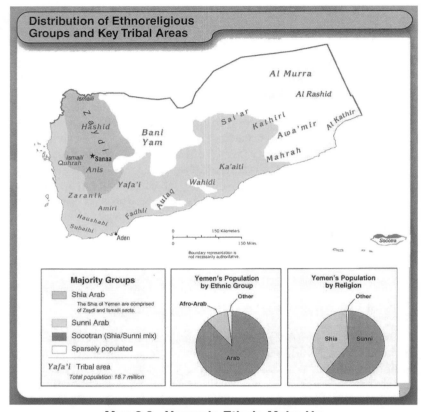

Map 8.3: Yemen's Ethnic Make-Up
(Source: Courtesy of General Libraries, University of Texas at Austin, from their website, for map designator "yemen_ethno_2002.jpg")

only carried by Iranian television (TV) and probably false.[13] As of January 2010, there was a shaky cease-fire between Yemeni forces and the Houthi rebels.

Al-Qaeda's Earlier Presence in Yemen

For many years, bin Laden had a communications center in one of the poorer neighborhoods of Sanaa, Yemen's capital. To this

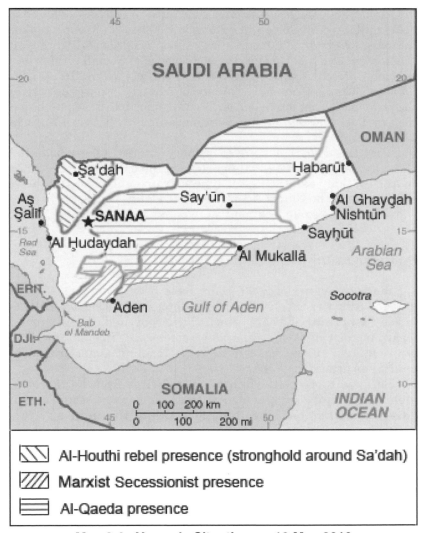

Map 8.4: Yemen's Situation on 12 May 2010
(Source: Map based on "Yemen Conflict Map," by Zimmerman, Frist, & Harnisch, CriticalThreats.org, 12 May 2010; Univ. of Texas at Austin map "yemen_sm_2010.gif")

building, his operatives supposedly called on their cell phones to report progress and request guidance.[14] Even after the U.S.S. Cole was damaged in Aden harbor by boat-borne *al-Qaeda* operatives

117

in October 2000, most Americans continued to believe *al-Qaeda* to be a landlocked organization. Then, in October 2002, supertanker Limburg was badly damaged in an attack by *al-Qaeda* fighters off the Yemeni coast.[15] This put the whole issue of Somali pirates into a much different light—particularly when *al-Qaeda*-affiliated *al-Shabaab* was discovered to be inhabiting the same spaces as most of the pirates. Osama bin Laden is, after all, known to have purchased his own fleet of freighters to operate presumably between Karachi and Dubai.[16]

That these sea lanes are of primary interest to any potential U.S. adversary became painfully clear in the early Spring of 2009. In April of that year, the PLA (Chinese) Navy sent its second three-ship flotilla to the Gulf of Aden.[17] A month later, Iran sent six more warships to the same location.[18]

Subsequent Developments in Yemen

Since December of 2009, there have been a number of U.S.-assisted attacks by Yemen's security forces on *al-Qaeda* elements inside that country. Those attacks have consisted of both ground forays against *al-Qaeda* cells and Yemeni air force or American cruise missile attacks against *al-Qaeda* training camps or leaders plotting to attack the West.[19]

Because those cells often receive shelter from local tribesmen who simply sympathize with their cause,[20] the Yemeni government has been hesitant to escalate the fight any further. Its longtime president Ali Abdullah Saleh is largely dependent for his political survival on the loyalty of such tribes. Yemeni authorities are worried too harsh a crackdown on *al-Qaeda* militants would further alienate a deeply conservative population that is already suspicious of the West. Additionally, *al-Qaeda* has often taken refuge in remote mountainous areas over which Sanaa has little control.[21]

Whether the Yemeni government wants to admit it or not, *al-Qaeda* may have serious designs on the whole southern part of the country. On 15 September 2010, *al-Qaeda* operatives blew up a gas pipeline in Southern Yemen.[22] Nine days later, regime troops were battling "the *al-Qaeda* militants involved in the pipeline incident" in Shawba Province near the village of Al-Hootah. This can only mean that *al-Qaeda* wants eventually to dominate the Marxist

118

Secessionist areas on Map 8.4.[23] That those areas abut the Gulf of Aden is no coincidence. The traditional smuggling route runs along this coast. (Refer back to Map 8.2.)

In early November 2010, AQAP mailed two packages from Yemen to the U.S. containing printer cartridges full of explosives. While the bombs were addressed to a Jewish center, Western authorities soon determined their purpose was instead to remotely detonate a fuel-laden cargo plane over a U.S. city. AQAP then took credit for the crash of another United Parcel Service (UPS) plane. On 9 November 2010, America's president banned any more commercial shipments to the U.S. from either Somalia or Yemen.[24]

Initial Summary for the Region

Prior to 1990, it was only the People's Democratic Republic of Yemen (PDRY) that bordered on the Gulf of Aden. The PDRY was a Marxist State. With little industrial output and agriculture for income, it probably welcomed any coastal smuggling gratuities. (See Figure 8.1.) After the PDRY's incorporation into Yemen, its Socialistic elements remained both restive and cash deprived. The Iranian-sponsored northern rebels and *al-Qaeda* supported eastern Sunnis had similar problems and goals. Thus, one may compare today's pressures on the capital of Yemen to those on the capital of Rhodesia before it became Zimbabwe. Instead of a pincers movement by a Chinese-proxy from one direction and Russian-proxy from another, Sanaa is under a three-sided attack. It must contend with the following extremist elements: (1) Shiites from the north; (2) Marxists from the south; and (3) Sunnis from the east. As the Sunni extremists and Marxists are now starting to cooperate, the Sanaa government may be in trouble. Or, the south may only want enough autonomy to monitor its own coastal trade. There is a certain Communist nation that would like nothing better than permanent naval access to the adjoining sea lanes. This nation would want *al-Qaeda* to facilitate the unlikely union between Yemeni Marxists and Islamists.

Yemen's Overall Prognosis Is Not Good

According to CBS's "60 Minutes," Yemen makes the perfect

Figure 8.1: Regime Has Little Control over Gulf of Aden Towns
(Source: Microsoft Office 2004 Clipart Gallery, image designator # j0090288)

"safe haven" for *al-Qaeda*. The poorest of the Arab nations, it has porous borders and ports, vast unregulated tribal areas, and a relatively powerless government. Ostensibly a U.S. ally in the War on Terror, its President Saleh is also the political ally of an *al-Qaeda* affiliate.

Formerly a member of the presidential council, Sheikh al-Zandani openly runs al-Eman University in Sanaa. With a number of *jihadist* graduates, this institution is "the cradle of extremism in Yemen." Sporting a red-dyed beard, its very vocal leader (al-Zindani) has been designated by the U.S. as a "specially designated global terrorist." He has a long history of working with Osama bin Laden, to include recruiting fighters and providing weapons. His vast following is what makes him a political necessity to Saleh's tenuous regime.[25]

The Widespread Demonstrations of Early 2011

After populist demonstrations unseated the autocratic leaders of Tunisia and Egypt at the first part of 2011, others in Syria and Yemen have continued to pressure their leaders.[26] Within Yemen, however, it was far from clear which of the three anti-government factions is mostly behind the demonstrations. On 17 February, two people were killed during riots in the southern port city of Aden.[27] Aden just happens to be at the center of the Marxist Secessionist area. (Refer back to Map 8.4.)

This Trouble Did Not Abate

After wondering who had been behind the demonstrations in Sanaa, Americans finally got a hint in late March 2011. On 24 March, Houthi rebels took over most of the key city Saada in the north.[28] Three days later *"al-Qaeda* supporters and separatists" took over the town of Jaar in Abyan Province just east of Aden.[29] Then on 3 April, the riots (and crackdown) spread to a city on the western edge of the Marxist Secessionist area — Taiz. (Refer back to Map 8.4.) This was about the time Washington announced it was ready for Saleh to step down.[30] Like *Hezbollah's* takeover of Lebanon, the Shiite victory in Northern Yemen seemed not to worry top U.S. leaders. Thus, there was no telling which populist element might end up ruling the rest of the country.

On 3 June, the Yemeni president was wounded in a rocket attack by "rebellious tribesmen" on his palace. After providing him with refuge for medical treatment, Saudi Arabia brokered a ceasefire of sorts. Then, something calling itself the "opposition coalition" started to celebrate Mr. Saleh's departure in Sanaa. Its precise composition remained unclear, as no Western news service seemed willing (or able) to fully analyze it. They would only say it was mostly tribal, with some "militant" representation. While professing to want a unity government,[31] this coalition most likely included no Shiite Houthis, but only a very troubling mix of Marxist and *al-Qaeda*-supporting Sunnis.

Within Yemen, there has been a direct *al-Qaeda* influence. The troublemakers in Somalia have only been labeled as *"al-Qaeda* affiliates."

Al-Qaeda's Takeover of Somalia

- Which Somali faction is *al-Qaeda's* current affiliate?
- How much land does the Somali government control?

Flag of Somalia.

(Source: Corel Galley Clipart, Flags, image designator "19B048.jpg")

The Old Trade Route Entrance to Africa

While Yemen is beset by *al-Qaeda* and secessionist elements in the south and Iranian-sponsored rebels in the north,[1] its largest African neighbor has its own problems. Though helped by Ethiopian reinforcements and then African Union peacekeepers, Somalia's government had been gradually losing control over its territory. Independence-minded Somaliland was relatively peaceful, but Puntland and the rest of Somalia were falling increasingly under *al-Qaeda's* influence. This influence has been undoubtedly enhanced by the flow of illicit drugs. (See Map 9.1.)

123

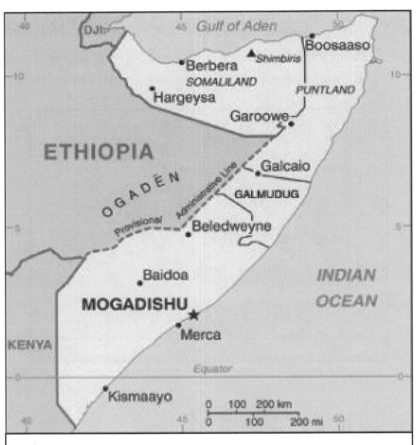

SOMALILAND: SELF-DECLARED REPUBLIC
PUNTLAND: SEMI-AUTONOMOUS REGION
GALMUDUG: SELF-DECLARED ADMINISTRATION (BENEFITS FROM
          SUPPORT OF AHLU SUNNA AND AL JAMA'A)
REST OF SOMALIA: ISLAMIST CONTROLLED (MOSTLY BY AL SHABAAB,
          WITH SOME HIZB AL ISLAM NORTH OF MOGADISHU

(SOURCE: "THE TERRORIST THREAT FROM SOMALIA," BY CHRISTOPHER HAMISCH,
AMERICAN ENTERPRISE INST. [CRITICALTHREATS.ORG], 12 FEB. 2010)

Map 9.1: Somalia Comprised of Several Autonomous Regions
(Source: Courtesy of General Libraries, University of Texas at Austin, from their website, for map designator "somalia_sm_2010.gif")

Somalia's Most Recent History

The *al-Qaeda* affiliate that now controls most of south central Somalia is *al-Shabaab*. In this nefarious role, it has succeeded both *al-Itihadd al-Islamiya (AIAI)* and the Union of Islamic Courts (ICU). Even when fighting U.S. forces in Mogadishu in 1993, *AIAI* had been an *al-Qaeda* ally.[2] The Ethiopian military intervention of 1996 drove it from the ports of Merka and Kismayo and inland center of Luuq. Then, much of *AIAI* may have taken up residence in Puntland—Somalia's component state at the "Horn of Africa." For a while, *AIAI* was even sending volunteers to fight with *al-Qaeda* in Afghanistan through Puntland's port of Boosaaso.[3] This would certainly explain why so much of the region's subsequent piracy originated from Puntland.[4] Puntland's government may have been complicit in this piracy,[5] or just unable to deal with all the foreign interest in its strategic location.

> "Now we are seeing Puntland essentially breaking down as an entity," said Rashid Abdi, Somalia expert at the International Crisis Group think-tank. "You're seeing a gradual takeover of the state by criminal gangs."[6]
> — Reuters News Service, 29 August 2008

As late as May 2009, northern Somalia was being called a safe haven for *al-Qaeda*.[7]

More about *al-Shabaab's* Predecessors

AIAI may have even had something to do with the temporary ouster of Puntland's leader in 2001. The Ethiopians certainly thought so.

> Washington . . . is likely to rely on neighboring Ethiopia—whose army has been fighting the al-Itihaad for at least four years. . . . There have already been allegations that Ethiopian troops have entered the breakaway Somali region of Puntland . . . to help the region's ousted leader, Abdullahi Yusuf [Ahmed].[8]
> — Center for Defense Info., 10 December 2001

Abdullah Yussuf Ahmed went on to administer Puntland until being elected as president of Somalia in October 2004. Contesting his leadership of Puntland had been a man by the name of Jama Ali Jama. He had been a Moscow-trained Socialist who went on to lead the opposition to Somalia's Transitional Federal Parliament (TFP).[9]

To consolidate all of Somalia under *sharia* law, the "Union of Islamic Courts" (ICU) began an offensive against the various warlords around Mogadishu in April 2006. As it had recently acquired a large arsenal and skilled militia,[10] the ICU was undoubtedly an *al-Qaeda* creation. Its leader was Hassan Dahir Aweys, a former cleric and head of *AIAI's* military wing.[11] In turn, those warlords formed the "Alliance for the Restoration of Peace and Counter-Terrorism." In April and May of 2006, it was reported to have U.S. backing, to include money and intelligence.[12]

By 5 June 2006, ICU forces had fully captured Mogadishu with the help of *jihadists* from Saudi Arabia, Yemen, and Pakistan.[13] An *al-Qaeda* recruiting video was made of their exploits.[14]

Then, ICU troops started pushing north to seize more territory. They were also moving west toward Baidoa where the fledgling Somali government was based.[15] By 19 June, the U.S. had turned the problem over to the Ethiopians. On this date, Sharif Sheikh Ahmed, ICU leader, reported hundreds of Ethiopian soldiers had crossed the border and were heading for Baidoa.[16] It was soon established that 300 Ethiopians had made the incursion and that ICU forces had already imposed *sharia* law on Jowhar—the other government bastion.[17] On 20 July, fully loaded Ethiopian armored personnel carriers were sent to Somalia at the request of its president.[18] Within days, the ICU was calling for a holy war to expel them.[19]

U.S. officials have since confirmed that Aweys was a high-level *al-Qaeda* operative who replaced Ahmed as head of the ICU.[20] Because Aweys had also controlled *AIAI's* military wing,[21] *Geostrategy-Direct* soon speculated that most of Somalia was under *al-Qaeda's* control.[22] Then, the Ethiopian invasion caused the ICU to break up. Among its splinter groups were *al-Shabaab* and *Hizb al Islam*. (Refer back to Map 9.1.)

Al-Qaeda's Longest-Existent Training Base in Somalia

The oceanside town of Ras Kamboni lies at the south end of

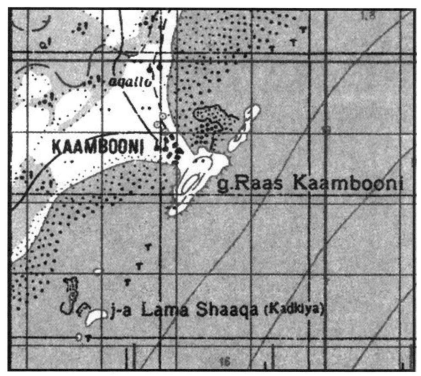

Map 9.2: Ras Kamboni at Somalia's Southern End
(Source: Courtesy of General Libraries, University of Texas at Austin, from their website, for map designator "ras_kaambooni.jpg")

Somalia, near its border with Kenya. (See Map 9.2.) For years, it and its coastline extrusion/island has been known as an *al-Qaeda* stronghold and training base.[23] The U.S.-gunship-supported Ethiopian invasion of Ras Kamboni in early 2007 only briefly altered this equation.[24] For, in April 2009, the *Christian Science Monitor* reported a recruit of *al-Qaeda*-affiliated *al-Shabaab* had just been trained there with hundreds of other young men.[25]

Things Are Changing in Puntland

On 6 June 2010, an ABC newsman on assignment in Boosasso videotaped a story about increasing *al-Shabaab* terrorist activity around the Puntland capital.[26]

His report is further proof of *al-Qaeda's* long-time presence in Puntland. Such a presence at the strategic Horn of Africa is no small matter.

Even Somaliland Is No Longer Safe from *al-Qaeda*

On 26 June 2010, NPR's "Morning Edition" News carried a story about Somaliland's upcoming elections. Though Somaliland is next to Djibouti and—from its very inception—pro-Western, it now has a big enough *al-Shabaab* contingent to openly warn the people not to vote.[27]

The Overall Picture

It's clear that most government-allied militias are from Gumu-dug. (Refer back to Map 9.1.) Somalia's Western backed transitional government only controls part of the capital, Mogadishu. After up to 80% of Somalia's police and soldiers defected to *al-Shabaab,* its security force is now "a composite of independent militias loyal to senior government officials . . . who profit from the business of war." In an effort to bolster the beleaguered government, the European Union (EU) has been training soldiers for its new army in Uganda. However, the U.N.'s Somalia monitoring group is not optimistic. In March 2010, it said, "Despite infusions of foreign training and assistance, government security forces remain ineffective, disorganized, and corrupt." In addition, they are severely underpaid.[28]

Meanwhile, *al-Shabaab's* influence had been growing dramatically. (See Maps 9.3 and 9.4.) After a rather unhappy Mogadishu experience, the U.S. military was in no hurry to again try to restrict this particular arm of *al-Qaeda.*

Then, on 12 July 2010, the pot boiled over. Two simultaneous blasts in Uganda's capital were claimed by *al-Shabaab. Al-Shabaab* had previously promised to attack Uganda and Burundi, if those countries were to fail to pull their peacekeepers out of Somalia.[29] Not only was *al-Qaeda's* African presence openly asserting itself, but it was also growing.

Proof Positive of *Al-Qaeda's* Longtime Presence

For years during the early 1990's, *al-Qaeda's* main body was being hosted by the government of Sudan—Somalia's western neighbor.[30] When finally asked to leave Sudan in 1996,[31] *al-Qaeda* moved enough of its infrastructure to Somalia to maintain several training camps at Ras Kamboni and Mogadishu.[32] At least part of this infrastructure has apparently stayed on.

> Somalia . . . is divided into three parts, each "ruled" by local warlords. . . . Al Qaeda has been transporting men and material through its vast, unguarded coastline for many years. . . .
> As the Islamist vanguard, it was incumbent on al-Qaeda to manifest Muslim displeasure at the U.S. intervention in the Horn of Africa [in 1993]. Beginning in early 1992, al-Qaeda established a network in Somalia. Al-Qaeda's then deputy Emir for military operations, Muhammed Atef, was entrusted with the mission, and frequently visited Somalia in 1992 and 1993. In early 1993, al-Qaeda's chief instructor, Ali Muhammad, came to train the attack team drawn from . . . *[AIAI]*, formerly known as the [Somali chapter of the] Muslim Brotherhood, an associate group of al-Qaeda. On October 3-4, al-Qaeda-trained *[AIAI]* . . . fighters attacked U.S. forces in Mogadishu, killing eighteen U.S. personnel. The blame focused on General Muhammad Farah Aideed, but Osama [bin Laden] was in fact behind this key operation. Although the world's attention was drawn to the deaths of American soldiers and the subsequent humiliating U.S. withdrawal, al-Qaeda-trained Somalis killed Belgian and Pakistani peacekeepers too. On the Somalia operation, referring to Osama's role in the attacks, the CIA later stated: "Information from our sources confirms his involvement *(Background on Osama Bin Laden and Al-Qa'ida,* CIA, Washington, D.C., 1998, 10)."

129

According to Indian intelligence interrogation of Maulana Masood Azhar, the then secretary of Harkat-ul-Ansar [an al-Qaeda affiliate in Pakistan], . . . a number of Arab mujahidin . . . moved to Somalia. . . . [S]ome 400 went to Sudan and thereafter to Somalia, where they joined *[AIAI]* . . . in 1993. . . .

Al Qaeda's role in expelling U.S. troops from Somalia is acknowledged by local Islamists. . . . On June 8, 1998, the U.S. Attorney General indicted Osama for his role in training the tribesmen who killed eighteen U.S. soldiers in Somalia in 1993.[33]

— *Inside al-Qaeda,* by Rohan Gunaratna

Public Broadcasting System's (PBS's) *Frontline* confirmed *al-Qaeda's* involvement with the U.S. withdrawal in 1993. It says, "Aideed's forces were getting help from Osama bin Laden's *al-Qaeda.*" Osama, after all, was still living in Sudan in 1993. It goes on to show that bin Laden had himself acknowledged *al-Qaeda's* intervention in Somalia in a 1998 interview. *Frontline* further

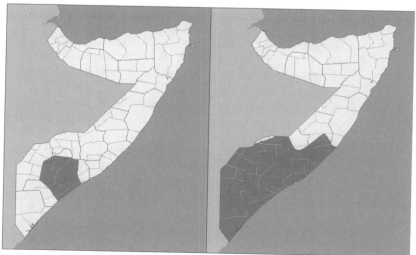

Map 9.3: *Al-Shabaab's* **Growth from 2009 to March 2010**
(Source: Wikipedia.org, s.v. "Harakat al-Shabaab Mujahideen," under provisions of GNU Free Documentation License, map designator "HSM_map.png" by Kermanshahi)

stated, "The U.S. Justice Department had indicted bin Laden for providing support to Somali fighters in the way of training and assistance."[34]

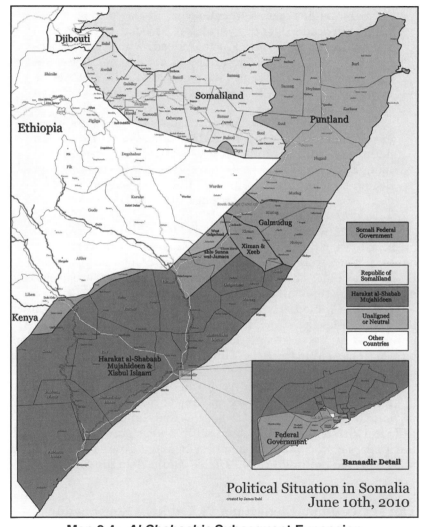

Map 9.4: *Al Shabaab's* **Subsequent Expansion**
(Source: Wikipedia.org, s.v. "Somalia," under provisions of GNU Free Documentation License, map designator "Somalia_map_states_regions_districts.png" by Iglo)

When asked to leave Sudan in 1996, Osama bin Laden almost certainly shifted key parts of his headquarters to nearby Somalia. The ICU forces that captured Mogadishu in early June 2006 had the help of *jihadists* from Saudi Arabia, Yemen, and Pakistan.[35] An *al-Qaeda* recruiting video was even made of their exploits.[36]

> Somalia has been a sanctuary for al-Qaeda since 1993, when bin Laden sent several top associates to provide assistance to Mohamed Farah Aideed, whose supporters eventually killed 18 American troops in Somalia. The country was again a center of al-Qaeda activity in 1998 as its members plotted the bombings of U.S. embassies in Kenya and Tanzania. . . .
> . . . In 1997, Ethiopia dispatched its troops to the western Somali town of Luuq to raid the offices of al-Itihaad. In addition to killing hundreds of the Islamic group's militiamen, Ethiopian forces reportedly seized three truckloads of documents detailing the group's link to al-Qaeda.[37]
> — Center for Defense Info., 10 December 2001

The *AIAI* was superseded by the ICU, and ICU troops were pushing toward Baidoa where the fledgling Somali government was based.[38] They were countered by another Ethiopian intervention. By 19 June 2006, Sharif Sheikh Ahmed, ICU leader, was reporting hundreds of Ethiopian soldiers crossing the border.[39]

Aweys—Ahmed's replacement as head of the ICU—was known to be a high-level *al-Qaeda* operative.[40] He had controlled *AIAI's* military wing,[41] so one could logically conclude the torch was being passed from AIAI to the ICU. Thus, much of Somalia was still under *al-Qaeda's* indirect control.[42]

On 27 December 2006, Aweys, along with several hundred fighters from the *Hizbul Shabaab* wing of the ICU fled Mogadishu, presumably to the former *AIAI* base at Ras Kamboni.[43] Forced into exile in Eritrea as the ICU collapsed,[44] Aweys started talking with the leaders of *al-Shabaab* and other Islamist groups—to include a newly formed umbrella called *Hisbul Islam* (Islamic Party).[45]

The Transitional Government's Unlikely New Leader

Greatly confusing an already complex situation in Somalia,

Sharif Sheikh Ahmed became head of Somalia's Transitional Federal Government (TFG) in January 2009. This is the same Islamist who, along with Aweys, had managed to take over most of Somalia by 2006 and was then ousted by the Ethiopians.

Ahmed had been allowed to join the U.N.-sponsored reconciliation process in Djibouti and was then elected Somalia's president days after the Ethiopian pullout.[46]

On 9 May 2009, Dahir Aweys' new group *(Hisbul Islam)* along with *al-Shabaab* and other allies tried to topple the Government of President Sharif Ahmed in a coup that failed.[47] Aweys had mostly complained about Ahmed permitting African Union peacekeepers into the country.

Mogadishu residents soon reported seeing foreign fighters in the frontline battle for the first time. This raised concerns that Somalia would become the next terrorist haven after Iraq and Afghanistan. Since then, foreign fighters have been further flocking to join *al-Shabaab*.[48]

Subsequent Developments

When the African Union announced in late July 2010 that it would send additional peacekeepers to Somalia, *al-Shabaab* was none too pleased. On 24 August, it launched an attack against a Mogadishu hotel that killed at least 30 people, including several members of the TFG parliament.[49] As it was, the TFG only controlled a few blocks of Mogadishu real estate. This was no ragtag guerrilla outfit like the one the U.S. had faced in 1993. A Reuters photograph of July 2010 shows its members to be well armed and wearing brand new Western-style utility uniforms.[50]

Political Situation in Somalia As of March 2011

The independent researcher who is responsible for Map 9.4 released an update on 24 March 2011. It contained some good news and some bad. The narrow government enclave along the Ethiopian border had subsequently been expanded southward, but the *al-Shabaab*-controlled region was now called "the Islamic Emirate of Somalia."[51] Luckily, the Western allies had also been busy. According to Reuters News, Somali troops backed by *Ahlu*

Sunna Waljamaca militia had just taken both Luuq and Beledhawo (Baydhabo), after "receiving logistical help from Ethiopian troops" (not necessarily those in the Africa Union peacekeeping force). With their main objective Baidoa, the former Somali capital, they were also pushing south along the Kenyan border.[52]

The researcher's new map also shows some kind of government initiative at the border of Somaliland with Puntland. *Al-Shabaab* had additionally gained some territory inside of Mogadishu and along the Shebele River north of there.[53] At least, the West was again pro-active in the region.

10 Much Depends on Pakistan

- Who's trying to overthrow the Zadari regime?
- Why doesn't Pakistan better impede the Afghan heroin flow?

Flag of Pakistan.

(Source: Corel Galley Clipart, Flags, image designator "19C025.jpg")

For Security Professionals Only

No Westerner should ever claim to understand Pakistan. As many nations in South Asia, it is a loosely controlled mix of widely divergent ideologies. All seem to blend quite easily into everyday life. But, therein lies the illusion, for many are still at odds. Yet, Pakistan's own researchers often cannot tell which faction was behind each manifestation of sectarian violence. That's what makes the following investigation so laborious. The average reader may want to skip through the composite analyses and closely read the summation.

135

Only while trying to think like an Asian, might an American come close to solving Pakistan's most perplexing current riddle— "Who or what is trying to overthrow the Islamabad government?" While Western "conventional wisdom" may lean toward al-Qaeda, local journalists aren't so sure. They think it's more likely that an internal faction has been vying for control—possibly with the support of some foreign nation. They may be right, because al-Qaeda would want a caliphate surrounded by Muslim nations.

For a number of reasons, the following analysis cannot obey all the parameters of a Western research paper. Most power plays in Asia resemble conspiracies. All perpetrators have carefully covered their tracks. The second problem is that most things Asian happen from the bottom up. Their only proof is in an accumulation of tiny clues. Such clues are difficult to corroborate. What necessarily results is a somewhat rambling discourse over every aspect of the incident. Within its "trends" lies the riddle's answer. Pakistan's most renown investigative journalists—like Wilson John and Ahmed Rashid—write this way, and that's the way this investigation must be structured. After embracing hundreds of clues, the reader then gets to pick the stalker of Islamabad.

A Telltale Admission from Pakistan

On 12 July 2010, an article appeared in *Newsweek* entitled "The Afghan Endgame." Within this article was a very disturbing admission. Pakistan had been advertising its ability to broker a deal between the Afghan president and "Pakistan's favored faction of the Afghan insurgency, led by Jalaluddin Haqqani."[1] A subsequent military journal article confirmed only that "the Haqqani network, with close connections to . . . Interservice Intelligence [ISI] and to al-Qaeda had begun exploratory talks using Pakistan as the intermediary."[2] However tactful the reference, the whole idea of Pakistan attributing any political status to Haqqani is ridiculous. Still, it comes as no surprise to inveterate FATA watchers. The Pakistani Army virtually ignored the Haqqani Network during its 2009-2010 sweep of the Waziristans.[3] Because Haqqani has long been the area's most celebrated drug smuggler, this carries with it some rather unpleasant implications.[4] Has Pakistan's drug syndicate become so powerful as to influence foreign policy? If so, it must be closely associated with its Army, ISI, or some very influential political party.

Figure 10.1: India's Proximity Affects Lahore Attitudes
(Source: Corel Clipart, image designator "28V033.jpg")

According to the CIA's *World Factbook,* Pakistan's military is its most potent political force. One highly respected local researcher thinks it's *JI* trying to overthrow the Islamabad regime.[5] *JI* does have considerable influence inside the Pakistani military (as almost 70% of the Army's officers and enlisted men are Punjabis, with most having attended schools in Lahore).[6] Still legal as a political party, *JI* has been only peripherally involved with the drug trafficking. Its military wing—*Hezb (Hezb-ul-Mujahideen)*—has been reportedly transporting heroin south to Karachi from northern FATA.[7]

Lahore is right next to India, so former residents (to include those in the military) might be more focused on the historical rift between Hindu and Moslem than on the Muslim extremist threat. (See Figure 10.1.)

More Than One Kind of Taliban in Pakistan

South Waziristan's *TTP* (*Tehrik-i-Taliban Pakistan* or "Pakistani Taliban") has been drawing most of the Pakistani Army's offensive wrath, but it is the "Punjabi Taliban" who have conducted many of the attacks against the government southeast of Islamabad. (See Table 10.1.) As such, the real enemy of the Pakistani regime may come not from FATA, but rather from Punjab.

The exact relationship between the Punjabi Taliban and the Pakistani Taliban is not completely clear. While both seem to include elements of the same radical factions, they still operate somewhat independently. It is usually believed that the former is just a Punjab-based component of the latter. However, the reverse is every bit as possible. Those attempting to overthrow the regime in Islamabad would be in no hurry to reveal the difference.

A Closer Look at Punjab

The capital of Punjab is Lahore. Greater Lahore is home not only to *JI*, but also to *Jamaat-ul-Dawa (JuD)*—formerly *Markaz-ud-Dawa-wal-Irshad (MDI)* and the parent of infamous *Lashkar e-Toiba (LET)*.[8] *LET* and Karachi drug lord Dawood Ibrahim have more than once cooperated to attack India (possibly under ISI direction). Ibrahim is known to have assisted some faction with the Mumbai attacks of 1993, and *LET* with those of 2003 and 2008. Whether he helped with the *LET* attacks on India's Parliament in 2001 and Mumbai train system in 2006 is not known.[9]

Though from different organizational models, *JI* and *JuD* have developed a certain degree of neighborly synergy. In December 2008, *JI* senators filed an adjournment motion in the Pakistani Senate against the government's decision to ban *JuD*.[10]

Of course, *JI and JuD* are not the only radical factions in Punjab Province. With a headquarters at Bahawalpur is *Jaish-e-Mohammed (JEM)*—an offshoot of the merger between *Harakat ul-Jihad-i-Islami (HUJI)* and the *Harakat ul-Mujahideen (HUM)* militia for the Fazlur Rehman faction of *Jamiat Ulema-i-Islam (JUI/F)*.[11] *Sipah-e-Sahaba (SSP)*—the parent of *Lashkar-e-Jhangvi (LeJ)*—coordinates its activities from Jhang.[12] Thus, comparing the locations of all four militant headquarters to those of the Punjabi

Taliban attacks might prove interesting. (See Maps 10.1 and 10.2.) All factions could be expected to defend their home turf against too much government snooping.

Only at Lahore, do the attack sites coincide with a suspected faction's headquarters. Yet, their armed wings—*Hezb* and *LET*—do not seem to be involved in any of the attacks. Most often implicated are *LeJ* and *JEM*, even in Lahore. Both factions specialize in squad assault (with the former being more suicide oriented), and both are closely allied with *al-Qaeda*.[13]

The Real Culprit Must Be Hiding

Whichever party, bureau, movement, or faction is trying to overthrow the Pakistan regime would draw unwanted attention by attacking with its own militiamen. Instead, it would hire the fighters of another faction and have some way to monitor/influence their activities. Many high-ranking officials believe the instigator to be a loosely aligned "syndicate of militant groups" that includes the *TTP*. More probably, it's an existing political entity that has been using those groups as proxies or scapegoats.

In October 2009, a key commander of the "Punjab-based *TTP* faction" [sometimes called the *Tehrik-i-Taliban Punjab]* was arrested at Bahawalpur. He is suspected of involvement in the following attacks: (1) Islamabad's Marriott; (2) Rawalpindi's Army Headquarters; (3) Lahore's Manawan Police Training School; and (4) Lahore's FIA Headquarters. His presence at Bahawalpur makes perfect sense, as *JEM* has its headquarters there, and this city is also an *SSP* stronghold.[14]

LeJ has been called *al-Qaeda's* "delta force,"[15] while *JEM* actively supported *JI*-offshoot *Tehreek-e-Nafaz-e-Shariat-e-Mohammadi (TNSM)* during its fight for the Swat Valley.[16] *Al-Qaeda* may thus seem the odds-on favorite for saboteur of the regime. Along with *LeJ*, *TNSM* and *JEM* are now part of Osama bin Laden's International Islamic Front (IIF).[17]

However, Pakistan's Interior Minister Rehman Malik has asserted, *"LeJ* and the *SSP* are working like contract killers and . . . being assisted both financially and strategically by the [FATA-based] *TTP* and *al-Qaeda."*[18] That's not quite the same as saying *TTP* and *al-Qaeda* are the hidden instigators. Yet, it eerily fits with several known facts. The Orakzai-based *Fedayeen-e Islam*—which has

2007 Feb—**Islamabad:** Bombings at Marriott and the international airport kill a number of people (BBC Timeline Pakistan).

2007 Jul—**Rawalpindi:** Someone tries to shoot down Pakistani President's plane from rooftop gun position (BBC, 6 Jul).

2007 Jul—**Islamabad:** Security forces storm the Red Mosque (Lal Masjid) complex after week-long siege (BBC Timeline Pakistan) with al-Qaeda-affiliated militants (Rediff, 15 July).

2007 Nov—**Sargodha:** Nuclear missile storage facility is attacked (EE, endnote 7-3).

2007 Dec—**Kamra:** Nuclear airbase attacked by suicide bombers (EE, endnote 7-3).

2007 Dec—**Rawalpindi:** Benazir Bhutto assassinated (BBC Timeline Pakistan).

2008 Jan—**Lahore:** Suicide bomber kills more than 20 policemen gathered outside the High Court ahead of anti-government rally (BBC Timeline Pakistan).

2008 Feb—**Lahore:** Two separate suicide attacks on Pakistani Army Medical Corps personnel—first its head, then bus-load of students (jamestown.org).

2008 Aug—**Wah Cantonment:** Several entry points to the nuclear weapons assembly plant came under attack by suicide bombers (EE, endnote 7-3).

2008 Sep—**Islamabad:** Marriott Hotel devastated in suicide truck bombing that leaves over 50 dead. Fedayeen-e-Islam claimed responsibility. JEM suspected and known to be the nucleus of the Fedayeen-e-Islam (EE, endnote 3-74).

2009 Mar—**Lahore:** Gunmen attack bus carrying the Sri Lankan cricket team. Five policemen are killed and seven players injured (BBC Timeline Pakistan).

2009 Mar—**Lahore:** Two dozen terrorists assault Police Training Center and hold over 400 people hostage. Fedayeen-e-Islam claims responsibility. Fedayeen-e-Islam comprised of members of JEM (EE, endnote 3-74).

2009 May—**Lahore:** Ground assault against Pakistan's ISI Headquarters, killing 23 people (EE, endnotes 3-58, 3-92, 7-92).

2009 Oct—**Islamabad:** Suicide bomber blows himself up at the U.N. World Food Program office killing five people (IANS, 15 Oct).

2009 Oct—**Rawalpindi:** National Army Headquarters stormed by terrorists who take 44 people hostage and only succumb after a 19-hour siege. Allegedly done by Punjabis (EE, endnotes 3-59, 3-66, 3-67). LeJ suspected (EE, endnote 3-72). Amjad Farooqi Group takes credit. Amjad Farooqi is TTP affiliated and known to contain elements of LeJ (EE, endnote 3-75).

2009 Oct— **Lahore:** Armed men dressed in military uniforms storm three targets: (1) Federal Investigation Agency (FIA) building; (2) headquarters and training center of "Elite [Police] Force"; and (3) Manawan police training school. This is the same school that was attacked in March. While the TTP claims responsibility, culprit is more likely a Punjab faction (IANS, 15 Oct).

Table 10.1: Taliban Attacks to Intimidate/Discredit Regime

2009 Oct— **Islamabad:** Eight people die and at least 18 wounded in the twin blasts at the International Islamic University (BBC, 2 Oct).

2009 Nov—**Rawalpindi:** Suicide bomber attacks people waiting to cash pay checks, including soldiers from Pakistani Army Headquarters (EE, endnote 3-81).

2009 Dec—**Islamabad:** Suicide bomber blows himself up at the entrance to the headquarters of Pakistan's Navy (AKI, 4 Dec. 2009).

2009 Dec—**Rawalpindi:** Six militants strike the mosque near military headquarters. They throw grenades and open fire, killing 27 civilians and nine soldiers, one a major general and another a brigadier (EE, endnote 3-82).

2009 Dec—**Multan:** Pakistani intelligence center assaulted (EE, endnote 7-94).

2010 Mar—**Lahore:** Two major bombings over five days. The first comes against the regime's "Special Investigation Agency" and is claimed by the "Pakistani Taliban." The second is directed at Army patrols (EE, endnote 3-83).

2010 Mar—**Lahore:** Suicide bombers strike at market (IANS, 28 May 2010).

2010 May—**Lahore:** Terrorists storm two mosques of the minority Ahmadi sect, taking hundreds of worshipers hostage and sparking gun battles with police that left at least 72 people dead. Tehreek-e-Taliban Punjab (not the TTP per se) takes the credit (IANS, 28 May).

2010 Jun—**Lahore:** Gunmen attack the Jinnah Hospital, killing at least 12 people, including four policemen, and injuring others. About three to four gunmen storm into the emergency ward where several injured people of Friday's mosque attacks had been admitted (IANS, 1 Jun).

2010 Jul—**Lahore:** Second Muslim shrine bombing in a month. This was at Data Darbar, Punjab's most revered Sufi shrine. (GW, endnotes 9-40 and 9-55).

2010 Sep—**Lahore:** Shiite procession targeted by three suicide bombers, killing 31 people and wounding 340 others. The TTP takes the credit (CNN).

2011 Jan—**Lahore:** Shiite procession hit by 13-year-old suicide bomber. To AFP, TTP says bombing in retaliation for drone strikes and military operations in tribal areas and warns "people to keep away from security forces and govt. property." To AP, its Fedayeen-e-Islam wing takes credit (BBC, 25 Jan.).

2011 Apr—**Multan:** TTP suicide bombers strike most important Sufi Shrine (AP).

Reference code:
  AKI: Italian News Service
  AP: Associated Press
  BBC: British News Service
  EE: Expeditionary Eagles
  GW: Global Warrior
  IANS: Indo-Asian News Service
  Rediff: Indian News Service
  CNN: Cable News Network

Table 10.1: Taliban Attacks to Intimidate/Discredit Regime (cont.)

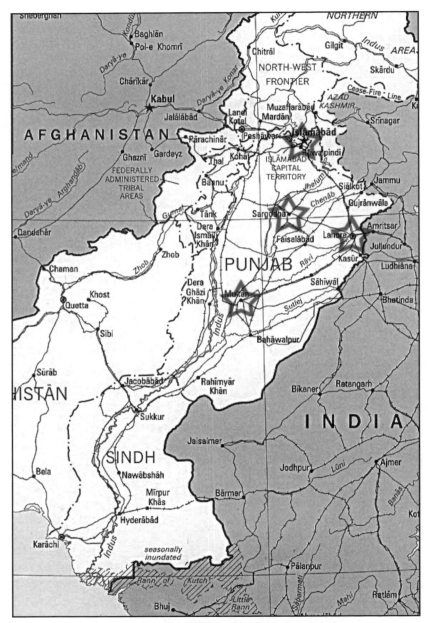

Map 10.1: Punjabi Taliban's Attack Locations
(Source: Courtesy of General Libraries, University of Texas at Austin, from their website, for map designator "pakistan_pol_1996.jpg")

Map 10.2: Headquarters of Militant Parties and Sects
(Source: Courtesy of General Libraries, University of Texas at Austin, from their website, for map designator "pakistan_pol_1996.jpg")

143

Map 10.3: *JuD's* Impromptu State

(Source: Courtesy of General Libraries, University of Texas at Austin, from their website, for map designator "txu-oclc-300481561-afghan_paki_admin_2008.jpg")

taken so much credit for attacks against the government—is comprised of elements of *TTP, LeJ, JEM,* and other militant factions. Nazir's South Waziristan militia has its own Punjabi component of "members of banned sectarian and Kashmiri militant groups."[19] It was Nazir who joined Bahadur and Baitullah Mehsud to sign the *Shura Ittehad-ul-Mujahideen (SIM)* agreement with Mullah Omar and Osama bin Laden in February 2009.[20] Since then, Nazir has been helping the Pakistani Army.

With this much "side-changing" going on, the regime's assailant won't be easy to identify. There's a lot of money in play, and the Pakistani Army virtually ignored both Haqqani and *JI*-affiliated Hekmatyar in its most recent sweep of FATA.[21] Haqqani is not only the region's biggest drug runner but also closely linked to *al-Qaeda's* new "Shadow Army."[22] Haqqani was also a member of *JI* originally.[28] Instead of a "Taliban network" trying to overthrow the central government, it's more probably an agency, political party, drug syndicate, or some combination thereof. *LeJ* and *SSP* could just as easily work for any one of them. The provincial government of Punjab is also somehow involved. Partially because of *JuD's* community service projects, Punjab's ruling body has largely ignored the nationwide ban on *JuD*. One wonders how much of *LET's* training it actually curtailed by taking over administrative control of the Murdikhe complex.[24] (See Maps 10.3 and 10.4.)

First Stab at the Hidden Instigator

To be suspected of a crime, one must have a motive. Within Pakistan, there are several entities giving the central regime grief. Likely after more autonomy for FATA, the *TTP* has long been accused of trying to control Peshawar as a stepping stone to Islamabad. Yet, only as a pawn of *al-Qaeda* would a nonpolitical fringe element embark on such an ambitious adventure. Likewise, *JuD* would happily stick to its fundamentalist haven to the north of Lahore.[25] (Look more closely at Map 10.4.) Not even an established political party—like *JI*—could create all of this chaos by itself.

There can't be all that many foreign players interested in toppling the Islamabad regime. India or any Western nation would be foolish to abandon the publicly elected and nonfundamentalist Zadari. This leaves a couple of other possibilities. After forming a separate alliance with *JI,* China is almost certainly interested in easier access to the Indian Ocean. And, as in Mexico, the international drug syndicate would love to bully the central government into more appeasement.

145

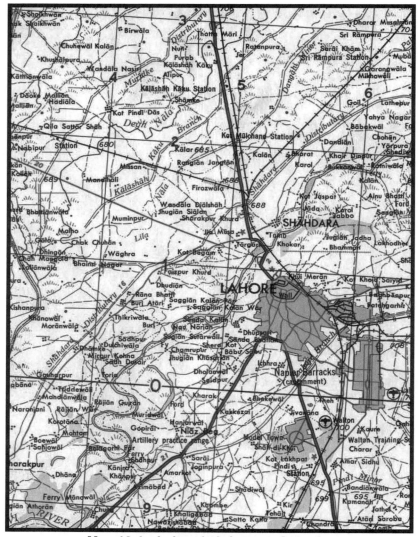

Map 10.4: *Lahore's Infamous Suburbs*
(Source: Courtesy of General Libraries, University of Texas at Austin, from their website, for map designator "lahore_amritsar_1963.jpg")

Most logically then, the culprit comes from within, but with still possible outside backing. The ISI has often been called a "state within a state." In the world of Islamist takeovers, this evokes unpleasant images of Nasrallah and al-Sadr developing their own alternative infrastructures in Lebanon and Iraq—complete with courts, police, schools, and relief agencies.

Only two "homegrown" factions have been constantly seeking to end the Zardari regime—*al-Qaeda* and *JI*. Since mid-June 2009, both bin Laden and al-Zawahiri have called for the destruction of the Pakistani state.[26] More than one local researcher has confirmed *JI's* stated agenda of taking over the Pakistani state from within.[27] In fact, what has always set *JI* apart from the Afghan-Taliban-supporting *JUI/F* is that the former wants a full "Islamic State" whereas the latter is willing to settle for more Islamic education and *sharia* law.[28]

If a political party wanted actively to cripple its own government while still remaining legal, it would do so discreetly. It might form improbable alliances and even position an anti-government proxy in the camp of a political rival. When Sufi Mohammad "quit" the *JI* in 1981, he did so in protest to its nonviolent political approach. He then supposedly began to copy the Saudi Wahhabis in action. Yet, upon returning from Afghanistan in 1989, he was reported to be "more convinced [than ever] of his religious ideals."[29] In other words, his original goals hadn't changed, only the way to achieve them. Thus, one cannot help but suspect *TNSM* of being a *JI* proxy in the *JUI/F's* Taliban camp. Both parents do, after all, come from the same Deobandi roots, and both are members of the *Mutahida Majlis Amal (MMA)*.

Such an arrangement would help to protect *JI's* interests in the FATA and Northwest Frontier Province (NWFP), while some other way was found to influence the Federal District, Baluchistan, Sindh, and the home province of Punjab. Any plan to take over the central government would require considerable funding. Like the ISI had done, *JI* might raise money through turning a blind eye to drug trafficking. Initially, Haqqani was also a member of *JI*. His dual affiliation has since helped him to build quite an empire.

Intentional Disinformation Must Be Expected

Much of the Taliban merger mirage comes from leaders of one militant faction assuming dual, honorary roles in other factions. All the while, their home group retains its original characteristics.

147

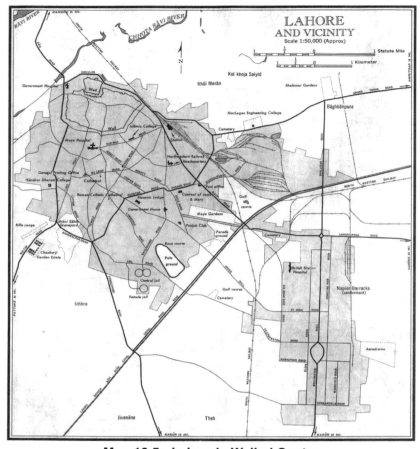

Map 10.5: Lahore's Walled Center
(Source: Courtesy of General Libraries, University of Texas at Austin, from their website, for map designator "lahore_vicinity_1963.jpg")

Temporary alliances of convenience are a fairly unique aspect of this region. Sometimes, those radical leaders even cooperate with the government for a while.

The Possibility of a Publicity Loving Scapegoat

With so many militant leaders changing sides, the most obvious attacker of Islamabad may only be a diversion. The real culprit will have preexisting political status, well-documented national aspirations, or a chaos-dependent methodology. With both ISI and Army headquarters under ground assault in Rawalpindi, Lahore, and Multan, one can pretty much rule out an agency-wide coup. (See Map 10.5.) That leaves only the ill will of some movement, party, cartel, faction, or rogue agency element. The most popular candidates for the first four possibilities are *al-Qaeda, JI,* Ibrahim syndicate, and *TTP.*

The southeastern assault on Islamabad has been often interpreted as a FATA reentry warning to the Pakistani Army from Waziristan-based *TTP.* Yet, it occurred as government forces were chasing *TNSM* and its *al-Qaeda* advisors out of the Swat Valley. So, the southeastern assault could have been to divert Pakistani forces from Swat. This would cast as much suspicion on *TNSM's* political affiliate.

Though only unhappy with the slowness of *JI's* political approach, *TNSM's* founder was soon categorized as a *JI* dissident and strictly Wahhabi.[30] More correctly, his group began to exhibit "Wahhabi and Deobandi leanings" (in true Salafist fashion).[31] That's not quite the same as being diametrically opposed to *JI's* goals.[32] In fact, there is evidence that Sufi Mohammad *(TNSM's* founder) remained loyal to the ideals of the man who originally established *JI.*

> He [Sufi Mohammad] argued that an Islamic state cannot be established through elections because the majority never votes in favor of Islamist parties. He started believing that the only way to establish an Islamic state is to follow the jihad philosophy of Maulana Maududi (1903-1979), the late founder of Jamaat-i-Islami.[33]
> — *Terrorism Monitor,* 16 July 2010

It has been alleged that *JI* intentionally weakened *TNSM* by tricking it into fighting the Americans in Afghanistan in 2001, and that *TNSM* now wants revenge against *JI.*[34] Such a claim is so wildly implausible as to be obvious disinformation. More probably

149

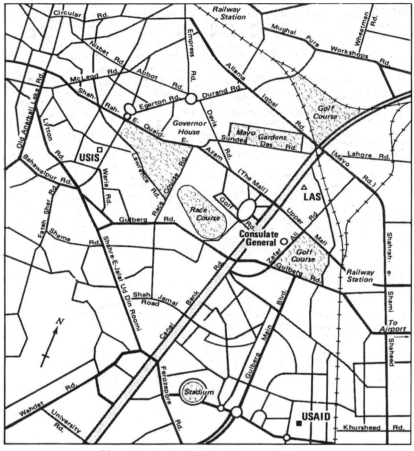

Map 10.6: Lahore's Newer Center
(Source: Courtesy of General Libraries, University of Texas at Austin, from their website, for map designator "lahore.jpg")

TNSM was a *JI* proxy at the time and just got badly hurt by the U.S. bombing along with everyone else. The extent of the current relationship between the two may lie in Sufi Mohammad's most recent *modus operandi*. He supposedly hated the political process but still wanted peace accords in the Swat Valley. Of late, he wants an Islamic system but now shuns violent methods and argues for peaceful ways to introduce *sharia*.[35] This sounds very much like political consensus with *JI*.

TNSM Has Never Been Part of the *TTP*

TNSM was not one of the five factions that originally formed the *TTP* (Pakistani Taliban) in Mohmand Agency in October of 2007.[36] Nor was it part of Baitullah Mehsud's later *SIM* agreement with Mullah Omar and Osama bin Laden. The *TNSM* and *TTP* have certainly cooperated over the years, but there is no proof of a permanent merger between them. An impromptu coalition of sorts may have occurred during the mutual fighting of December 2007,[37] but it never led to a mixing of resources or agendas.[38] If it had, the media would not have reported *TNSM* as a separate entity throughout 2008, 2009, and 2010. Yet, the *TNSM* is still mistakenly thought to be an extension of the *TTP*. Might a wily foe have used a little deception to distance itself from the northern instrument of its overall strategy?

If that assault on Islamabad from the southeast was in support of the *TNSM,* then it may have been launched by *al-Qaeda* or *TNSM's* original parent. The Lahore mosque attacks look more like the work of an extremist organization than of a rogue government agency or drug cartel. While *JuD* and *JI* both qualify, only the latter has nationalistic aspirations. Somewhere in Lahore lies the link between the Islamabad stalker and its southern proxies—*LeJ* and *JEM*.

Ongoing Events in Lahore

While Pakistan's central government has almost certainly been the main target of the terrorist attacks, Table 10.1 also shows an inordinate amount of activity in Lahore. (See Map 10.6.) This activity has not only taken the form of armed attacks against government facilities, but also against religious gatherings. Either someone wants Lahore as the new seat of national government, or the Islamabad stalker does not like this much security-agency attention in its own backyard. (Refer back to Map 10.2.) The religious interface has become so large (up to 1,500 people held hostage) that one suspects some sort of serious doctrinal discord. Yet, the first denomination to be targeted was the minority Ahmadi sect. The Ahmadis are considered by many mainstream Muslims to be heretics because they believe their founder in 1889 was the messiah foretold by Muhammad.[39] As such, they have often suffered discrimination and could easily be the disorder that local authorities seem powerless to prevent.

On 1 July 2010, Lahore's second Muslim shrine bombing in a month took place. It occurred at Punjab Province's largest and most revered Sufi shrine.[40] This horrific event prompted accusations that the local authorities could no longer protect the people and that Punjab's government was "soft" on the militants. This government appeared to be either afraid of, or in collusion with, those militants.[41] Punjab had not included the *TTP* in its list of 17 banned radical organizations, nor had it cracked down very hard on *LET, JuD,* and *JEM.*[42]

Full Composition of the Punjabi Taliban

While most of the Punjabi Taliban's heavy work has been conducted by *LeJ* and *JEM,* there are other members. Like the ISI's Army of Islam in Kashmir, the Punjabi Taliban contains elements of *SSP, LeJ, JEM, LET,* and *Hezb.*[43] As simply the parent of *LeJ, SSP* is not too surprisingly a contributor. Yet, having the militias of *JI* and *JuD* included may make quite a difference. They may be there merely to protect their parent's interests. The presence of non-Wahhabi *Hezb* tends to rule out *al-Qaeda* as being the overall coordinator.

Which Taliban Faction Is in Charge?

Some claim the *TTP* works for Mullah Omar or *al-Qaeda.* Others say it works for Haqqani. If either were true, the *TTP* might be calling the anti-establishment shots in Punjab. But, the *TTP* and Punjabi Taliban are only loosely connected. In fact, there seem to be more Punjabi advisers in FATA, than FATA advisers in Punjab. FATA isn't Pakistan's traditional hotbed of political/religious dissent. That dubious honor belongs to Punjab Province. Thus, there is a good chance the hidden stalker of the Zadari regime has been concurrently influencing the Pakistani Taliban from FATA and Punjabi Taliban from Lahore.

> From 2006 to date [July 2010], Punjab has witnessed no fewer than 174 terrorist attacks, which killed 1,312 security forces personnel and civilians. These attacks include 39 suicide attacks as well, out of which 15 [were] reported in Lahore.
> The situation can be compared with 1996-98 when sectarian violence had gripped the province with 204 terrorist attacks, killing 361 people. Lahore, alone had shared the 64 attacks. Lashkar-e-Jhangvi, Sipah-e-Sahabah, and Sipah-e-Muhammad were major culprit[s] behind these attacks.[44]
> — *Friday Times* (Lahore), 7-15 July 2010

The Punjabi Taliban is said to be comprised of splinter elements from major militant factions (most notably *LeJ* and *JEM)* and new terrorist cells. A good example of the latter is the Yaqoob Awan Group. Yaqoob Awan was an active member of *Jamaat-e-Islami* in Punjab. In 2007, he formed a group now affiliated with the *TTP.* Before the proliferation of Punjabi Taliban, two discourses were dominant in Pakistan. The first was of Islamization and sectarian supremacy through political means. *JI* and *SSP* were among those subscribing to this approach. The second was *jihad* against certain external forces (and authorities who cooperated with them). In discussing this, one Pakistani journalist divulges the Punjabi Taliban's original goal. "[T]he Punjabi Taliban appropriated both agendas and pursued them through violent means as illustrated by their targeting of sectarian, communal, foreign, political and security institutions, and their support to the militants in Swat."[45]

More than 37 groups have been called "Punjabi" Taliban, and this list even includes groups from Karachi and the Dera Ismail Khan district of NWFP. When such militants launched their terrorist operations inside Pakistan in October 2001, law enforcement agencies tagged them all as members of *"Lashkar-e-Jhangvi" (LeJ).*[46] Now, two of the most infamous in the assembly are *Fedayyen-e-Islam* and the Amjad Farooqi Group. This first is from FATA while the second has most lately been based in Sindh Province.[47]

The *Fedayeen-e-Islam* is itself an alliance of six Punjabi Taliban factions: *Illyas Kashmiri, Asmat Maaviya, Qari Zafar, Rana Afzal, Qari Hussain,* and Commander Tariq groups. *Fedayyen-e-Islam* took credit for the Marriott bombing in Islamabad and police training center attacks in Lahore.[48]

The *Fedayeen-e-Islam* is believed to be comprised of members of the *Jaish-e-Mohammad [JEM]* . . . a banned terror group that operates in South Waziristan. The *Fedayeen-e-Islam* has direct links to . . . Baitullah Mehsud as well as to *al-Qaeda*. The *Fedayeen-e-Islam* claimed it carried out the devastating Marriott Hotel suicide attack [in Islamabad] in September 2008.[49]
— *Long War Journal,* 30 March 2009

The group is made up of members of the Pakistani Taliban, the Lashkar-i-Jhangvi, Jaish-e-Mohammed, and other Islamist terrorists from Pakistan. It is based in Arakzai and South Waziristan.[50]
— *Long War Journal,* 17 November 2009

The Amjad Farooqi Group took credit for the Army Headquarters attack in Rawalpindi. Farooqi was the member of *HUJI* involved with many terrorist attacks in Islamabad including two assassination attempts against Musharraf in 2003. He was killed in an encounter in 2004 in Sindh Province. His peers formed the group now active in Islamabad and Rawalpindi.[51]

The Amjad Farooqi Group is . . . a mishmash of Pakistani jihadi groups from all regions of the country. . . While the Amjad Farooqi Group is largely made up of members from the Harkat-ul-Jihad-Al-Islami, members from the [Pakistani] Taliban, the Lashkar-e-Jhangvi [LEJ], the Lashkar-e-Taiba [LET], and other groups can be called on to fill out the ranks.[52]
— *Long War Journal,* 10 October 2009

The Attack Coordinator May Not Be *al-Qaeda*

More than one Pakistani researcher believes the element encouraging all the terrorist outfits to be the severely anti-American *JI*. *JI's* stated methodology, after all, is taking over the state of Pakistan from within.

> The fountainhead of religious extremism in our country is Mansoora, the headquarters of the JI, in Lahore. Unless Pakistan and the U.S. seriously take a look at the activities of the JI, any meaningful progress in stopping extremism feeding this terror will be impossible. The JI actively works on Pakistan's largest university campuses to spread its doctrine of hate and bigotry not just against other countries such as the U.S. but religious and sectarian minorities in Pakistan. . . . The JI seeks to infiltrate the army, the air force and the civil bureaucracy to weaken the state's resolve against extremism in Pakistan. Key members of the JI [who] sit in departments such as education introduce nothing but poison in Pakistan's young minds.[53]
> — *Daily Times* (Pakistan), 20 May 2010

The Religious Attacks

Pakistan is a pretty volatile place. Not all of its violence can be linked to some master plan. Among the worst is that associated with religious preference.

> The concentration of religious organizations in urban areas has an economic and political background. Lahore, Rawalpindi and Dera Ghazi Khan faced 19 terrorist attacks in 2009. The same trend was followed in 2007 and 2008. South Punjab is often highlighted as a troubled zone, but distribution characteristics show that religious organizations exist in all regions of the province. The most affected districts are Lahore, Gurjranwala, Rawalpindi, Faisalabad, Jhang, Multan and Dera Ghazi Khan.[54]
> — *Friday Times* (Lahore), 16-22 July 2010

By reviewing all reported targets, one might be able to sift out the signature actions *(modus operandi)* of the perpetrator with designs on Islamabad.

155

Attacks on security forces: Army and Security forces personnel are the primary targets of terrorists. Security forces have faced 33 terror assaults from 2006 to 2010. . . .

Sectarian violence: Eleven major sectarian terrorist attacks have been reported in Punjab during [the] last five years. The Tehrik-e-Taliban Pakistan and its affiliate[d] groups have claimed responsibility. . . . [T]he horrific terrorist attack on Data Darbar is a manifestation of the expanding sectarian agenda.

Communal targeting: Communal targeting has also increased in the province. During 2009 targeting of a Christian neighborhood in the Punjabi town of Gojra on August 1 was the most horrific instance. . . . This year Ahmadiyya community's places of worship were brutally attacked in an organized guerrilla style leaving a hundred worshippers dead.

Attacks on cultural and secular symbols: When Punjabi Taliban visit their native areas, they motivate the local people to take action against what they call anti-Islamic activities of barbers, cosmetics sellers and CD [Compact Disc] shops. The intent of the Taliban was clear when they attacked markets crowded with women, such as the Moon Market in Lahore. . . . [A]ttacks on cultural festivals, theaters and cinemas indicate the growing radicalization and the presence of violent radical cells in the city.[55]

— *Friday Times* (Lahore), 9-15 July 2010

Hezb's Only Apparent Role in the Punjabi Taliban

The media organs of militant outfits play a critical role in propagating their *jihadist* ideologies throughout Pakistan. Within the Punjabi Taliban camp, there is most evidence of *Hezb* operating in the media arena. Its parent—*JI*—is actively involved as well. "Jamaat-e-Islami and its subsidiary groups have at least 22 media publications to promote a jihadi outlook," according to a well-respected Lahore journalist.[56]

Various banned Pakistani organizations have now turned to community service projects to refresh their once flagging opportunities.

Banned organizations have ostensibly transformed into charities and under law their publications cannot be banned until these charities are declared defunct. Jaish-e-Muhammad [JEM] is now operating as Al-Rehmat Trust, Lashkar-e-Taiba [LET] as Jamaat ud-Da'awa [JuD] and Jamaatul Furqan as Al-Asar Trust.[57]
— *Friday Times* (Lahore), 23-29 July 2010

Six major militant outfits–Jamaat ud-Da'waa (Lashkar-e-Taiba), Tehrik Khuddam-ul-Islam (Jaish-e-Muhammad), Al-Rasheed Trust, Jamaatul Mujahideen, Hizbul Mujahideen [Hezb] and Sipah-e-Sahaba [SSP]–publish a wide range of periodicals, specifically to influence the minds of children, youth, women or the general reader.[58]
— *Friday Times* (Lahore), 23-29 July 2010

The Possible Mirage

The world is a far more complicated place than normally portrayed by the U.S. media. This is particularly true of Asia, where deception of all types has long been the norm. Yet, within America, the "duty solutions" have been far too simple since 9/11. *Al-Qaeda* has gladly taken credit for every obscenity worldwide. To this day, it remains the U.S. security establishment's only target. Yet, after 10 years of concerted North Atlantic Treaty Organization (NATO) targeting, *al-Qaeda* is also thought to have been reduced to a movement that can only function as an umbrella for other outfits. Both assessments cannot be simultaneously correct. Either *al-Qaeda* is getting stronger, or it has been given too much credit for the chaos.

During the early part of the U.S. occupation of Iraq, something calling itself *"al-Qaeda* in Iraq" started taking responsibility for every terrorist act in the northern part of the country. Every time the Sadr Brigade needed a break from the fighting in the south, *"al-Qaeda* in Iraq" claimed another atrocity in the north. Now in Lahore, the FATA-based *TTP* is taking credit for most of the mayhem. As the *TTP* is thought to be closer to *al-Qaeda* than the other militant factions, many U.S. service members seem content with this conclusion. *Al-Qaeda* did formerly have a headquarters on the *TTP's* home turf, but its new "Shadow Army" is supported by an independent and elsewhere-located Haqqani. *Al-Qaeda*-affiliated Uzbeks (from the IMU) also accompanied *TNSM* fighters on their Swat envelopment of Islamabad. After all, the *TNSM* is now part of Osama bin Laden's IIF. Yet, only to the extent that the other IIF members—*LeJ* and *JEM*—are currently *al-Qaeda* instruments, does *al-Qaeda* seem to have a significant presence in the Punjabi Taliban.

Thus, one has to wonder if the Pakistani chaos has instead been generated by an inner coalition or some foreign power wanting more control over the country. In April 2008, the Bush Administration finally admitted that Iran (as opposed to *al-Qaeda)* had been behind most of the trouble in Iraq.[59] Perhaps, the real culprit in Pakistan has been also hiding. Pakistan does have governmental agencies and political parties that are perfectly capable of a coup. With control over 90% of world's heroin, it also has a very powerful criminal element. To further complicate things, it has a blatantly expansionist neighbor. After successfully subverting Nepal, China is almost certainly behind India's growing Maoist (Naxalite) rebellion. Now, China has its own pact with *JI*,[60] an avowed opponent of the Islamabad government. *JI's* student wing, the *Islami Jamiat-i-Talaba (IJT)* is, after all, modeled after the National Socialist Party.[61] Thus, it would be a big mistake to believe *al-Qaeda* alone responsible for all the Pakistani destabilization in some spiritual quest for a new caliphate.

A Faction within the Pakistani Military May Be to Blame

To narrow down a field of suspects, one looks at motive, past history, and possible cohorts. Through its trucking company, the Pakistani Army was deeply involved in the drug trade during the Soviet-Afghan War.[62] The militarily staffed ISI has since supported both drug runners and Taliban.[63] As a military dictator, Musharaff was definitely playing both ends against the middle. Only since the civilian Zadari took over has there been any widespread hope for improvement. Yet, as is often the case in a Communist-targeted nation, Zadari has been often accused of corruption. Corruption is something that occurs to some extent in all duly elected governments, but it is still preferable to military rule. According to *Time* on 18 October 2010, Pakistan's military is again "calling many of the government's shots." Among other things, it vetoed Zadari's plans to "civilianize" the ISI and improve relations with India. Even more disturbing for an Army that may still overlook illicit trade, Pakistan's new finance minister is of its choosing.[64]

As did the U.S. military during its various Central American adventures, the Pakistani Army may have negotiated directly with the PLA in its bid to enter Gilgit-Balistan. Such decisions are best left to the foreign-policy department of a duly elected government. Most Westernized military establishments too seldom consider the full spectrum of political and economic variables.

The Deteriorating Situation inside Pakistan

On 4 January 2011, the progressive governor of Punjab (and political ally of President Zadari) was gunned down in Islamabad by a bodyguard who objected to his speaking out against Muslim extremism. The breaking point had apparently come when the governor wanted to ease the application of anti-blasphemy laws to a Christian woman.[65] The very same day, Islamabad's ruling coalition collapsed after a key party defected.[66]

The party defecting was the *MQM,* whereas Zadari and the deceased governor were from the Pakistan People's Party (PPP).[67] *MQM* has been a longtime affiliate of the Pakistani Army.

Many in Pakistan will see the hand of the country's powerful military behind the crisis. The MQM . . . is reputedly close to the military establishment.[68]

— *The Guardian* (UK), 4 January 2011

Though *MQM* rejoined the government a few days later (after Islamabad backed down on a fuel price hike),[69] the writing was still on the wall. With two years left of Zadari's five-year term, the Pakistani Army had been flexing its muscles in the political arena. Even more distressing had been its method—political destabilization. One has to wonder what this Army, or some ultra-conservative clique within it, has been concurrently doing in other arenas.

[T]he [Pakistani] military has worked behind the scenes in the past to end civilian governments and also periodically staged coups.[70]

— *The Guardian* (UK), 4 January 2011

This is not the only insight from the incident. *JI* and *MQM* had been recently conferring in Lahore. What were they conferring about? *JI* is known to favor regime change.[71]

The Probable Stalker of Islamabad Emerges

Somewhat distrustful of the Zadari regime, the Pakistani military has kept a tight hold over how foreign and defense policies are implemented.[72] Its relationship with China's PLA might help to explain the recent events in Gilgit-Baltistan.

After the coalition's temporary collapse, the Associated Press made a startling claim.

> Pakistan's powerful army could use the lack of political consensus to avoid operations that clash with its perceived strategic interests.[73]
> — Associated Press, 4 January 2011

Pakistan and all of its governmental departments are still extremely short of funds. Without the monetary kickbacks from various forms of trade, its Army will be much less able to pursue those strategic interests. That's why—during its recent invasion of the Waziristans—the Army may have left the Haqqani Network alone.[74]

Possibly also to save money, the Pakistani Army may have put to work at least one of the radical militias. In December 2010, Qari Saifullah Akhtar—longtime leader of *HUJI*—was released for the fourth time from Pakistani custody. *The Long War Journal* cites this as proof of *HUJI*'s support by both Army and ISI.[75]

Of course, not all of the Army wants a return to military dictatorship. Otherwise Army Headquarters would never have been attacked. As was the case in previous coups, it is more likely a powerful clique within the Army has been stalking the central government. To what extent this clique has been cooperating with *al-Qaeda* is not completely clear. On 1 May 2011, U.S. SEALS did finally manage to kill Osama bin Laden in Abbottabad, an affluent community some 35 miles from Islamabad. The make-up of this community and location of bin Laden's compound are both quite troubling.[76]

The compound is about 100 yards from a Pakistani military academy, in a city that is home to three army regiments and thousands of military personnel.[77]
— CBS's Online News, 1 May 2011

HUJI May Be This Clique's "Hardball" Coordinator

HUJI is, in many ways, distinct from the other extremist militias. Though formed in Punjab in the 1980's, it became an affiliate of *al-Qaeda* while battling the Soviets in Afghanistan. After helping the Taliban to resist the U.S. invasion of 2001, it sent most of its people over to fight the Indians in Jammu/Kashmir.[78] Though not normally listed as one of the ISI's proxies, it must have been somebody's surrogate to have this kind of record. More recently, it has been linked to a number of terrorist attacks inside Pakistan.[79] The most notable are as follows: (1) two assassination attempts on Musharraf in 2003;[80] (2) the attack against former Prime Minister Benazir Bhutto in 2007;[81] (3) the Islamabad Marriott Hotel bombing in 2008;[82] and (4) the Rawalpindi Army Headquarters attack in 2009.[83] That all were launched against upper-echelon targets was no coincidence. Bhutto's posthumously released book says Akhtar tried to overthrow her second regime in the 1990's.[84]

Of course, *HUJI* is also a member of Osama bin Laden's IIF.[85] Its members fought with *al-Qaeda's* Brigade 313 during Afghanistan's Taliban regime,[86] and still participate in its new "Shadow Army."[87] However, the repeated release of *HUJI's* leader from Pakistani custody points to a "regime changer" other than *al-Qaeda*. That changer may be an ultra-Islamist or drug-funded segment of the Pakistani Army. Coups often involve armed clashes between sister military units. Why couldn't a political overthrow also include mortal intimidation of military superiors? On 7 July 2011, NPR reported that some Pakistani military officers had been arrested "because of ties to a militant group advocating the overthrow of the central government."[88] Of all the groups, *HUJI* most closely fits that description.

Best Evidence Yet of a Little Foreign "Encouragement"

After the March 2010 Lahore bombing, there appeared a very

161

interesting videotaped interview from Associated Press. In it, Punjab's Law Minister (like an Attorney General) said the Army was hunting those responsible for these incidents. He further stated that "foreign countries are backing them [the miscreants]." Because that minister—Rana Sanaullah Khan—did not directly accuse India,[89] the guilty nation may be a little farther away and to the northeast.

11 The Resupply Routes into Afghanistan

● Why can't the Afghan drug flow be abated?
● To what extent is the Pakistani Taliban involved?

Old Flag of Afghanistan.

Another Piece to the Afghan Puzzle

Already established is that the Afghan regime is rife with corruption and its president's brother facilitating the drug flow. Only left to be determined is how those outbound opiates escape NATO detection. A *Christian Science Monitor* article on 19 July 2010 may help to solve this riddle. It seems the brother—Ahmed Wali Karzai—is the most powerful man in Kandahar. He is not the provincial governor, but rather the head of the provincial council. He is also the head of the Popalzai tribe.[1]

During the Soviet-Afghan War, some opiates were exiting Afghanistan on Pakistani-Army-run NLC (National Logistics Cell) trucks that had somehow managed to enter the country.[2] Those trucks had probably just secretly delivered Western war supplies to the *mujahideen*. Because the Soviets were unable to impede this form of cross-border flow, one might expect a similar scheme today. Contemporary trucks would need protection.

Wherever protection is necessary in a corrupt environment, "protection rackets" appear. Such rackets are none too particular about whom they help. Their services would be as available to illicit traders. Ahmed Wali Karzai is now allegedly receiving "a cut of the hundreds of millions of dollars spent on guarding the trucks that deliver food, fuel, and ammunition to NATO forces." If some of those trucks were carrying hidden drugs on the return trip to Karachi, Dawood Ibrahim might be quite appreciative. Another of the president's brothers—Hashmat Karzai—runs one of Afghanistan's largest security contractors—Asia Security Group.[3] This may help to explain why U.S. security contractors have been so unwelcome of late.

If the Afghan government were the only one in the region to be peripherally mixed up with the drug trade, things would be a lot simpler. Unfortunately, Pakistan's regime is as well. Ibrahim only avoided extradition to India for the 1993 Mumbai bombings by making a huge "loan" to Pakistan's failing central bank. The ISI has long funded its proxy armies through protection payoffs from the drug runners.[4]

How the Pakistani Turmoil Has Affected the Afghan War

The ISI is known to have run the war against the Soviets and rumored to be still helping the Taliban. To what extent it (and the Pakistani military) may try to influence the composition of Afghanistan's new coalition government, no one really knows. Yet, President Karzai is certainly aware of the pressure. Though a former member of the Northern Alliance himself, Hamid Karzai has recently become much more conciliatory toward the Taliban. According to one military journal, he has begun to remove over 50 Taliban commanders from the U.N.'s list of terrorists. He has also been conferring with Hekmatyar and Haqqani. In April 2010, Karzai was even heard to say he would "join the Taliban" if the West continued to meddle in Afghan affairs.[5]

While a coalition regime may provide a useful transition from open warfare to political debate, it should never be allowed to include a narco-guerrilla. Pakistan's endorsement of Haqqani for the new Afghan administration is very troubling.[6]

Neither are President Karzai's motives completely clear. He appears to be quite serious about forging new links with the Afghan Taliban in deference to his Northern Alliance roots. In the late summer of 2010, he replaced the decidedly anti-Taliban Minister of Interior and Director of Security. To survive politically, one military journal believes President Karzai will allow a "traditional" degree of corruption within his ranks.[7]

Hekmatyar's Continuing Influence

It was not merely Haqqani whom the Pakistani Army ignored during its sweep of FATA, but also *JI*-affiliated Hekmatyar.[8] In February 2011, Hekmatyar—in another bid to join an Afghan coalition government—offered to protect the full length of the Turkmenistan natural-gas pipeline. He did this despite the fact that the pipeline will run through areas not presently under his control.[9]

Haqqani's Troubled Background

While Jalaluddin Haqqani is a legendary drug runner and probably still calling the shots for the Haqqani Network, his son now runs its day-to-day operations. This Network has had a long-standing affiliation with *al-Qaeda*. In Afghanistan, it has been using not only Uzbek advisors,[10] but also *LET* commandos. *LET* maintains close ties to the Haqqani Network and has participated in Haqqani-led operations against Indian targets inside Afghanistan over the past several years. It has been further speculated that *LET* was involved in the Haqqani Network's February 2011 bank attack in Jalalabad which killed 38 soldiers, police, and civilians.[11] This partnership between Haqqani and *LET* may help to explain the sophistication of the raids in Kabul. Within both Afghanistan and Pakistan, "political pressure" may more often take on a violent dimension. *LET* has also been Dawood Ibrahim's choice for high-visibility attacks on India proper. Despite known ties to *al-Qaeda*, he has been routinely protected by the ISI.[12]

165

Most troubling is the conclusion of the Institute for the Study of War in Washington, D.C. It claims the drug-running Haqqani Network has been functioning as a proxy for part of Pakistan's security establishment.[13]

Apparently, NATO must do more to reverse this traditional source of income for both the Afghan and Pakistani governments. In October 2010, President Karzai denounced—as a "violation of Afghan sovereignty"—a large-scale drug raid into Nangarhar Province. In this raid, U.S. forces and Russian drug agents were helped by his own counter-narcotics police. Nangarhar just happens to be host to many of Haqqani's heroin labs.[14]

A Telling Oversight by Pakistan

Though longtime insurgent and drug smuggler, Jalaluddin Haqqani and his network were almost completely ignored by the Pakistani Army during its October 2009 sweep into FATA. Prior to this sweep, it even made a nonaggression pact with Bahadur, the warlord of the area in which Haqqani had his headquarters. Then, it never bothered his part of North Waziristan. The U.S. envoy to Kabul has since divulged that only six of FATA's seven tribal agencies were ever entered during the Army operation. The sacrosanct seventh agency had to be Kurram. On 15 November 2010, NPR confirmed that Haqqani had withdrawn to upper Kurram and blocked all of its entrance roads. Protecting Haqqani may have had as much to do with politics as drugs, for he was subsequently nominated by the Pakistani government to be part of Afghanistan's new coalition administration.[15]

The NATO Resupply Effort Takes a Turn for the Worse

Having targeted the older Haqqani with drone-fired missiles since at least October 2008, the U.S. military and CIA aimed a veritable barrage at him in December 2009. Then, in September 2010, another 21 drone missiles were launched against Haqqani targets in the highest monthly toll for such attacks.[16] This may not have pleased the part of the Pakistani government that depends on Haqqani for political and financial support. When a U.S. helicopter mistakenly fired on a Pakistani border post in Kurram agency at

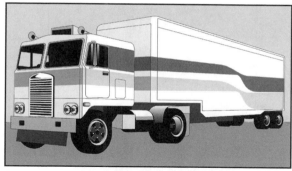

Figure 11.1: Most NATO Supplies Enter Afghanistan by Truck
(Source: Corel Clipart, Image designator "44D017.jpg")

the end of September, Pakistan closed the Torkham (Khyber Pass) border crossing to all NATO-bound vehicles. (See Figure 11.1.) This, in turn, sparked an all-out assault on fuel tankers coming up from Karachi. Within the original connection may lie some much needed answers.

The Overall Resupply Effort

Half of all NATO supplies enter Afghanistan through Pakistan via Torkham (on the road to Kabul from Peshawar) and Chaman (on the road to Kandahar from Karachi). (See Map 11.1.) Another thirty percent enter through Central Asia. The only confirmed overland northern route is from Kazakhstan through Uzbekistan. The "Transit Center" at Manas Air Base, Kyrgyzstan, only refuels Afghanistan-bound cargo planes. Even this may be only temporary. The riots that forced Kyrgyzstan's President Bakiyev from power in April 2010 had to do with resentment over resident Uzbeks. According to BBC News, "[S]ome in the group now taking control in

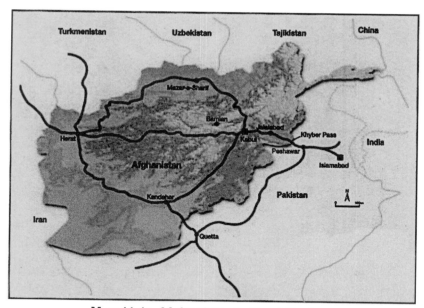

Map 11.1: Afghanistan's Road System
(Source: Courtesy of General Libraries, University of Texas at Austin, from their website, for map designator "afghanroad.tif")

Kyrgyzstan . . . have their eyes on the Manas base." To keep the base open, America has since had to pay a much higher rent.[17] Very few supplies make it by highway into Afghanistan through Tajikistan, because the remaining 20 percent of NATO's more sensitive where-withal (to include weapons and ammunition) supposedly comes in by air.[18]

Key Events Pursuant to the Torkham Border Closing

Torkham is the little town on the Afghan side of the famous Khyber Pass. Before reaching Peshawar and all points south, the road from Torkham runs through the FATA town of Landi Kotal. Probably carrying most Afghan heroin out are the same Pakistani trucks that have just carried NATO supplies in. Secret compart-ments would be hardest to find in the fuel tankers. In the fall of 2009, there was a rather suspicious incident involving two fuel tankers in

Kunduz Province. After being allegedly hijacked by the Taliban, one truck got stuck in a riverbed and was bombed by a NATO plane as villagers pilfered its contents.[19] While a little farfetched, the story still sounds plausible. However, within Asia, one must always look beyond the obvious. Any evidence of heroin transport would also have been incinerated.

On 1 October 2010, right after the Torkham border closing, 27 Afghanistan-bound fuel trucks were attacked at Shikarpur in Sindh Province.[20] One could more easily connect their burning to the helicopter incident if other tankers had not been formerly lost. As many as 100 fuel trucks had already been destroyed inside Pakistan. Most such ambushes had occurred in either the Khyber tribal region of northwestern Pakistan or in Balochistan.[21] But, 10 tankers had also been torched in Karachi in early August.[22] And "dozens" of NATO-bound trucks (to include fuelers) had been set ablaze in Rawalpindi in early June 2010.[23]

It's what happened next that may point to the real reason for the Torkham border closing. After NATO's Secretary General formally apologized on 4 October for the helicopter's killing of the three Frontier Corps personnel, the trucking attacks continued.[24] On the very day he apologized, 28 more fuel tankers were set afire in a poorly guarded terminal on the outskirts of Islamabad (in Rawalpindi).[25] On 6 October (in the sixth such event in a week), two dozen more tankers were destroyed in Quetta *en route* to the open Chaman crossing.[26]

While the border closure and truck burnings seemed directly related, there may have been another more obscure connection. Clearly, the trucks were more vulnerable while waiting for the Torkham crossing to open. Yet, not only the Torkham-bound trucks were being hit. Those at Shikarpur had been heading for the open Chaman crossing. Thus, the whole trucking disruption may have been a way for some faction to blackmail NATO into being less aggressive along certain parts of the Pakistani border. As the area's principal drug runner, Haqqani has considerable clout inside of Pakistan. He may have resented the CIA's drone missile attacks on what was previously his safe refuge. Such resentment could have led to duress on the Pakistani government as well as help from insurgent allies. Islamabad was probably already under pressure from the West to keep China out of occupied Kashmir. All this unsolicited interest in its internal affairs may have made the Zadari regime a little nervous.

Looking beyond the Border Incursion

Prior to the helicopter incident and border closing, many NATO-bound convoys had already been attacked. Almost all had to have some trucks carrying petroleum.[27] So, the only thing that had changed was the intensity with which the fuel tankers were being destroyed without much interference from Pakistani authorities. Rather than the Pakistani Taliban trying to help the Afghan Taliban, it is far more likely that Haqqani and his entourage of corrupt officials had been trying to pressure NATO into leaving their drug operation alone. Even the Pakistani Taliban have admitted the fuel truck attacks had more to do with the latest barrage of drone missiles than with the helicopter incident.

> A spokesman for the Pakistani Taliban, Azzam Tariq, told CNN that . . . the attacks were retaliation for U.S. drone strikes in Pakistan. . . .
> September saw 21 drone strikes in Pakistan, a record number, with three more strikes occurring so far in October, reports Reuters.[28]
> — *Christian Science Monitor,* 5 October 2010

When the Torkham crossing was again opened on 11 October 2010, as many as 150 fuel carriers lay in smoldering heaps of twisted metal.[29] No specific reason was ever given for the Pakistani government's final easing of the border-crossing restriction. Still, a very disturbing pattern had been established.

The Tanker Disruption Continues from All Sides

In mid-October 2010, two more fuelers were attacked inside Pakistan on their way to the Khyber Pass. On 11 November, an additional two were torched on their way to the Chaman crossing into Afghanistan. Three days later, 12 fuel trucks were set ablaze in Afghanistan's Nangarhar Province, east of Kabul. With regard to the latter, Afghan militants also promised to keep attacking fuel tankers until there is an end to the drone missile attacks against their tribal areas.[30]

Whatever the original reason for tanker hits inside Pakistan, they continued at the southern Chaman crossing. By the end of 2010, a yearly total of 136 NATO tankers had been destroyed by 56 attacks inside of Baluchistan alone.[31]

Then, by mid-January 2011, Iran was also embargoing all oil and gas shipments to Afghanistan so "they could not be used by NATO."[32] Not only had one of the opposition's principal strategies become clear, but also its international sponsorship.

On 1 April, two or three NATO fuel tankers were again set ablaze in the Khyber Agency, and three more sprayed with gunfire from motorcyclists near the Quetta crossing.[33] Local newspapers now readily admit that the NATO tankers are being regularly targeted inside Pakistan.

After Osama bin Laden was discovered living within 100 yards of Pakistan's premiere military academy in May 2011, a vital hint to the tanker riddle emerged. During "military discussions" on the floor of the Pakistani Parliament, it was suggested that any more U.S. incursions onto Pakistani soil be met with a full "disruption" of Afghanistan-bound supplies.[34] Implicit in this suggestion was that previous disruptions had shared both purpose and sanction. Three days after the parliamentary discussions, another U.S. helicopter was taken under fire by Pakistani border guards.[35] Four days later, 15 more NATO fuel trucks were attacked inside Pakistan.[36]

Meanwhile, Enemy Reinforcements Are Plentiful

As was clearly evident in the last chapter, there is no shortage of replacement fighters for Afghanistan. While the ordnance travels in pieces, the new fighters travel in pairs. Their mission is not just to confront NATO in open combat. Among them are highly trained suicide bombers and commando raiders. As there is often no way to tell who is Afghan born, some end up as members of the Afghan security forces. Many will facilitate raids by leaving gates open or ladders handy, but others will strive to intensify distrust between allies.

In 2010, there was an upsurge in the killing of NATO troops by Afghan security personnel. During the spring or summer, an Afghan policeman suddenly turned his automatic weapon on his U.S. advisors.[37] In December, an Afghan army recruit killed two more Americans with a suicide bombing.[38] Then, in February 2011, another Afghan soldier gunned down nine German peacekeepers for no apparent reason.[39] By late April, it was disclosed that seven such attacks had occurred in 2011, with 24 Americans so far dead at the hands of supposed allies.[40] The assassins had almost certainly been enemy infiltrators bent on undermining the all-important trust between Afghan and NATO forces. That's how a foreign entity might use a Sun-Tzu-like strategy to destabilize the place. More than one Asian entity would certainly like to.

On 24 April 2011, the Taliban used a mile-long tunnel to free 500 inmates from a high-security prison in Kandahar.[41] This was no precedent, as almost 900 others had been sprung by a spectacular assault from this same place in 2008.[42] So, the enemy will have no shortage of seasoned personnel for the 2011 season.

NATO Not Sufficiently Active in All Parts of Afghanistan

With limited resources, NATO has only focused on the most volatile Afghan regions. This can be risky where opportunistic rebels are involved, particularly when there is hard evidence of Iranian, Pakistani, and Chinese interest in the place. As of mid-January 2011, three widely respected news services had reported an upsurge in Taliban activity in the previously quiet northern and western quadrants of the country.[43]

A Country That Is Strategically Vital to Several Neighbors

Not only Iran, but also China has been trying to influence the action in Afghanistan. Bamian Province is not only home to the Mongol-appearing yet uniquely Shiite Hazaras, but also the corridor through which the PRC hopes to ship home its Iranian petroleum. Details on how the Chinese have previously helped the Taliban and *al-Qaeda* have been published in other titles and will not be repeated here.[44] This is the forum for recent news. Should the U.S. decide not to lend Pakistan as much money in the wake of bin Laden's discovery within 100 yards of its premier military academy, China has offered to make up the difference.[45]

Below is also a very interesting excerpt from a 13 February 2009 State Department cable signed by Tatiana C. Gfoeller, the U.S. ambassador to Kyrgyzstan.

pro.

"Kyrgyz officials had told her that China had offered a $3 billion financial package to close Manas Air Base . . . [so she] asked for the [Chinese] ambassador's reaction . . . ,˜ the cable stated. "Visibly flustered, Zhang [that ambassador] temporarily lost the ability to speak Russian and began spluttering in Chinese to the silent aide."[46]
— *Washington Times,* 2 December 2010

Then, the *Washington Times* goes on to claim the following: "The cable highlights what observers say has been China's behind-the-scenes, anti-U.S. strategy of seeking to undermine U.S. global counterterrorism efforts."[47] So direct an allegation may not mesh well with Washington's current devotion to its lenders. On 7 June, NPR disclosed that Kazakhstan (the northern ground portal for key U.S. supplies into Afghanistan) was being so broadly invested by China as to fear losing its independence.[48] So, not only have the radical Shiites been helping radical Sunnis, but the Communists may have been indirectly assisting both. While bogged down in expensive anti-Islamist wars, America would be much less able to resist Communist expansion.

173

12 Why All the Trouble _____ in Thailand?

- How is Thailand part of the current world crisis?
- What two commodities make Thailand strategically vital?

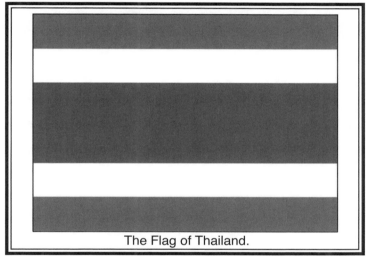

The Flag of Thailand.

(Source: Corel Galley Clipart, Flags, image designator "19C029.jpg")

All Can Agree on Thailand's Strategic Significance

Since the 1960's, China has been working hard on any number of ways to bypass the Straits of Malacca with its natural-resource shipments. It has established an overland route to Iran through occupied Kashmir and Afghanistan. It has gone to extraordinary efforts to create an outlet to the Indian Ocean through Nepal and either India or Bangladesh. It has spent billions on an oil conduit up the Irrawaddy River and then along the Old Burma Road. Finally, it has long wanted a canal across the Kra Isthmus of Thailand.[1] (See Maps 12.1 and 12.2.) Unfortunately, the existing government

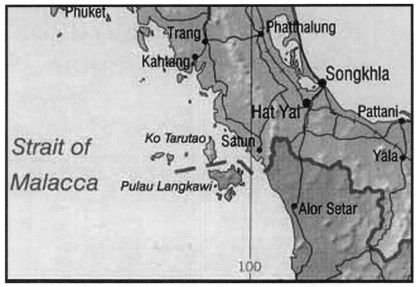

Map 12.1: The Kra Isthmus Is Narrow and Low
(Source: Courtesy of General Libraries, University of Texas at Austin, from their website, for map designator "thailand_rel_2002.pdf")

of Thailand must first endorse such a project. Thai Prime Minister Chavalit Yongchaiyudh endorsed its construction in 1996 but was soon replaced after a major financial crisis. In fact, over the last 40 years, Thailand's ruling system has been constantly in flux, with no fewer than three military coups interspersed with contested elections. There has been so much uncertainty that something of a cycle has developed in its governance pattern. Riots bring down any military regime, and then the duly elected government again lacks stability.[2] As Thailand has been long recognized as the anti-Communist bastion of the region, most of those coups must have been in response to a real or imaginary leftist threat. Once again,

Map 12.2: Only Thai Peninsula Stands between Oceans
(Source: Courtesy of General Libraries, University of Texas at Austin, from their website, for map designator "thailand_sm_2010.gif")

in September 2006, the military entered national politics by carrying out a bloodless coup against populist Prime Minister Thaksin Shinawatra.[3]

All the while in Thailand's extreme south, there had been a fairly large Muslim separatist uprising killing thousands. Whether its proximity to the canal's most likely route (from Satun to Songkhla) means anything or not, no one can really say. (Refer back to Map 12.1). Yet, oil routes, Muslim uprisings, and Chinese "enterprises" have been all present at once in other strategically important locations—like Nigeria and Sudan. There, it appears as if China has welcomed the societal unrest that invariably limits Western competition.

Such a canal would cost a lot of money, of course—money that the government of Thailand no longer has after its current rash of riots. This means China would likely end up funding the project. The Chinese would also handle its construction with the same massive work force that has recently completed the Three Gorges Dam Project.

With worldwide Chinese expansion a given for all but the most casual of readers, the complete lack of media attention to China's possible meddling in Thai affairs can no longer be ignored. After Nepal's recent slide into servitude, Mao's most subtle follow-up methods have almost certainly been refined. With public demonstrations as a hammer, it may now resemble more of a democratic push toward more equitable treatment for the rural poor. The words "democratic" and "republic" do both appear as part of North Korea's official title. Any evidence of Chinese intrigue in Thailand will almost certainly be circumstantial and limited. This is in no way proof of its absence. Deception is the name of the game in Asia, and the U.S. better start realizing it.

Those Red-Shirts Are Pretty Well Organized

While the color red does not always equate with Communism, it certainly can. In Venezuela, Hugo Chavez's supporters wear red shirts. Throughout much of 2009 and early 2010, red-shirted protestors virtually crippled Bangkok. While there was little evidence of Communist agitation, it is still suspected.

The focus of the red-shirts was, of course, on Thaksin Shinawatra—the prime minister ousted by military coup in 2006.

Mr. Thaksin [Shinawatra] . . . was very popular among the rural poor, because he initiated policies that benefited them, such as funding for health-care and education.[4]
— *BBC News Profile,* 20 April 2010

Voters from Thailand's north and northeast had returned Thaksin Shinawatra's allies to power, only to see the new government fall to a series of opposition protests and court rulings. So, in March 2009, the red-shirts came out on the streets of Bangkok, as the United Front for Democracy against Dictatorship (UDD). UDD's members are mainly rural workers from outside Bangkok, but its ranks also include students and activists. Their protest began with a series of sit-ins outside of government offices, but quickly escalated. In April 2009, they forced the cancellation of a summit of the Association of Southeast Asian Nations (ASEAN) after storming the summit's designated building in the seaside resort of Pattaya. Then, violence erupted in Bangkok. Clashes involving troops, protesters, and Bangkok residents left many people hurt. As Thai troops finally massed, the red-shirts called off their protests. UDD leaders said they didn't want any more loss of life. Yet, the anger that had triggered their action did not go away. In April 2010, they called for more protests in Bangkok aimed at toppling the regime. They occupied Bangkok's historic and commercial districts and at one point stormed Thailand's parliament building. They also assaulted a satellite transmission site, in a bid to restart a station that had been shut down by the government. Then, the protests turned more and more violent. On 11 April, four soldiers and 17 civilians were killed as the army tried to disperse the red-shirts. The red-shirts subsequently announced they would not go home until parliament was dissolved.[5]

Communism Is No Stranger to Thailand

Though Thailand has been the regional bastion of anti-Communist effort since the Vietnam War, it has still had its own internal struggles with Communism. The Communist Party of Thailand (CPT) was active from 1942 until the 1990's. By the early 1970's, the CPT had become the second largest Communist movement in Southeast Asia. At its political peak, the party effectively acted as a state within a state. For rural support, it had over four million people, from whom it recruited 10,000-14,000 armed fighters.[6] The CPT's influence was not merely concentrated in the Northeastern and Northern parts of the country, but it also extended to the "Southern region."[7] At the country's mid-section, most Thai citizens are believed to have still supported America's anti-Communist agenda. (See Figure 12.1.) Following a series of internal and external "pressures" (mostly government imposed), the CPT all but disappeared from Thailand's political scenario in the early 1990's.

The Pieces Are Starting to Fit

While Thaksin Shinawatra's profile reveals no visible Communist connections, most of his supporters do come from regions that were previously home to the CPT. Like the CPT, Mr. Shinawatra has been pushing for health-care and education for the disenfranchised poor.

> [CPT] alliances with the hill tribes were made by offering services such as health, education, and assistance to the poor and by attacking outside enemies such as the Thai army, the forestry companies, and various gangs.[8]
> — *International Journal of Socialist Renewal,* 2009

Shinawatra is instead a telecommunications magnate who has managed to amass considerable financial holdings. Yet, the Thai Supreme Court has recently stripped his family of $1.4 billion in contested assets.[9] So, he may now be interested in an additional cash flow from a foreign backer. After more than five years in power, he was ousted after being accused of corruption and abuse of power. Now in self-imposed exile, he faces a two-year jail sentence if he returns to Thailand.[10] Thaksin Shinawatra has no military background, but the prime minister who originally endorsed the canal does—Chavalit Yongchaiyudh. A "pro-canal" partnership between the two could generate some serious income.

> [Current] Prime Minister Abhisit Vejjajiva Thursday urged the public not to panic after former prime minister Thaksin Shinawatra announced the formation of the people's army

with Pheu Thai chairman Chavalit Yongchaiyudh serving as the supreme commander.[11]
— *The Nation* (Thailand), 29 October 2010

The words "People" or "People's" do not necessarily infer Communism either. Though seen as the reincarnation of Thaksin Shinawatra's banned Thai Rak Thai party, the People Power Party (PPP), ruled Thailand from December 2007 until December 2008. Then, it too was banned for suspected corruption.[12] However, the word "army" is more troubling. The CPT called its military wing the People's Liberation Army (PLAT).[13] Therefore, the choice of words in Mr. Shinawatra's announcement is either very telling or very unfortunate. From this single statement, one can definitely detect a Chinese connection (whether the shared agenda be political or just financial). A national leader has only to be leftist and strapped for cash to be the unwitting pawn of the Chinese.

Figure 12.1: Thailand Has Been Best U.S Ally in the Region
(Source: FMFM 2-1 [1967], p. 115)

After "a carefully stage-managed election campaign," Thaksin Shinawatra's businesswoman sister was elected Thailand's next prime minister on 4 July 2011.[14]

13 All This over Ocean Chokepoints?

- Is *al-Qaeda* trying to control the world's trade?
- Which foreign entity is?

Warfare is no longer limited to shooting and explosions.

(Source: Corel Gallery Clipart, image designator "21C043.jpg")

Pakistan Provides a Way to Avoid Malacca

Part Two has discussed how recent events in several nations relate to ocean chokepoints. It is through those chokepoints that the flow of natural resources might be restricted in time of war. Yemen and Somalia are at the entrance to the Suez Canal, Thailand abuts the Straits of Malacca, and Pakistan provides a way to bypass those Straits. All three locations are also on major drug conduits. From Pakistan, one runs east, and the other west. Together they carry much of the world's heroin to market. Coastal Yemen lies along the westward leg that runs through Dubai, across Somalia and the Lower Sahara, and then down to Venezuela. The eastern leg runs through nations with direct access to the Central Pacific. The CIA's *World Factbook* still lists Thailand as "transit point for illicit heroin en route to the international drug market from Burma and Laos."[1] Some of the eastward bound Afghan heroin might end up there as well. So, from two different standpoints, these three separate locales have strategic significance for the world's aspiring superpowers. What those superpowers have been doing there is now at issue.

Afghanistan Cannot Be Saved Until Pakistan Changes

Pakistan's instability is the real threat to world peace in South Asia. The radical takeover of its government could be enough to precipitate a missile exchange. Almost as loosely ruled as Afghanistan, Pakistan plays host to the region's most powerful extremists and smugglers. To have any hope of stabilizing it, President Zadari would have to shut down hundreds of *madrasas*. Sadly, Pakistan has too little national school system to replace them. Plus, such a move would almost certainly doom any chances of Zadari's reelection. As president of a now almost bankrupt nation, he may also be more susceptible to financial influence than was his saintly wife. That Pakistan is now backing Haqqani for inclusion in Afghanistan's unity government means its drug syndicate holds enough political sway to affect foreign policy.[2] Of course, this syndicate is not the only self-absorbed element at work in the country. Some radical faction has also been trying to overthrow Pakistan's central government. Both offending parties may be one and the same, and the mostly likely candidate is part of the Pakistani Army. An Army-run trucking company was hauling Afghan drugs to Karachi during the Soviet-Afghan War,[3] and all three successful coups have been by members of the Army. In fact, the Army has ruled Pakistan for over half of its history.[4] That Pakistani Army Headquarters was assaulted by extremists in 2008 need not alter this conclusion. This is a security establishment that regularly uses religious factions as proxies outside the country. Why couldn't a mutinous segment of the Army also use one inside the country to bully the top brass? This hypothesis is also consistent with the Army's political affiliations. Among its biggest supporters is *JI* (the country's largest religious party) and *MQM*.[5] It was a *JI* offshoot (*TNSM*) that ran the Swat Valley envelopment of Islamabad in 2009,[6] and *MQM* that caused the government temporarily to collapse in January 2011.[7]

For the "core" faction during the Army Headquarters attack, *HUJI* is the odds-on favorite, though *LeJ* and *JEM* may have also helped. After the attack, somebody calling themselves "the Punjabi Taliban" actually took the credit.[8] But, the Punjabi Taliban undoubtedly consists of elements from several different factions, and *HUJI* most often targets the central government. It was *HUJI* that Benazir Bhutto thought was trying to overthrow her second regime.[9] *HUJI's* history is also somewhat different from the other extremist militias. It helped the Afghan Taliban to resist the U.S. invasion of Afghanistan but then did not become one of the more obvious ISI proxies in Kashmir.[10] Some 30,000 of its fighters survived the U.S. airstrikes and then moved back to Karachi, Lahore, Faisalabad, Rawalpindi, and Azad Kashmir.[11] Some *HUJI* cadres took refuge in South Waziristan while others went to the Buner part of Pakistan's NWFP.[12] Many *HUJI* leaders were thus well positioned to link up with the *TTP*. Actual credit for the Army Headquarters attack was taken by a group founded by a *HUJI* member.[13] There is no inconsistency in the fact that attack's mastermind (Qari Ishtiaq) was also a *TTP* commander,[14] because in this region individuals sometimes hold leadership roles in two different organizations at once. Like the above-mentioned *HUJI* member,[15] Ishtiaq has also been linked to the Islamabad Marriott bombing.[16] Though banned, *HUJI* may still maintain branch offices in 40 districts and revenue divisions across Pakistan, to include Sargodha, Dera Ghazi Khan, Multan, Khanpur, Gujranwala, Gujrat, Mianwali, Bannu, Kohat, Waziristan, Dera Ismail Khan, Swabi, Peshawar, and Islamabad.[17] In December 2010, Qari Saifullah Akhtar—the longtime leader of *HUJI*—was released for the fourth time from Pakistani custody. *The Long War Journal* cites this as proof of *HUJI's* support by both the Pakistani Army and ISI.[18]

Additional proof surfaced on 22 May 2011 that the faction trying to overthrow the Zadari regime was also deeply involved with the drug trafficking. On this date, the Pakistani Taliban went far outside of its normal range to attack Pakistan's naval aviation base at Karachi. In that attack, well-equipped militants destroyed two P-C3 Orion aircraft recently acquired from the U.S. Those planes were undoubtedly intended for the maritime surveillance of drug shipments.[19]

China's Interest in All This

Of course, the Communist PRC cares deeply about what happens to Pakistan as well. It wants to ship home the Middle Eastern petroleum through Afghanistan or Gwadar and then up the Karakoram Highway, and it has big plans for the rest of occupied Kashmir. As such, it has already formed a pact with *JI*.[20] Without the concurrence of the Pakistani Army, it could not have stationed its troops in Gilgit-Balistan.[21] Always mindful of what another world war would entail, it has been trying for many years to bypass the Straits of Malacca.

The Unfortunate Likelihood

Whoever is trying to overthrow the Islamabad government is likely also helping to expel NATO from Afghanistan. The regional drug syndicate would certainly like to. Karachi drug lord Dawood Ibrahim has used *LET* on more than one occasion to attack India.[22] The culprit's *modus operandi* during several commando raids on Kabul would certainly suggest *LET*.[23] The Pakistani ISI (which is made up mostly of Pakistani Army personnel) is still suspected of aiding the Afghan Taliban.[24] The ISI has already been shown to fund some of its foreign adventures through "drug-route-protection" payoffs.[25] Perhaps part of the Army does as well. Wherever drug money is involved, corruption is sure to follow. Who's to say where the corruption stops. It could very well extend all the way to the intended market.

As for the Suez Region

The month of January 2011 proved very hard on the pro-Western autocratic regimes along the various approaches to the Suez Canal. First, street demonstrations forced the leaders of Tunisia and Egypt to step down, and then that of Yemen to promise not to run for reelection. In many U.S. circles, these events were viewed as a normal progression toward democracy. In others, there was more concern.

Started in Egypt, the Muslim Brotherhood has long been the proponent of Islamic statehood. With all subversive activities closely monitored there, the Muslim Brotherhood has had to shift its center of "external" operations to Sudan. There, it managed to spawn Sudan's ruling party.[26] Most Islamist destabilization of North Africa has since sprung from Sudan,[27] which in turn gets most of its arms shipments from China.[28] Through Abdallah Zusuf Azzam and Ayman al-Zawahiri, the Muslim Brotherhood has also spawned both *Hamas* in Palestine and *al-Qaeda* in Pakistan.[29] An avowed enemy of "Western decadence," it has been trying for quite some time to consolidate anti-Western sentiment in North Africa and the Levant.[30] While not very capable militarily, the Muslim Brotherhood is quite good at fomenting public discord.

In recent years, the Islamists have been showing a lot of interest in the Suez region. *Al-Qaeda* now runs most of Somalia (to include Puntland), and is very influential in Yemen. *Hezbollah* has been fighting in North Yemen and just took over the Lebanese government. *Hamas* has won the elections in the Gaza Strip near the canal. Thus, one wonders if a Sunni caliphate and Shiite imamate may be forming side by side.

The Communists don't care as much as the Islamists about the Suez Canal. They don't need it to carry any natural resources home, so their only real interest would be its blockage in time of war. However, the Communists may still be using the West's obsession with *al-Qaeda* as a screen. As more than adequately evidenced by recent events in Nepal and the Western Hemisphere,[31] they now know how to subjugate countries through loans and the electoral process. Should their "foreign-aid and democratic assistance" package not achieve immediate results, they can always fall back on rioting and insurrection. The Communists would still want some control over the ancient trade route through the Gulf of Aden to Africa. Several years after Marxist South Yemen went away, a North Korean vessel was detained with Scud missiles bound for Yemen.[32] That's why it is not now completely clear who is asking the Yemeni president to step down. They may not be Islamist.

This "pro-democracy" effort mobilized Tunisian and Egyptian youth through Facebook and Twitter.[33] While the Islamists are certainly capable of such things, it would more likely occur to the Communists. As on the battlefield, most Communist attacks are not main efforts at all, but rather feints. The Maoists' "politicization" campaign went after the youth in Nepal,[34] and the PLA has been thoroughly enthralled with cyber warfare for the last ten years.[35] Instead of Lebanon, the ultimate target may have been Yemen.

Rioting is what contemporary Communists do after the political intrigue stalls (e.g., Calcutta [36]). Open insurrection is their last resort (e.g., Peru and Colombia).

Making a Lasting Positive out of this Negative

After borrowing that much money from China, U.S. leaders aren't likely to question its motives. Yet, if there is the slightest chance the PRC is guilty of worldwide subversion, they must still take protective measures. In the final analysis, it matters little whether the Communists, Islamists, criminals, or fast-food franchises are trying to take over the planet. Neither does it matter that the global expanse of the destabilization may be coincidental. All that matters is that someone do something about it. In this new age where warfare no longer requires shooting, those protective measures need not be openly provocative. Instead of more defense contracts with pro-Western dictators, the U.S. should try more of the "bottom-up" approach. It's less likely to spark another arms race.

To preclude a problem—however hypothetical—one must still look at it squarely in the face. Few can deny China's meteoric rise to power. Economically and then politically to control most of the globe, it has only to avoid an all-out war with the West. The Islamists and criminals have also done quite well. Yet, much of the chaos—from whatever source—can still be peaceably arrested. If the Pentagon were to ask all deployed infantry battalions to disperse into 50 "foreign-assistance" squads, things would get a lot better. There aren't enough U.S. Special Forces teams to cover even one of the nations so far beleaguered. These new "special-infantry" squads would be trained in four nontraditional areas: (1) "bottom-up" (vice standard) instruction of indigenous militiamen; (2) certain police procedures; (3) 4GW (multifaceted societal awareness); and (4) UW (escape and evasion). Within the next Part will be tactical techniques for this mission.

Part Three

Averting WWIII through Tiny Detachments

"Rejoice young men in your youth." — Ecclesiastes

(Source: Attributed to *Old Testament* figure, Ecclesiastes)

14 How Eastern Players ___ Influence Things

- Why is the world changing so drastically?
- Do other nations have anything to do with it?

Asians are more discreet in their wartime activities.

(Source: MCRP 3-02H [1999], p. 1-5)

Traditional U.S. Foreign Assistance

The U.S. government has for years provided foreign aid to pro-spective allies with repressive regimes. While this money may have been intended for their beleaguered populations, it has all too often ended up in someone's retirement account. Such is the nature of top-down diplomacy. The PRC doesn't operate that way. It not only requires payment for every favor rendered, but also puts enough "boots on the ground" to ensure it. Of late, the Communist Chinese have been magnanimously expanding the road and rail systems of many developing nations. Several of those systems just happen to carry natural resources back to China. Most have been built by corporate extensions of the PLA. Some—like those in Sudan and Pakistani Kashmir—have uniformed Chinese troops guarding them.[1] While China's politics are not to be emulated, its bottom-up way of monitoring foreign aid should be. If America had followed that process in Haiti, its population would have far fewer problems.

Time for a Serious Reality Check

What one hears in church also rings true in warfare: "We don't see things the way they are; we see things the way we are." Threatening to turn an offending Eastern nation into a parking lot shows an inherent misunderstanding of Oriental culture. Depending on the nation, it may already be a parking lot. Asians like to work from the bottom up. This means they don't need much of an equipment pool, supply chain, or command apparatus to operate. North Vietnam and North Korea are perfect examples. America and its allies dropped more aerial bombs during the Vietnam War than in all of WWII, yet still lost the conflict.[2] Had Hanoi been totally flooded by the Red River and Haiphong Harbor completely blocked, the outcome would have been the same. With the world's most accomplished light infantrymen, North Vietnam needed only what it could steal from its oversupplied foe—and no tanks, planes, or heavy artillery—to win. North Korea is the same way today. While North Korea's sizeable garrison could possibly be starved into submission, it only has to move a few miles to the south to stay continuously resupplied. Its infiltration skills and hidden tunnels make such a move much less problematic. There are no military targets visible anywhere between Pyongyang and the border.[3] Even if there were, the country is so poor as to be relatively devoid of infrastructure. Armies like these don't need a fancy "command and control" system or supply chain. That's because its various components are largely self sufficient. During active combat, additional wherewithal is simply shifted to the underground depot nearest the fighting. Then, any intruder must contend with a veritable swarm of highly opportunistic opponents. Those who doubt this assessment have only to study the well-seasoned and fully supported U.S. forces' attempt to enter North Korea in 1953. This is when the Communists first tried a below-ground version of their elastic, positional defense.[4]

During that time [just preceding the 1953 Korean hill battles], anyone who happened to enter the mountainous area of our positions could hear the sound of earthwork. . . . Gradually, a defense system took shape. It was backed up by supporting [strong] points with tunnel fortifications as main structures. . . . Here one could find all kinds of facilities . . . as well as defended fortifications, communications entrenchments, and crisscrossing main tunnels and branch lines. . . . Even though the enemy continued dropping thousands of bombs that exploded on top of the mountains, our commanders were able to sit down and peacefully read books and newspapers or play cards and chess.[5]
— *Mao's Generals Remember Korea*

These are not the only "bottom-oriented" Asian countries. Some are so diverse at their lower echelons as to be almost impossible to rule. Lack of governmental control is what makes Pakistan such a difficult proposition. Its physical "infrastructure" has been all but ignored by home-grown rebels. That's because it too little affects societal functioning to target. Every time a bridge breaks in Pakistan, the locals go back to fording the river on muleback. For this reason, Western forces could never hope to match the Pakistani Army in reestablishing the proper mix of local variables. Instead of making fun of the Easterner's lack of technology, perhaps the Pentagon should more closely try his light-infantry methodology. This methodology is not only more flexible and cheap, but also based on more centuries of experience.

How the Rest of WWIII May Be Fought

Whether the various "revolutionary" governments have been conspiring during their expansion is not that important. Only important is that they have been collectively doing quite well at it—not so much in the martial sense, as in the economic and political sense. This is why many now feel that a 4GW-based global conflict is already underway. To win it, all the Islamist, Communist, and criminally oriented countries have to do is to avoid an all out war with the West. None is so foolish as to militarily confront the West with anything but a proxy. Wherever the economic and political agenda does poorly, small contingents of government "operatives" will work as force multipliers for indigenous guerrillas. When viewed in this way, what is now occurring throughout the world could logically go by several different names: (1) multi-faceted *jihad;* (2) Chinese "comprehensive warfare";[6] or an international variant of organized crime. To stop it, the West can no longer rely on its technological edge or willingness to risk collateral damage. It must look for another solution. To prevent any escalation to the ongoing struggle, it may have to adopt a more discreet way of war.

The World's Other Way of Doing Things

"Top-down" systems regularly cover up lackluster results, preferring all members to "think positively," "play team ball," or "fix all organizational problems from within." Islamist and Communist movements are more "bottom-up" in their approach. As such, they more readily acknowledge mistakes and more easily learn from history. Not all bottom-up systems have negative intent. In fact, Revolutionary War "Minute Men" operated almost exclusively by the seat of their pants in 1776. And contemporary companies that regularly take the advice of technicians are some of the most successful in America.

Most U.S. military leaders see no particular problem with the organizational structure that has so richly rewarded them. Yet, "top-down" systems are known to have other limitations. While they may seem responsive to their commander's every whim, their bottom echelons often don't "get the word" in time to fully support it. Nor are they properly prepared to follow it without the enemy's knowledge. Nor do they generally think it will work (as the situation has already changed). In fact, the bottom echelons often consider their leaders to be almost as stupid, as those leaders consider them. To compensate for this unfortunate leadership dynamic, top-down organizations choose charismatic leaders.

To paraphrase General Patton, "The rank and file still have a good nose for what is true." They don't see all this mandatory optimism, team ball, and cloistering of problems as better preparing them for combat. To them, it is mostly self-serving "spin." Yet, those same wonderful GIs still assume their grandfathers' and fathers' lessons to have been somehow assimilated, and American operations to be generally valid because of it. Any other belief would be too hard on unit cohesion. That's why U.S. leaders so seldom see any need to apprise the troops of strategic issues or elsewhere-developed small-unit maneuvers. Why jeopardize unit cohesion with too broad a viewpoint? For those to whom the American system has bequeathed "all the answers of any consequence," it's all about control. From the Commander in Chief on down, every order must be obeyed to the letter. That it may be executed after the situation has changed, the enemy has gotten wind of it, or a better idea has come up from the bottom is of no matter.

Yet, too much is now at stake to be mired in traditionalism. America's most recent combat outings—in Vietnam, Iraq, and Afghanistan—have had something very important in common. All have proven that Eastern wars can no longer be waged from the top down. It is therefore time to look for another organizational model for U.S. security elements to partially emulate. Models in no way retain the politics of their previous user. Whatever is morally distasteful in one can often be removed without changing its overall design. Thus, those of past and future adversaries deserve consideration.

China More Indirectly Influences Things

America has always been fairly direct in its approach to foreign policy. Such diplomatic integrity is commendable, but overwhelming force while coming to someone's aid can be a little hard on their health. That's why the numbers of civilian casualties at Normandy, Seoul, and other places are so seldom discussed. As the wars in Iraq and Afghanistan have shown, a less violent way of war is now required. This way need not delve as much into deception as Sun Tzu's descendents. Still, the Asians—including the Chinese—are the acknowledged experts on unconventional warfare.

The Price of Cooperation

Three fourths of all Western Hemisphere governments now lean toward the left. Only at issue is whether they have arrived at all leftward-leaning agendas on their own. If one were forced to accept continual favors from the Chinese, there is no telling how many political concessions it would have to make. The trend toward Socialism in Central and South America appears to be the work of Communist proxies.[7] The Soviet Union can no longer be their sponsor, as most of its influence went away in 1990. Cuba could not be doing it alone. So, it must have the only remaining Communist power as its new Sugar Daddy. As the acknowledged forefather of military deception, China would leave very few clues of such an arrangement. Almost all evidence of its involvement in America's drug deluge, political intrigue, and financial crisis has been strictly circumstantial. U.S. leaders are now so bogged down with internal crises, that they will only respond to the most blatant foreign subversion.

How Better to Resist Any Chinese Intrusion

Western-style bureaucracies tend to resist change, however useful. That's why established procedures so often outlive their usefulness. Those in the Pentagon sometimes even mistake pressure toward tactical reform as "aiding and abetting" the enemy. South American militaries have all too often resisted left-leaning civilian leaders with coups and secret wars against "subversives." This should never happen here. After a very suspicious Kennedy assassination, there should be no more ultraconservative horseplay. Democracy, whether overly liberal or even corrupt, is still preferable to any other form of government. The best way to thwart China's long-term designs on America is better to counter its incursions worldwide. As was the case with the Romans 2,000 years ago, the perfect strategy is Christian.

The Similarities in Method between Culprits

All three threats to America are now primarily applied from the bottom up. The criminal threat involves making money at minimal risk to the perpetrator. Its particulars can best be left up to the reader's imagination. In Mexico, the cartels have become so bold as to intentionally destabilize that country's governing fabric. Islamist and Communist infiltrators will sometimes try to destabilize an entire population.

The standard Islamist formula is as follows: (1) rabble rousing; (2) destruction of physical infrastructure; and (3) constantly demonstrating that the incumbent government can neither maintain order nor provide other basic services.

The Western Hemisphere variant of the Communist method looks very similar: (1) making false promises to the working class; (2) accusing the incumbent regime of corruption; (3) supporting an opposition candidate through local drug proceeds or smuggled foreign funding; and (4) infrastructure obstruction through strikes and riots.

Throughout all three varieties of incursion, the targeted-nation's police establishment must bear the brunt of the onslaught. Further to overload those police, the Islamists and Communists both use organized crime as a strategic tool.

As for PRC instigation of any of the above, there is little hard evidence of such. That's because it's a tiny, secretive portion of China's overall foreign policy. As an aspiring superpower, it has almost limitless needs. Those needs can best be met through economic and then political expansion. The more obvious steps to this expansion are as follows: (1) so flooding each nation's economy with low-price trade goods that its local manufacturers go broke; (2) massive immigration; (3) using PLA business enterprises to build the transportation corridors to extract natural resources; and then (4) acquiring diplomatic concessions through conditional loans.

Why Isn't Washington Worried?

U.S. foreign policy has traditionally been about big issues with other nations. This new threat operates from within other nations, but often beyond the reach of their central governments. Understandably protective of both sovereignty and internal politics, those governments have been hesitant to accept too much "drone-oriented" assistance. As in Washington, elected officials look bad every time their promised security is impugned (or a foreigner fires a missile onto their soil).

A More Holistic Compilation of Little Pictures

To see what a bottom-up adversary is up to, one must graphically display all the little clues, however mundane, and whether

Figure 14.1: The Invisible Way to Resupply an Army
(Source: Corel Gallery Clipart, Totem, Man, image designator "28V011")

or not they are fully supported. That's how *modus operandi* police investigations are conducted. The evidential trends then become obvious, and the misinformation peripheral. With a highly deceptive bottom up adversary, broad brush strokes will never adequately portray past activities—much less predict future ones. As in the famous "dot picture" of Jesus, the dots will only define the image when viewed from a few steps back. The same is true of any Eastern methodology. (See Figure 14.1.)

Brute Force Not Much Good at Removing Criminal Elements

All three threats resemble opportunistic criminal activity. As in police work, distressed societies can best be helped through highly aggressive, yet largely nonviolent methods. America's enemies are no more humane than before, just more psychologically sophisticated. The U.S. military must follow suit. It can no longer treat every host country resident like an enemy sympathizer. Just as the citizens of a depressed U.S. neighborhood, a foreign population can sometimes have elements too brutal to individually challenge. U.S. police departments can't burn buildings in which felons take refuge, and neither should the CIA or Pentagon blow up residences in which terrorists are thought to be hiding. The same rules of behavior apply to both criminal and insurgent environments.

Help Will Be Needed in More Places at Once

There are few countries in the Developing World that do not now have sizable Chinese communities and work projects. Any further U.S. aid to those countries should include boots on the ground—either specially trained security detachments or civilian firms who regularly report to the U.S. government. Both will need special training on how independently to operate in hostile environments. Their tactical orientation will be the focus of the last few chapters.

199

15

A U.S. Version of the Chinese Model

● Aren't there Asian Americans?

● Why isn't more of their cultural heritage utilized?

Surprise creates no collateral damage.

(Source: MCRP 3-02H [1999], fig. 1-2)

America's Cultural Blind Spot

Whether officially acknowledged or not, all cultures have their weaknesses. Two examples—one from the East and one from the West—should be sufficient to make the point. Through a heritage of Sun-Tzu-like military deception, the Chinese may be more prone to integrity lapses during all sorts of transactions. Having descended from monarchy emigrants, most Americans see all the inequities of "top-down" bureaucracy as unavoidable.

Western-style governmental agencies have many members, each with their own substantive or geographical area of expertise. The only problem is that their superiors then have trouble consolidating such specialized advice. As such, much of their expertise goes for naught. Meanwhile, the advice from the general membership of an Eastern bureaucracy is more holistic in nature and easy to utilize. It should come as no surprise then, that the Asian organizational model is more efficient in many ways.

"Counterculture" is a difficult topic to pursue without further explanation. Among the most unfortunate truths about Western-style bureaucracies is that "top-down" organizations tend to be least proficient at their lowest echelons. Their leaders not only fail to acquire many ideas from the bottom, but they also insufficiently inform, train, and utilize the bottom. Because the bottom is where the "rubber meets the road," what routinely results is insufficient performance against any "bottom-up" adversary. To try to compensate for this little "organizational weak spot," Western-style bureaucracies have come up with some grossly illogical strategies over the years. Among the best examples are Agent Orange, whatever caused the Gulf War Syndrome, and too much bombardment in a 4GW environment. Then, to compound the mistake, lackluster results are suppressed for the sake of "national unity."

The easiest solution to this self-imposed handicap involves a paradox. While the greatest threat to the world now comes from Asia, the Asian version of bureaucracy (minus any Communist or Islamist influences) is in many ways superior to its Western counterpart. Effectively to counter the new Eastern threat, America's security agencies may have to somewhat alter their organizational structures.

In Which Ways Is the Asian Model More Productive?

The Communist victors of Vietnam applied their *"Kiem Thao* sessions" to more than just the North Vietnamese Army—and quite possibly to all government agencies.[1] Through such sessions in military units (where the lower ranks were encouraged to criticize superiors), they could improve unit performance between battles. Then, by encouraging those same riflemen to monitor the official battle chronicles, they additionally made sure that all tactical mistakes were widely disseminated.

In *Kiem Thao* sessions, the [enemy] soldiers offered judg-

ments of their comrades and listened to evaluations of their own performances. The meetings sometimes featured discussions of tactics from the unit's recent engagements or suggestions . . . sent from the army command. *Kiem Thao* sessions could become extremely heated and emotional. For some soldiers the sessions were especially traumatic, as they heard their weaknesses and failings denounced publicly and then had to respond to those charges.[2]
    — *Vietnam Experience,* by Maitland and McInerney

North Vietnam's Commander-in-Chief Vo Nguyen Giap is known to have adapted Mao Tse-Tung's model for a revolutionary war to the situation in Vietnam. Since 1928, Mao had given all soldiers freedom of assembly and speech, as well as inspection rights to the "account" books.[3] From this, one can reasonably conclude that the Chinese bureaucratic model may produce better results than its American counterpart in at least two ways: (1) more tactical proficiency at the small-unit level; and (2) more incorporation of the lessons learned into the organizational body of knowledge (the manuals). In essence, the Communists had removed the hierarchal blockage between top and bottom perspectives—making them more compatible. The generals would no longer regard the privates as stupid (or *vice versa),* and more organizational cohesion could therefore be realized. So, at least this part of the Chinese model could prove useful to the U.S. military. It worked just fine for the Marine Raider battalions of WWII, and they were patterned after Mao Tse-Tung's 8th Route Army.[4] It or other Eastern methodologies (like bottom-up training) need not replace traditional GI instruction, but just supplement it.

The Hidden Costs of "Top-Down Control"

It has already been suggested that Western-style bureaucracies could more easily gain knowledge in a different way. Now, it is further suggested that they may unwittingly destroy their own body of experience. U.S. military personnel have been everywhere and done everything. Without such an organizational quirk, how else could their small-unit tactical techniques have fallen so far behind those of the Eastern world? This may be why non-state actors and even individuals can so easily outsmart a Western intelligence or security agency. Any U.S. soldier or Marine who has ever served as a training exercise "aggressor" can attest to how easy an American unit is to fool. And anyone who has ever worked as U.S. public servant can attest to the loss of valuable knowledge every time his or her turnover file got thrown away.

Not only does knowledge gathering suffer from America's top-down system, but also intelligence gathering. As in Vietnam, the latter has only to do with the overall picture, and generally leaves the company commander blind as to what might be happening in his local Tactical Area of Responsibility (TAOR).[5] Every "Chinese commander"—of any echelon—is responsible for all of his own intelligence gathering. As such, so are the company and platoon commanders. This alone gives them a significant edge over their Western counterparts.

> Every commander must organize reconnaissance within his unit's zone of activities. He must not wait for instructions from his superior, nor must he seek his superior's decision as to whether he should organize reconnaissance. The reconnaissance he organizes must be carried out without cessation to comply with the combat mission through each successive period and phase of combat. Each new mission requires immediate organization of reconnaissance. The conduct of continuous reconnaissance during combat is vitally important.[6]
> — Regulations for contemporary Chinese PLA

Even National Security Is Based on Input from the Bottom

Thanks to the hard work of tens of thousands of dedicated U.S. security agency workers, there has been no major terrorist attack in America since 9/11. However, there has been no restructuring of their "top-heavy" parent organizations either. America's duly elected politicians don't realize how fortunate they've been. The long-term answer is not in how many intelligence agencies are operating, but in how much their respective specialists talk with each other. For without comparing notes on multiple factors and parts of the world, few will ever fully appreciate a global foe's *modus operandi*. Those who do figure it out on their own will be lucky to get their interpretations noticed. In long chains of command, not all elements of information rise to the top. Whether they match the current administration's foreign policy should have nothing to do with it. Word of something as big as 9/11 had to have been on the world's streets for weeks in advance. Yet, since 9/11, the U.S. government has only compounded its original error. According to *Newsweek,* it has since created or redirected 263 organizations to handle the "War on Terror." Many must be intelligence oriented, as the cost for that service has increased 250 percent to over $75 billion a year. Some 33 new building complexes have been built for intelligence bureaucracies alone, occupying the spacial equivalent of 22 U.S. Capitols and three Pentagons. Housed at the largest site will be most of the Department of Homeland Security's 230,000 workers.[7] Through it all, the Mexican border will remain just as porous as ever.

The truth is inescapable. More holistic information gathering and shorter chains of command would work better. The creation of a DNI seems to have partially satisfied the latter requirement, but there's a limit to how many intelligence agencies one person can solely coordinate. As in active combat, too much information can make it much harder to tell which is important.

China's Bottom Infantry Echelon

The U.S. Marine Corps' official pamphlet on its famed "Raider" battalions briefly describes them being trained as guerrillas.[8] (Asian Communist armies normally train all troops in positional, mobile [like maneuver], and guerrilla warfare.[9]) Guerrilla warfare and E&E are the two types of UW that apply to infantrymen.[10] Ergo, the Raiders may have been the first U.S. troops to be trained in any kind of UW (as all now should be). (See Figure 15.1.) Sadly, many former Raiders don't fully appreciate the significance of this, nor have they studied enough guerrilla history to know which parts of their training applied. Most remember only broad categories of training, like speed marches, nighttime stealth, hand-to-hand combat, obstacle crossing, etc. Of note, they also recall most of their instruction being conducted by their own squad leaders and platoon sergeants. The extent to which squad techniques (like football plays) were addressed during these individualized sessions is important. The curriculum variance between units would have created more learning synergy than standardized training. Plus, the end result would have been more surprise-oriented maneuvers. One former 3rd Battalion Raider remembers only company-size group movements — probably similar to the whistle-directed Chinese sweeps at the Chosin Reservoir. (Something this large doesn't really qualify as "technique," as it allows too little individual initiative.) He also

Figure 15.1: The Marine Raiders of WWII
(Source: Official recruiting poster, image designator "post_usmc_168th-birthday_ww2.jpg," retrieved from U.S. Nat. Archives and Records Admin. by www.bluejacket.com)

remembers mostly reconnaissance-type missions (looking for Japanese base camps with the help of local citizens), and point men not being allowed to fire their weapons so as to preserve the element of surprise.[11]

The people writing the pamphlet may have had a slightly better feel for how guerrilla warfare fit into the overall scheme of things. They credit Evans Carlson with thinking "guerrilla warfare was the wave of the future." They also say James Donovan was concurrently urging President Roosevelt to "create a guerrilla force that would infiltrate occupied territory and assist resistance groups." Unfortunately, they make no mention of Raiders being shown the Asian art of short-range infiltration (i.e., how to crawl unnoticed between opposition fighting holes).[12] So which advanced guerrilla techniques those Raiders learned and how, may soon be largely lost to history. When the Raiders were finally integrated into the more conventional 4th Marine Infantry Regiment in early 1944, less of those "hip-pocket" type classes would have been authorized. Still, the Raider motto of "Gung Ho" was not so easily obliterated. This little motto would go on to inspire future generations of Marines to not only work more closely together, but also to experience the same hardships as subordinates. It has thus become an integral part of their magnificent heritage.

16 _ How Best to Make a 4GW Difference

- Can occupying every town better protect a population?
- How does drug trafficking affect counterinsurgency?

The GI's load will dictate how easily he can avoid bullets.

A New Starting Point for Tactical Technique

Posterity Press titles are not just about counterinsurgency and 4GW. They also show how to more effectively conduct Second and Third Generation Warfare (2GW and 3GW). U.S. service personnel are the "best in the world" at using their equipment. Too much equipment can get in the way of movement and surprise. Most U.S. troops have yet to match the maneuverability of their 1917 enemy counterparts. Among their substandard or missing techniques are the following: (1) assault on a prepared enemy position; (2) ambushing; (3) walking point; (4) tracking; (5) stalking; (6) occupying an observation post; (7) E&E; and (7) fighting like a guerrilla. This deficiency—with regard to what other armies can do—has become so chronic as to be almost criminal. It has resulted in the unnecessary loss of thousands of U.S. lives, and at least one war. If ever officially acknowledged, it would be easy to fix—over the long run—through decentralizing control over training. To correct it in a hurry, commanders would have to direct all rifle companies to follow the fully refined bottom-up squad training methodology in Appendix A. So far, it has been shown to 43 battalions and special-operations units. Of the few that tried it, all confirm it works.[1] It can be concurrently implemented with existing training programs without any additional expenditure of command section time or money. That's because only the NCOs and troops are actually involved—with one SNCO as facilitator. They would execute their new training regimen in half-hour increments every time the trucks are late.

What all Three Threats to America Have in Common

Communist guerrillas, Islamist terrorists, and drug smugglers all follow the same organizational format. Better to deceive authorities, exploit opportunity, and discourage failure, that format is largely devoid of structure. More often than not, the members of each cell get to decide how best to make a strategic difference. They have received no orders from above, only tactical guidelines and technical or financial assistance. When asked to participate in a joint mission, they often do so without ever knowing who else is involved. That's one of the more effective ways of "working from the bottom up" in the Eastern vernacular. As Western culture is mostly coordinated from the "top-down," U.S. leaders have trouble wrapping their minds around this "bottom-up" way of doing things. Fully to understand it, one must be either a student of the Eastern mindset, or at the bottom of a rather big Western heap. The U.S. military establishment's junior enlisted personnel would certainly qualify. For this reason, it is they who must be allowed to take on the Communist guerrillas, Islamist terrorists, and drug runners. Through their severe lack of status, those young soldiers and Marines can more easily see how the enemy thinks. Until their overprotective leaders let them carry the fight, things will get no better in any of the three contests. The following example should adequately illustrate the point

America's Lack of Tactical Interest Is Nothing New

America has—since WWI—depended almost entirely on its technological and financial superiority to win wars. In the process, it has paid too little attention to squad tactics. Here's what two of this era's best-respected military trainers had to say about the problem.

> We can still lose this war. . . . The Germans are colder and hungrier than we are, but they fight better.[2]
> — Gen. George S. Patton during Battle of the Bulge

> Since 1941 . . . our forces were not as well trained as those of the enemy. . . . After the buildup of forces, when we went on the offensive, we did not defeat the enemy tactically. We overpowered and overwhelmed our enemies with equipment and firepower.[3]
> — Lt.Gen. Arthur S. Collins Jr., U.S. Army (Ret.), 1978

Even a modern-day battlefield expert says that nothing has changed. In a courageous admission of guilt, he confirms the U.S. tactical shortfall was as true in Vietnam as it is today. After his unit was severely hurt on a firebase overlooking the A Shau Valley, he realized the following:

> The loss was mainly my fault. I wasn't new at the job. This was my fourth command so I thought I knew what I was doing. A much smarter and better trained . . . enemy taught me that I did not.[4]
> — Maj.Gen. Robert H. Scales, U.S. Army (Ret.), 2010

In respectful deference to the good general's admission, this researcher can categorically promise that whatever happened wasn't all his fault. It was primarily the fault of a system that has never paid much attention to any enemy's tactical capabilities. If this enemy is to be summarily steamrolled, why worry about it? Unfortunately, the North Vietnamese—like the Japanese before them—were as aware of the tactical advances of WWI German Stormtroopers as of their own *Ninja* heritage. To this day, Hanoi still has the world's best light infantry.

The problem is not with the quality of gear issued to contemporary U.S. infantrymen. It is in their responsibility to always wear it. One's battlefield mobility is largely dictated by what jangles at the front of his web belt. Without anything there, he can more easily crawl through the microterrain that provides the majority of cover from those ever-present bullets. The best way to take care of the troops is not by burying them in the latest gadgets, but by showing them how to generate a little surprise. This takes individual, buddy-team, fire team, and squad movement techniques (like football stunts and plays). The troops' training must go far beyond the use of their equipment. It must show them how to more discreetly move around the battlefield. Surprise and firepower are virtually interchangeable in war.

When it comes to state-of-the-art squad tactics, no officer-manned "warfighting laboratory" can take the place of widespread experimentation at the company level. Such experimentation has almost never been encouraged because it flies in the face of "top-down" control. Yet, modern-day battles are no longer fought at the battalion, regiment, or division levels. They involve mostly individual and small-unit maneuvers.

Until U.S. leaders realize the limitations of their Western approach to squad proficiency, things will get no better in the fight against Communist, Islamist, and criminal expansion. Even for the most progressive of America's war planners, this habitual prioritizing of equipment over maneuver obscures the solution. That's because the solution, however simple, would seem "countercultural" to any military organization modeled after the French and British.

> These challenges can be met only by demanding that our national-level-policy and planning staffs look at war from the ground up rather than the top down.[5]
> — Maj.Gen. Robert H. Scales, U.S. Army (Ret.), 2010

Increased tactical proficiency cannot be achieved by assigning the task to more headquarters staffs. Since WWI, all Eastern offenses and defenses (of whatever size) have been based on the lone rifle squad. A rifle squad made each of their initial offensive penetrations, and a rifle squad anchored each of their defensive strongpoints. Thus, the answer almost certainly lies in harnessing the infantry NCOs' inherent understanding of squad chemistry. To do better in war, the Pentagon has only to decentralize control over all but the most elementary of squad classes. The way to do so has already been fully tested in the Fleet Marine Corps. No more studies, boards, or after-action reports will be needed to identify its particulars. Its most refined variation is there for everyone to see in the appendices to this book and *Tequila Junction.*[6] Though decidedly "bottom-up" in format, this squad training method in no way interferes with any "top-down" requirements. That's because only the junior enlisted personnel are involved. Aren't they the ones with the most time on their hands? For each rifle company, the standardization of all tactical techniques will still be possible. Its techniques will simply vary from those of other companies — creating an excellent learning dynamic.

Organizational Pride Must Give Way to Small-Unit Initiative

Within the U.S. security establishment, it's widely believed the people at the bottom control no strategic action. This doesn't help with their ability to contribute. Neither does it help to win wars. America's battlefield commanders would have more tactical options, if their squads were more proficient. Like the German Stormtroopers of 1918, each squad should to be able to attack or defend against many times its number. That only commanders rate any credit for battlefield victories is a cultural myth. No U.S. commander would have won anything if each of his riflemen had not first defeated the enemy soldier to his front. Thus, supplementing the existing squad training with that from Posterity Press could help to win WWIII.

For All Those Who Oppose Light Infantry

Over the years, there have been any number of military reform attempts in Washington. While a few have proposed more genuinely "light" infantry and shorter chains of command, the usual debate has been over "high-end" equipment, strategies, and leadership. Almost never mentioned is that less frequently changed gear and more often allowed small-unit autonomy would permit a very interesting "bottom-up" power projection alternative. This alternative would not only cost less initially, but would later avoid having to fix as much collateral damage. Now that the Head of the Joint Chiefs of Staff has publicly proclaimed that the biggest security threat to America is her debt,[7] perhaps more of those reformers will revisit the core problem. This problem is that a severely bloated and technology-driven military bureaucracy has traditionally helped to fuel the U.S. economy. Most other shortcomings are simply products of this ill-advised marriage. Three of the easiest ways to streamline bureaucracy are to shorten chains of command, discard outmoded procedures, and encourage bottom-echelon initiative. However, the latter will never be permitted in America's ground forces until the troops can be better trained. That necessarily includes more than just how to operate the latest gadget. Those who are about to get their heads blown off might also like to see a little state-of-the-art tactical technique for when that gadget gets wet. Yet, they are still being provided with premachinegun vintage maneuvers. The latest excuse is that all U.S. infantrymen must now be mechanized, so they will no longer need any way to surprise an enemy strongpoint on foot. Those past and present military leaders who now espouse this belief are more than dangerous, they are criminally deficient in their care of their enlisted subordinates. The Chinese used to have a way of correcting this syndrome. They would make all staff officers above company grade (of any occupational specialty) into infantry privates for six months out of every year.[8]

A few reformers have also become way too impressed with their own experiences in a very complicated arena. Only their way will do, and no others can be combined. Col. Douglas MacGregor has seen fit to impugn not only the entire light-infantry concept, but also all of Posterity Press's 20-year body of research.[9] He may have commanded a tank unit in Iraq, but this in no way qualifies him to discuss light-infantry subjects. In fact, only those who have faced "world-class" light infantry really rate an opinion. Some of the Marines in Iraq were unknowingly fighting some pretty good *Hezbollah* light infantry, but most of the U.S. experience with this particular subject dates back to the Vietnam War. In that war, tanks almost never got anywhere close to the heavy action (through no fault of their crews, only the old "land-mine-on-a-string" trick). By then, the Germans and Japanese had both made extensive studies of how to kill tanks barehandedly. Throughout WWII, they had also used a single squad to precede every assault and be the building block of every strongpoint defense.[10] That's because light-infantry skills are not just good for counterinsurgency and 4GW, but they also work in conventional warfare. In essence, they give the conventional commander more ways to generate surprise. The terrain was wrong for mechanized units in Vietnam, and so is any precipitous, vegetated, or urban part of the world.

So, only pre-1973 war veterans and the current crop of junior grunts have much business assessing the worth of "lighter" U.S. infantry units. Luckily, there is one man with enough rank and stature to rebuff the firepower fanatics. Col. Robert Killebrew, a retired infantry colonel who served with the Special Forces in Vietnam, has repeatedly called for as many light infantrymen as there are mechanized in the U.S. Army.[11] Those who would take issue with his recommendation may have too little knowledge of the following history: (1) what the contemporary world's best light infantrymen did to the U.S. phalanx in Vietnam; (2) what their unsupported border militia did to a fully supported Chinese invasion force in 1979;[12] and (3) what *Hezbollah* light infantry did to the mechanized Israeli force with full air cover that entered Southern Lebanon in 2006.[13] As was done by *Hezbollah* in Lebanon, light infantry can be easily combined with remotely controlled tank-killing systems. Or, like the Russians, it can be equipped with thermobaric "bazookas"—thereby eliminating the need for proximity artillery support.[14] So, the belief that light infantrymen will always lose to armor is no longer true. As the tactical shortfall of the light infantryman decreases, so too does his need for any equipment at all. This is the paramount lesson of Vietnam that has been so carefully hidden by the U.S. arms manufactures. All the NVA/VC needed to win were some plastic explosives, blasting caps, timers, and 61-mm mortars to create the impression that U.S. bases were under mortar attack every time their ammo dumps exploded.

What is currently called "light infantry" in the U.S. military establishment really isn't. It is "line infantry" that travels mostly by mine-resistant truck and depend almost entirely on supporting arms.

Whether or not the above arguments are accepted, the bottom line is this. American infantry squads still cannot outmaneuver their Eastern counterparts; and GIs are still being killed because of it. Until their manuals place more emphasis on surprise than firepower, this will always be the case. For any U.S. "grunt" or special operator who finds this state of affairs unacceptable, a few more tactical techniques (of Eastern origin) are offered. Without them (and those in previous titles), he and his buddies will have a much harder time winning any stage of WWIII.

17   Opportunity-Based _____ Offense

● Do U.S. security patrols close quickly with all foes?

● What might be gained from more aggressive patrolling?

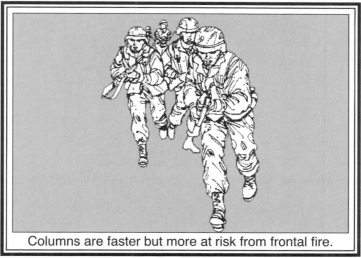

Columns are faster but more at risk from frontal fire.

Momentum Is Still the Key to Victory

For any battlefield confrontation, momentum belongs to the side that strings together consecutive victories. This goes for all sizes of combatants and every kind of victory. Thus, the American squad helping to garrison an Afghan village better contributes to the war effort by keeping its local Taliban off balance. Those Taliban should not be permitted to predict, trail, or target any U.S. patrol. This takes more stealth and speed than most U.S. infantrymen are able to combine. To help in this regard, the following technique is offered.

Figure 17.1: All Nighttime Patrols Were Conducted in Column
(Source: FM 7-8 [1984], p. 3-52)

Single-Formation Patrolling

U.S. nighttime patrols have traditionally been run in squad size and single file. (See Figure 17.1.) That's because there's no reason for flankers wherever the patrol cannot clearly be seen. The same thing holds true for patrols through heavily vegetated terrain. If the enemy can't see them, he can't accurately shoot at them. Modern technology hasn't changed this age-old movement axiom all that much. In the woods on dark rainy nights, image-intensification devices have very little ambient light, and even thermal imaging can't see through the bushes. Under such conditions, contemporary patrols still need no flankers or anything but a single file. The resulting increase in speed would create its own type of security. If the patrol were spotted by anyone, it would be gone before they could get permission to do anything about it. All of this assumes, of course, that the patrol has been properly handling all danger areas. This takes traversing straight stretches of trail and small clearings a few people at a time.

Every time an opposition group was detected by one of these traditional U.S. patrols, the fourteen or so GIs would get on line and then slowly approach it. If the enemy force seemed more numerous than their own, they would form a defensive circle and call for indirect fire. Unfortunately, both formation changes required either rehearsal or squad leader direction. (See Figure 17.2.) Both diverted attention from the foe's most likely avenue of approach. Both made it hard to keep friendly fire teams together. And both created a major "movement" signature.

Figure 17.2: Instead of Lanes Being Slowly Assigned
(Source: FM 22-100 [1983], p. 185; FM 90-10-1 [1982], pp. B-3, B-4)

Figure 17.3: Whole Column Turns Left, Stops, and Faces Right
(Source: FM 7-8 [1984], p. B-2)

There is no need for all this formation changing on security patrols through poorly illuminated or heavily vegetated terrain—even in the daytime. When an enemy unit is spotted on the move, the U.S. column can discreetly change direction to move perpendicular to (and block) the enemy's direction of march. (See Figure 17.3.) Then, to engage the target, the GIs have only to face left or right and move forward.

If an opposition presence is only suspected to one flank, the American column could "echelon" left or right as in marching and move on line to that side. (See Figures 17.4 and 17.5.) Then, as before, all U.S. members could engage the target without masking each others' fires. If no enemy were found, all patrol members could—on their leader's signal—simultaneously pivot to form a column in the

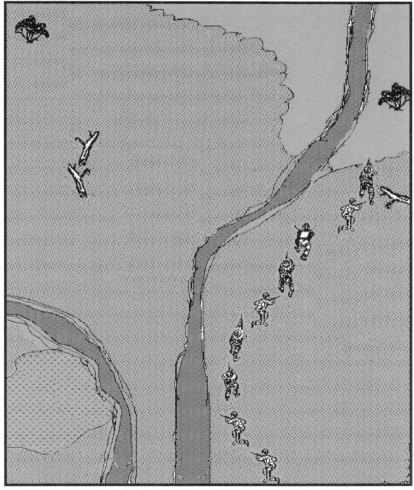

Figure 17.4: Squad Moves in Column through Darkness or Brush
(Sources: FM 7-8 [84], p. 3-28; FM 5-103 [85], p. 4-6; FM 7-70 [86], p. 4-20; FM 7-11B1/2 [78], pp. 2-II-A-1.2, 2-IV-B-10.2; MCI 03.66a [86], p. 2-9; FMFM 6-7 [89], p. 1-13)

original direction. The patrol's movement would be uninterrupted, and the new trace only slightly offset from the original. Needless to say, such a method builds more confidence among new patrol members than the current habit of stopping every time there is a break in the brush.

Figure 17.5: Squad Moves Sideways to Check Possible Sighting
(Sources: FM 7-8 [84], p. 3-28; FM 5-103 [85], p. 4-6; FM 7-70 [86], p. 4-20; FM 7-11B1/2 [78], pp. 2-II-A-1.2, 2-IV-B-10.2; MCI 03.66a [86], p. 2-9; FMFM 6-7 [89], p. 1-13)

To go on the defense, the squad leader would have only to halt the column, close it up, alternately face its members outboard, and place its automatic weapons at either end. (See Figures 17.6 and 17.7.) Then, his tiny unit would have interlocking bands of auto-

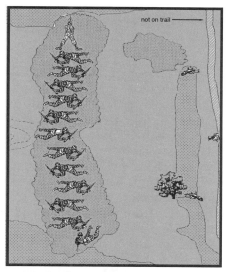

Figure 17.6: Squad-Sized Linear Defense
(Sources: FM 22-100 [1983], p. 66; FM 7-70 [1986], p. 4-20; MCI 03.66a [1986], p. 2-8; FM 7-11B1/2 [1978], pp. 2-II-A-5.2, 2-III-E-8.2)

Figure 17.7: Close Enough for Half to Sleep
(Sources: FM 5-103 [1985], p. 5-2; FM 21-75 [1967], p. 67)

matic-weapons fire with which to repel an assault from either side. It would also avoid all the movement associated with forming a circle in uncertain terrain.

This is one way to more aggressively patrol, and its central precepts have been in the Asian military literature for decades. In combat, U.S. squads that don't operate like football teams should have very little expectation of momentum.

Deja Vu

In Vietnam, whole platoons of NVA soldiers could safely traverse the rice-paddy-infested coastal plain south of Danang within full view of U.S. artillery observers. Even without getting proper clearance, those observers could do nothing about them. That's because the NVA columns were traveling in single file and so fast that no artillery barrage—however quickly summoned—could effectively bracket them. Those "brush-covered snakes" were a sight to behold. Traveling through heavily outposted regions at dusk (before the U.S. ambush patrols were out), their members carried little gear and moved along the village trails and paddy dikes at a steady (and highly confident) shuffle.[1]

Neither was the "single-line" defense illogical to an NVA unit on the move. In October 1966 at a place called "Three Gateways to Hell" on the main trail between Gio Linh and Con Thien, a U.S. Marine company had little luck assaulting such a formation.[2] Located just south of the Demilitarized Zone (DMZ) along one of the interior legs of the Ho Chi Minh trail, it was a ragged line of hastily constructed fighting holes connected by land line. Only many years later, did a member of the relief company realize that the NVA routinely established linear defenses like this. They were most commonly composed of two parallel lines.[3] That way, much of the U.S. supporting-arms fire would land harmlessly between them.

When an NVA unit in transit was ready to go on defense, a bend in the trail didn't bother its commander any. He merely moved everyone off the trail a few yards to where they had better cover/ concealment and fields of fire. When in a bent line, they enjoyed the more lethal crossfire of a "firesack." If disturbed, his troops had only to "hug" the attacking force's formation to escape its artillery and air strikes. (A bent line defense would only work for U.S. troops if fire sectors were carefully assigned.) NVA units also used a "paral-

Figure 17.8: NVA "Double-Line" Security Arrangement

lel-line" defense in their overnight bivouacs and more permanent base camps. (See Figure 17.8.) The second line not only provided a fallback position, but also helped with evacuation.

> Under the dense canopy of vegetation, two lines or belts of fortifications were constructed fifty to two hundred meters apart.[4]
> — *Inside the VC and the NVA, 1992*

To provide crossfire, these strings of defensive positions would occasionally follow the shape of an "L," "U," or "V." The distance between them was often just far enough so that the second would not be visible from the first. This second line provided the defenders with a place to come if pushed out of the first line. From there they could either break contact or counterattack to regain the first string.[5]

Of course, those NVA soldiers had an even better reason for all this deception. As have other armies facing a well-supported foe, they wanted to limit the damage from any standoff weaponry. First, they would construct dummy positions to draw in any artillery or air strikes. Then, they would leave the area between their actual lines vacant, in the hopes that the Americans would think them part of a perimeter with strategic assets and a command element in the center.

In Vietnam, even the adversary's most permanent base camps followed the same two-belt design as for their temporary bivouac sites. (Look at Figure 17.8 again.) However, in the base camps they often added a third belt and better constructed fighting positions and bunkers. Then, to counter the American's "surround and pound" methodology, they would "hug their opponent" rather than withdraw to the second belt of defenses. As the U.S. infantrymen pulled back to escape the fragmentation from their own artillery and air strikes, the NVA troops would leave their fortifications and follow them.[6]

Why Not Use the Same Formation on Defense and Offense?

During the vast majority of past offensive operations, U.S. units have bivouacked every night in some sort of circular formation. Then, when it came time to resume the attack in the morning, they would take a while to get into the proper formation (sometimes within full view of the enemy). Thus, the whole idea of attacking in the same formation as was assumed on defense becomes very appealing. With a "two-up-and-one-back" attack formation, some semblance of a circular defensive array would still be possible. As the last paragraph so aptly demonstrates, such a tactical shortcut has many precedents in Asia.

Why Not Also Plan for the Loss of Surprise?

As U.S. ground attacks have traditionally counted on firepower to carry the day, they make little provision for any loss of surprise. Yet, friendly mistakes do happen, and the foe will almost certainly fight back. Thus, the whole idea of somehow prearranging ways to regenerate surprise becomes almost necessary. While deliberate attacks should be discontinued in which all surprise has been forfeited, just fooling a quarry as to direction of the main effort is often enough to defeat him.

As long as U.S. commanders continue to use what they see

through their binoculars as their only reconnaissance of an attack objective, they could usefully plan for the unexpected. (See Figure 17.9).

In this vein, three schematics and associated tables are pro-vided—one for each type of ground attack. Figure 17.10 and Table 17.1 contain ways to rebuild surprise after the most common inter-

Figure 17.9: Binocular "Recon" Leaves Many Things Unknown
(Sources: Ft. Sill Military Clipart Library, retrieved from the following U.S. Army website—www.hqda.army.mil/aoguide/clipart)

ruptions to a daylight attack. Please note that the friendly secret being most closely guarded is that the actual objective has any American ground troops interested in it, much less near enough to assault.

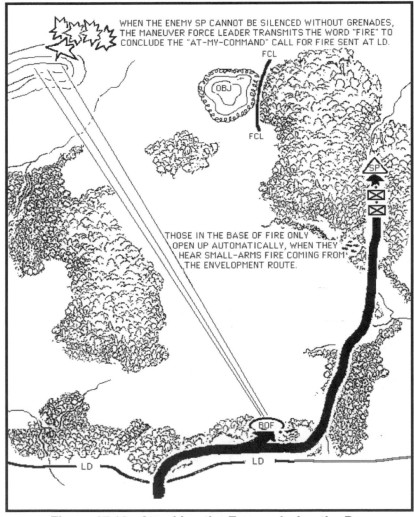

Figure 17.10: Attacking the Enemy during the Day

LOSS OF SURPRISE	PLANNED FRIENDLY RESPONSE	INTENDED OPPOSITION IMPRESSION
SHOOTING IN ENVELOPMENT ROUTE	BoF MG OPENS UP IMMEDIATELY AT HILL BEHIND OBJECTIVE	THAT OTHER NEARBY HILL UNDER LONG-RANGE MG FIRE FOR SOME REASON
EXPLOSION IN ENVELOPMENT ROUTE	BoF MK-19 OR 60MM MORTAR FIRES IMMEDIATELY AT HILL BEHIND OBJECTIVE	THAT OTHER NEARBY HILL UNDER LONG-RANGE MK-19 OR MORTAR FIRE FOR SOME REASON
UNWANTED ENEMY ATTENTION TO THE ATTACK POSITION JUST BEHIND FCL	PREREGISTERED PINPOINT ARTILLERY BARRAGE ON ENEMY HILL BEHIND OBJECTIVE ("AT MY COMMAND BUT DON'T LOAD" MISSION SENT AT LoD)	THAT HILL BEHIND OBJECTIVE ACTUALLY THE ONE UNDER ATTACK, BUT ONLY BY LONG-RANGE FIRE
FURTHER DISCOVERY IN THE ATTACK POSITION JUST BEHIND FCL	DEMONSTRATION BY FIRE TEAM THAT HAS CRAWLED INTO TREES LEFT OF OBJECTIVE	THAT THE OBJECTIVE IS ONLY UNDER OBSERVATION FROM ITS LEFT SIDE
BANGALORE NEEDED TO BREACH WIRE	WHILE BARRAGE MOVED TO OBJECTIVE	THAT IT IS ALL PART OF SHIFTED BARRAGE
ARTILLERY SMOKE TO SCREEN ASSAULT LANDS IN WRONG PLACE	HAND SMOKES THROWN AT TIME OF IMPACT OF SECOND ARTILLERY SMOKE	DISTANT ARTILLERY OBSERVER HAD TO MOVE SPOTTING SMOKE ROUND TO BETTER SEE IT
ASSAULT FORCE DISCOVERED BEFORE LEAD FIRE TEAM CAN ENTER FOE'S WIRE	POSTPONE THE ASSAULT UNTIL AFTER DARK AND WITHDRAW TO LoD	THAT THE ATTACK FORCE HAS BEEN BEATEN AND WILL NOT BE BACK
ASSAULT FORCE DISCOVERED AFTER SOME OF SQUAD ALREADY THRU WIRE	EVERYONE DROPS TO THE GROUND AND CRAWLS DURING REST OF THE ASSAULT	THAT EVERYONE IN THE ATTACK FORCE HAS BEEN WOUNDED OR KILLED

Table 17.1: Regenerating Surprise during a Daylight Attack

Then, Figure 17.11 and Table 17.2 show how surprise might
be regenerated during a night attack. Here, the Probable Line of
Deployment (PLD) and attack position are just inside the foe's wire,
as no night attack against a fortified position should ever be tried
unless the troops can advance that far undetected.

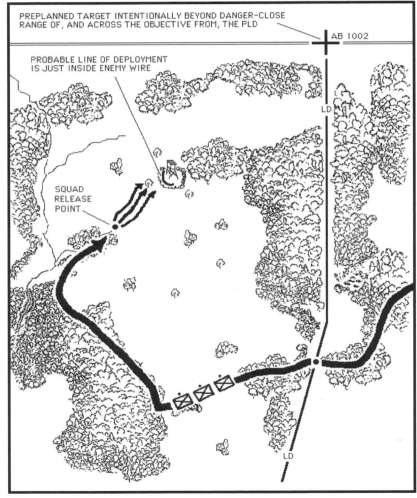

Figure 17.11: Attacking the Enemy at Night

LOSS OF SURPRISE	PLANNED FRIENDLY RESPONSE	INTENDED OPPOSITION IMPRESSION
Explosion at listening post	Instant series of grenades by rear party at LoD	That closer explosion just double impact of distant mortar barrage
Shooting at listening post	Instant automatic weapons fire into the ground by rear party at LoD	That closer reports just initial part of distant fire fight
Enemy trip flare set off	Half-hour delay in attack sequence	That trip flare triggered by small animal
Enemy recon by fire or illumination of assault force	If not well directed, no BoF MG fire from just outside enemy wire	That no attack force is present
Unwanted interest in staging area just outside enemy wire	Prearranged artillery barrage on other position behind objective	That other position is the one being attacked, but only by long-range indirect fire
Discovery in the staging area just outside enemy wire	Demonstration by fire team sent to opposite side of objective	That reconnaissance scouts are present, but no attack force
Bangalore needed to breach wire	While barrage moved to objective	That it is all part of the shifted artillery
Discovery before lead fire team can get thru enemy wire to FCL	Postpone assault, withdraw, and attack from other side later	That the attack force has been beaten and will not be back
Discovery after some of squad already at FCL inside enemy wire	Tree-mounted BoF MG fires over heads of crawling assault force	That assault force cannot be coming from same side as grazing MG fire

Table 17.2: Regenerating Surprise during a Night Attack

Finally, some tricks for more easily performing short-range infiltration are provided in Figure 17.12 and Table 17.3. Here, locally generated diversions are more difficult, but not impossible.

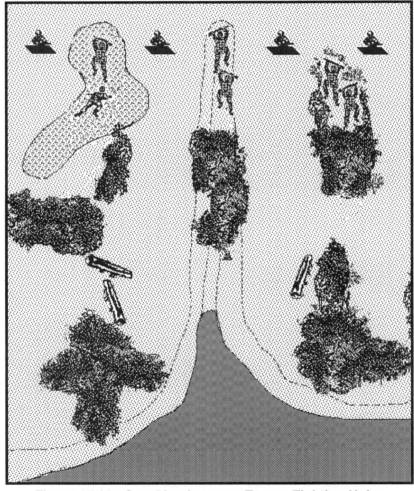

Figure 17.12: Sneaking between Enemy Fighting Holes

Natural Diversion	Enemy-Caused Diversion	Friendly-Planned Diversion
Aerial flare or lightning behind penetration try temporarily negates foe's night vision options	Any light whatsoever in enemy hole (even smoking cigarette) distracts and temporarily blinds its occupant	Continuous indirect-fire illumination mission far behind infiltration attempt ruins almost all enemy night vision capabilities
Heavy rain, fog, or vegetation negates thermal-imaging	Rain on helmet or poncho disrupts sentries' hearing and concentration	Crawling through standing water makes infiltrators less visible to thermal imaging
Moon goes behind cloud or throws dark shadows	Shift to or from night vision device temporarily distracts sentry	Friendlies try to crawl mostly thru shadow and never before light background
External event distracts sentries or covers sound (helo, barrage, fire fight, thunder, wind, rain)	Even having to slap mosquito will temporarily disrupt sentry	Twig intentionally cracked in lane other than one drawing too much attention
Internal event distracts sentries	Enemy lines checked by superior Watch relief by another person Chow time Prayer time Bathroom break Talking with hole partner Decreased alertness in wee hours	Diversionary movement in other lane where subsequent approach almost totally obscured by microterrain
Microterrain or low vegetation makes it hard to see crawlers	Any sentry behind military crest can't see crawler to his front	Friendlies take full advantage of all cover and concealment encountered en route

Table 17.3: Diversions during Short-Range Infiltration

A Much Needed Change to the Way Things Are Done

Supposedly to limit casualties, U.S. ground forces have seldom attempted any squad-sized penetrations of prepared enemy positions. That's not a very good way to keep pace with evolutionary assault technique. With less emphasis on firepower, American units might discover more ways to initially build and subsequently maintain surprise on offense. Against an accomplished adversary, that would be cheaper in ordnance expended and lives lost. Of course, world-class defenders also utilize surprise.

18 Opportunity-Based Defense

- Shouldn't every defense seem to the foe like an ambush?
- How could this be most easily achieved in heavy foliage?

Not every defense has to look like one from a distance.

(Source: Air Univ., Army/Marine Clipart, image designator "1-13b.gif," retrieved from www.au.af.mil/au/awc/awcgate/cliparmy.htm)

The Most Powerful Type of Defense

In U.S. military discussions, the term "defense" has come to mean "self protection." In practice, however, this tactical option most usefully robs the attacker of momentum. Two schemes are well suited to this latter purpose: (1) the positional defense that so startles the foe as to throw him off balance; and (2) the backwards moving defense that so disperses the foe as to make him susceptible to piecemeal annihilation. While both are more often practiced in the Orient,[1] there is no reason why GIs couldn't use them as well. That's why the finer points of each are next discussed. Because

235

both choices require more surprise than the traditional U.S. "fire superiority demonstration," both must be based on examples from Asia.

The Hidden Positional Defense

During the battle for Hue City in February 1968, a U.S. Marine battalion—though fully supported by tanks, artillery, naval gunfire, and close air—required four full days to cross a two-lane street.[2] While the NVA's defense of Mai Thuc Loan or "Phase Line Green" had many ingenious aspects, most impressive was its almost total obscurity from the front. Its defenders and their barrier plan were so well hidden that the first Marines to reach Mai Thuc Loan merely sauntered along its sidewalks.[3]

Sadly, this "obscurity" did not go away with the first shots being fired. Then, not only were the sources of NVA fire hidden, but sometimes even the areas they targeted. Collectively, they covered almost every square foot of frontage. (See Figure 18.1.) Much of this all-encompassing destruction came along interlocking diagonals from building recesses. From the front, the veil of destruction appeared to have no particular origin.

In his years at the [Basic] school, [Major Bill] Eshelman had never heard of an integrated defensive plan as comprehensive as what he saw on the ground in the Citadel.[4]

As at Iwo Jima, the NVA's "front line" was actually parallel rows of mutually supporting strongpoints—with those strongpoints now being buildings. Sometimes two of the rearward bastions could place interlocking machinegun (MG) fire across the front of one forward. More often, the rearward positions could fire into the forward structures and then cover their occupants' withdrawal. Between the various strongpoints were trenches and covered crawl ways. Every time a forward fort was penetrated, its defenders would move to one in the rear row. This was not done on a grand scale as along the three belts on Iwo Jima, but more in the miniature format of that island's last holdout.

In attacking these positions [in the Gorge], no Japanese were to be seen, all being in caves or crevices in the rocks and so disposed as to give an all-around interlocking, ghost-like defense to each small compartment. Attacking troops were subjected to fire from flanks and rear more than from their front. It was always difficult and often impossible to

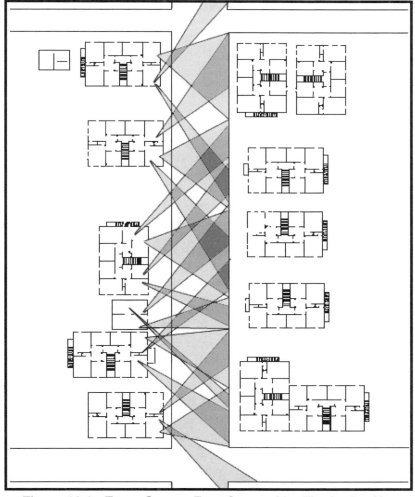

Figure 18.1: Every Square Foot Covered by Fire in the City
(Sources: TC 90-1 [1986], p. 3-53)

locate exactly where defensive fires originated. The field of fire of the individual Japanese defender in his cave position was often limited to an arc of 10° or less; conversely he was protected from fire except that coming back on this arc. The Japanese smokeless, flashless powder for small arms, always advantageous, was of particular usefulness here. When the position was overrun or threatened, the enemy retreated farther into his caves where he usually was safe from gunfire, only to pop out again as soon as the occasion warranted unless the cave was immediately blown.[5]
— 5th Mar. Div. Intel. Report of 24 March 1945

The U.S. Rural Equivalent

Heavy plunging fire is most possible in the city, but the NVA's other Hue City methods would work just fine in a rural setting. In urban terrain, U.S. forces will also partially disguise defended streets. Yet, in the country, they seldom take this precaution. As a result, their rural defenses are more vulnerable to attack and less likely to stop a determined aggressor.

While American fighting holes are partially camouflaged, their fields of fire almost always give away their locations. If those fields of fire were not as well cleared, something like the Phase Line Green ambush would be possible. With full vegetation to the immediate front of those fighting holes, the holes themselves wouldn't need much disguising. If the overall position then looked like everything around it, the foe would less often hit it with preparatory fire. Many parts of the world are heavily foliated. There, complete fields of fire are virtually impossible to clear anyway. (See Figure 18.2.)

Observation and Fire Lanes

Observation lanes are diagonal corridors built through the vegetation to give some defenders a momentary glimpse of enemy approaching other defenders. (See Figure 18.3.) The most useful are those with only the lowest branches removed to keep any upright trespasser from noticing his exposure. When, a machinegun or other weapon is placed at the head of an observation lane, it becomes a fire lane.

Figure 18.2: Think before Clearing Those Fields of Fire
(Sources: FM 100-20 [1981], p. 178)

Figure 18.3: Observation Lanes Better Preserve Surprise
(Sources: FM 7-1181/2 [1978], p. 2-II-B-3.3; Corel Print House, Plants, Tree 9; Gallery Graphics, Mac/EPS, Flowers, Trees, and Plants 2, "Shrubs")

Enough interlocking fire lanes would provide a "kill zone" through which no attacking force—however big—could advance. With command-detonated claymores or grenade launcher "concentrations" in any defiladed portion of an otherwise flat frontage, such a defense could decisively rob any intruder of momentum. Perhaps that's what happened to the 3rd Battalion, 27th Marines' company, which—according to rumor—was cut to pieces after trying to chase a few VC into a field of elephant grass in 1968.[6] This may have been part of the Operation Allenbrook fight for Phu Dong (2) so well recounted at one of the 27th Marines' websites.[7] Next time, it will be enemy soldiers in such a trap. Why have a state-of-the art defense without trying it out?

The Backwards-Moving Defense

Enough has been written about this maneuver as not to require many examples. It was most famously used at Hue City and Seoul, so one might think it Communist in origin and best suited to urban terrain. Yet, it was also used by the Turks at Gallipoli's Sulva Bay and by the Japanese at Iwo Jima. So, the concept is actually quite universal throughout the Eastern World. The whole idea is to draw a larger foe into a series of mishaps that make him more vulnerable to attack. At Sulva Bay, the Turks kept moving backwards until the British ran so short of water that one whole company may have bared their backs to a line of Turkish spider holes.[8] At Iwo Jima, every apparent gap in "enemy lines" was instead a firesack, and all defenders could withdraw to well-hidden reverse-slope emplacements.[9] (See Figure 18.4.)

A U.S. Version of the Falling-Back Exercise

For a tiny unit, there are two ways to safely withdraw under pressure: (1) through a ditch while a sister element provides overhead fire; and (2) by the quickest route while a sister element distracts the attacker. (For an example of the latter, see Figure 18.5.) Here, the first team retreats after drawing the lead tank's attention (to make it more vulnerable to the second team). As the next tank goes after this second team, the third team then has a clear shot at it. Such are the dynamics of a rearward moving ambush.

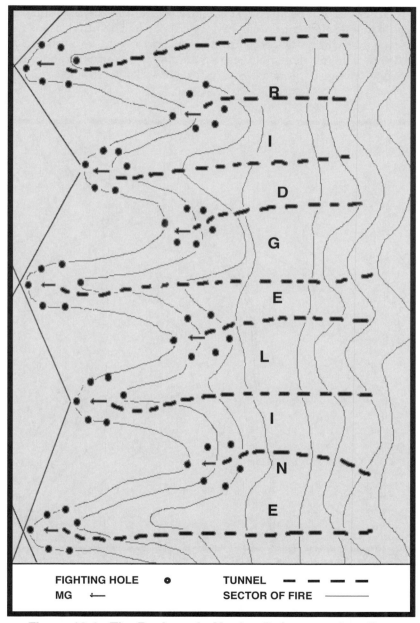

FIGHTING HOLE	⊙	TUNNEL	▬ ▬ ▬ ▬
MG	←	SECTOR OF FIRE	──

Figure 18.4: The Backwards-Moving Defense on Iwo Jima

Other variations on this theme are best left to the ingenuity of highly mobile elements. Still, history offers some helpful lessons for baiting and killing. Ways to lure the quarry range from a false trail to fleeing soldiers. Kill methods include claymore series, preplanned barrage, and grazing machinegun fire. (See Table 18.1.)

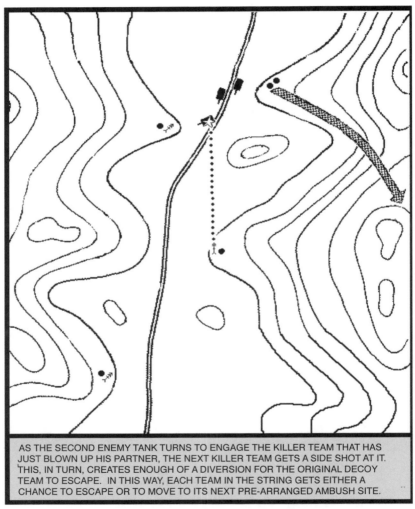

AS THE SECOND ENEMY TANK TURNS TO ENGAGE THE KILLER TEAM THAT HAS JUST BLOWN UP HIS PARTNER, THE NEXT KILLER TEAM GETS A SIDE SHOT AT IT. THIS, IN TURN, CREATES ENOUGH OF A DIVERSION FOR THE ORIGINAL DECOY TEAM TO ESCAPE. IN THIS WAY, EACH TEAM IN THE STRING GETS EITHER A CHANCE TO ESCAPE OR TO MOVE TO ITS NEXT PRE-ARRANGED AMBUSH SITE.

Figure 18.5: Tiny Ambushes in Series

WAYS TO SPLIT AND GUIDE AN ENEMY FORCE	WAYS TO TRAP A MANAGEABLE PART OF THAT ENEMY FORCE
DUAL & EQUALLY ACCESSIBLE LINES OF DRIFT TO SPLIT FOE	COMMAND-DETONATED CLAYMORES IN SERIES ALONG NARROW DEFILE
DUAL SIGNS OF PASSAGE TO SPLIT FOE	PREREGISTERED PRECISION MORTAR CONCENTRATION
SNIPER SHOTS TO DRAW FOE TOWARD THEM	FRIENDLY UNITS FORM OPEN CIRCLE AROUND LOW GROUND
TREE MARKINGS OR STONE PILES ALONG DESIRED WAY	FIELD OF ELEPHANT GRASS SET AFIRE FROM ALL FOUR SIDES AT ONCE
REMAINS OF CAMP FIRE ALONG HOPED-FOR ROUTE	HEAVILY VEGETATED BUT FLAT AREA SWEPT WITH GRAZING MG FIRE
BRUSH DISCREETLY CLEARED ALONG DESIRED BEARING	
DISCARDED GEAR ALONG SOUGHT-AFTER LEG	
ONE OR TWO FRIENDLIES FLEE IN APPROPRIATE DIRECTION	
FAKE MINEFIELD TO PREVENT DETOUR	
CLUMPS OF OLD WIRE OR BRUSH TO BLOCK ACCESS	
EXTRA FOOTPRINTS TO DISCOURAGE LEAVING THE TRAIL	
STREAM DAMMED TO LIMIT ENTRANCE INTO SIDE DRAW	
TREE DISCREETLY FELLED TO PRECLUDE PASSAGE	

Table 18.1: Options for Dividing, Canalizing, and Trapping Foe

How U.S. "Grunts" Might Set the Trap

As the intent of the backwards-moving defense is to string out and disperse one's attacker, two ancient Chinese formations may be helpful. The first is colloquially referred to as the "Three-Shaped" Battle Array." It was more properly for attacking a demoralized foe.[10] (See Figure 18.6.) As offense and defense often blur in the Orient, it might easily apply to a withdrawal that turns into a trap. The dual opening faces the enemy force. As this force is divided, its halves are encircled.

Something similar happened to a Marine company ambushed during Operation Buffalo in July 1968. After sending one platoon after a sniper, its main column was breached from the side in several places. Then, the detached platoon and each column segment were systematically encircled.[11] Luckily, help arrived in time, and most of those Marines lived to tell the tale. Herein may lie the basics for a GI-operated trap. If the center of the "three" were a terrain feature or some other reason for the enemy force to split, then half of this force might be lured into a semi-circular kill zone.

Figure 18.6: The "Three-Shaped" Battle Array

The ancient Chinese had another formation for wearing out a foe. It was the "Obstructing and Blocking Array."[12] (See Figure 18.7.) It's not quite clear why the concentric-circle openings face the foe. Perhaps they are intended as a firesack that can be closed with long-range weaponry.

A Much Needed Exception to Doctrine

It would take a full U.S. company to form even one of these concentric "C's" in most terrain. However, along particularly narrow defiles, the nine fire teams of a platoon might be enough. Unfortunately, there are doctrinal issues involved. Any encirclement is technically in violation of U.S. doctrine. However, in this case, there is an almost foolproof way to avoid fratricide. What if all members of the circle only fired downwards because of the enemy's lower elevation? Then, swarming in for a "turkey shoot" might work as well as it did for the "Minute Men" of 1775.

Figure 18.7: The Obstructing and Blocking Array

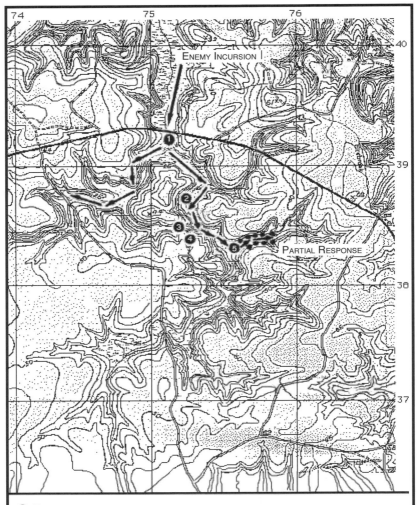

① FOOTPRINT TRAIL PARTS AT THE STREAM JUNCTION CAUSING ENEMY UNIT TO SPLIT.

② SNIPER SHOOTS ONE ROUND CAUSING ENEMY UNIT TO FOLLOW.

③ MINEFIELD SIGNS CAUSE ENEMY UNIT TO IGNORE SIDE DRAW.

④ PILES OF OLD WIRE AND DEAD BRUSH CAUSE ENEMY TO IGNORE SIDE DRAW.

⑤ TWO FRIENDLIES FLEE UP SIDE DRAW AT OTHER SIDE CAUSING ENEMY TO FOLLOW.

● NINE SQUADS/FIRE TEAMS WAITING IN "C" FORMATION TO ALL FIRE DOWNWARDS.

Map 18.1: Divide, Guide, and Conquer

How Such a Scheme Might Look

If a quarry of manageable size could be lured into a narrow draw, then the friendly squads or fire teams along the sides of this draw could all safely target the quarry at once. While waiting, those squads or fire teams would be in an elongated perimeter formation and thus equally capable of defense. If there were not enough of them to complete the "C," then mines or mortar concentrations could be added. Once the quarry was inside the trap, long-range fire could effectively cover the C's" mouth, thereby trapping its occupant. For how an enemy force could be divided, and then lured in pieces to its destruction, closely follow the steps on Map 18.1.

19 Rifleman Tactics

● Of what else is the U.S. rifleman capable?
● How might he better help America to win the next war?

U.S. riflemen are only as good as allowed.

(Source: Air Univ., Army/Marine Clipart, image designator "1-3d.gif," retrieved from www.au.af.mil/au/awc/awcgate/cliparmy.htm)

How the Rest of the World Sees Things

"Beauty is in the eyes of the beholder," the old saying goes. America takes such pride in providing its military with the latest equipment, that the Pentagon does little more than handle defense contracts. Meanwhile, less prosperous armies have only human initiative with which to close the gap. That's the dynamic—equipment versus people. Unbeknownst to most Americans, being the richest country in the world does have its downside. When it's all about the equipment, the people tend to be treated like troublesome peripherals.

249

Once U.S. School of Infantry graduates reach their line outfits, they are generally treated like "new guys who don't know much." In some Oriental armies, every rifleman is prepared to make a strategic difference. Why the variation in perspective? Aren't Americans every bit as capable as Asians? Many Oriental armies enjoy more of the following: (1) actual fighters (as opposed to support troops or officers); (2) battlefield versatility; (3) influence by the fighters on operational-decision making; (4) comprehensive training of the fighters; and (5) strategic briefing of the fighters. It's almost as if U.S. infantrymen are considered a sideshow to the main event— overwhelming firepower. If conventional firepower had prevented more WWII casualties, managed more than a tie in Korea, won in Vietnam, more cheaply pacified Iraq, or befriended more Afghan civilians, who would care? But it didn't.

More Actual Fighters

The percentage of all U.S. troops dedicated to ground combat will astound most readers. After every aerial duel must come the occupation. In 2009, the number of Army infantrymen was barely 10% of the whole.[1] Meanwhile, the WWII Japanese considered infantrymen so important that they had five different pay grades of private.[2]

Over the years, the Chinese Army has vacillated between having and not having ranks. From its inception, the only distinction between personnel was "leader" (or commander) and "fighter." (See Figure 19.1.) Then, in 1955, the PLA tried an assortment of ranks. Within ten years, the wearing of rank was again abolished.[3] Nine years after China's disastrous 1979 border war with Vietnam, it reinstated the rank system—presumably to provide more coordination.[4] Whether this trend continues is unimportant. China has more enlisted fighters with whom to locally garrison multiple war zones.

Greater Versatility on the Battlefield

While U.S. military doctrine now allows for more maneuver, its battlefield format is still "high-tech" 2GW—i.e., technologically overpowering one's enemy. American forces still do very little maneuvering below platoon level, and what happens on defense can best be described as "old-fashioned" positional warfare.

Since 1949, all Chinese troops have been prepared for positional, mobile, and guerrilla warfare.[5] The three options make them more versatile.

More Influence over Operational-Decision Making

The American infantry private may weekly share a few words with his platoon leader. In *Kiem Thao* sessions during the Vietnam War, NVA privates were encouraged to regularly correct both commanders and battle chronicles.[6]

Each soldier and officer criticized his own actions and the other members of the company regardless of rank. After each confession or criticism, a general [group] discussion ensued. . . . [I]t gave the soldiers a sense of participation in the unit's decision-making process. They viewed themselves, therefore, not as witless cannon fodder, but as thinking members of a team.[7]

As adequately evidenced by this quote from Mao, all Communist armies (and guerrillas) give their lower echelons more of a say in what goes on. Along with the increase in cohesion would come a more comprehensive assessment of the last battle and current frontline situation.

[T]he reason why the Red Army can sustain itself . . . is its practice of democracy. . . . [O]fficers and men receive equal treatment; soldiers enjoy freedom of assembly and speech; cumbersome formalities and ceremonies are done away with; and the account books are open to the inspection of all.[8]
— Mao Tse-Tung

More Comprehensive Training

American Boot Camp training is excellent, but what then happens at the School of Infantry is only a taste of what has to be the

251

Figure 19.1: The 1955-Vintage Chinese Soldier
(Source: GlobalSecurity.org, s.v. "PLA Uniforms and Insignia," image designator "uniform-1955.jpg")

most complicated of all occupational specialties. Meanwhile, all Chinese infantrymen are shown how productively to contribute to positional, mobile, and guerrilla warfare.[9] And all North Korean soldiers are trained in both conventional and unconventional warfare. Included in the latter are E&E and guerrilla methods.[10]

Keeping the Actual Fighters Fully Informed

In comparison, U.S. grunts will be lucky to learn what their platoon leader has planned for the afternoon. Since the Korean War, lowest-echelon Chinese soldiers have been kept regularly apprised of the tactical and strategic "intents" of all leaders up their respective chains of command.[11]

What This All Means to the Next Global Conflict

In effect, the Eastern way of war depends more on the opinions (and initiative) of frontline fighters than does its Western counterpart. This is no recent revelation. Since 1917, the Germans and Eastern Russians have followed the same format. Despite all the "team pressure" against it, a few U.S. military leaders have also realized the paradox. America's top commander in WWI may have literally meant the following:

> The deadliest weapon in the world is a Marine and his rifle.[12]
> — U.S. Army Gen. John J. "Black Jack" Pershing

How Helpful Is this Individual and Small-Unit Edge

Anyone who has ever tried to research a Communist nation's small-unit tactics can attest to their particulars being protected like missile dimensions. Their wartime leaders intentionally write in circles with very little mention of specific maneuvers used.[13] That's because the lowliest rifleman is—in truth—the Asians' secret weapon.

Meanwhile in America, all the emphasis on rank and technology has so undermined the U.S. rifleman's status as to make him seem like excess baggage. While his Eastern counterpart is being rewarded for initiative, the GI is punished for it. Of course, there's a reason for the inequity. "The Easterner's culture has made him more receptive to group effort," so the argument goes. Still, once the Western recruit's independent spirit has been sufficiently "dampened" at Boot Camp, it must be reestablished before combat. Otherwise, the young GI will either rush a machinegun, or wish he were home. He is instead needed to apply continual pressure to an unrelenting foe.

What's Ultimately at Stake Here

To win a global conflict against the current assortment of bottom-up adversaries, the Pentagon will have finally to permit its lowest infantry ranks to reach their full potential. Just knowing a few Americanized *jujitsu* moves and how to operate one's equipment will not be enough to defeat a longtime student of *ninjutsu* and unconventional warfare. Unless the U.S. training regimen is immediately lengthened, young Americans will remain at a decided disadvantage in any one-on-one encounter. The representative of an under-supplied (and tactically emphatic) aggressor will automatically have the edge. Among the GIs' greatest threats will be the "soldiers" of all Communist, Islamist, and criminal outfits. While such adversaries will have varying degrees of combat proficiency, all come from a bottom-up environment in which they were forced to learn the hard way. In the process, they couldn't help but face their own strengths and weaknesses. This gives them the edge over those who are constantly told how good they are, but can only mimic elementary training. Such a pointed comparison is nothing new, just politically incorrect to say too loudly.

> If I had to train my regiment over again, I would stress small group training and the training of the individual.... Our basic training is all right. . . . In your [Fleet] training put your time and emphasis on the squad and platoon rather than on the company, battalion and regiment.
>
> In your scouting and patrolling, . . . have the men work against each other. Same thing [goes] for squads and platoons in their problems. . . .
>
> . . . With proper training, our Americans are better [than the Japanese], as our people can think better as individuals. Encourage your individuals and bring them out.[14]
> — Col. Merritt A. Edson after Guadalcanal
> *FMFRP 12-110*

The Most Likely Opponent Next Time Around

On 10 March 2011, the DNI publicly stated before the Senate Armed Services Committee that China and Russia still pose the greatest risk to the U.S.[15] While such an assessment was not very popular politically, it is almost certainly correct. If such a threat is ever realized, it will be quite different from before. Instead of mechanized armies vying for the Russian Steppe or North Africa, there will be proxy-led disturbances all over the planet. There's only one way the U.S. military could respond. Instead of one Texas Ranger per riot, it will have to employ 13 U.S. grunts per hundred square miles.

No infantry enlistee has more potential than the American (of any generation). In 2011, he must be a hero simply to survive high school. Whether or not this potential is ever realized is what is at issue here. More bottom-up training would better prepare him for what is to come.

The Chinese soldier is considered one of the most highly motivated soldiers in the world today.[16]
— U.S. Defense Intel. Agency, 1976 and 1984

Though often stereotyped as an illiterate peasant, the Chinese soldier is actually quite self-assured and well disciplined. Among his societal responsibilities are the following "eight points of attention": (1) speak politely; (2) pay fairly for what you buy; (3) return everything you borrow; (4) pay for anything that you damage; (5) do not hit or swear at people; (6) do not damage crops; (7) do not take liberties with women; and (8) do not ill-treat captives.[17] He is therefore as capable as a Western soldier of locally assuming the moral high ground. One of the lessons of Vietnam, Iraq, and Afghanistan is that so doing has become almost a prerequisite of winning 21st Century wars.

The Communist armies have less moral intentions, but more shrapnel-free methods. In these times of near-lethal national debt, there is no reason why the West could not borrow a few of their light-infantry techniques. (See Figure 19.1.) Think of the money it would save, not to mention the number of lives and ignominious pull-outs. All infrastructure left in tact during the next foreign-population rescue wouldn't have to be reconstructed.

The North Koreans were like ghosts. They passed over the countryside and left no mark on it in many ways. But when you use the rock crusher techniques of an American

Figure 19.1: Night Fighting Has Always Been the Safest
(Source: Courtesy of Sorman Information and Media, from Soldf: Soldaten i falt, © 2001 by Forsvarsmakten and Wolfgang Bartsch, Stockholm, p. 133)

army you hurt your friends. And that was true in Vietnam
as well as in Korea.[18]
> — Maj.Gen. Edwin Simmons USMC (Ret.)
> former Director of History and Museums, HQMC
> PBS Special *Korea—the Unknown War*

20   Acquiring Enough Individual Skill

● Is it enough to know how to use one's gear?

● What else does the infantryman need to understand?

Fancy gear doesn't make one any less of a target.

(Source: Corel Gallery Clipart, image designator "45A106.jpg")

The Inescapable Truth

Over the last 70 years, America has fought four major wars in the Pacific. In each, GIs have seldom seen the very people they were fighting. Though over 20,000 strong, the Japanese defenders of tiny Iwo Jima were nearly impervious to bombardment and return fire.[1] Five years later, "the North Koreans were like ghosts" during their invasion of the South.[2] Then, no fewer than ten Chinese divisions secretly reached the Chosin Reservoir.[3] During the Vietnam War, NVA and VC sappers regularly sneaked into U.S. strongpoints just for reconnaissance purposes alone.[4]

257

This "near invisibility" of the Asian adversary was not only noticed by U.S. commanders. The frontline troops were painfully aware of it.

> We hardly ever saw an enemy [on Iwo Jima]. The Japanese had every inch of ground covered by fire.[5]
> — Navaho Marine veteran
> "Japanese Codetalkers," History Channel

> Seldom on Iwo, from D-day until the battle was over [36 days later], did you see the enemy—just the sights and sounds of deadly fire from his weapons.[6]
> — Marine infantryman on Iwo Jima

Within the U.S. military establishment, there are "duty" explanations for this Asian phenomenon. Among the more popular are that the foe was more culturally patient, reluctant to fight, or operating in his own backyard. The truth of the matter is that his frontline fighters were more extensively trained than their U.S. counterparts. The Japanese soldier's aptitude for escaping detection became first apparent on Guadalcanal. There, if the leaves weren't moving, the Marines had nothing to shoot at. Many were experienced deer hunters from Appalachia (See Figures 20.1 and 20.2.)

> There must be training in difficult observation. . . . It is my observation [determination on Guadalcanal] that only 5% of the men can really see while observing.[7]
> — Col. Merritt A. Edson, in *FMFRP 12-110*

What the Real Problem Was

The "country-boy" Marines on Guadalcanal could see just fine. The problem was that their adversary had received more training on camouflage and obscure movement. Since 1913, every Japanese soldier had been given a detailed appreciation of nighttime movement.[8]

As might be expected, more extensive troop ability gives the Asian commander more maneuver options. He can then quite safely

Figure 20.1: A Japanese Infantry Private from 1942
(Source: Courtesy of Cassell PLC, from World Army Uniforms since 1939, © 1975, 1980, 1981, 1983 by Blandford Press Ltd., Part I, Plate 156)

Figure 20.2: The Problem the Marines Had on Guadalcanal
(Source: "A Concise History of the Unites States Marine Corps 1775-1969," by Capt. William D. Parker, sketch by Capt. Donald L. Dickson, Hist. Div., HQMC, 1970, p. 62)

attempt everything from sapper to encirclement tactics. Because he and his men are still considered second rate by most Americans, this will take further proof.

In essence, U.S. infantrymen are the best trained in the world at *how to use the latest equipment*. Some of this equipment may help them to shoot enemy soldiers, but none of it makes them any less visible themselves. Too much of it so erodes their mobility as to make them veritable "sitting ducks." If there were no money and politics involved, such a realization would generate more interest in the Asian curriculum.

At the start of WWII, the Japanese may have overestimated what highly trained riflemen could accomplish on their own. On Guadalcanal, they tried to run too many troops through each breach in the Marines' barbed wire. Yet, by 1965, the Asian way of compensating for too little firepower had been fully refined. While casualty counts vary, Vietnamese light infantry did—with no tank, artillery, or aerial support—hold their own against the full might of the U.S. war machine from 1965 to 1973. In 1979, Vietnamese militia repeated the feat against a powerful neighbor. While this neighbor may now practice a less-Western approach to invasion, U.S. troops must still be ready to dodge its (or somebody else's) "high-tech" weaponry. More easily to survive, most would be very interested in the East Asian methods. Their leaders must walk—for just a moment—in their shoes.

The Japanese Soldier of WWII

With a martial arts heritage, the Nipponese knew well the benefits of rehearsal. By 1913, their enlisted men were intensively drilling on how to do the following at night: (1) march quietly; (2) participate in connecting files; (3) act as a messenger; (4) cross rough ground; (5) throw grenades; (6) bayonet fight; (7) entrench; (8) stand guard; (9) recognize friendly troops; (10) fire their weapons; (11) patrol; and (12) perform a hidden patrol.[9] Of note, these drills were conducted *as experiments and often involved statistical feedback*. Each man was given the opportunity to gauge his own progress and to share with the rest of his group any techniques he had discovered.[10] The Japanese practiced many of these battledrills with dummy rifles.[11]

Additionally, there was competition between units. A 1935 photograph had on it the following inscription: "Wall-scaling drill in a competition between the Imperial Bodyguard and the Army's First Division."[12] Wall scaling was one of the *ninja's* many ways of "penetrating fortresses." As with the Germans, these battledrills took up much of each day and were followed by a "free-play" exercise.

Before WWII, Japanese infantrymen were often asked to work on their individual skills after normal working hours or during maneuvers. They trained 14 hours a day, six days a week. While often marching 25 miles a day, they celebrated holidays with a "sham" battle.[13] The Japanese drills for individuals may have gone far beyond what the Germans attempted. Each so-called "basic" was subdivided many times. During the "hearing" drill, the Japanese private had to distinguish between the sounds of "digging with a pick, driving a shovel strongly into the ground, pushing a spade into various kinds of ground, and a squad entrenching freely."[14] During messenger training, he not only learned terrain association techniques (advanced land navigation), but also how to memorize nighttime routes.[15] Right before WWII, the members of one Japanese company arose at 4:00 A.M. just to participate until dawn in a "bayonet-fighting tournament."[16]

The Chinese

Since 1949, all Chinese troops have been prepared for positional, mobile, and guerrilla warfare. Their specialty is still night fighting.[17]

Chinese troops are trained differently than U.S. troops. Instead of attending central schools, they acquire most of their advanced knowledge through practical application at each line unit. There, instead of sitting in class, they most likely learn (and help to refine) the tactical techniques they will use through battledrill rehearsal. Battledrills are nothing new to the PLA. During the Korean War, such drills were quite evident. It was there the Chinese learned that whole companies can't maneuver as in marching, but their component squads can. What looked to Americans like a several-row-deep human wave was really squad columns on line, with each using German Stormtrooper technique from WWI.[18]

Following basic training, the [modern Chinese] soldier is integrated into a regular unit where here receives advanced individual training.[19]
— DIA's *Handbook on the Chinese Armed Forces*

The [Chinese] armies [entering Korea] had two phases of drills before going into battles. . . . The first phase focused on the exercises of small-group combat tactics, including shooting, throwing grenades, demolition, anti-aircraft training, and nighttime anti-air-raid practice. The second phase stressed courses of [larger] group-attack tactics. . . . These exercises were aimed at the demolition of enemy defense works under enemy fire. . . .
All armies offered classes in antitank training.[20]
— *Mao's Generals Remember Korea*

The North Koreans

North Korean infantrymen also depend heavily on battledrills. All dedicate two months a year to squad-level training.[21]

Each [unit's biannual] cycle consists of approximately 760 hours of training, which progresses from individual . . . exercises to joint service maneuvers.[22]

[All North Korean soldiers] are trained in both conventional and unconventional warfare (E&E and fighting like a guerrilla).[23]

The North Vietnamese

Within every NVA line company, tiny elements diligently practiced many maneuvers. There were drills for almost every aspect of the offense and defense.

Sapper units were also considered light infantry and were taught how to operate as an infantry unit. This training was the basis of specialized sapper training anyway, and sapper units trained hard so that they could do these small unit drills better than regular infantry units. Such tactics covered how to deploy on the battlefield for various types of operations (deliberate attack, hasty attack, meeting engagement, withdrawal, hasty and deliberate defense, regular patrolling, etc.).[24]

North Vietnamese soldiers who showed exceptional aptitude were sent to commando school. There they would drill on scouting and the more sophisticated aspects of short-range combat. As full-fledged commandos, many returned to the line outfits as teaching cadre. One can therefore conclude that all NVA infantrymen received at least some of the following:

Sappers recruited in North Vietnam . . . were given six to twelve month's training. The key subjects were:

Assault Techniques. . . . A lot of these assault techniques were drill, to make the right moves automatic. . . .

Breaching Obstacles. Sappers were carefully trained on the best techniques for getting through barbed wire, minefields, and floodlit areas. A lot of this was just practice, practice, practice. . . .

Camouflage. . . . This was best accomplished by knowing how to hide yourself in plain sight. . . .

Exfiltration. . . .

Explosives. Sappers used explosives to blow up obstacles and to destroy enemy fortifications and equipment. . . .

Infiltration. . . . Sappers were known for their ability to sneak through the most formidable obstacles. . .

Navigation. . . . Sappers spent a lot of time in the field practicing. . . .

Planning. . . . Sappers were trained on how U.S. and South Vietnamese bases were laid out and what [strategic] installations were found in all of them. So more reconnaissance was done until the model of the enemy base was complete. . . .

Reconnaissance. . . .

Small Unit Tactics. . . .

Special Equipment Training. . . .

Weapons Training.[25]

The Viet Cong

Every few months, VC riflemen would receive refresher technique training from a "mobile infantry school."[26] Techniques are best learned through battledrills, so battledrills were probably the method of instruction. The curriculum generally included more than one crawling technique,[27] so the instructors were probably NVA commandos.

Even village-defense-force members received instruction in sniper fire, trench warfare, use of grenades and mines, tunneling, and construction of homemade weapons. Meanwhile, the district-maneuver-force personnel were trained in surprise raids, trench fighting, ambushing, and demolition work.[28] The VC who were to become sappers practiced demolition rigging and "observation and reconnaissance techniques."[29] Only another commando would have understood the latter well enough to teach it.

The Teaching Trends among Oriental Armies

All four Asian groups seem to have received some training in the following: (1) advanced land navigation (upon approach); (2) short-range infiltration (for *ninja*-style assault); (3) demolitions (after entering the enemy bastion); (4) dodging bombardment (during consolidation); and (5) "barehanded" tank fighting (on defense). With troops this talented, the Asian commanders could do a lot. Such subordinates helped to offset their chronic shortage of supplies and largely eliminated any need for tank, artillery, and air support. In essence, troop training had—with more surprise—supplanted the loss of firepower.

Whereas the American soldier was learning only the most elementary aspects of "shooting," "moving," and "communicating," the Asian soldier was learning much more. It included the following: (1) micro-terrain appreciation; (2) harnessing the senses; (3) night familiarity; (4) nondetectable movement; (5) guarded communication; (6) discreet force at close range; (7) combat deception; and (8) one-on-one tactical-decision making.[30]

For all four Asian groups, the preferred method of instruction was technique formulation through interactive drilling. Not too long ago, U.S. troops also practiced drills. However, theirs strictly followed what was in the manuals. The Asian drills are different. They are for refining technique, whereas the American ones are for enforcing an established procedure. Did not the Japanese soldiers conduct "experiments"? The only experiment a U.S. private ever conducts is how to avoid being punished after deviating from an illogical norm. To make the training even more dynamic, the Asians even incorporated competition and free play.

Finally, all four Asian armies seem to have shown their enlistees how to instruct friendly militia and guerrillas. This gave them additional utility as force multipliers.

The U.S. Gladiator Could Also Use a Lower Profile

Like the fire teams and squads, U.S. riflemen have too few movement skills to match up well with their Asian counterparts. Traditionally allowed only to follow orders, many have too little practice at dodging enemy fire and using available cover. They also suffer from too little tactical-decision-making experience and initiative. For many, their "free-spirited nature" was usefully dampened at boot camp, but not adequately restored. Such things make U.S. riflemen less survivable in combat. Cumbersome and finicky "high-tech" gear only adds to the handicap.

Too little decision making and initiative can best be corrected by letting infantry NCOs—as a group—determine and correct their own tactical deficiencies, as in Appendix A. That's because such a thought process is similar to what squad leaders must do in combat. Over the last 15 years, this "bottom-up" training method has been fully tested (and refined) throughout the Fleet Marine Corps. During a progressive CO's tenure, several battalions have already adopted it.[31] Never intended to replace the existing individual-through-squad training curriculum, this new way simply supplements it. Its sessions occur during all of those short unavoidable delays in each training day (like when the trucks to the ranges are late), and requires no additional funding. As such, it will not make the civilian contractors very happy. Yet, the advantages of letting professionals train themselves far overshadow any political downside. Given enough time, this new training method could also fix the shortfall in movement technique. To do so quickly, a few Asian precedents must be added to the commanders' guidance.

At various times in recent history, every line infantryman from Japan, China, North Korea, and Vietnam has received some training in both *ninjutsu* (secretly crossing obstacles) and barehanded tank killing.[32] The former is tantamount to short-range infiltration—the safest of all assault options. Additionally, every Communist soldier has been trained in UW (E&E and guerrilla methods).[33] Just to survive, any insurgent must learn some of these same skill sets. One way or another, GIs must be given the same opportunity.

Firepower and Technology Can Only Do So Much

U.S. infantrymen are now mostly road bound and supporting-arms dependent. There may be a scenario in which this would work, but it hasn't lately. The days of U.S. riflemen blindly following orders are over. The sooner their commanders realize this, the fewer casualties they will suffer, and the more wars they will win. While fully capable of following orders, U.S. servicemen must also be able to think for themselves. How else can they win the inevitable one-on-one encounter?

Two axioms usefully summarize the infantry dynamic. When close to a foe who realizes it, everything at the squad level must be done by the numbers. When far from a less cognizant foe, looser control generates better results. During both sets of circumstances, squads that have practiced some applicable maneuver do better. In combat, things happen quickly, and there are many situational variables. That's what makes the continual practice and refinement of applicable techniques so important. Then, instead of time-consuming orders, the squad members are guided by "numbered techniques" in which each member has some degree of leeway. As in football, this situational leeway works a lot better against a thinking opponent than always depending on some standard (and fully predictable) method. (See Appendix B.)

At the squad level, the wave of the future is "guidelines" and "technique refinement/rehearsal" vice "doctrine" and "detailed instructions." With more proficient squads will come more surprise-oriented options for parent-unit commanders. Sounds simple, doesn't it? It's also completely logical. This is why the best Eastern armies operate this way. The problem is that it flies squarely in the face of Western-style bureaucracy.

Figure 20.3: A Truly "Special-Ops-Qualified" Infantryman
(Source: Podgotovka Razvegchika: Sistema Spetsnaza GRU, © 1998 by A.E.Taras and F.D. Zaruz, p. 330)

What's Been Done So Far

This small-unit deficiency has now been acknowledged at the U.S. Army's Fort Leavenworth think-tank. To help with the problem, the Pentagon has been increasing its inventory of special operators. Yet, U.S. special operators are still very reconnaissance oriented. More appropriate might be some truly light infantrymen (the modern equivalent of Carlson's Raiders or Merrill's Marauders). (See Figures 15.1 and 20.3.) For this ever to happen, more voting Americans would have to demand it. The problem lies in the political allure of costly equipment over free tactical innovation. The latter would not make the military-industrial complex very happy. It would prefer to perpetuate the myth that light infantrymen can't stand up to conventional forces. What, on earth, do they think happened in Vietnam? That may be what dual-medal-of-honor winning Marine Gen. D. Smedley Butler was complaining about in his 1932 classic *War Is a Racket*. The good general wasn't finally rebelling at authority, he was just tired of seeing his beloved brethren in arms killed through a self-imposed aversion to maneuver.

In football, teamwork and muscle memory are achieved through the practice of plays and stunts. In combat, teamwork and muscle memory are achieved through the rehearsal of movement techniques. Squads, fire teams, buddy teams, and individuals all need them. Like companies, platoons have too many moving parts for any prearranged scheme to work smoothly.

America's Best Chance for the Future

Asian armies more often train and operate from the bottom up. That's why they so easily see that bottom-up experimentation results in more individual skill than force-fed instruction. By 2005, a few of the 100,000 special operators in North Korea's "Light Infantry Training Guidance Bureau" were already attached to each of its line companies as instructors. Additionally, 320,000—or a full 20% of China's 1.6 million man ground force—had been converted to special operators.[34] What if the PLA were widely to disperse 25,000 squad-sized teams to every corner of the earth to act as force multipliers for indigenous Communist militias? Would the United States and NATO have enough of the right kind of people to counter such a strategy?

Sadly, the news has recently gotten worse. By 2009, North Korea had increased its force of infiltrating commandos to 180,000, and (by some estimates) the PRC had a million special operators.[35] This means the next global conflict may take far more manpower than the U.S. and its allies can quickly muster. They will have to make better use of their existing inventory. After boot camp and infantry training, every U.S. infantry private must help develop a company-wide technique portfolio. If experimental in format and anything like the Asian equivalent, this effort will sufficiently develop his movement skills, decision making, and initiative. See Appendices A and B. Better performance through technique rehearsal is not a new concept, just too seldom required. Without fully understanding the terms, people too easily confuse adaptive technique with mandatory procedure.

> Using football as an analogy, my players knew how to play the game, but had no team plays, much less any rehearsal of these plays. . . .

. . . [So, I told them,] "My purpose is not to teach you anything but to pull our collective knowledge together, to get our purpose, our plays, our timing down to a razor edge."

. . . "We will spend two hours each day here talking and walking ourselves through some offensive tactics that I feel are needed."[36]

— Lt. Wesley Fox (former SNCO & future MoH winner) upon assuming command of A/1/9 in Vietnam

21

Policeman Tactics

- Are there new challenges for first responders to a crime?
- Should their tactics be more paramilitary?

A "homeland siege" must be finally defeated by policemen.

(Source: Educational-purpose police clipart, image designator "police.png," retrieved from http://www.cksinfo.com/clipart/society/police)

Contemporary Policemen Have More to Worry About

The U.S. continues to be the world's largest market for illicit narcotics. That makes it the main target for international organized crime. Nothing will unravel a society quicker than drugs, so America's enemies may try to exploit this unfortunate circumstance. Communists and Islamists are both known to use destabilization as part of their takeover strategies. If such a ploy were in progress in the U.S., it would severely test an already overstretched law enforcement community.

The *Posse Comitatus* law and associated directives from the

Department of Defense (DoD) mostly disallow the use of U.S. troops to counter cross-border smuggling and infiltration.[1] As such, beat patrolmen will be America's first line of defense against any drug-related aspects of 4GW. With local law enforcement now largely responsible for national security, a few pointed questions might be in order. Have all entry-level U.S. policemen been told about 4GW? Would knowledge of the U.S. military's mostly 2GW infantry methods give those policemen the best chance of winning all future one-on-one encounters? Do current police training regimens instill enough movement technique, tactical-decision making, and initiative into their students?

The First Sign of Real Trouble

Now, as the 21st Century moves into its second decade, the number of U.S. police officers being killed in the line of duty is beginning to escalate. While questionable judgment and insufficient training may be to blame, this unfortunate statistic reflects great promise. Like ground warfare, street combat is inherently danger- ous. Any force (military or otherwise) that suffers too few casualties at the local level may be insufficiently engaged at that level. No "bottom-up" conflict can be won this way. With all the casualties so far suffered, America's police departments are clearly very much engaged. As such, they and all members are richly deserving of the nation's thanks.

Those officers are probably getting killed by charging directly into trouble with too little cover (bullet-resistant objects between them and the suspect). Such courage could be easily channeled into more advanced maneuvering. It also takes nerve to sneak up alone on a professional killer. Without this much determination, only the most elementary of attacks would be possible (those in which the quarry is simply overpowered by a much larger force). That the suspects are being quickly neutralized is good. That too many casualties are being suffered in the process is not so good. However, the latter can be remedied.

A Mutual Frame of Reference

On 21 March 2009, a convicted felon first killed two Oakland motorcycle police during a traffic stop and then later killed two Special-Weapons Assault Team (SWAT) members during an arrest attempt at the apartment of the felon's sister.[2] While all problems with the second evolution aren't clear, the suspect's use of a handgun initially may have caused the SWAT members to expect one later. That's not what they encountered. The desperate quarry then displayed all the cunning of a Stalingrad veteran. He ambushed those SWAT personnel from inside a closet. Wielding either an AK-47 or SKS assault rifle, he shot them right through its door and drywall.[3] Disturbingly, he could have as easily done so through the partition of an adjoining room. Only necessary would have been a tiny peephole through its wallpaper. Such things are difficult to spot in a background pattern.

For a blow-by-blow account of the encounter, one must look at the report of the Board of Inquiry convened by Oakland's Acting Police Chief. It shows an eight-man *ad hoc* SWAT team making the arrest attempt about 3:00 P.M. after conferring in the middle of the street within full view of the suspect's apartment. First, the apartment door was forced. Then Officer #2 followed Officer #1 inside. Both were immediately shot, with Officer #2 being killed and Officer #1 continuing on with the mission. Neither had fired a shot as there was no visible target and an unarmed woman had coming running past them. Upon also entering the apartment, Officer #3 observed the suspect holding an assault rifle beside a rear bedroom door. He fired at him as he retreated into the bedroom and closed the door. Next, Officer #4 (now in the apartment) was mortally wounded as he passed through that back bedroom door. Officer #1 had followed him into the bedroom but luckily tripped, thereby narrowly escaping another gunshot. Able to see the suspect sitting on the floor of a closet with its door partially open, he then took him under fire. So did Officer #3 and Officer #5.[4] Officer #5 had been part of the outer perimeter force, so the initial entry team probably consisted of four people. Officer #1, though wounded, had finished clearing the front room and then followed Officer #4 into the back bedroom. Extreme courage had finally solved the puzzle, but at too high a cost.

The Moral of this Story

The Oakland SWATs had not too greatly deviated from their own established procedure. Yet, the use of an *ad hoc* team implicitly removed rehearsal, and the Board of Inquiry has attested to a lack of reconnaissance.[5] So, in essence, the arrest team had relied too much on "shock and awe" while running a hasty attack against a prepared enemy position. After watching the much-heralded U.S. military do the very same thing during its invasion of Iraq, who could blame them? Unfortunately, the U.S. military is not always the best model to follow in combat. It's not nearly as proficient at maneuver as it claims at budget time. Nevertheless, it does publish attack guidelines. All patrolmen and SWAT members would be wise to follow more of these guidelines. Within Table 21.1 has been amassed nine paramilitary axioms for approaching every suspect. They should help all U.S. policemen decide how best to approach each suspect. While so doing, they must carefully watch for two types of indicators: (1) that the suspect knows they are there; and (2) that he is fully prepared to repel them.

Big-city SWAT teams are probably the best at room entry of any member of the U.S. security establishment. Unlike the military, the Oakland SWAT team at least had the sense to precede entry with concussion (vice fragmentation) grenades. However, ultra-thin interior walls won't stop AK-47 rounds, so it's often more dangerous for policemen to search structures. Luckily, most criminals have yet to discover the most effective building defense methods ever devised militarily. Even publishing such a list would be poorly advised. Suffice it to say, all SWAT teams—however well trained—should be willing to call off an arrest in any building obviously rigged for defense. While expensive, some suspects may require temporary "restriction to quarters." For the latest particulars on hostage rescue, another publication is offered.[6]

By occasionally coming in crawling, U.S. SWAT teams could usefully sacrifice a little speed for better cover. Then, once the general direction of the suspect's fire had been established, it could be quickly eliminated (through the walls if necessary). This is one of the basic lessons of intense combat. Wherever a desperate quarry is involved, no one in their right mind would burst—standing up and in a "diamond-shaped" formation—into his home strongpoint. This is as true today as it was on Iwo Jima.

> This wasn't the Hollywood version of men going into battle [on Iwo Jima]....
> They move in small units; fire teams scamper, one

man at a time, in a low, running crouch from one hole to another, from one ravine to another, from one burned-out bunker to another. Live troops win battles, and cover is the key to survival. When a man has no cover, he doesn't stand, he crawls. Only when it is thought an area is secure and cleared of enemy will men move in anything like a Hollywood style formation, even then, they are vigilant, wary, and keep distance between each other.[7]

If hostages are at stake, a high-intensity "flash" grenade (like Swedish soldiers use) could be tossed to temporarily blind the hostage-taker. (See Figure 21.1.) Momentum is useful in combat, but not always achieved by going fast. The arresting officers must only move more quickly than the quarry expects. Thus, police momentum may be more usefully acquired by quietly and sequentially solving the puzzle. Speed only helps to reduce killing shots from the quarry.

Cultural Habits Can Sometimes Get in the Way

Within the U.S. law enforcement community, there is a long-standing tradition of never showing fear and always taking immediate action. For highly trained officers in desperate situations, the second can be more productive than waiting for the cavalry. Fear is the body's early warning system. When properly managed, it can greatly help the combatant. There's a big difference between caution and cowardice. The whole idea is to win every engagement. Sometimes the best way to do so is by going more slowly or taking three steps backwards. Where no hostages are likely, there should be very few future occasions in which several police officers come charging through the same exterior doorway. Where possible, they should first kick it in and then "pie-off" the front room from both sides of a reenforced entryway.

What if the target isn't quite that passive? In an age where criminals leave prison more dangerous than before, extra care must be taken. Previously convicted felons may be capable of wildly ingenious ruses. While most Western police and soldiers are trained to think faster than their opponent (to keep him off balance), their Eastern counterparts are trained in the art of delay. It involves

Figure 21.1: Some Grenades Only Cause Temporary Vision Loss
(Source: Courtesy of Sorman Information and Media, from Soldf: Soldaten i fält, © 2001 by Forsvarsmakten and Wolfgang Bartsch, Stockholm, p. 300)

showing one's adversary approximately what he is expecting, waiting for him to make the wrong first move, and then attacking him from an unexpected direction. When trying to arrest someone as desperate as the Oakland felon, one can't take anything for granted. All manner of early warning tricks, diversions, and ambushes must be expected.

Against a particularly dangerous suspect, well-seasoned policemen will sometimes use a different tactic. They first hide nearby and then wait for a natural opportunity to make the arrest—like when the suspect retrieves his mail. This just happens to be the basic difference between Eastern and Western approaches to "closing with an opponent." The Easterner waits for nature to provide an opening. The Westerner pays little attention to natural flow of things and barges right in. While Western security personnel are regularly told how their equipment makes them superior, their Eastern cousins embrace their own shortcomings so that the bar

1. ONLY DURING "CHANCE CONTACT" CAN A "HASTY ATTACK" (ONE LACKING REHEARSAL AND RECONNAISSANCE) BE EXPECTED TO SUCCEED.

2. MARINE LEGEND CHESTY PULLER THOUGHT THE BEST WAY TO HANDLE CHANCE CONTACT WAS TO HEAD STRAIGHT AT THE OPPOSING FORCE WITH LITTLE REGARD FOR ITS SIZE (AGAINST SEASONED REGULARS HE MAY HAVE CALLED IN A MORTAR MISSION BEHIND THEM AS BACKUP).

3. A "PREPARED ENEMY POSITION" IS ONE IN WHICH THE ENEMY HAS HAD THE CHANCE TO DIG IN, PUT OUT EARLY WARNING DEVICES AND MINES, ARRANGE FOR INTERLOCKING MG FIRE, ETC. INSIDE A BUILDING, MOST (OR THEIR EQUIVALENT) ARE STILL POSSIBLE.

4. EVERY ATTACK, HOWEVER RAPIDLY LAUNCHED, AGAINST A PREPARED ENEMY POSITION, MUST HAVE BEEN REHEARSED AND RECONNOITERED. HOW THAT POSITION LOOKS FROM SEVERAL DIFFERENT PERSPECTIVES AT THE TIME WILL SOMETIMES SUFFICE AS RECONNAISSANCE.

5. THE NEXT BEST THING TO REHEARSAL IS TAKING A MOMENT TO THOROUGHLY "VISUALIZE" ONE'S SUBSEQUENT ACTIONS.

6. EVERY ATTACK, HOWEVER RAPIDLY LAUNCHED, AGAINST A PREPARED ENEMY POSITION, MUST INVOLVE SURPRISE. THAT SURPRISE CAN BE MAINTAINED THROUGH A SERIES OF PRECONCEIVED DECEPTIONS. ONCE ALL SURPRISE HAS BEEN COMPROMISED, THE ATTACK MUST BE RESCHEDULED.

7. WHEN THE SUSPECT KNOWS HE HAS COMPANY, EACH STEP IN HIS NEUTRALIZATION MUST BE ACCOMPLISHED BEFORE THE NEXT STEP CAN PROCEED. ONLY THEN WILL ONE'S OWN MOTION CREATE A SMALLER TARGET.

8. WHEN THE SUSPECT DOESN'T KNOW HE HAS COMPANY, THERE IS MORE ROOM FOR IMPROVISATION. THEN, SPEED OFTEN SERVES NO PURPOSE.

9. ALL AVAILABLE COVER MUST BE USED DURING ANY APPROACH. A STALKER ALSO KEEPS AN OBJECT BETWEEN HIMSELF AND HIS QUARRY.

Table 21.1: Policeman's Paramilitary Approach to a Suspect

can be raised. One regularly operates within his own skin, and the other doesn't. In a one-on-one encounter, which has the better chance? A good rule of thumb for all tiny contingents of American soldiers and police is this: "Unless some semblance of surprise can be maintained, all attack/arrest attempts must be postponed (and then altered in format)."

In an ideal world, U.S. police departments would each develop their own state-of-the-art techniques, and then their officers be allowed to somewhat deviate from them during execution. In the meantime, the tradition of "do what you're told" and "high diddle diddle right up the middle" will persist. Often, the only way to salvage such a plan is through heroism.

As in police work, Marine heroism on Iwo was also largely a matter of habit and peer pressure. While those group-oriented "Gyrenes" took many casualties, they still managed to accomplish the nearly impossible. Yet, to do so, they first had to overcome a still-prevalent cultural misconception. If a nation's premiere fighting force had to deal with it, so too must its police officers.

> Patrick Couplet, a twenty-five-year-old Fifth Division corporal from New Brunswick, New Jersey, put it more succinctly: "All the bombardment did was let the Nips know we were coming at them again. It stirred them up like a hornet's nest, and the sonsab. . . were waiting in their caves and bunkers to kill more Marines just as they had every. . . day since we landed."[8]

With no preliminary announcement of an impending assault, more things are possible. Chesty Puller liked to handle every chance contact with a hasty frontal assault. This only works when the opposition isn't ready for it. Contrary to popular opinion, Asian soldiers prefer secretive infiltration to stand-up assault. Many of those so-called "human waves" were elaborate diversions. As a multicultural society, Americans might now want to copy some of their infiltration methods.

More Options Possible with Better Technique

Like "plays" and "stunts" in football, prerehearsed techniques provide teamwork and muscle memory to soldiers and policemen alike. That way, every step in a fairly common evolution need not be individually directed. While patrolmen normally interact with nondangerous individuals, they should still be shown how to conduct short-range infiltration and all of its associated diversions. (Refer back to Figure 16.12 and Table 16.3.) With such skills, they could safely get much closer to the exceptions. Going a little slower would also help the rookies to think more clearly, build confidence, and avoid getting shot.

In the two-man infiltration technique,[9] one partner draws a bead on the quarry, while the other sneaks past the quarry. Then, the partners reverse roles. For more advanced infiltration techniques, one has only to study *ninjutsu.*[10] Just think how easy a hostage rescue would become if a single SWAT member could first sneak within easy closing distance of the hostage taker.

There are many other police-applicable movement skills.[11] Stalking is accomplished by keeping some object between oneself and the quarry and then moving only when he isn't looking.[12] Night movement is a multifaceted art.[13] Among its more useful variations is "shadow walking."

The New Pre-Contact Thought Process

Impromptu-tactics is what has been getting many of those police officers killed. Only the most seasoned of street veterans have enough ice water in their veins to do *ad lib* tactics that consistently work. Everyone else needs to do the following: (1) embrace the paramilitary axioms (like never attacking a barricaded suspect without surprise); (2) continually rehearse three techniques for each enemy situation (to build muscle memory); and (3) then have some way to settle down. Going with the adrenalin flow may feel like courage, but it does little to promote the thought process.

The Best Way to Maximize the Odds

In today's more threatening environment, street cops can no longer play the role and hope for the best. They must find a more reliable way to stack the odds in their favor. This takes a different way of training. To refine existing technique, they gauge minor

1. WARN PARTICIPANTS THAT MOVING UP A STREET IS TOO RISKY IN WAR BUT A GOOD WAY TO LEARN HOW TO AVOID THE FIRST BULLET.

2. LIST FOR THEM THE MOST PROBABLE WAYS OF GETTING SHOT IN THE CITY.

   A. BY BULLETS DEFLECTED ALONG WALLS
   B. FROM MACHINEGUNS AT THE ENDS OF THE STREET
   C. FROM UPPER STORIES TO THE FRONT OR REAR
   D. FROM SPACES BETWEEN BUILDINGS
   E. FROM WINDOWS AND OPEN DOORS
   F. FROM TINY WALL APERTURES (LIKE INLET VENTS)
   G. THROUGH CLOSED DOORS OR THIN WALLS

3. PLACE AGGRESSORS NEXT TO THE WALLS ON BOTH SIDES OF THE STREET NEAR ITS END.

4. HAVE AGGRESSORS ASSESS THEIR KILLS BY THREE-SECOND SIGHT PICTURES OF FULLY EXPOSED HUMAN BEINGS.

5. SEND PARTICIPANTS, TWO AT A TIME, UP OPPOSITE SIDES OF THE STREET WORKING ON THE FIRST THREAT.

6. HAVE AGGRESSORS RECORD AND APPRISE THEIR RESPECTIVE RUNNERS OF HOW MANY TIMES THEY GOT KILLED.

7. REPEAT THE DRILL AND ASK STUDENTS TO BEAT THEIR OWN PREVIOUS SCORES.

8. HAVE AGGRESSORS MOVE TO PROVIDE THE SECOND THREAT.

9. SEND PARTICIPANTS, TWO AT A TIME, UP OPPOSITE SIDES OF THE STREET TO WORK ON THE SECOND THREAT.

10. REPEAT THE DRILL AND ASK STUDENTS TO BEAT THEIR PREVIOUS SCORES.

11. FOLLOW THE SAME PROCEDURE FOR EACH OF THE REMAINING THREATS.

12. THEN HAVE THE PARTICIPANTS WORK ON TWO THREATS AT ONCE, THEN THREE, THEN FOUR, THEN FIVE, THEN SIX, THEN ALL SEVEN.

Table 21.2: Urban Fun Run

adjustments against simulated casualty assessment. To create new technique, they must take a show of hands from 20 or more of their compatriots and then field test that on which three-fourths can agree.

Even the most promising "street moves" are likely to fail unless continually practiced. Each officer should have no fewer than three regularly rehearsed tactical techniques for the most common criminal scenarios. Then, when the suspect shows up, that officer will already have the "muscle memory" of a generally appropriate response. This should allow him more quickly to adapt to unique circumstances.

The Most Useful Training Is Also the Most Enjoyable

The whole idea is to concentrate more on surprise than on firepower. In combat, they are interchangeable. There are as many indicators of surprise as there are methods. Many are easily measured. In addition to casualty assessment, there are speed, noise, and distance (as in how close one can sneak). Then, training becomes a series of competitions between tiny contingents, or against one's own past record.

Some of the best military-technique rehearsal courses could be easily converted to police use. In "the two-man fire and movement" course, the pair take turns providing cover fire and rushing.[14] In the "movement through urban terrain" course, participants progressively learn how to avoid getting shot in the city.[15] (See Table 21.2.)

The Duty Solution

Letting each group of 20 or more patrolmen or SWATs collectively decide, build, and test their own portfolio of "most-needed" movement techniques is the way to go. If every section or department were a mirror image of the others, their actions would be far too easy for the law breakers to predict. By training in this way, every officer's self-confidence and survivability would be automatically enhanced. That's because developing maneuvers takes the same thought process as tactical-decision making. U.S. policemen need more individual movement skills than do the GIs—because they more often have to close with an adversary alone. It's high time that they be better prepared for this role.

Tactical-decision games are best conducted in an actual street environment. Those in a classroom too often ignore micro-terrain. It is far better for a cop or soldier briefly to experience every possible door lock and furniture arrangement, than for him to become too accustomed to any particular set of circumstances.

Free play is the most enjoyable and productive of all the training mediums. The side with the fewest simulated casualties wins. GIs don't always have Multiple Integrated Laser Engagement System (MILES) gear, so instead they use three-second sight pictures on upright humans to determine casualties. For additional details, see Appendix A.

While Each Department Ponders

Before closing with any future suspect, all American policemen should attempt an East Asian procedure. After rehearsing in their minds (through visualization) each step of their movement toward the quarry, they arrive at what to do if he attacks. All U.S. military "point men" should do likewise. One's own life is definitely worth saving, and the 4GW assault on freedom-loving nations is far from over.

It's now or never for every part of the U.S. security establishment—whether intelligence, ground combat, or law enforcement—to streamline their operations. With the huge number of bottom-up adversaries now arrayed against the United States, their new agency-wide focus must be on lowest-echelon productivity.

22 _____ Conclusion

- How can the Pentagon more cheaply protect the world?
- Which part of its team has been grossly underutilized?

Grunts should be more than subservient gun platforms.

(Source: Courtesy of U.S. Air Force, from its website, www.af.mil, "Aim High" graphic by Tech.Sgt. Cody Vance, afg_030409_002.jpg)

The Problem in Layman's Terms

America has inherited a "top-down" way of doing things from its mostly European immigrants. While basing decisions on well-substantiated facts, its leaders determine all strategy. That's why the news stories are so carefully researched, the non-fiction publications so heavily edited, and the intelligence bureaucracy so huge. Yet, because only "big" issues can be fully corroborated, the governmental body of knowledge consists mostly of overall conclusions. Many of the associated details are too mundane or seemingly insignificant to confirm. Even if regularly reported by low-ranking personnel, they seldom reach the desk of their organizational leaders. This is what causes some of the more illogical governmental conclusions. We're losing in Vietnam, so one of Southeast Asia's most pristine jungles must be defoliated. There are illegal aliens crossing the Mexican border, so an electronic fence must be built across its entire 2,000-mile width. Or the enemy in Iraq has IEDs, so very expensive counter-IED technology is needed. In each case, a more simplistic (and cheaper) option is also available. In Vietnam, some world-class light-infantry training might have helped. Along the Mexican border, each stretch of territory might require its own defensive scheme. And in Iraq, dismounting the vehicles and then living off the local economy would have limited the number of IED targets.

This all-American way of doing business is fine when one's adversary comes from anywhere but Germany in Western Europe. However, it works less well on a student of Asian warfare. Throughout Asia, the culture is decidedly bottom up. That means more opportunities are realized through bottom-echelon sightings and exploited through collective effort. So doing is not inherently Communistic or bad. In fact, this is how the Americans of 1776 managed to do so well against the British.

Still, that's not the extent of the bad news. Since the end of the Korean War, several Asian armies have been further refining their ways to defeat the traditional foe—a technologically superior and fully supported Western military. Of late, they have come up with some very formidable improvements to Mao's already proven guerrilla formula. That makes studying the details of each Asian initiative absolutely crucial to a Western security agency, whether those details can be fully substantiated or not. Had U.S. leaders realized they were losing too many war supplies to half-naked saboteurs in Vietnam, things might have also turned out differently there. Sounds a lot like the Afghan *mujahideen's* strategy of "guerrilla war of a thousand cuts,"[1] doesn't it? That's because even non-state actors have learned how to do it.

To have much luck with a 4GW-wise Eastern foe, the very way this knowledge is collected in America must change. More emphasis must be put on the probable details of bottom-echelon enemy activity—whether they be martial, economic, political, psychological, or fully corroborated. As in police work, every aspect of the *modus operandi* must be studied.

A Slightly More Polite Way of Saying the Same Thing

Americans have had trouble defeating Asian foes because of the differences in their respective cultures. Through an unwanted heritage of European monarchy, the U.S. government continues to generate most of its actionable knowledge from the top. The president establishes the diplomatic/strategic focus, and then his intelligence agencies focus in on all associated threats. If Saudi Arabia, for example, were designated an official friend, then only the most blatant evidence of worldwide subversion by Saudi Arabia would ever be considered.

In the Orient, actionable knowledge is more often generated from the bottom. A low-ranking scout spots an enemy weakness, and then his commanders exploit this weakness. This diametrically opposed way of problem solving is cultural in nature and thus largely transcends any particular style of government. Yet, wherever a little "counterculture" might seem appropriate, proud Americans often abstain. The very distinct possibility of now losing an unconventionally fought WWIII might give them reason for pause.

The U.S. government can no longer "have it both ways." It must now choose between absolute control from the top, and enough lower-echelon flexibility to handle a "bottom up" foe. Whether that foe be Communist, Islamist, or criminal, he will exploit all grassroots opportunities. Even without an adversary, the lowest U.S. security echelons have trouble meshing "chain-of-command-delayed" orders with a constantly changing situation. The only way it can additionally handle a grassroots opponent is through an inordinate expenditure of manpower, ordnance, and money. Even that wasn't enough in Vietnam. With military manufacturing largely driving the U.S. economy, Washington wants no "equipment-free" solutions. Though U.S. troops performed well, it shouldn't have taken that much money and time to defeat the Iraqi insurgency. Unlike the Viet Cong, its members had no previous experience with guerrilla warfare.

The Most Reasonable "Nontraditional" Solution

This book may seem a little confusing to some. On one hand, it says China poses the greatest risk to U.S. security. On the other,

285

it recommends copying some of the PRC's very different organizational characteristics. Even if China were trying to collapse America from within, borrowing these particular management ideas could in no way accelerate this process. That's because Chinese bureaucracy is not solely the product of Mao Tse-Tung. The idea of collective thinking and bottom-up problem solving predates Communism by thousands of years. It's what the Asians have learned from far more societal experience. Considering America's present state of emergency, that which may seem a little counter-intuitive should still be considered. How Jesus proposed to "save everyone from their enemies" was as well.[2]

Something has been dragging America down, and it's not the political system. A representative republic is far superior to the veiled totalitarianism modern-day Chinese endure. Bureaucratic structure is not intractably wedded to any particular political system. It can be easily molded to fit any tenant or overseer. U.S. agencies could now embrace shorter chains of command and more bottom-up problem solving without endangering their missions. Nor would so doing risk a more Socialistic form of government. No one wants the erosion to individual freedoms that such a thing would entail.

Sadly, what is wrong with America can no longer be fixed at the ballot box (until nationwide referendums are allowed). Some President and Congress must at some point overhaul all national security agencies (to include the U.S. military). It makes little difference whether they be Republican or Democrat. While the former have always professed to like smaller government, they have yet to engineer a major bureaucratic shake-up. The size of each agency is not as important as its level of efficiency. Many could operate nearly as well with far fewer departments. Sadly, Western-style bureaucracies seem to take on a life of their own. They resist any change, however productive. Even their top executives have trouble altering the most mundane of procedures. Still, their organizations do still work for the U.S. government. They must obey its instructions. Almost every American security deficiency can be traced back to some structural excess or outmoded procedure.

Once enough streamlining has been accomplished, things will get a lot better. In the meantime, Appendices A and B have shown how—in a frontline unit—to counterbalance some of this headquarters inertia.

The External Threat

While Islamic insurgents often follow Mao's guerrilla method, it's now time to face the much greater threat posed by Mao's homeland. The PRC's ruling party has been much more subversive than it is politically correct to acknowledge. In effect, it has been manipulating both *jihadists* and West to achieve worldwide economic (and then political) domination.

After all, Mao's guerrilla method does already have its own "politicization" phase.[3] Of the six Western Hemisphere countries that still had rightist governments in mid-June 2011, three also had Maoist rebellions—Colombia *(FARC),* Peru (Shining Path), and Mexico *(EPR, EZLN,* and now *FARC*-assisted cartels). Honduras, Panama, and the Guianas also host Communist elements that operate more discreetly. While *FARC* was originally Marxist, it is now Maoist in both intent and method.[4] Its operatives have been spotted not only in Venezuela, Bolivia, Ecuador, Nicaragua, Mexico, Peru, Paraguay, and Brazil, but also in Honduras and Panama.[5] The PRC is Cuba's new "Sugar Daddy" and thus the hidden mentor of Cuban satellite Venezuela.[6] On 20 June 2011, *Time* reported that Ollanta Humala, longtime supporter of Hugo Chavez, had been elected Peru's next President.[7] Washington said nothing. It would appear that the old "Domino Theory" was finally being fulfilled.

Fully to realize that the U.S. is now under 4GW attack from China, one should only need evidence of similar aggression in other free countries. Here, the proof is almost always circumstantial. There, it can be more direct. Still, enough circumstantial evidence can—by itself—convict in any U.S. court of law.

For Those Who Missed It the First Time

Few now deny the global ramifications of China's economic expansion. There's even a website that documents it.[8] Still, as is clearly evident throughout the Western Hemisphere,[9] the ultimate Chinese objective is not economic, but rather political (with the trade and loan portion only its precursor).

China's "comprehensive warfare" strategy wears down enemy using non-military means. . . .

287

AVERTING **WWIII** through **Tiny Detachments**

. . . Col. Meng Xiansheng . . . defined the term as "the means of defeating enemies without waging a war through deploying a wide range of political, economic, cultural, diplomatic and military tactics."

Meng said "comprehensive warfare" [not only] advocates the use of non-violent means in handling state-to-state disputes, . . . but also fits with China's grand strategy of "peaceful development."[10]
— *Geostrategy-Direct,* 2 August 2006

A few of the lesser-known "coincidences" surrounding 9/11 are once again offered. The attack was not planned in Pakistan or Afghanistan as is commonly thought. Most of what happened on this tragic date had been envisioned by *al-Qaeda* operatives (as part of Operation Bojinka) in the Philippines in 1994. This is a matter of public record in the State of New York.[11] In February 1999, the PLA Publishing House released *Unrestricted Warfare* further discussing the effectiveness of "plane hijackings," "tall building(s)," "a bombing attack by bin Laden," and "a major explosion at the World Trade Center."[12] In January 2000, two of the 9/11 participants attended a "Terrorist Summit" in Kuala Lumpur.[13] Then, the same two may have accompanied their handler—Khallad—all the way to Hong Kong.[14] After the attack, one of original Operation Bojinka planners fled with his Chinese-Malaysian wife to pro-Chinese Cambodia.[15]

Among the subcategories of China's *Unrestricted Warfare* doctrine are the following: (1) financial; (2) trade; (3) resources; (4) regulatory; (5) smuggling; (6) drug; (7) diplomatic; (8) sanction; (9) economic aid; (10) network; (11) media; (12) information; (13) intelligence; (14) ideological; and (15) terrorist.[16] Wouldn't a long-term "drug" deluge cause more civilian casualties than any amount of "terrorism"? Yet, most Western leaders still see smuggled drugs as strictly a law enforcement challenge. On their watch, any combination of the other—more subliminal—types of *Unrestricted Warfare* might go completely unnoticed.

So the threat to the world appears to be much more serious than an economic downturn and shift toward democracy. Hopefully, this book has sufficiently demonstrated not only its Chinese, Islamist, and criminal make-up, but also its "quasi-expeditionary" solution. As before previous world wars, appeasement and isolationism are not the answer.

288

With the Pentagon mostly dedicated to new defense contracts, this book's cost-free proposal has very little chance of happening. When it's all about the equipment, people will always be a troublesome peripheral. The last three and most future wars can only be won through special-operations-qualified squads acting as force multipliers for indigenous forces. Those U.S. squads won't be able to do so in a really dangerous area without more light-infantry and UW ability. Both are best acquired through experimentation at the company level (which is generally not encouraged). As per maneuver warfare doctrine, control of these squads must be through "guidelines" and "technique refinement/rehearsal" vice "doctrine" and "detailed instructions." That's the only way to be in enough places at once to preclude a worldwide takeover by America's enemies.

The Asians—through their bottom-up cultural perspective—more easily see this. By some estimates, the number of Chinese special operators has now risen to one million of what used to be a 1.6 million man ground force. In 2009, the North Koreans also upped the number of commandos in their "Light Infantry Training Guidance Bureau" from 100,000 to 180,000.[17] That's how the Communists plan to exploit the Western mindset to bypass its firepower. Only this time, there will be "death by a thousand razor cuts" on a much larger scale and then a veritable sweep of leftist election victories.

Appendix A:
Bottom-Up Training

1. In 4th-Generation Warfare, U.S. grunts will always be outnumbered.

2. For enough skill to operate alone and in small units, they will need "bottom-up" training.

    a. There can be no true "Maneuver Warfare" capability without some decentralization of control and more bottom-echelon initiative.

    b. Each company must learn to operate as nine semi-independent maneuver squads.

        (1) Squads can fight like football teams.

            (a) If they've practiced and numbered several "plays" for each category of enemy contact.
            (b) If the squad leader asks his fire team leaders (by hand-and-arm signal) which play to run before picking.
            (c) If that play need not be run exactly as rehearsed (so individuals can react to unforeseen circumstances).

        (2) Each squad leader will have adequate control if all plays practiced in varied terrain before attempted in war.

        (3) Training for squad combat is like football too.

            (a) Individual, buddy team, fire team, and squad drills are followed by force-on-force scrimmage.
            (b) Instead of daily physical training (PT), squads do battledrills on cross-country runs with boots and rifles.

    c. Training must give every squad member initiative, tactical-decision-making practice, and nonpredictability.

        (1) Best way is to let the junior NCOs of each company collectively identify and fix their own tactical deficiencies.

(2) Companies no longer need identical squad maneuvers.

(3) Only through local experimentation can the lowest
echelons of a "top-down" organization
gain "world class" tactical proficiency.

d. Officers must control "bottom-up" training indirectly.

(1) By providing options from history.

(2) By choosing situations to be solved.

(3) By monitoring improvement in surprise
generated and simulated-casualties suffered.

3. Planning Phase.

a. CO and plt. leaders publish "mission-type" training order to
Gy.Sgt.—short list of squad combat situations to be solved.

(1) E.g., security patrol, counterambush, ambush, chance
contact, day attack, night attack, short-range infiltration,
urban attack, urban defense, sapper-oriented defense.

(2) Best are those involving large numbers of enemy soldiers,
because they will require total surprise.

b. Gy.Sgt. will function as facilitator of group knowledge (as
opposed to enforcer of organizational procedure).

c. Gy.Sgt. convenes NCO conference to record on the blackboard
what will be needed to comply with officers' goals.

(1) Group arrives at prerequisite skills for each situation—what
squads, fire teams, buddy teams, and individuals must do.

(2) Elementary "basics" will no longer be enough.

(a) All must be able to covertly shoot, move, and communicate.
(b) All must have microterrain appreciation, harnessing of
senses, night skills, deception, decision practice as well.

d. Gy.Sgt. then schedules supplementary instruction for
progressively larger elements (individuals first).

(1) Any weapons training will have one of two formats.

    (a) Explain, demonstrate, imitate, practice, test.
    (b) Create situation for students to solve (more
        retention and applicable to enemy weapons).

(2) Established tactical maneuvers taught through battledrills.

    (a) Attention gainer and lecture.
    (b) Demonstration and practical application.
        1 Outdoors.
        2 Blackboard or overhead projector.
        3 Sand table with miniatures.
    (c) Practical application testing (e.g., count U.S. losses).

(3) New tactical maneuvers taught thru "situation stations" (with participants allowed to arrive at own solutions).

(4) NCO assigned to each period of instruction.

    (a) Leaders of next-higher echelon will do the teaching.
    (b) Situation station "experiments" given to NCOs with
        "by-the-book" mentalities.

(5) Instructors told to refer to *The Last Hundred Yards* and *The Tiger's Way* for guidance on what to teach.

    (a) Fully tested maneuver warfare methods.
    (b) No squad-level maneuver in conflict with U.S. doctrine.

(6) All instruction will takes place near unit's headquarters or barracks with rubber rifles and makeshift training aids.

4. Execution Phase.

  a. Training is conducted for whole company at once.

    (1) Either sequentially or in "round-robin" format.

    (2) Normally in 20-minute sessions for 12-man "sticks."

    (3) Assigned instructor can ask any number of peers to help.

    (4) Most training consists of movement technique rehearsal.

(a) Success measured through surprise generated (speed, stealth, deception) or simulated-casualties suffered.

(b) Individuals and subunits are asked to compete with each other or improve themselves on successive tries.

(c) "Super squad" determined for each training period.

(5) Instructors statistically track how well the techniques they are teaching work, and keep notes on how to improve them.

b. Next comes the "Tactical Demonstration."

(1) Officers arrange training support and recreate situations.

(2) Squads run through situations under simulated fire.

(a) Machinegun and artillery simulators add realism.

(b) Surprise indicators and friendly casualties measured.

(3) Only recourse for dissatisfied officers is to change situations or pick another group facilitator (SNCO).

c. Then comes "Free Play" — a force-on-force exercise in which the side with the fewest simulated casualties wins.

(1) Sides required to solve—twice—certain situations for which technique was taught (e.g., two assaults on foe's camp).

(a) One side reverses its shirts.

(b) Sides assigned command posts (CPs) not too far apart.

(c) One third of each force defends own CP with no outposts.

(d) Two thirds of each force must assault enemy CP.

(e) Each man records any 3-second sight picture of upright foe or flour grenade hit within 10 feet of himself.

(f) Casualties reenter problem via own CP after short delay.

(g) Secretly seizing the enemy's flag nets bonus points (flag must be unattached and at ground level in CP).

(h) Umpires assess demerits for any bodily contact or not doing required events.

(2) At end of the event, sides are moved beyond earshot of each other while all counts are made and winner determined.

d. Finally, "Lessons-Learned Field Day" is held.

(1) All junior enlisted personnel are assembled in bleachers.

(2) Privates given chance to demonstrate better ways.
(3) Gy.Sgt. gauges worth of each way through show of hands.
(4) No promises made as to training changes.
(5) Troops reminded of existing "NCO-Conference" techniques
(6) New PT method demonstrated.

5. All squads are expected to practice existing NCO Conference movement techniques during daily PT.

   a. First some combat warm-ups.

      (1) Crawling races (with squad leader participating).
      (2) Duck walking as if as under a wall aperture.
      (3) Practice in window entry over any horizontal obstruction.

   b. Then each squad takes its own combat run with boots and rifles.

      (1) Move in "Indian" file (column) through all types of terrain.
      (2) Periodically slow to practice one of the squad techniques.
      (3) Make mental note of terrain limitations to each maneuver.

6. Gy.Sgt. convenes all NCOs quarterly to modify the company's portfolio of squad, fire team, buddy team and individual techniques, and to plan the next training evolution.

   a. Shortfalls in last training session identified.

      (1) If fewer mock casualties possible than with existing techniques.
      (2) Whether all instructor modifications considered.
      (3) Whether officers' and privates' expectations met.
      (4) Whether overall organizational doctrine still followed.

   b. All techniques modified as necessary.

7. Gy.Sgt. arrives at next training schedule.

8. This "bottom-up" cycle becomes a recurring and supplementary part of each company's training program (whether in garrison or deployed).

9. Only now is each battalion fully capable of employing its new tactical doctrine—Maneuver Warfare.

10. Only now can the theater commander employ the state of the small unit art—by starting an attack with a squad-sized penetration or building a defensive matrix from squad-sized strongpoints.

295

Appendix B:
What's Now Possible in War

Tall, "top-down" military organizations tend to be least proficient at their lowest echelons. Junior ranks get too little practice at initiative, decision making, and technique development. As a result, parent units underperform at short range in both conventional or unconventional combat. Both U.S. infantry services have long sought a way to correct this deficiency—to somehow harness their NCOs collective experience so as to help each individual to reach his/her own potential. That way has now been found. It has already been adopted (during a single Commanding Officer's tenure) by three Marine battalions. By making it mandatory throughout the infantry establishment, the Pentagon could fully compensate for this unfortunate by-product of its top-down structure.

Designed for use at the company level, this method accomplishes several different things simultaneously: (1) better tactical technique (through experimentation); (2) less predictability (no two companies alike); (3) better learning dynamic (competition between units); and (4) better morale, initiative, and tactical-decision making at the lowest echelons (every NCO a trainer).

When a company's squad leaders are allowed to train this way, they collectively develop three (or more) "numbered" maneuvers for each of the most probable combat scenarios (e.g., counterambushing). They then practice those maneuvers daily with their squads (during boots-and-rifles PT). When the enemy shows up (after deployment), the squad leader has only to ask his deployed fire team leaders (by gesture) which number to run. By simply considering their advice, he makes possible a "deliberate attack" (one already reconnoitered and rehearsed). As most professional tacticians can attest, trying to carry a "prepared enemy position" with anything less will result in too many casualties. That the squad leader can launch a deliberate attack so quickly makes possible the Holy Grail of short-range combat—momentum. This was the German Stormtroopers' secret to so much success in the Spring Offensives of 1918. Appendix A is the method that would make all of this possible.

Notes

SOURCE NOTES

Illustrations:

Picture on page vi reprinted under provisions of GNU Free
Documentation License, from *WIKIPEDIA ENCYCLOPEDIA,* s.v.
"Political Posters" and "Cultural Revolution." With file designator
"Destroy_the_old_world_Cultural_Revolution_poster.jpg," it
also appears as "Fair Usage" material under the following url:
www.api.freebase.com/view/m/0ccpgvv. Repro@iisgl.nl writes that
China may have trouble claiming copyrights retroactively to
any image created prior to the mid-1980's. As an educational
nonprofit, Posterity Press considers its reproduction to be fair usage,
but others must be more mindful of its possible copyright.
Copyright © n.d. All rights reserved.

Maps on pages 17, 22, 58, 60, 101, 112, 116, 124, 127, 142, 143, 144, 146,
148, 150, 168, 176, and 177 reproduced after written assurance from the
GENERAL LIBRARIES OF THE UNIVERSITY OF TEXAS AT
AUSTIN that they are in public domain.

Map on page 23 reprinted with permission of fordam.edu/halsall.
Entitled "The Muslim Empire: 750 CE," it comes from MEDIEVAL
SOURCEBOOK (http://www.fordham.edu/halsall/sbookmap.html),
and originally from H.G. Wells, *A Short History of the World*
(London: 1922). Copyright © indeterminate. All rights
reserved.

Map on pages 24, 61, and 62 reprinted under provisions of GNU Free
Documentation License, from *WIKIPEDIA ENCYCLOPEDIA,* s.v.
"Gilgit-Baltistan." They have map designators "Old_World_820.png,"
"Pakistan Northern.png," and "Northern_Areas_Pakistan.png." As an
educational nonprofit, Posterity Press considers its reproduction to be
fair usage, but others must be more mindful of its possible copyright.
Copyright © n.d. All rights reserved.

Map on page 25 reproduced after being unable to contact *RUPEE NEWS* (India). This image appears in its online article " 'Pakistan' Existed 5,000 Years Ago*" of* 27 November 2007. Appearing to be locally produced, it has map designator "indus-civilization-map.jpg." Copyright © 2007 by Rupee News. All rights reserved.

Picture on page 47 reprinted after written assurance from GLOBAL SECURITY that it does not own its copyright or know if it has one. This image appears at globalsecurity.org under "PLA History," and has file designator "C14053PictPowPpleArmy53.jpg." The same picture appears at Wikipedia.org, s.v. "People's Liberation Army," with file designator "peoples_army.jpg" and would be covered by the provisions of GNU Free Documentation License. It's not for sale as part of the 1ISH Collection at ChinesePosters.net. Repro@iisgl.nl writes that China may have trouble claiming copyrights retroactively to any image created prior to the mid-1980's. As an educational nonprofit, Posterity Press considers its reproduction to be fair usage, but others must be more mindful of its possible copyright. Copyright © n.d. All rights reserved.

Map on page 56 reproduced after being unable to contact the INSTITUTE OF CONFLICT MANAGEMENT (India). This illustration appeared in "A Spectre Haunting India," *The Economist,* 17 August 2006. Copyright © 2006 by Inst. of Conflict Management. All rights reserved.

Map on page 63 appears to have been produced by the GOVERNMENT OF PAKISTAN and is therefore deemed fair-usage material under certain conditions. The image appears in "Pakistan's Newest Province 'Gilgit-Baltistan'," *Rupee News,* 29 August 2009, and has map designator "karakorum-highway-chitral." As an educational nonprofit, Posterity Press considers its reproduction to be fair-usage, but others must be more mindful of its possible copyright. Copyright © n.d. All rights reserved.

Maps on pages 66 and 81 reproduced with permission of the United Nations Cartographic Section and Office on Drugs and Crime. They come from "Afghanistan," Map Number 3958, Revision 5, October 2005, and a composite of Maps 3 through 5, *WORLD DRUG REPORT 2010*, and China_India_Pakistan_map_tmp.pdf. The boundaries and names shown and the designations used on the latter do not imply official endorsement or acceptance by the United Nations. Copyrights © 2005 and 2010 by United Nations. All rights reserved.

Picture insert on pages 68, 86, and 259 reproduced after written
assurance from Cassell PLC (London, UK), that the copyright holders
for *WORLD ARMY UNIFORMS SINCE 1939,* text by Andrew Mollo
and Digby Smith, color plates by Malcolm McGregor and Michael
Chappell, can no longer be contacted. The illustrations are from
Parts I and II of an Orion Books reprint. Copyrights © 1975,
1980, 1981, 1983 by Blandford Books Ltd. All rights reserved.

Pictures on pages 84, 85, 256, and 276 reproduced with permission of
the SWEDISH ARMED FORCES and written assurance from Sorman
Information/Media (Vaxjo, Sweden) that the illustrator can no longer
be contacted, from *Soldf: Soldaten I Falt,* by Forsvarsmakten, with
illustrations by Wolfgang Bartsch. These drawings appear on pages
31, 145, 133, and 300 of the Swedish publication. Copyrights © 2001 by
Wolfgang Bartsch. All rights reserved.

Map on pages 113, 130, and 131 reprinted under provisions of GNU
Free Documentation License, from *WIKIPEDIA ENCYCLOPEDIA,*
s.v. "Somalia." They have map designators "HSM_map.png"
(by Kermanshahi), "Somalia_map_states_regions_districts.png"
(by Iglo), and "Silk_route.jpg" (from NASA/Goddard Space
Flight Center). Copyright © n.d. All rights reserved.

Map on page 117 created from University of Texas at Austin map
designator "yemen_sm_2010.gif" and CRITICALTHREATS.ORG map
designator "Yemen_Conflict_Map_Jan21201.gif. The latter comes
from "Yemen Conflict Map," by Katherine Zimmerman, Jonathan
Frist, and Chris Harnisch, American Enterprise Institute for Public
Policy Research, 12 May 2010. The boundaries and names shown, and
designations used, do not imply official endorsement or acceptance by
CriticalThreats.org. Copyright © 2010. All rights reserved.

Picture on page 206 was created by a government agency and is thus
deemed in the public domain. This is an official recruiting poster, image
designator "post_usmc_168th-birthday_ww2.jpg," retrieved from U.S.
Nat. Archives and Records Administration, by www.bluejacket.com.

Picture on page 252 reprinted after written assurance from GLOBAL
SECURITY that it does not own the copyright. This image appears at
its website under "PLA Uniforms and Insignia." Repro@iisgl.nl says that
China may have trouble claiming copyrights to any image created prior
to the mid-1980's. As an educational nonprofit, Posterity Press considers
its reproduction to be fair usage, but others must be more mindful of its
possible copyright. Copyright © n.d. All rights
reserved.

Picture on page 259 was created by a government agency and is thus deemed in the public domain. It comes from *A Concise History of the Unites States Marine Corps 1775-1969,* by Capt. William D. Parker, sketch by Capt. Donald L. Dickson (Washington, D.C.: History Division, Headquarters Marine Corps, 1970), p. 62.

Picture on pages 267 reproduced with permission of Dr. Anatol Taras, Minsk, Belarus, from *PODGOTOVKA RAZVEGCHIKA: SISTEMA SPETSNAZA GRU,* by A.E. Taras and F.D. Zaruz. The illustration is from p. 330 of the original work. Copyright © 1998 by A.E. Taras and F.D. Zaruz. All rights reserved.

Picture on page 271 reprinted after asking permission of CKSINFO. Advertised as free only for educational purposes, this picture appears at the following url: www.cksinfo.com/clipart/society/police/police.png. Copyright © n.d. by cks.info. All rights reserved.

Picture on page 283 was created by a government agency and is thus deemed in the public domain. It comes from the U.S. Air Force website, www.af.mil. Entitled "Aim High," this graphic by Tech.Sgt. Cody Vance has image designator afg_030409_002.jpg.

Text:

Reprinted after asking permission of *THE AUSTRALIAN CONSERVATIVE,* from the following article: "Iran's Global Terrorist Reach," by Dr. Walid Phares, 12 July 2010. Copyright © 2010 by the Australian Conservative. All rights reserved.

Reprinted after being unable to contact *THE DAILY STAR* (Lebanon), from the following article: "The Battle That Helped Change the Course of the 'Israeli' Occupation," 6 September 2000. Copyright © 2000 by the Daily Star. All rights reserved.

Reprinted with permission of *GEOSTRATEGY-DIRECT,* from the following article(s): (1) "Iran's Improved Fajr-5 Rockets Can Be Fired Remotely," 31 May 2006; and (2) "China's 'Comprehensive Warfare' Strategy Wears Down Enemy Using Non-Military Means," 2 August 2006. Copyrights © 2006 by East-West Services. All rights reserved.

Reprinted after being unable to contact *DEBKAFILE* (Israel), from the following article: "New Warfront Opens in Iraq Three Months before Handover," by Art Theyson, 5 April 2004. Copyright © 2004 by DEBKAfile. All rights reserved.

Reprinted with permission of the CENTER FOR STRATEGIC AND INTERNATIONAL STUDIES (Washington, D.C.), from the following article(s): (1) "Iran's Developing Military Capabilities," working draft, by Anthony H. Cordesman, 14 December 2004; and (2) "Iran's Revolutionary Guards, the Al Quds Force, and Other Intelligence and Paramilitary Forces," working draft, by Anthony H. Cordesman, 16 August 2007. Copyrights © 2004 and 2007 by Center for Strategic and International Studies. All rights reserved.

Reprinted with permission of *GLOBAL SECURITY* (Alexandria, VA), from the following databank entry: "Tibet," n.d. Copyright © n.d. by Global Security. All rights reserved.

Reprinted with implicit permission of *SOUTH ASIA INTELLIGENCE REVIEW,* Institute for Conflict Management (www.satp.org in India), from the following databank entry: "People's Liberation Army of NE India," n.d. Copyright © n.d. by the South Asia Intelligence Review. All rights reserved.

Reprinted with permission of CHENNAI CENTRE FOR CHINA STUDIES (India), from the following article: "China Corrects Diplomatic Faux Pas, but Maintains Presence in Gilgit-Baltistan," B. Raman, C3S Paper No. 586, 5 September 2010. Copyright © 2010 by Chennai Centre for China Studies. All rights reserved.

Reprinted after asking permission of *NEWSMAX* (West Palm Beach, FL), from the following article: "U.S. Bombs Chinese Network in Afghanistan, PRC Sold Taliban Advanced Air Defense System," by Charles R. Smith, 20 October 2001. Copyright © 2001 by Newsmax. All rights reserved.

Reprinted after asking permission of COUNCIL ON FOREIGN RELATIONS (New York), from the following databank entry: "Modernizing the People's Liberation Army of China," by Carin Zissis, Backgrounder, 5 December 2006. Copyright © 2006 by Council on Foreign Relations. All rights reserved.

Reprinted after being unable to contact the INTERNATIONAL INSTITUTE OF SOCIAL HISTORY (Holland), from the following databank entry: "Military Industrial Complex," n.d. Copyright © n.d. by International Institute of Social History. All rights reserved.

Reprinted with permission of the United Nations (New York), from *WORLD DRUG REPORT 2010, by* United Nations Office on Drugs and Crime. Copyright © 2010 by United Nations. All rights reserved.

Reprinted after being unable to contact *REDIFF NEWS* (India), from the following article: "Pakistan Is Handing over De-Facto Control of the Strategic Gilgit-Baltistan Region," 28 August 2010. Copyright © 2010 by Rediff News. All rights reserved.

Reprinted after being unable to contact *TIMES OF INDIA* (India), from the following article: "Pak Ceded Control of Gilgit to China," by Chidanand Rajghatta, 10 September 2010. Copyright © 2010 by Times of India. All rights reserved.

Reprinted after asking permission of the AMERICAN FOREIGN POLICY COUNCIL (Washington, D.C.), from its following investigative report: "The Panama Canal in Transition: Threats to U.S. Security and China's Growing Role in Latin America," by Al Santoli, 23 June 1999. Copyright © 1999 by Al Santoli. All rights reserved.

Reprinted with permission of CENTER FOR DEFENSE INFORMATION (Washington, D.C.), from "Eliminating Terrorist Sanctuaries: The Case of Iraq, Iran, Somalia and Sudan," 10 December 2001. Copyright © 2001 by Center for Defense Information. All rights reserved.

Reprinted after asking permission of C. Hurst & Co., Ltd. (London), from *INSIDE AL-QAEDA: GLOBAL NETWORK OF TERROR,* by Rohan Gunaratna. Copyright © 2002 by Rohan Gunaratna. All rights reserved.

Reprinted after being unable to contact *FRIDAY TIMES* (Pakistan), from the following series of articles: "Governance Crisis," by Mohammad Amir Rana, Parts I through V, 7 July - 11 August 2010. Copyright © 2010 by Friday Times. All rights reserved.

Reprinted after being unable to contact *DAILY TIMES* (Pakistan), from the following article: "Jamaat-e-Islami: The Fountainhead of Religious Extremism," by Yasser Latif Hamdani, 20 May 2010. Copyright © 2010 by Daily Times. All rights reserved.

Reprinted after asking permission of *LONG WAR JOURNAL* (Pakistan), from the following articles: (1) "Waziristan-Based Terror Group Takes Credit for Lahore Assault," by Bill Roggio, 30 March 2009; (2) "Pakistani Military Hits Taliban in Orakzai," by Bill Roggio, 17 November 2009; and (3) "Pakistani Commandos Break Siege on Army Headquarters," by Bill Roggio, 10 October 2009. Copyrights © 2009 by Public Mulitmedia Inc. All rights reserved.

ENDNOTES

Preface

1. Arkady Shipunov and Gennady Filimonov, "Field Artillery to be Replaced with Shmel Infantry Flamethrower," *Military Parade* (Moscow), issue 29, September 1998.
2. General Patton, as quoted in *Hitler's Last Gamble,* by Trevor N. Dupuy, David L. Bongard, and Richard C. Anderson, Jr. (New York: HarperPerennial, 1994), pp. 498, 499.
3. Lt.Gen. Arthur S. Collins Jr., U.S. Army (Ret.), *Common Sense Training — A Working Philosophy for Leaders* (Novato, CA: Presidio Press, 1978), p. 214.
4. Maj.Gen. Edwin Simmons USMC (Ret.), in "An Entirely New War," *Korea — the Unknown War* (London: Thames TV in assoc. with WGBH Boston, 1990), NC Public TV, n.d.
5. Maj.Gen. Robert H. Scales, U.S. Army (Ret.), *Firepower in Limited War* (Washington, D.C.: Nat. Defense Univ. Press, 1990), pp. 4, 5.
6. Memorandum for the record by H.J. Poole.
7. Ibid.
8. Pope John Paul II, as quoted in *Dragon Days,* by H. John Poole (Emerald Isle, NC: Posterity Press, 2007), p. xxix.

Chapter 1: *Introduction*

1. Memorandum for the record by H.J. Poole.
2. Rohan Gunaratna, *Inside al-Qaeda: Global Network of Terror* (Lahore: Vanguard, 2002), pp. 178-181; Mir, *The True Face of Jihadis* (Lahore: Mashal Books, 2004), pp. 183, 184; "Sipah-e-Sahaba," by Animesh Roul, *Unmasking Terror,* vol. I, ed. Heffelfinger (Washington, D.C: Jamestown Foundation, 2005), p. 314; "Comprehensive Report on Suspected Terrorist Support Network" (N.p., n.d.), p. 1, from *Inside al-Qaeda,* by Gunaratna, p. 178.
3. "Path to 9/11," ABC's News Online, 10 September 2006; Global Security (globalsecurity.org), s.v. "Project Bojinka"; *Wikipedia Encyclopedia,* s.v. "Oplan Bojinka" and "Ramzei Yousef."
4. "Philippines: U.S. Missed 9/11 Clues Years Ago," by Maria Ressa, CNN Online, 26 July 2003.
5. "The Spy Factory," PBS's *Nova,* NC Public TV, 3 July 2010; Gunaratna, *Inside al-Qaeda,* p. 196.

6. H. John Poole, *Dragon Days: Time for "Unconventional" Tactics* (Emerald Isle, NC: Posterity Press, 2007), pp. 42-44; Nat. Commission on Terrorist Attacks upon the United States, chapt. 5 of its report, footnotes 59-61; "The Emir," *Unmasking Terror,* vol. I, ed. Heffelfinger (Washington, D.C: Jamestown Foundation, 2005), pp. 402, 403.

7. "Philippines: U.S. Missed 9/11 Clues Years Ago," by Ressa.

8. "Profile: Al-Qaeda 'Kingpin'," BBC's News Online, 28 September 2006; Erika Kinetz, "U.S. Congress Warms to Cambodia," *Christian Science Monitor,* 14 March 2007, p. 4; *Wikipedia Encyclopedia,* s.v. "Responsibility for the September 11, 2001 Attacks" and "Riduan Isamuddin."

9. "FBI Informant Says Agents Missed Chance to Stop 9/11 Ringleader Mohammed Atta," by Brian Ross and Vic Walter, ABC's News Online, 10 September 2009.

10. Michael Lee Lanning and Dan Cragg, *Inside the VC and the NVA: The Real Story of North Vietnam's Armed Forces* (New York: Ivy Books, 1992)*,* p. 211.

11. Ibid., pp. 99-102.

12. DEA Chief Jack Dawn in testimony before the Senate Intel. Committee, and CIA assessment in September 1988, as quoted in *Seeds of Terror,* by Gretchen Peters (New York: Thomas Dunne Books, 2009), pp. 28, 51.

13. *National Drug Threat Assessment (for) 2009,* NDIC, December 2008; *National Drug Threat Assessment (for) 2010,* NDIC, February 2010; *World Drug Report 2009,* UNODC, November 2009; *World Drug Report 2010,* UNODC, 25 June 2010.

14. *National Drug Threat Assessment (for) 2010,* NDIC.

15. Texas police officer, in conversation with author on 16 May 2011.

16. ABC's Nightly News, 29 March 2010; "Hooked: Seattle High School Battles Heroin Addiction," ABC's News Online, retrieved in October 2010.

17. "White House Czar Calls for End to 'War on Drugs'," by Gary Fields, *Wall Street Journal Online,* 14 May 2009; "Drug Policy Changes Under New Director," NPR's News Online, 3 November 2009; Drug Czar, as quoted on NPR's "Morning Edition" News, mid-2010.

18. Akhtar Rehman (Pakistani ISI head), as quoted in *Silent Soldier,* by Brigadier Yousaf (South Yorkshire, UK: Leo Cooper, n.d.).

Chapter 2: *The National Intelligence Estimate*

1. *CIA—The World Factbook* (www.cia.gov)*,* s.v. "China."

2. Adm. Mike Mullen, as quoted by NPR's "Morning Edition" News, 6 July 2010.

3. "Blair's Resignation Follows Rocky Ride as DNI," CNN Online, 21 May 2010.

4. "Analysts: By 2025, U.S. Won't Be Top World Power," by Tom Gjelten, NPR's "Morning Edition" News, 21 November 2008, review of *Global Trends 2025: The National Intelligence Council's 2025 Project,* as still available from this url: www.dni.gov/nic/NIC_2025_project.html. (This work will henceforth be cited as "Analysts: By 2025.")

5. CBS's "Sixty Minutes," 29 August 2010.

6. "Analysts: By 2025."

7. Ibid.

8. Ibid.

9. Ibid.

10. Ibid.

11. Ibid.

12. *CIA — The World Factbook* (www.cia.gov), s.v. "China."

13. U.S. Customs Service Report, as quoted in *The China Threat,* by Bill Gertz (Washington, D.C.: Regnery Publishing, 2002), pp. 90, 91.

14. H. John Poole, *Expeditionary Eagles: Outmaneuvering the Taliban* (Emerald Isle, NC: Posterity Press, 2010), pp. 46-48.

15. "Russia's Georgia Invasion May Be About Oil," by Rachel Martin, ABC's News Online, 16 August 2008.

15. "Trio Sign Up for Turkmen Gas," *Upstream* (Internat. Oil and Natural Gas Newspaper, Norway), 25 April 2008; "Afghan Pipeline Raises Security Questions," by Travis Lupick, *Global Research,* 21 July 2008; *Wikipedia Encyclopedia,* s.v. "Trans-Afghan Pipeline."

17. Amiuzadeh (Deputy Minister of . . . Iran), "Special Address to the Federation of Indian Chambers of Commerce and Industry," New Delhi, 22 July 2003; "Ambassadors in Pakistan Visit Gwadar Port," Xinjua News Agency, 11 January 2002; *Wikipedia Encyclopedia,* s.v. "Hazara" and "Karakoram Highway."

18. Bill Gertz, *The China Threat* (Washington, D.C.: Regnery Publishing, 2002. p. 187; Energy Info. Administration Map, from "A Natural-Gas Gang," *Time,* 16 April 2007, p. 16; Robert A. Manning, *The Asia Energy Factor* (New York: Polygrave, 2000), in *China: The Gathering Threat,* by Constantine Menges (Nashville, TN: Nelson Current, 2005), p. 379.

19. Poole, *Dragon Days,* pp. 60, 61.

20. Maria rost Rublee, "Foreign Policy Responses to Aggressive Territorial Moves: The Case of the Spratley Islands," *International Affairs Review,* Summer 1996, in *China: The Gathering Threat,* by Constantine Menges (Nashville, TN: Nelson Current, 2005), p. 295.

21. NPR's "Morning Edition" News, 28 April 2010.

22. "China in Angola: An Emerging Energy Partnership," by Paul Hare, Jamestown Foundation, *China Brief*, vol. 6, issue 22, 8 November 2006; "China and Angola Strengthen Bilateral Relationship," by Loro Horta, *Power and Interest News Report*, 23 June 2006; *China's Rising Power in Africa,* Part 3, "China, Congo Trade for What the Other Wants," by Gwen Thompkins, NPR, 30 July 2008.

23. "Ecuador Offers Concession of Manta Air Base to China, Declines to Renew Contract with U.S.," by Vittorio Hernandez, AHN News (Ecuador), 26 November 2007.

Chapter 3: *The Islamist Threat*

1. *Pakistan: A Country Study,* ed. Peter R. Blood, Fed. Research Div., Library of Congress, Area Handbook Series, Hdqts. Dept. of the Army, DA Pamphlet 550-48 (Washington, D.C.: U.S. Govt. Printing Office, 1995), pp. 4-5; "Divine Calendars Testify of Abraham, Isaac, and Jacob," by John P. Pratt, *Meridian Magazine,* 11 September 2003.

2. Gregory D. Johnson, "Yemen Accuses Iran of Meddling in Its Internal Affairs," Jamestown Foundation, *Terrorism Focus,* vol. 4, issue 2, 20 February 2007"; "Yemen Intercepts Iranian Ship with Arms," UPI, 28 October 2009.

3. "APNewsBreak: Nigeria Links Iran to Arms Shipment," by Bashir Adigun and Jon Gambrell, Yahoo News, 11 November 2010.

4. Gretchen Peters, *Seeds of Terror: How Heroin Is Bankrolling the Taliban and al-Qaeda* (New York: Thomas Dunne Books, 2009), p. 159; "Afghan Rebels Using Iranian Arms: Canadian Defense Minister," from AFP, 26 December 2007.

5. "Changes in War Against Latin America's Illicit Trafficking," by David A. Fulghum, *Aviation Week,* 27 April 2010.

6. *Tehran's War of Terror and Its Nuclear Delivery Capability*, by Stephen E. Hughes (Victoria, Canada: Trafford Publishing, 2007), p. 158. [This work will henceforth be cited as *Tehran's War of Terror.]*

7. "Iran: U.S. Concerns and Policy Responses," by Kenneth Katzman, CRS Report for Congress, Order Code RL32048, 26 October 2010, p. 35.

8. *Al-Hadath* (Jordan), in FBIS-NES-96-108, May 27, 1996, p. 9, and in *Al-Sharq Al-Awsat,* FBIS-NES-96-110, June 5, 1996, pp. 1, 4; A. J. Venter, "Iran Still Exporting Terrorism," *Jane's Intelligence Review,* November, 1997, pp. 511-516; both from Anthony H. Cordesman, "Iran's Revolutionary Guards, the Al Quds Force, and Other Intelligence and Paramilitary Forces," working draft (Washington, D.C.: Ctr. for Strategic and Internat. Studies, 16 August 2007, p 8.

9. Anthony H. Cordesman (Strategy Chair), "Iran's Revolutionary Guards, the Al Quds Force, and Other Intelligence and Paramilitary Forces," working draft (Washington, D.C.: Ctr. for Strategic and Internat. Studies, 16 August 2007), pp. 3, 8; Abdul Hussein al-Obeidi, AP, "Holy City Najaf Fighting Worst Since Saddam Fell," *Jacksonville Daily News* (NC), 7 August 2004, pp. 1A, 4A; Babak Dehganpisheh, "A War's Hidden Hands," *Newsweek,* 6 September 2004, pp. 52-53; "Shiite Radicals Join with Sunni Insurgents in Ramadi," *DEBKAfile*, 7 April 2004.

10. "Exporting the Revolution: Iran's al-Quds Force," Red Cell Intel. Group, course announcement, n.d.; Cordesman, "Iran's Revolutionary Guards . . . ," pp. 3, 8; Barbara Slavin, "Iran Helped Overthrow the Taliban, Candidate Says," *USA Today,* 10 June 2005, p. 14A.

11. "Iran: U.S. Concerns and Policy Responses," by Katzman, pp. 20, 38, 40, 42, 45.

12. Cordesman, "Iran's Revolutionary Guards . . . ," p. 9.

13. Anthony H. Cordesman (Strategy Chair), "Iran's Developing Military Capabilities," working draft (Washington, D.C.: Ctr. for Strategic and Internat. Studies, 14 December 2004), pp. 35-38.

14. Gunaratna, *Inside al-Qaeda,* pp. 40, 206; Ahmed Rashid, "Taliban Ready for 'Decisive' Push," *Daily Telegraph* (London), 22 July 1999, in "Afghanistan: Crisis of Impunity," by Robin Batty and David Hoffman, *Human Rights Watch,* vol. 13, no. 3(c), July 2001, p. 32.

15. Edward Cody and Molly Moore, "Analysts Attribute Hezbollah's Resilience to Zeal, Secrecy and Iranian Funding," *Washington Post,* 14 August 2006.

16. "Iran's Improved Fajr-5 Rockets Can Be Fired Remotely," *Geostrategy-Direct,* 31 May 2006.

17. Cordesman, "Iran's Revolutionary Guards . . . ," p. 10.

18. Maj.Gen. Robert H. Scales, U.S. Army (Ret.), "Infantry and National Priorities," *Armed Forces Journal,* December 2007, pp. 14-17.

19. Ibid.

20. Lee Glendinning, "The Secret World of Palestinian Tunnels," *Times Online* (UK), 27 June 2006; ABC's Morning News, 12 July 2006.

21. Sam Ghattas, AP, "Nine Israeli Soldiers Killed in Fighting in South Lebanon," *Jacksonville Daily News* (NC), 27 July 2006, pp. 1A, 2A; ABC's Nightly News, 18-20 July 2006.

22. ABC's Nightly News, 28 July 2006.

23. Ibid.

24. Embassy World, s.v. "Embassy Listings for North Korea," from its website, www.embassyworld.com; British private website, http://uk.geocities.com/hkgalbert/kpdo.htm.

25. "North Koreans Assisted Hezbollah with Tunnel Construction," Jamestown Foundation, *Terrorism Focus,* vol. III, issue 30, August 2006.

26. Ghattas, "Nine Israeli Soldiers Killed in Fighting in South Lebanon," pp. 1A, 2A.

27. Hala Jaber, "Hezbollah: We've Planned This for 6 Years," *The Sunday Times* (London), 30 July 2006.

28. Hamza Hendawi, "Israel Hits Beirut; Hezbollah Rockets Israel," from AP, 3 August 2006.

29. "Hizbullah Using Tunnels, Bunkers to Frustrate Israelis' Advance," *World Tribune* (Springfield, VA), 7 August 2006.

30. Ibid.

31. Nicholas Blanford, Daniel McGrory, and Stephen Farrell, "Tactics That Have Kept the Middle East's Most Powerful Army at Bay," *The Times* (UK), 10 August 2006.

32. Kevin Peraino, Babak Dehghanpisheh, and Christopher Dickey, "Eye for an Eye," *Newsweek,* 14 August 2006, p. 22; Ravi Nessman, AP, "Israelis Step Up Offensive," *Jacksonville Daily News* (NC), 10 August 2006, p. 2A.

33. Blanford et al, "Tactics That Have Kept the Middle East's Most Powerful Army at Bay."

34. Cody and Moore, "Analysts Attribute Hezbollah's Resilience to Zeal, Secrecy and Iranian Funding."

35. Nicholas Blanford, "Hizbullah's Resilience Built on Years of Homework," *Christian Science Monitor,* 11 August 2006, p. 4.

36. Scott Peterson, "Unresolved: Disarming Hizbullah," *Christian Science Monitor,* 15 August 2006, pp. 1, 10.

37. "Why Did Armored Corps Fail in Lebanon," by Hanan Greenberg, Israeli News, 30 August 2006.

38. Ali Jalali and Lester W. Grau, *Afghan Guerrilla Warfare: In the Words of the Mujahideen Fighters* (St. Paul, MN: MBI Publishing, 2001), p. 401.

39. Lt.Cmdr. Youssef H. Aboul-Enein, "The Hezbollah Model: Using Terror and Creating a Quasi-State in Lebanon," *Marine Corps Gazette,* June 2003.

40. David Gardner, "'Israel': Hizbollah Sharpens Up Its Tactics," *London Financial Times,* 1997.

41. Lt.Col. David Eshel (IDF, Ret.), "Counterguerrilla Warfare in South Lebanon," *Marine Corps Gazette,* July 1997, p. 42.

42. Yossi Melman, "Ambush of Naval Squad 'No Accident'," Ha'aretz (Tel Aviv), 13 August 1998.

43. Scott Peterson, "In a War It Cannot Win, Israel Tries New Tactics," *Christian Science Monitor,* 9/20 October 1997.

44. Melman, "Ambush of Naval Squad 'No Accident'."

45. Martin van Creveld, *The Sword and the Olive: A Critical History of the Israeli Defense Force* (New York: PublicAffairs, Perseus Books, 1998), p. 304.

46. Melman, "Ambush of Naval Squad 'No Accident'."

47. "The Battle That Helped Change the Course of the 'Israeli' Occupation," *Daily Star* (Lebanon), 6 September 2000.

48. Naomi Segal, Jewish Telegraphic Agency, "IDF Absolved of Blame in Deaths of Naval Commandos in Lebanon," *San Francisco Jewish Community Publication,* 31 October 1997.

49. Grand Floridian hotel waitress (first-generation Lebanese immigrant), in conversation with author on 20 December 2008.

50. *Nationmaster Encyclopedia* (www.nationmaster.com), s.v. "Hezbollah," as retrieved 5 July 2004.

51. G.I. Wilson, "Iraq: Fourth Generation Warfare (4GW) Swamp," *Militarycom,* 18 June 2004.

52. "Shiites March throughout Middle East," from AP, *Jacksonville Daily News* (NC), 22 May 2004, p. 10A; "Hizbullah Offers to Pay Up to Five Times More for Suicide Attacks," *Geostrategy-Direct,* week of 22 February 2005.

53. "Hizbullah Suspected of Joining Sunni Insurgents," *Iraqi News,* 17 February 2005.

54. Michael Rubin, "Ansar al-Sunna: Iraq's New Terrorist Threat," *Middle East Intelligence Bulletin,* vol. 6, no. 5, May 2004.

55. H. John Poole, *Militant Tricks: Battlefield Ruses of the Islamic Insurgent* (Emerald Isle, NC: Posterity Press, 2005), p. 63; Company commander of 3rd Battalion, 7th Marines, in conversation with author during training evolution of 15, 16 January 2005.

56. Scott Peterson, "Shadows of Tehran over Iraq," *Christian Science Monitor,* 19 April 2004, pp. 1, 10.

57. Art Theyson, "New Warfront Opens in Iraq Three Months before Handover," *DEBKAfile* (Israel), 5 April 2004.

58. Ibid.

59. Howard Lafranchi, "Anti-Iran Sentiment Hardening Fast," *Christian Science Monitor,* 22 July 2002, pp. 1, 10.

60. Aaron Mannes, *Profiles in Terror: Guide to Middle East Terror Organizations* (Lanham, MD: Rowman & Littlefield, 2004), p. 163.

61. Nicholas Blanford, "Hizbullah Reelects Its Leader," *Christian Science Monitor,* 19 August 2004, p. 6; Baer, *See No Evil,* and Faye Bowers, "A Collaboration between al-Qaeda and Hizbullah . . . ," *Christian Science Monitor,* n.d., in *Warring on Terrorism,* by Stephen E. Hughes, part I (internet piece), 2005, p. 35.

62. "Top Iranian Defector on Iran's Collaboration with Iraq, North Korea, Al-Qa'ida, and Hizbullah," Middle East Media Research Inst., Special Dispatch No. 473, 21 February 2003.

63. Peter Ford, "A Suspect Emerges As Key Link in Terror Chain," *Christian Science Monitor,* 23 January 2004, pp. 1, 7.

64. Michael D. Maples, Director of Defense Intel. Agency, before the Committee on Senate Select Intelligence, 11 January 2007, in Cordesman, "Iran's Revolutionary Guards . . . ," p. 8.

65. "Yemen: A Hezbollah Withdrawal," *STRATFOR Weekly,* 10 February 2010; Islami Davet Islamic Politics and Cultural Website (Turkey), as viewed on 26 November 2010.

66. "Yemen's War," *The Economist,* 19 November 2010.

67. "Iranian Proxies: An Intricate and Active Web," by Scott Stewart, *STRATFOR Weekly,* 3 February 2010.

68. "Iran's Global Terrorist Reach," by Dr. Walid Phares, *The Australian Conservative*, 12 July 2010.

69. NPR's "Morning Edition" News, 17 February 2011.

70. Ibid.

71. Ibid.

72. "Iranian Proxies," by Stewart

73. Ibid.

74. "Iran's Global Terrorist Reach," by Phares.

75. "Why West Africa Cannot Break Its Drug Habit," by Rose Skelton, BBC's News Online, 21 June 2010; *World Drug Report 2009,* U.N. Office on Drugs and Crime, p. 74, 168; "Mystery Surrounds Alleged Hezbollah Links to Drug Arrests in Curacao," by Chris Zambelis, Jamestown Foundation, *Terrorism Monitor,* vol. 7, issue 18, 25 June 2009; "Guinea Bissau: Hezbollah, Al Qaida and the Lebanese Connection," by Marco Vernaschi, pulitzercenter.org, 19 June 2009; "Drug Seizures in West Africa Prompt Fears of Terrorist Links," by Jamie Doward, *Guardian Observer Online* (www.guardian.co.uk), 29 November 2009.

76. "Iran's Global Terrorist Reach," by Phares.

77. "Hezbollah Chooses Lebanon's Next Prime Minister," by Anthony Shadid, *New York Times Online,* 24 January 2011.

78. "Rogues' Gallery," by Bobby Ghosh, *Time,* 2 May 2011.

79. NPR's "All Things Considered," 27 February 2011; "Will Arab World's Freedom Wave Reach Iran or China," by John Hughes, *Christian Science Monitor,* 21 March 2011, p. 33.

80. H. John Poole, *Terrorist Trail: Backtracking the Foreign Fighter* (Emerald Isle, NC: Posterity Press, 2006), p. 8; Gunaratna, *Inside al-Qaeda,* pp. 139, 152, 153, 158; "Eliminating Terrorist Sanctuaries: The Case of Iraq, Iran, Somalia and Sudan," Ctr. for Defense Info. (Washington, D.C.), 10 December 2001.

81. "Special Report: Iran and the Saudi's Countermove on Bahrain," by George Freidman, *STRATFOR Weekly,* 14 March 2011.

82. Robin Wright and Peter Baker, "Iraq, Jordan See Threat to Election from Iran," *Washington Post,* 8 December 2004, p. A01.

83. "U.S. Resists Role for Iraq Cleric," by Sam Dagher, *Wall Street Journal Online,* 6 October 2010.

84. Peterson, "Shadows of Tehran over Iraq," pp. 1, 10; Ann Scott Tyson, "Sadr's Militia Regrouping, Rearming," *Christian Science Monitor,* 15 July 2004, pp. 1, 7; Jamie Tarabay, AP, "U.S. Chopper Downed amid Fierce Fighting in Iraq," AOL News, 5 August 2004.

85. "U.S. Resists Role for Iraq Cleric," by Dagher.

86. "Iraq's New Government," editorial, *Washington Post Online,* 13 November 2010.

87. Robin Batty and David Hoffman, "Afghanistan: Crisis of Impunity," *Human Rights Watch,* vol. 13, no. 3(c), July 2001, pp. 35-39; Poole, *Militant Tricks,* pp. 139-141.

88. "Afghanistan's President: Partner or Obstacle," by Soraya Sarhaddi Nelson, NPR's "Morning Edition" News, 24 March 2010.

89. "Sacks of Cash," by Sami Yousafzai and Ron Moreau, *Newsweek,* 8 November 2010, p. 8; "Afghan President Hamid Karzai . . . Accepts Bags of Money," News in Brief, *Christian Science Monitor,* 8 November 2010, p. 9; "Show Me the Money," *Time,* 8 November 2010, p. 33.

90. Richard Clarke (former U.S. antiterrorism czar), on ABC's Morning News, 7 June 2007.

91. "Sacks of Cash," by Yousafzai and Moreau, p. 8.

Chapter 4: *The Communist Threat*

1. *CIA — The World Factbook* (www.cia.gov), s.v. "Cuba," "China," "Korea, North," "Laos," and "Vietnam."

2. "South Korea Says North Torpedoed Ship," by Jack Kim and Ross Colvin, Reuters Online, 20 Mary 2010; "North Korea Launched an Artillery Barrage . . . ," News in Brief, *Christian Science Monitor,* 6 December 2010, p. 9.

3. David G. Winneck, "The South China Sea Dispute Background Briefing," manuscript, 11 February 1999, and Maria rost Rublee, "Foreign Policy Responses to Aggressive Territorial Moves: The Case of the Spratley Islands," *Internat. Affairs Review,* Summer 1996, both in *China: The Gathering Threat,* by Constantine Menges (Nashville, TN: Nelson Current, 2005), pp. 294-297.

4. Energy Info. Administration Map, from "A Natural-Gas Gang," *Time,* 16 April 2007, p. 16.

5. *Wikipedia Encyclopedia,* s.v. "Hainan Island Incident."

6. "U.S. Navy Provoked South China Sea Incident, China Says," by Mark Mcdonald, *New York Times Online,* 10 March 2009.

7. "China's Young Officers and the 1930's Syndrome," by Ambrose Evans-Pritchard, *The Telegraph Online* (UK), 7 September 2010.

8. "Syrian Reactor Detailed," by Pamela Hess and Deb Riechmann, AP, *Jacksonville Daily News* (NC), 25 April 2008, p. 1; "How Big a Threat Is N. Korea," by Kristen Chick, *Christian Science Monitor,* 24 May 2009, p.12; "Top Iranian Defector on Iran's Collaboration with Iraq, North Korea, Al-Qa'ida, and Hizbullah," Middle East Media Research Inst.; "North Koreans Assisted Hezbollah with Tunnel Construction."

9. *Encyclopedia Britannica Online,* s.v. "Communism."

10. *Columbia Encyclopedia,* sixth ed., 2008, s.v. "Communism," as retrieved through the following url: www.encyclopedia.com/topic/communism.aspx.

11. Caracas art store owner, in conversation with author on 16 August 2008.

12. "Country Profile: Venezuela," Library of Congress, Fed. Research Div., March 2005.

13. Peter Brookes, "Venezuelan Vagaries," *Armed Forces Journal,* July 2007, pp. 12, 13.

14. H. John Poole, *Tequila Junction: 4th-Generation Counterinsurgency* (Emerald Isle, NC: Posterity Press, 2008), part one.

15. "Colombian Army Adaption to FARC Insurgency," by Thomas Marks, PUB18.pdf, Stategic Studies Inst., January 2002, p. 16; "Betancourt, 3 US Hostages Freed From FARC Rebels," from AP, 2 July 2008; "An Unacknowledged War," by Toby Westerman, *Canada Free Press,* 27 August 2009; "Colombia: FARC Linked to Peruvian Guerrillas," by Brett Borkan, *Colombia Reports,* 8 March 2010; *Wikipedia Encyclopedia,* s.v. "Socio-Economic Structure of the FARC-EP" and "Jacobo Arenas" (as retrieved in early 2008); Sara Miller Llana, "El Salvador Joins Latin Leftward Tilt," *Christian Science Monitor,* 17 March 2009, pp. 1, 11; Brookes, "Venezuelan Vagaries," pp. 12, 13; "Four Spies for the U.S. Have Been Caught by Venezuelan Security," World News in Brief, *Christian Science Monitor,* 21 August 2006, p. 7.

16. "Chavez Eyes China, Russia, More on 'Strategic'-Interest Tour," from AFP, 20 September 2008.

17. Bill Gertz, "Chinese Military Trains in West," *Washington Times,* 15 March 2006; Gertz, *The China Threat,* p. 97.

18. H. John Poole, *Homeland Siege: Tactics for Police and Military* (Emerald Isle, NC: Posterity Press, 2009), intro. and part one; Poole, *Dragon Days,* part one; Poole, *Tequila Junction,* part one; Poole, *Terrorist Trail,* part one.

19. *Global Security* (globalsecurity.org), s.v. "Tibet."

20. *Handbook on the Chinese Armed Forces,* DDI-2680-32-76 (Washington, D.C.: Defense Intel. Agency, July 1976), pp. 1-4, 1-7.

21. *CIA — The World Factbook* (www.cia.gov), s.v. "China."

22. Poole, *Homeland Siege*, intro. and appendix; "A Former Maoist Guerrilla Was Sworn in Monday As Nepal's First Prime Minister," World News in Brief, *Christian Science Monitor,* 19 August 2008.

23. NPR's "Morning Edition" News, 18 February 2010; Anuj Chopra, "Maoist Rebels Spread across Rural India," *Christian Science Monitor,* 22 August 2006, p. 6; "Maoists Attack," The World, *Time,* 19 April 2010, p. 19; "Are India's Maoist Rebels Winning the War," BBC's News Online, 28 May 2010.

24. Randeep Ramesh, "Inside India's Hidden War," *The Guardian* (UK), 9 May 2006; *Wikipedia Encyclopedia,* s.v. "Naxalbari," "Naxalite," "West Bengal," and "Kolkata."

25. *South Asia Intelligence Review* database (satp.org), s.v. "People's Liberation Army of NE India."

26. Poole, *Dragon Days,* pp. 30-35.

27. "All Travelers to Bhutan Must Arrive . . . ," World News in Brief, *Christian Science Monitor,* 21 March 2008.

28. "About Sikkim," from the official website of the Government of Sikkim, as retrieved on 15 June 2009, in *Wikipedia Encyclopedia,* s.v. "Sikkim."

29. Constantine Menges, *China: The Gathering Threat* (Nashville, TN: Nelson Current, 2005), pp. 395, 398; Gertz, *The China Threat,* pp. 82, 94.

30. "China's Discreet Hold on Pakistan's Northern Borderlands," by Selig Harrison, *New York Times,* 26 August 2010.

31. Ibid.

32. "Pakistan Is Handing Over De-Facto Control of the Strategic Gilgit-Baltistan Region," *Rediff News* (India), 28 August 2010.

33. "China Corrects Diplomatic Faux Pas, but Maintains Presence in Gilgit-Baltistan," by B. Raman, Chennai Centre for China Studies, C3S Paper No.586, 5 September 2010.

34. "No De-Facto Control of Gilgit Baltistan to China," Zee News (India), 1 September 2010.

35. "China Puts 700,000 Troops on Alert in Sudan," *Newsmax* (West Palm Beach, FL), 27 August 2000; Bill Gertz, "Notes from the Pentagon," *Washington Times,* 5 March 2004; "China Winning Resources and Loyalties of Africa," *The Financial Times* (UK), 28 February 2006.

36. Longtime owner of Khartoum hotel, in conversation with author on 31 May 2006.

37. Gilbert King, *The Most Dangerous Man in the World* (New York: Chamberlain Bros., a Penguin imprint, 2004), chapt. 7; "Organized Crime, Intelligence and Terror: The D-Company's Role in the Mumbai Attacks," by Tom Burghardt, *Global Research,* 13 December 2008; "Dawood Ibrahim Had Played an Important Role in the Smuggling of Nuclear Weapons," by S. Balakrishnan, *Times of India,* 4 August 2004.

38. "China Corrects Diplomatic Faux Pas, but Maintains Presence in Gilgit-Baltistan," by Raman.

39. "China's Kashmir Gambit: Stakes in India-Pakistan Dispute," *Rupee News* (India), 7 September 2010.

40. "More Than Troops, Chinese Projects in PoK Worry India," by Pranab Dhal Samanta, *Indian Express* (Delhi), 5 September 2010, reprinted by Yahoo News, 5 September 2010.

41. "China Corrects Diplomatic Faux Pas, but Maintains Presence in Gilgit-Baltistan," by Raman.

42. Trip Atlas (tripatlas.com), s.v. "Peoples Liberation Army."

43. Menges, *China: The Gathering Threat,* pp. 395, 398; Gertz, *The China Threat,* pp. 82, 94.

44. "Chinese Company Gets EU Afghan Road Contract," *Dawn* (Pakistan), 2 December 2003; "Karzai Attends Starting Ceremony of Road Project," Pakistani News Service, 28 August 2006; "Chinese Gunned Down in Afghanistan," CNN Online, 10 June 2004; "Chinese Company to Reconstruct Afghan Road," *People's Daily* (China), 28 August 2006.

45. Amiuzadeh (Deputy Minister of . . . Iran), "Special Address to the Federation of Indian Chambers of Commerce and Industry," New Delhi, 22 July 2003; *Wikipedia Encyclopedia,* s.v. "Hazara"; "China's Global Reach," *Christian Science Monitor,* 30 January 2007, p. 13; Fred Weir, "Big Powers Jockey for Oil in Central Asia," *Christian Science Monitor*, 28 March 2007, p. 1.

46. Carlotta Gall, "Afghan-Iranian Road Opens," *New York Times,* 28 January 2005.

47. *Wikipedia Encyclopedia,* s.v. "Trans-Karakoram Tract."

48. *China's Rising Power in Africa,* part 3, "China, Congo Trade for What the Other Wants," by Gwen Thompkins, NPR, 30 July 2008.

49. "More Than Troops, Chinese Projects in PoK Worry India," by Samanta.

50. Mohan Malik, *Dragon on Terrorism: Assessing China's Tactical Gains and Strategic Losses Post-September 11* (Carlisle, PA: Strategic Studies Inst., U. S. Army War College, October 2002), table 1.

51. Scott Baldauf, "How Al Qaeda Seeks to Buy Chinese Arms," *Christian Science Monitor,* 23 August 2002; Malik, *Dragon on Terrorism,* table 1.

52. "Global Double Crossing," by Charles R. Smith, *Newsmax* (West Palm Beach, FL), 27 February 2003.

53. Charles R. Smith, "U.S. Bombs Chinese Network in Afghanistan, PRC Sold Taliban Advanced Air Defense System," *Newsmax* (West Palm Beach, FL), 20 October 2001; Malik, *Dragon on Terrorism,* p. 12.

54. Introductory video, CEIEC's website, ceiec.com.cn.

55. "China Railway Construction Corp. Plans $3.4B IPO," by Vivian Wai-yin Kwok, *Forbes Magazine,* 4 January 2008.

56. "China Corrects Diplomatic Faux Pas, but Maintains Presence in Gilgit-Baltistan," by Raman.

57. "China Railway Construction Seeks End-Feb HK IPO-Source," from Reuters Online, 15 January 2008.

58. CRSSG's website, crssg.com/english.

59. *Wikipedia Encyclopedia,* s.v. "Modernization of the Peoples Liberation Army."

60. Ibid., s.v. "People's Liberation Army."

61. *Global Security* (globalsecurity.org), s.v. "People's Liberation Army."

62. *Wikipedia Encyclopedia,* s.v. "People's Liberation Army."

63. "Modernizing the People's Liberation Army of China," by Carin Zissis, Backgrounder, Council on Foreign Relations (New York), 5 December 2006.

64. Chinese Posters (hosted by Internat. Inst. of Social History in Amsterdam), s.v. "Military Industrial Complex" (at the following url: http://chineseposters.net/themes/military-industrial-complex.php.)

65. *Wikipedia Encyclopedia,* s.v. "Category: Central-Owned Enterprise of the People's Republic of China."

66. Ibid.

67. CEIEC's website, ceiec.com.cn; CRBC's website, crbc.com/cn; and CSCEC's website, app.cscec.com.cn.

68. Hutchison Whampoa's website, hutchison-whampoa.com.

69. Ibid.

70. CCCCLTD website, ccccltd.com.cn.

71. *Wikipedia Encyclopedia,* s.v. "Category:Central-Owned Enterprise of the People's Republic of China."

72. "A Means of Maintaining Social Order," part II, Partners in Crime Series, by Fredric Dannen, *The New Republic,* 14 & 21 July 1997.

73. "More Than Troops, Chinese Projects in PoK Worry India," by Samanta.

74. Ibid.

75. Ibid.

76. Ibid.

77. Ibid.

78. "Beijing's Afghan Gamble," by Robert D. Kaplan, *New York Times,* 7 October 2009.

79. "More Than Troops, Chinese Projects in PoK Worry India," by Samanta.

80. "China's Discreet Hold on Pakistan's Northern Borderlands," by Harrison.

81. Ibid.

82. "Pakistan Is Handing Over De-Facto Control of the Strategic Gilgit-Baltistan Region."

83. "China's Discreet Hold on Pakistan's Northern Borderlands," by Harrison.

84. "Pak Ceded Control of Gilgit to China," by Chidanand Rajghatta, *Times of India,* 10 September 2010.

85. "Averting Blame in China," by Isaac Stone Fish, *Newsweek,* 6 December 2010, p. 8.

86. "The Caucus Papers: A Conversation on China," by Congressman J. Randy Forbes, p. 9.

87. NPR's "Morning Edition" News, 21 September 2010.

88. Ibid., 24 September 2010.

89. "Cadillac Sponsors Communist Propaganda Film," *China Auto Web—A Guide to China's Auto Industry,* 2 September 2010.

90. "SAIC-GM-Wuling (SGMW)," *China Auto Web—A Guide to China's Auto Industry,* n.d.

91. NPR's "Morning Edition" News, 24 September 2010.

92. Memorandum for the record from H.J. Poole.

93. "Foreign Journalists Beaten during Communist Party Crackdown," *Newsweek,* 14 March 2011, p. 15.

Chapter 5: *The Criminal Threat*

1. NPR's "Morning Edition" News, 16 September 2010.

2. ABC's Nightly News, 16 September 2010.

3. *National Drug Threat Assessment (for) 2009, NDIC,* "Drug Trafficking Organizations."

4. *National Drug Threat Assessment (for) 2010,* NDIC, p. 111.

5. ABC's Nightly News, 31 October 2010; NPR's "Morning Edition" News, 27 April 2011; ABC's Nightly News, 27 April 2011; "Afghan Military Officer Kills 8 U.S. Troops," New Briefs/Wire Reports (AP), *Jacksonville Daily News* (NC), 28 April 2011.

Chapter 6: *Where Threats Combine*

1. H. John Poole, *Phantom Soldier: The Enemy's Answer to Firepower* (Emerald Isle, NC: Posterity Press, August 2001), p. 157.
2. Chanakya Sen, review of *Karachi: A Terror Capital in the Making,* by Wilson John, *Asia Times Online,* 17 January 2004; Peters, *Seeds of Terror,* p. 31; Lawrence Lifschultz, "Pakistan, the Empire of Heroin," in McCoy and Block, "War on Drugs," p. 320, and Lifschultz, *Heroin Empire,* pp. 71-72, and *The Herald* (Pakistan) during 1985, all in *Seeds of Terror,* by Peters, p. 37.
3. "A Godfather's Lethal Mix of Business and Politics," *U.S. News & World Report Online,* 5 December 2005; "How Pakistan's ISI Funds Its Proxy War," by Syed Nooruzzaman, *The Tribune* (India), 28 November 1999.
4. Peters, *Seeds of Terror,* p. 129.
5. "Afghan Policeman Kills Six U.S. Troops," from AP, *Jacksonville Daily News* (NC), 30 November 2010, p. 10; U.S. Army indigenous police trainer, in conversation with author in early January 2011; Channel 12 News (WCTI, New Bern, NC), 17 May 2011.
6. "China's 'Comprehensive Warfare' Strategy Wears Down Enemy Using Non-Military Means," *Geostrategy-Direct,* 2 August 2006.
7. *Unrestricted Warfare,* by Qiao Liang and Wang Xiangsui (Beijing: PLA Literature and Arts Publishing House, February 1999), pp. 191, 223 (footnote 2).
8. Al Santoli, "The Panama Canal in Transition: Threats to U.S. Security and China's Growing Role in Latin America," American Foreign Policy Council Investigative Report, 23 June 1999.
9. "Do I Look Dangerous to You," part I, Partners in Crime Series, by Fredric Dannen, *The New Republic,* 14 & 21 July 1997.
10. "A Means of Maintaining Social Order," by Dannen; *Unrestricted Warfare, by* Liang and Xiangsu.
11. "Everyone Wants Cut in Afghan Drug Trade," from McClatchy News Service, *Jacksonville Daily News* (NC), 10 May 2009, p. A8.
12. Rachel Ehrenfield, *Funding Evil: How Terrorism is Financed and How to Stop It* (Chicago: Bonus Books, 2005), in *Warring on Terrorism,* by Stephen E. Hughes, part I (internet piece), 2005, pp. 24-26.
13. Poole, *Homeland Siege,* chaps. 2, 3, and 4.

14. Harris Whitbeck and Ingrid Arneson, "Terrorists Find Haven in South America," CNN, 8 November 2001, in *Tehran's War of Terror,* by Hughes, p. 150; Antonio Garrastazu and Jerry Haar, "International Terrorism: The Western Hemisphere Connection," OAS, *America's Forum North-South Center Update,* 2001; Sara Miller Llana, "Nicaragua Plans a Big Dig to Rival Panama Canal," *Christian Science Monitor,* 1 December 2006, pp. 1, 5.

15. *Tehran's War of Terror,* by Hughes, p. 148; U.S. Customs Service Report, as quoted in *The China Threat,* by Gertz, pp. 90, 91; Gunaratna, *Inside al-Qaeda,* pp. 164, 165.

16. "U.S. Designates Dawood Ibrahim As Terrorist Supporter," U.S. Treasury Dept. Press Release, 16 October 2003.

17. Peters, *Seeds of Terror,* p. 177.

18. "Analysts: By 2025."

19. "Eliminating Terrorist Sanctuaries: The Case of Iraq, Iran, Somalia and Sudan," Ctr. for Defense Info. (Washington, D.C.), 10 December 2001; Gunaratna, *Inside al-Qaeda*, p. 158; "China Winning Resources and Loyalties of Africa," *The Financial Times* (UK), 28 February 2006.

20. "Israel Intercepts Dual-Use Military Shipment from China to Gaza, *World Tribune,* 4 May 2006; "Explosive Powder Found on Chinese Ship," FOX's News Online, 8 November 2006.

21. Brookes, "Venezuelan Vagaries," p. 14; Simon Romero, "Files Released by Colombia Point to Venezuelan Bid to Arm Rebels," *New York Times,* 30 March 2008, p. 1.

22. Poole, *Homeland Siege,* p. xxvi.

23. David Luhnow and Jose de Cordoba, "The Perilous State of Mexico," *Wall Street Journal,* 21 February 2009.

24. NPR's "Morning Edition" News, 18 February 2010; Anuj Chopra, "Maoist Rebels Spread across Rural India," *Christian Science Monitor,* 22 August 2006, p. 6; "Maoists Attack," The World, *Time,* 19 April 2010, p. 19; "Are India's Maoist Rebels Winning the War," BBC's News Online, 28 May 2010.

25. Thomas A. Marks, "A Model Counterinsurgency: Uribe's Colombia (2002-2006)," *Military Review,* March-April 2007, photo caption, p. 42; LaVerle Berry, Glenn E. Curtis, John N. Gibbs, Rex A. Hudson, Tara Karacan, Nina Kollars, and Ramon Miro, "Nations Hospitable to Organized Crime and Terrorism," Fed. Research Div., Library of Congress, October 2003.

26. *CIA — The World Factbook,* s.v. "China."

27. *National Drug Threat Assessment (for) 2010,* NDIC, p. 10.

28. ABC's Nightly News, 16 September 2010.

29. *National Drug Threat Assessment (for) 2010,* NDIC, p. 111.

30. "Mexico's Sinaloa Gang Grows Empire, Defies Crackdown," by Anahi Rama Anahi Rama, Reuters Online, 19 January 2011.

31. "How Mexico Fares in Drug War," by Sara Miller Llana, *Christian Science Monitor,* 17 January 2011.

32. "Mexicali Called Hub for Smuggling Chinese into the United States," *Geostrategy-Direct,* 22 February 2005; "Smuggled Chinese Travel Circuitously," by Irene Jay Liu, NPR's "Morning Edition" News, 20 November 2007; "Terror Hoax Uncovers Border Threat," by David Hancock, CBS's News Online, 7 February 2005.

33. *CIA—The World Factbook* (www.cia.gov), s.v. "China."

34. "Dawood's ISI Links Could Trouble Musharraf," by Wilson John, Observer Research Foundation (New Delhi), *Strategic Trends,* vol. I, issue 5, 4 November 2003

35. "Alleged Drug Trafficker Arrested in Maryland," *Washington Times,* 24 July 2007; *Wikipedia Encyclopedia,* s.v. "Zhenli Ye Gon."

36. *Hong Kong Taxation: Law and Practice, 2010-2011,* by Garry Laird and Ayesha Macpherson (N.p.: Chinese Univ. Press, 1 October 2010), one page excerpt.

37. "Alleged Drug Trafficker Arrested in Maryland."

38. U.S. Embassy in Mexico, Press Release 07, "Largest Cash Seizure in History Product of U.S.-Mexico Counter-Narcotics Cooperation," statement by Ambassador Antonio O. Garza, 20 March 2007.

39. Ten or more Mexican media articles (all in Spanish) visible from "googling" Zhenli Ye Gon on 22 January 2011.

40. "Do I Look Dangerous to You," by Dannen.

41. Ibid.; "A Means of Maintaining Social Order," by Dannen.

42. "Asian Organized Crime and Terrorist Activity in Canada, 1999-2002," by Neil S. Helfand, Fed. Research Div., Library of Congress, July 2003, pp. 25, 26.

43. *National Drug Threat Assessment (for) 2008,* NDIC, October 2007, "Drug Transportation."

44. Menges, *China: The Gathering Threat,* pp. 395, 398; Santoli, "The Panama Canal in Transition"; Gertz, *The China Threat,* pp. 82, 94.

45. China's State Commission of Science, Technology and Industry for Nat. Defense, as quoted in "Chinese Military to Make Billions through Capitalism," *Geostrategy-Direct,* 16 January 2008; Hutchison Whampoa, from its website, www.hutchisonwhampoa.com.

46. "Do I Look Dangerous to You" and "A Means of Maintaining Social Order," by Dannen.

47. Santoli, "The Panama Canal in Transition"; Gertz, *The China Threat,* p. 94.

48. *Tehran's Wars of Terror,* by Hughes, p. 151.

49. Ibid., p. 148.

50. *Unrestricted Warfare,* by Liang and Xiangsui, p. 146.

51. "Drug Trafficking and North Korea: Issues for U.S. Policy,"
by Ralph F. Perl, Congressional Research Service Report RL32167,
last in a series of updates, 27 November 2006; Bill Powell and Adam
Zagorin, "The Sopranos State," *Time,* 23 July 2007.
52. Ibid.; U.S. Dept. of State, Internat. Narcotics Control
Strategy Report [INCSR], March 2003, p. VIII-43, in "Drug Trafficking
and North Korea," by Perl, p. 8.
53. NPR's "Morning Edition" News, 31 December
2010.
54. Poole, *Terrorist Trail,* p. 7; "Guinea Bissau: Hezbollah,
Al Qaida and the Lebanese Connection," by Marco Vernaschi,
pulitzercenter.org, 19 June 2009.
55. "Drug Seizures in West Africa Prompt Fears of Terrorist Links,"
by Jamie Doward, *Guardian Observer Online* (UK), 29 November 2009;
World Drug Report 2010, pp. 84, 242-244.
56. Lt.Col Patrick Meyers and Patrick Poole, "Hezbollah, Illegal
Immigration, and the Next 9/11," *Front Page Magazine,* 28 April 2006;
Ehrenfield, *Funding Evil,* in *Warring on Terrorism,* by Hughes, part I
(internet piece), 2005, pp. 24-26.
57. "Lebanese Find Troubles Fertile Ground for Cannabis," by Tom
Perry, Reuters Online, 26 September 2007; *World Drug Report 2010,*
tables 14 and 15.
58. "Hezbollah Uses Mexican Drug Routes into U.S.," *Washington
Times,* 27 March 2009; Gunaratna, *Inside al-Qaeda*, pp. 164, 165; Chris
Zambelis, "Radical Islam in Latin America," in *Unmasking Terror,*
vol. III, p. 484.
59. "Hezbollah Uses Mexican Drug Routes into U.S."
60. Ibid.
61. Keith Bradsher, "North Korean Ploy Masks
Ships under Other Flags," *New York Times,* 20 October 2006.
62. U.S. special operator, in conversation with author
on 2 January 2011.
63. *World Drug Report 2010,* pp. 84.
64. Ibid., p. 242.
65. Ibid, p. 244.
66. Ibid.
67. Ibid. p. 242.

Chapter 7: *If Current Trends Continue*

1. U.S. Congressional Testimony, in "Iran Continues Support of
Terrorism," Voice of America, 17 February 2005; Peterson,
"Shadows of Tehran over Iraq," pp. 1, 10; "Hezbollah Fighters Said
to Be in Iraq," *World Net Daily,* 21 June 2004.

2. Nicholas Blandford, "Lebanon Defuses Crisis," *Christian Science Monitor,* 22 May 2008, pp. 1, 11; Andrew Lee Butters, "Welcome to Hizballahstan," *Newsweek,* 26 May 2008, pp. 30, 31.

3. "Lebanon Government Collapsed," News in Brief, *Christian Science Monitor,* 24 January 2011. p. 9.

4. Nahal Toosi, AP, "Troubled Pakistan Faces Ruling Coalition Collapse," *Jacksonville Daily News* (NC), 4 January 2011; "Pakistani Government in Turmoil after Coalition Party Quits over Fuel and Taxes," by Saeed Shah, *Guardian Online* (UK), 2 January 2011.

5. NPR's "Morning Edition" News, 27 January 2011.

6. "Iran Responsible for 1983 Marine Barracks Bombing, Judge Rules," CNN Online, 30 May 2003.

7. Lawrence Pintak, *Seeds of Hate: How America's Flawed Middle East Policy Ignited the Jihad* (London: Pluto Press, 2003), p. 292.

8. Poole, *Terrorist Trail,* pp. 35-37.

9. Meyers and Poole, "Hezbollah, Illegal Immigration, and the Next 9/11"; Ehrenfield, *Funding Evil,* in *Warring on Terrorism,* by Hughes, part I (internet piece), 2005, pp. 24-26.

10. "Yemen: A Hezbollah Withdrawal."

11. "Hezbollah Uses Mexican Drug Routes into U.S."

12. "Hezbollah Leader Vows Not to Give Up Weapons," from AP, *Jacksonville Daily News* (NC), 23 September 2006, p. 4A; Ed Timperlake, "Clues How Chinese Missile Ended Up in Hezbollah's Arsenal," as posted on 26 July 2006 at G2-forward.org.

13. David Ignatius, "Hezbollah's Success," *Washington Post,* 23 September 2003, p. A27; "Suicide Bomber Kills Peacekeeper, Civilian in Afghan Capital," World Briefs Wire Reports (AP), *Jacksonville Daily News* (NC), 28 January 2004.

14. Poole, *Militant Tricks,* pp. 237-244.

15. Poole, *Homeland Siege,* intro. and appendix.

16. "A Victory for Hizballah," *Time,* 7 February 2011, p. 13.

17. "Rioting Spreads across Tunisia, Unrest Also Reported in Algeria," by Alexandra Sandels, *Los Angeles Times Online,* 8 January 2011.

18. NPR's "Morning Edition" News, 27 January 2011.

19. Hillary Rodham Clinton, U.S. Secretary of State, in interview with Chris Wallace, FOX's News Online, 30 January 2011.

20. NPR's "Morning Edition" News, 31 January 2011.

21. "Inside the Muslim Brotherhood," by Christopher Dickey and Babak Dehghanpisheh, *Newsweek,* 14 February 2011, pp. 3-5.

22. John Hunwick, "Africa and Islamic Revival: Historical and Contemporary Perspectives," extracted verbatim from MSA News by Univ. of Georgia, p. 7; *Britannica.com,* s.v. "Muslim Brotherhood"; *Wikipedia Encyclopedia,* s.v. "Wahhabi" and "Salafi."

23. ABC's Nightly News, 31 January - 9 February 2011; NBC's Noon News, 11 February 2011.

24. "Hizballah," *Patterns of Global Terrorism, 2002 Report* (Washington, D.C.: U.S. Dept. of State, April 2003); "Hezbollah," *Encyclopedia* (www.nationmaster.com), 5 July 2004.

25. "Bush Leaves Opening for Hezbollah Move to Political Mainstream," National Briefs Wire Reports (AP), *Jacksonville Daily News* (NC), 16 March 2005, p. 7A.

26. Wright and Baker, "Iraq, Jordan See Threat to Election from Iran," p. A01.

27. "In Iraq, a U.S. Enemy Returns," by Jane Arraf, *Christian Science Monitor,* 24 January 2011, p. 8.

28. Jason Burke, "Waiting for a Last Battle with the Taliban," *The Observer* (UK), 27 June 1999; Mir, *The True Face of Jihadis,* p. 29.

29. "Varja Sky over Tibet," by John Bush, *Journey into Buddhism Series,* PBS, NC Public TV, 27 January 2011.

30. "Muslim Brotherhood Declares War on America," by Barry Rubin, Global Research in Internat. Affairs (GLORIA) Ctr. (Israel), 7 October 2010, from G2-Forward.org.

31. *Financial Times,* as quoted on NPR's "Morning Edition" News, 18 January 2011.

32. Adm. Mike Mullen, as quoted by NPR's "Morning Edition" News, 6 July 2010.

33. Abdel Bari Atwan, *The Secret History of Al-Qaʻida* (London: Abacus, an imprint of Little, Brown Book Group, 2006), p. 122.

34. "The Emir," *Unmasking Terror,* vol. I, ed. Heffelfinger (Washington, D.C: Jamestown Foundation, 2005), pp. 402, 403; "Path to 9/11"; Nat.Commission on Terrorist Attacks upon the U.S., chapt. 5 of its report, footnotes 59-61; Gunaratna, *Inside al-Qaeda,* p. 196; *Wikipedia Encyclopedia,* s.v. "Oplan Bojinka" and "Ramzei Yousef."

35. "The Spy Factory"; Gunaratna, *Inside al-Qaeda,* p. 196.

36. Memorandum for the record by H.J. Poole.

Chapter 8: *Latest Developments in Yemen*

1. Johnson, "Yemen Accuses Iran of Meddling in Its Internal Affairs."

2. "Middle East: Strait Shooting," *STRATFOR Weekly*, 8 June 2011.

3. J. Stephen Morrison, "Africa and the War on Terrorism," House Internat. Relations Committee, Capitol Hill Hearing Testimony, Washington, D.C., 15 November 2001, in *Inside al-Qaeda,* by Gunaratna, p. 156; ABC's Nightly News, 6 June 2010.

4. "Country Profiles," BBC's News Online, s.v. "Yemen"; map display, in *Wikipedia Encyclopedia,* s.v. "Somalia"; "Somali Pirates a Growing Threat to Shipping," from Reuters Online, 29 August 2008.

5. "Guarding Troubled Waters," by Sarah A. Topol, News in Brief, *Christian Science Monitor,* 19 June 2010.

6. "Somali Pirates a Growing Threat to Shipping."

7. "Country Profiles," BBC's News Online, s.v. "Yemen."

8. Johnson, "Yemen Accuses Iran of Meddling in Its Internal Affairs."

9. "Al-Qaeda's Influence in Yemen," by Jeremy Bowen, BBC's News Online, 5 January 2010; "Profile: Al-Qaeda in the Arabian Peninsula," loc. cit., 3 January 2010; "Country Profiles," loc. cit. s.v. "Yemen."

10. "Civil War Fears As Yemen Celebrates Unity," BBC's News Online, 21 May 2009.

11. "Yemen Conflict Map," by Katherine Zimmerman, Jonathan Frist, Chris Harnisch, Ctr. for Defense Studies (Washington, D.C.), *Critical Threats,* 21 January 2009.

12. Ginny Hill, "Cold War Roots of Yemen Conflict," BBC's News Online, 17 September 2009.

13. "U.S. Fighter Jets Attack Yemeni Fighters," Press TV Online (Iran), 14 December 2009; *Wikipedia Encyclopedia,* s.v. "Houti Rebels."

14. "The Spy Factory."

15. "Country Profiles," BBC's News Online, s.v. "Yemen: Timeline."

16. Sen, review of *Karachi,* by John.

17. "Chinese Navy Sends New Escort Ships to Somali Waters," *China Defense Mashup,* as reprinted from Xinhua, 1 April 2009.

18. "Iran Sends 6 Warships to International Waters in 'Saber Rattling' Move," FOX's News Online, 25 May 2009.

19. "Yemen Conflict Map," by Zimmerman et al; Brian Ross; Richard Esposito, Matthew Cole, Luis Martinez, and Kirit Radia, "Obama Ordered U.S. Military Strike on Yemen Terrorists," ABC's News Online, late December 2009.

20. Ibid.

21. "U.S. Secret War against *al-Qaeda* in Yemen Idles," World Briefs Wire Reports (AP), *Jacksonville Daily News* (NC), 16 October 2010.

22. "Al-Qaeda Blows Up Gas Pipeline in Yemen," *Hindustan Times* (India), 15 September 2010.

23. "Civilians Flee From Battle In Southern Yemen," by Soraya Sarhaddi Nelson and Steve Inskeep, NPR's "Morning Edition" News, 24 September 2010.

24. "Al Qaeda Yemen Wing Claims Parcel Plot, UPS Crash," from Reuters Online, 6 November 2010; NPR's "Morning Edition" News, 9 November 2010.

25. "Yemen, America's Uneasy Ally in War on Terror," CBS's "Sixty Minutes," 14 January 2011.

26. NPR's "Morning Edition" News, 2 February 2011.

27. "Bahrain Protests Joined by Arab Anger in Libya," News Briefs/Wire Reports (AP), *Jacksonville Daily News* (NC), 17 February 2011.

28. "Insurgents Take Control of Yemeni City," by Abigail Fielding-Smith, *Financial Times,* 24 March 2011.

29. "Yemenis Rally against Government," by Cynthia Johnston and Mohammed Ghobari, Reuters Online, 28 March 2011.

30. "U.S. Shifts to Seek Removal of Yemen's Leader, an Ally," by Laura Kasinof and David Sanger, *New York Times,* 3 April 2011.

31. "Yemen Opposition Backs Power Transfer . . . ," BBC's News Online, 6 June 2011; NPR's "Morning Edition" News, 6 June 2011.

Chapter 9: *Al-Qaeda's Takeover of Somalia*

1. Johnson, "Yemen Accuses Iran of Meddling in Its Internal Affairs."

2. "Eliminating Terrorist Sanctuaries," Ctr. for Defense Info.; Gunaratna, *Inside al-Qaeda,* pp. 154-156.

3. J. Stephen Morrison, "Africa and the War on Terrorism," House Internat. Relations Committee, Capitol Hill Hearing Testimony, Washington, D.C., 15 November 2001, in *Inside al-Qaeda,* by Gunaratna, p. 156.

4. "Somali Pirates a Growing Threat to Shipping," by Daniel Wallis, Reuters Online, 29 August 2008.

5. "New Pirate Raids Expose International Efforts to Secure Trade Routes," AFP, 12 December 2008.

6. "Somali Pirates a Growing Threat to Shipping," by Wallis.

7. ABC's Nightly News, 30 November 2008; senior member of Gen. Petraeus' staff, on CBS's "Sixty Minutes," 22 February 2009.

8. "Eliminating Terrorist Sanctuaries," Ctr. for Defense Info.

9. "Analysis: Somalia's Powerbrokers," BBC's News Online, 8 January 2002; *Wikipedia Encyclopedia,* s.v. "Jama Ali Jama."

10. Chris Thomlinson, AP, "U.S. Backing Somali Militants against Islamic Extremists," *Jacksonville Daily News* (NC), 10 April 2006, p. 3A.

11. Harun Hassan, "Somalia Twists in the Wind," from harowo.com, 13 April 2006, through G2-forward.org; "Militia Hunt Al-Qaeda in Somalia," from AFP, 5 May 2006.

12. Edward Girardet, "Clashes Worsen Somalia Food Crisis As Drought Sets In," *Christian Science Monitor,* 19 April 2006, p. 4.

13. ABC's Nightly News, 5 June 2006; Rob Crilly, "Islamist-Warlord Clashes Hinder Somalia's New Government," *Christian Science Monitor,* 5 June 2006, p. 4.

14. Chris Thomlinson, "Video Shows Arabs Fighting in Somalia," from AP, 5 July 2006.

15. "Chanting, 'We Don't Want Islamic Courts . . . '," World News in Brief, *Christian Science Monitor,* 7 June 2006, p. 7.

16. "Hundreds of Soldiers from Neighboring Ethiopia Crossed into Somalia," World News in Brief, *Christian Science Monitor,* 19 June 2006, p. 7.

17. Rob Crilly, "Foreign Intervention in Somalia," *Christian Science Monitor,* 21 June 2006, pp. 1, 2.

18. "Ethiopian Troops Lend Aid to Somali Allies," World Briefs Wire Reports (AP), *Jacksonville Daily News* (NC), 21 July 2006, p. 4A.

19. Rob Crilly, "Somalia on the Edge of Full-Scale War," *Christian Science Monitor,* 25 July 2006. p. 7.

20. "Al Qaida Now Controls Somalia," *Geostrategy-Direct,* Middle East Report, 30 June 2006.

21. Hassan, "Somalia Twists in the Wind"; "Militia Hunt Al-Qaeda in Somalia," from AFP.

22. "Al Qaida Now Controls Somalia."

23. Bill Gertz, " 'White Man' Training Al Qaida Terrorists in Wilderness Camp near Kenya," *Geostrategy-Direct,* week of 14 December 2004.

24. "U.S. Launches New Somalia Raids," *Guardian Online* (UK), 9 January 2007.

25. Scott Baldauf and Ali Mohamed, "Cash Lures Somali 'Holy' Warriors," *Christian Science Monitor,* 19 April 2010, p. 19.

26. ABC's Nightly News, 6 June 2010.

27. BBC's News, Public Radio East, 26 June 2010.

28. Max Delany, "West Trains Army to Fight in Somalia," *Christian Science Monitor,* 21 June 2010, p. 13.

29. ABC's Nightly News, 12 July 2010; NPR's "Morning Edition" News, 12 July 2010.

30. Mannes, *Profiles in Terror,* p. 21; interview with U.S. intel. community, February 2000, from *Inside al-Qaeda,* by Gunaratna, p. 158.

31. Gunaratna, *Inside al-Qaeda,* p. 159.

32. "Islamists Training in Somalia," by Bill Gertz, *ERRI Daily Intelligence Report,* vol. 11, no. 363, Emergency Net News, 31 December 2005, through *Geostrategy-Direct.*

33. Gunaratna, *Inside al-Qaeda,* pp. 154-156.

34. "Ambush in Mogadishu," by William Cran, PBS's *Frontline,* in conjunction with WGBH, Boston, 2002, videotape.

35. ABC's Nightly News, 5 June 2006; Crilly, "Islamist-Warlord Clashes Hinder Somalia's New Government," p. 4.

36. Chris Thomlinson, "Video Shows Arabs Fighting in Somalia."

37. "Eliminating Terrorist Sanctuaries," Ctr. for Defense Info.

38. "Chanting, 'We Don't Want Islamic Courts . . . '," p. 7.

39. "Hundreds of Soldiers from Neighboring Ethiopia Crossed into Somalia," p. 7.

40. "Al Qaida Now Controls Somalia."

41. Hassan, "Somalia Twists in the Wind"; "Militia Hunt Al-Qaeda in Somalia," from AFP.

42. Al Qaida Now Controls Somalia."

43. "Former Members of Radical Somali Group Give Details of Their Group," Voice of America, 6 January 2007, from *Wikipedia Encyclopedia,* s.v. "Hassan Dahir Aweys."

44. "Somalia's Kingmaker Returns," by Mohamed Mohamed, BBC's News Online, 28 April 2009.

45. Ibid.

46. "U.N. Somalia Envoy Accuses Islamist of Coup Attempt," from AFP, 14 May 2009.

47. Ibid.

48. Ibid.

49. "Al Shabaab Takes Aim," *Time,* 6 September 2009, p. 12.

50. Kevin Peraino, "Somalia Strkes Out," *Newsweek,* 26 July 2010, p. 42.

51. Map entitled "Political Situation in Somalia, March 24, 2011," by Iglo, *Wikipedia Encyclopedia,* s.v. "Somalia."

52. "Somali Troops, Militia Take Two Towns from Rebels," from Reuters Online, 28 March 2011.

53. Map entitled "Political Situation in Somalia, March 24, 2011."

Chapter 10: *Much Now Depends on Pakistan*

1. "The Afghan Endgame," by John Barry, Sami Yousafzai, and Ron Moreau, *Newsweek,* 12 July 2010, p. 45.

2. Joseph J. Collins, "The Way Ahead in Afghanistan," *Armed Forces Journal,* July/August 2010, pp. 36-38.

3. Gordon Lubold, "Mullen's Charm Offensive," *Christian Science Monitor,* 17 January 2010, p. 19; Samina Ahmed, Internat. Crisis Group, as quoted in "Crackdown on Taliban Shifts U.S.-Pakistan Ties," by Julie McCarthy, NPR's "Morning Edition" News, 10 March 2010; South Asia Intel. Review database (satp.org), s.v. "Harkat-ul-Ansar"; "Jaish-e-Mohammed (JEM) Backgrounder," South Asia Analysis Group (India), paper no. 3320, 10 March 2001; "Harakat ul-Mujahidin," *Patterns of Global Terrorism, 2002 Report* (Washington, D.C.: U.S. Dept. of State, April 2003).

4. Peters, *Seeds of Terror,* p. 129.

5. Wilson John, Observer Research Foundation, *Coming Blowback: How Pakistan Is Endangering the World* (New Delhi: Rupa & Co., 2009), pp. 37-39; Vali Nasr, *The Vanguard of the Islamic Revolution: The Jama'at-i-Islami of Pakistan* (Berkeley: Univ. of California Press, 1994), in *Coming Blowback,* by John, p. 38; *CIA — The World Factbook* (www.cia.gov), s.v. "Pakistan."

6. John, *Coming Blowback,* pp. 39, 184.

7. "Opium Trade Is Halal in Islam: Bara Scholar," *Pakistan Daily News,* 21 January 2005, in *Seeds of Terror,* by Peters, p. 143.

8. NPR's "Morning Edition" News, 12 October 2009; "Pakistan's 'New Zone of Militancy'," BBC's News Online, 12 October 2009; "Taliban Claim Pakistan Army Raid," BBC's News Online, 12 October 2009.

9. "Smoking Al Qaeda Out of Karachi," by B. Raman, South Asia Analysis Group, Paper No. 519, 14 September 2002; "Dawood Gang Provided Logistics to Lashkar Militants," from Press Trust of India, and "Dawood's Drug Net Financed 26/11: Russian Intelligence," as both retrieved from NDTV Online (Mumbai) on 18 December 2008; *Wikipedia Encyclopedia,* s.v. "Dawood Ibrahim"; Craig Whitlock and Karen DeYoung, "Attributes Suggest Outside Help," *Washington Post,* 28 November 2008, p. 1; "Three Guilty in 2003 Mumbai Bombings Trial," by Salil Panchal, AFP, 27 July 2009; "Islamic Extremism in India (page 2)," Internat. Inst. for Strategic Studies (London), vol. 15, issue 3, April 2009; "Govt Blames LeT for Parliament Attack, Asks Pak to Restrain Terrorist Outfits," from Rediff News (India), 14 December 2001.

10. "Jamaat-e-Islami Moves Pak Senate on Jamaat-ud-Daawa Ban," from ANI, *Malaysia Sun,* 14 December 2008.

11. "Markets Closed, Traffic Thin: 135 Arrested in Lahore," by Intikhab Hanif and Ahmad Fraz Khan, *Dawn Newspaper Group Online* (Karachi), 10 November 2001; John, *Coming Blowback,* pp. 20, 42, 167; *South Asia Intelligence Review* database (satp.org), s.v. "Lashkar e-Toiba"; Mir, *The True Face of Jahadis,* pp. 183, 184.

12. Amir Mir, *Talibanisation of Pakistan* (New Delhi: Pentagon Press, 2010), pp. 118-120; "India Wants Him, Pak Uses Jaish Chief to Defuse Mosque Tension," by Pranab Dhal Samanta, *India Express* (Delhi), 7 July 2009; *Jaish e-Mohammed* profile, *Global Security News & Reports,* Overseas Security Advisor Council, from its website, www.ds-osac.org; Danny Pearl, as quoted in *A Mighty Heart,* by Mariane Pearl, p. 75; Pearl, *A Mighty Heart,* p. 74; South Asia Intel. Review database (satp.org), s.v. "Sipah-e-Sahaba Pakistan."

13. *South Asia Intelligence Review* database (satp.org), s.v. "Lashkar i-Jhangvi"; "Lashkar-e-Jhangvi & Al Qaeda," by B. Raman, Paper No. 2526, 31 December 2007 (same as *International Terrorism Monitor,* Paper No. 337, n.d.) and "Jaish-e-Mohammed (JEM) Backgrounder," Paper No. 3320, 10 March 2001, all from South Asia Analysis Group (India); Mir, *The True Face of Jihadis,* p. 218.

14. "GHQ Attack Mastermind Apprehended in Bahawalpur," from ANI, Thaindian News Online, 28 October 2009; South Asia Intel. Review database (satp.org), s.v. "Sipah-e-Sahaba Pakistan."

15. Mir, *The True Face of Jihadis,* p. 137.

16. B. Raman, "The New Trojan Horse of Al Qaeda," South Asia Analysis Group (India), *International Terrorism Monitor,* Paper No. 301, 10 November 2007.

17. Ibid.

18. "Lashkar-e-Jhangvi, Sipah-e-Sahaba Working Like 'Paid Killers' for Taliban: Malik," from ANI, Thaindian News Online, 3 July 2010.

19. "Pakistani Military Hits Taliban in Orakzai," by Bill Roggio, *Long War Journal,* 17 November 2009; "South Waziristan's Maulvi Nazir: The New Face of the Taliban," by Hassan Abbas, The Jamestown Foundation, *Terrorism Monitor,* vol. 5, issue 9, 14 May 2007.

20. Gall et al, "Pakistani and Afghan Taliban Unify in Face of U.S. Influx"; Khan, "Taliban Rename Their Group," *The Nation* (Pakistan), 23 February 2009; "Three Taliban Factions Form Shura Ittehad-ul-Mujahiden," *The News* (Pakistan), 23 February 2009; all in *Wikipedia Encyclopedia,* s.v. "Tehrik-i-Taliban Pakistan."

21. Lubold, "Mullen's Charm Offensive," p. 19.

22. "Al Qaeda Deploys Paramilitary 'Shadow Army'," by Bill Roggio, *Long War Journal,* 10 February 2009.

23. *Friday Times* (Pakistan), 30 March 2007, *Daily Times* (Pakistan), 9 January 2009, in "South Waziristan's Maulvi Nazir," by Abbas.

24. "Taliban's Presence in Pak Punjab Officially Accepted," from ANI, Thaindian News Online, 17 May 2010.

25. "Pak's 'Friendly Attitude' towards JuD Bound to Raise Eyebrows: Pak Editorial," from ANI, Thaindian News Online, 7 July 2010; Mir, *Talibanisation of Pakistan,* pp. 78, 79.

26. "Al-Qaeda on Pakistan: Dr. Ayman al-Zawahiri's Morning and the Lamp," Jamestown Foundation, *Terrorism Monitor,* vol. 8, issue 11, 19 March 2010.

27. "Pakistani Islamists Sign Deal With China," by Farhan Bokhari, CBS's News Online, World Watch, 18 February 2009.

28. Vali Nasr, *The Vanguard of the Islamic Revolution: The Jama'at-i-Islami of Pakistan* (Berkeley: Univ. of California Press, 1994), in *Coming Blowback,* by John, p. 38; "Jamaat-e-Islami: The Fountainhead of Religious Extremism," by Yasser Latif Hamdani, *Daily Times* (Pakistan), 20 May 2010; *Pakistan Country Study;* Tini Tran, AP, "Tape Targets Clerics," *Jacksonville Daily News* (NC), 25 November 2004, pp. 1A, 4A.

29. "The Black-Turbaned Brigade: The Rise of TNSM in Pakistan," by Hassan Abbas, Jamestown Foundation, *Terrorism Monitor,* vol. 4, issue 23, 30 November 2006.

30. *South Asia Intelligence Review* database (satp.org), s.v. *"Tehreek-e-Nafaz-e-Shariat-e-Mohammadi."*

31. "Taliban Attacks, Establishes Control over Emerald Mine in NWFP," from ANI, *News Track India,* 2 April 2009.

32. Neamatollah Nojumi, *The Rise of the Taliban in Afghanistan* (New York: Palgrave, 2002), pp. 101, 189.

33. "Pakistani Taliban Widen Jihad with Strikes on Fellow Muslims," by Arif Jamal, Jamestown Foundation, *Terrorism Monitor*, vol. 8, issue 28, 16 July 2010.

34. Ibid.

35. "Daily Mashriq (Pakistan)," 24 April 2008, in "Militant or Peace Broker? A Profile of the Swat Valley's Maulana Sufi Muhammad," by Imtiaz Ali, Jamestown Foundation, *Terrorism Monitor,* vol. 7, issue 7, 26 March 2009.

36. *Global Security* (globalsecurity.org), s.v. "Baittulah Mehsud."

37. Ibid., s.v. *"Tehreek-e-Nafaz-e-Shariat-e-Mohammadi."*

38. Kamran Rehmat, "Swat: Pakistan's Lost Paradise," Al Jazeera, 27 January 2009, in *Wikipedia Encyclopedia,* s.v. "Tehreek-e-Nafaz-e-Shariat-e-Mohammadi."

39. Jane Perlez, "Attackers Hit Mosques of Islamic Sect in Pakistan," *New York Times,* 29 May 2010.

40. "Half-Hearted Security Operations in Punjab Do Little to Restrain Taliban Attacks," by Arif Jamal, Jamestown Foundation, *Terrorism Monitor,* vol. 8, issue 31, 5 August 2010; NPR's "Morning Edition" News, 5 July 2010.

41. Perlez, "Attackers Hit Mosques of Islamic Sect in Pakistan."

42. "Half-Hearted Security Operations in Punjab Do Little to Restrain Taliban Attacks," by Jamal.

43. Issam Ahmed, "Pakistan's Old Jihadis Pose New Threat," *Christian Science Monitor,* 6 December 2009, pp. 8, 9.

44. "Punjab: A New Battlefield," part I, Governance Crisis Series, by Mohammad Amir Rana, *Friday Times* (Lahore), 7-15 July 2010.

45. "Unholy Alliances," part V, Governance Crisis Series, by Mohammad Amir Rana, *Friday Times* (Lahore), 5-11 August 2010.

46. "Unpacking 'Punjabi Taliban'," part IV, Governance Crisis Series, by Mohammad Amir Rana, *Friday Times* (Lahore), 30 July-5 August 2010.
47. Ibid.
48. Ibid.
49. "Waziristan-Based Terror Group Takes Credit for Lahore Assault," by Bill Roggio, *Long War Journal*, 30 March 2009.
50. "Pakistani Military Hits Taliban in Orakzai," by Roggio.
51. "Unpacking 'Punjabi Taliban'," by Rana.
52. "Pakistani Commandos Break Siege on Army Headquarters," by Bill Roggio, *Long War Journal,* 10 October 2009.
53. "Jamaat-e-Islami: The Fountainhead of Religious Extremism," by Yasser Latif Hamdani, *Daily Times* (Pakistan), 20 May 2010.
54. "Proliferation of Religious Organisations in the Punjab," part II, Governance Crisis Series, by Mohammad Amir Rana, *Friday Times* (Lahore), 16-22 July 2010.
55. "Punjab: A New Battlefield," by Rana.
56. "Militants' Media Power," part III, Governance Crisis Series, by Mohammad Amir Rana, *Friday Times* (Lahore), 23-29 July 2010.
57. Ibid.
58. Ibid.
59. H. John Poole, *Tactics of the Crescent Moon: Militant Muslim Combat Methods* (Emerald Isle, NC: Posterity Press, 2004), chapt. 8; Bush Administration admission, on ABC's Nightly News, 12 April 2008.
60. "Pakistani Islamists Sign Deal With China," by Bokhari.
61. "Jamaat-e-Islami: The Fountainhead of Religious Extremism," by Hamdani.
62. Sen, review of *Karachi,* by John; Peters, *Seeds of Terror,* p. 31; Lawrence Lifschultz, "Pakistan, the Empire of Heroin," in McCoy and Block, "War on Drugs," p. 320, and Lifschultz, *Heroin Empire,* pp. 71-72, and *The Herald* (Pakistan) during 1985, all in *Seeds of Terror,* by Peters, p. 37.
63. "Pakistan Trims Top ISI Chairs," from PTI Islamabad, *The Economic Times* (Chennai), 13 August 2009, p. 3; "A Godfather's Lethal Mix of Business and Politics"; "Dawood's ISI Links Could Trouble Musharraf," by John; John, *Coming Blowback,* p. 187.
64. Aryn Baker, "Pakistan's Army Flexes Its Muscles," *Time,* 18 October 2010. p. 58.
65. "Assassination Intensifies the Crisis," The World, *Newsweek,* 17 January 2011, p. 14; NPR's "Morning Edition" News, 5 January 2011.

66. Toosi, "Troubled Pakistan Faces Ruling Coalition Collapse."

67. "Pakistani Government in Turmoil after Coalition Party Quits over Fuel and Taxes," by Saeed Shah, *Guardian Online* (UK), 2 January 2011; "Assassination Intensifies the Crisis," p. 14.

68. "Pakistani Government in Turmoil . . . ," by Shah.

69. "Coalition Partner Rejoins Pakistani Government," Voice of America News (www.voanews.com), 7 January 2011.

70. "Pakistani Government in Turmoil . . . ," by Shah.

71. "MQM, JI Discuss Political Situation," Dawn Online (Pakistan), 22 December 2010; John, *Coming Blowback,* pp. 37-39.

72. "Pakistani Government in Turmoil . . . ," by Shah.

73. Toosi, "Troubled Pakistan Faces Ruling Coalition Collapse."

74. Lubold, "Mullen's Charm Offensive," p. 19; Samina Ahmed, Internat. Crisis Group, as quoted in "Crackdown on Taliban Shifts U.S.-Pakistan Ties," by Julie McCarthy, NPR's "Morning Edition" News, 10 March 2010; *South Asia Intelligence Review* database (satp.org), s.v. "Harkat-ul-Ansar"; "Jaish-e-Mohammed (JEM) Backgrounder," South Asia Analysis Group (India), Paper No. 3320, 10 March 2001; "Harakat ul-Mujahidin," *Patterns of Global Terrorism, 2002 Report* (Washington, D.C.: U.S. Dept. of State, April 2003).

75. "Pakistan Releases Top Terrorist Leader," by Bill Roggio, *Long War Journal,* 4 January 2011.

76. NPR's "Morning Edition" News, 2 May 2011.

77. "Osama bin Laden Is Dead," CBS's Online News, 1 May 2011.

78. Ibid., Federation of American Scientists website (www.fas.org), s.v. "Harakat ul-Jihad-I-Islami (HUJI)."

79. "Pakistan Releases Top Terrorist Leader," by Roggio.

80. "Unpacking 'Punjabi Taliban'."

81. "Pakistan Releases Top Terrorist Leader," by Roggio.

82. Ibid.; "The Marriott Blast," by B. Rahman, South Asia Analysis Group (India), *International Terrorism Monitor,"* Paper No. 449, 22 September 2008.

83. "Unpacking 'Punjabi Taliban'."

84. "Pakistan Releases Top Terrorist Leader," by Roggio.

85. Mir, *The True Face of Jihadis,* pp. 31, 328; Raman, "The New Trojan Horse of Al Qaeda."

86. "Harakat-ul Mujahideen Al Alami (HMA)," Memorial Inst. for the Prevention of Terrorism (MIPT) database, an affiliate or member of the U.S. Dept. of Homeland Security, 24 July 2005; *South Asia Intelligence Review* database, s.v. "Lashkar i-Jhangvi."

87. "Al Qaeda Deploys Paramilitary 'Shadow Army'," by Roggio.

88. NPR's "Morning Edition" News, 7 July 2011.

89. Rana Sanaullah Khan (Punjab Law Minister), in "Dozen Dead in Suicide Bombing," videotaped news story, from AP, 8 March 2010, as viewed at Youtube on 5 February 2011.

Chapter 11: *The Resupply Routes into Afghanistan*

1. Dan Murphy, "The Other Karzai Boss," *Christian Science Monitor,* 19 July 2010, pp. 8, 9.
2. Sen, review of *Karachi,* by John; Peters, *Seeds of Terror,* p. 31; Lawrence Lifschultz, "Pakistan, the Empire of Heroin," in McCoy and Block, *War on Drugs,* p. 320; Lifschultz, *Heroin Empire,* pp. 71-72; *The Herald* (Pakistan) during 1985; and "Heroin in Pakistan: Sowing the Wind," a CIA report leaked to and printed by Pakistan's *Friday Times,* 3 September 1995—all in *Seeds of Terror,* by Peters, pp. 37, 60; Poole, *Expeditionary Eagles,* p. 82.
3. Murphy, "The Other Karzai Boss," pp. 8, 9.
4. Sen, review of *Karachi,* by John; "How Pakistan's ISI Funds Its Proxy War," by Syed Nooruzzaman, *The Tribune* (India), 28 November 1999; "Hunting for Dawood Ibrahim," by B. Raman, South Asia Analysis Group (India), Paper No. 1952, 16 September 2006 (same as *International Terrorism Monitor,* Paper No. 122, n.d.); King, *The Most Dangerous Man in the World,* p. 15.
5. "Karzai's Exit Strategy," by Dan Green, *Armed Forces Journal,* September 2010, pp. 38, 39.
6. "The Afghan Endgame," by Barry et al, p. 45; Peters, *Seeds of Terror,* p. 129.
7. "Karzai's Exit Strategy," by Green, pp. 38, 39.
8. Lubold, "Mullen's Charm Offensive," p. 19.
9. Tom A. Peter, "An Afghan Insurgent Tries Politics," *Christian Science Monitor,* 28 February 2011., p. 12.
10. Thomas Joscelyn, "Report: Al Qaeda Disarms Select Taliban Commanders," *Threat Matrix,* 8 September 2010, in "The Haqqani Network," by Jeffrey A. Dressler, Inst. for the Study of War (Washington, D.C.), Afghanistan Report #6, October 2010.
11. "The Haqqani Network," by Jeffrey A. Dressler, Inst. for the Study of War (Washington, D.C.), Afghanistan Report #6, October 2010, p. 14; "ISW in Brief: Trouble Ahead in Afghanistan's East," by Jeffrey A. Dressler, loc. cit., Works by Our Authors, 17 March 2011.
12. "A Godfather's Lethal Mix of Business and Politics"; Poole, *Expeditionary Eagles,* pp. 78, 115-117; Poole, *Homeland Siege,* intro.; "The Haqqani Network," by Jeffrey A. Dressler, p. 37.
13. "The Haqqani Network," by Jeffrey A. Dressler, p. 37.
14. "Karzai Denounces U.S.-Russian Drug Raid in Afghanistan," *Los Angeles Times,* as reprinted in *Jacksonville Daily News* (NC), 31 October 2010, p. 26; Peters, *Seeds of Terror*, p. 129.

15. "The Afghan Endgame," by Barry et al, p. 45; interview of interim U.S. envoy to Kabul, NPR's "Morning Edition" News, 15 November and 17 December 2010; Joseph J. Collins, "The Way Ahead in Afghanistan," *Armed Forces Journal,* July/August 2010, pp. 36-38; Ben Arnoldy, "South Asia," World (in Summary), *Christian Science Monitor,* 27 December 2010, p. 10.

16. "U.S. Drone Strike Kills Rebels in Pakistan," from AFP, *Sydney Morning Herald* (Australia), 5 October 2010.

17. Liam Stack, "Fifth NATO Tanker Attacked in Six Days since Pakistan Sealed Border Post," *Christian Science Monitor,* 5 October 2010; "Future of U.S. Base in Kyrgyzstan in Question, by Paul Reynolds, BBC's News Online, 9 April 2010.

18. Ibid.

19. "NATO Airstrike on Afghanistan Fuel Truck Kills 40," *Telegraph* (UK), 4 September 2009.

20. "NATO Tankers Torched in Pakistan, but Alternative Routes to Afghanistan Limited," by Ben Arnoldy, *Christian Science Monitor,* 1 October 2010.

21. "NATO Tankers Torched in Pakistan," BBC's News Online, 1 October 2010; "Four NATO Trucks Torched in Quetta," from ANI, Thaindian News Online, 16 July 2010; "NATO Oil Tankers Destroyed by Militants in Pakistan," from IANS, Thaindian News Online, 29 August 2010.

22. "10 Trucks Torched in Issa Nagri," by Roy Jawad Hussain, *Pakistan Criminal Records,* 4 August 2010.

23. "Gunmen Torch NATO Trucks in Rawalpindi," *Dawn* (Pakistan), 9 June 2010.

24. Stack, "Fifth NATO Tanker Attacked in Six Days since Pakistan Sealed Border Post."

25. "Militants Hit NATO Tankers Again," World Briefs Wire Reports (AP), *Jacksonville Daily News* (NC), 4 October 2010.

26. NPR's "Morning Edition" News, 6 October 2010.

27. "Four NATO Trucks Torched in Quetta," from ANI, Thaindian News Online, 16 July 2010; "NATO Oil Tankers Destroyed by Militants in Pakistan," from IANS, Thaindian News Online, 29 August 2010.

28. Stack, "Fifth NATO Tanker Attacked in Six Days since Pakistan Sealed Border Post."

29. Alex Rodriguez, "Pakistan Reopens Checkpoint," *Wilmington Star News* (NC), 11 October 2010, p. 4A.

30. "Two Fuel Tankers for NATO Attacked in Pakistan," by Nasir Habib, CNN Online, 1 November 2010; "NATO Tankers Torched in Afghanistan," Press TV Online (Iran), 14 November 2010; "More NATO Tankers Attacked in Pakistan," Press TV Online (Iran), 11 November 2010; NPR's "Morning Edition" News, 14 November 2010.

31. "Gunmen Torch 14 NATO Oil Tankers in Pakistan," News Briefs Wire Reports (AP), *Jacksonville Daily News* (NC), 16 January 2011, p. 14.

32. NPR's Evening News, 18 January 2011.

33. Ibid., 1 April 2011.

34. FOX's Nightly News, 14 May 2011.

35. NPR's "Morning Edition" News, 17 May 2011.

36. NPR's "Morning Edition" News, 21 May 2011.

37. U.S. Army indigenous police trainer, in conversation with author in early January 2011.

38. "Attack Kills 3 Coalition Troops in Afghanistan," News Briefs Wire Reports (AP), *Jacksonville Daily News* (NC), 6 December 2010.

39. "Afghan Soldier Fires on German Troops, Killing 3," from AP, *Jacksonville Daily News* (NC), 19 February 2011.

40. ABC's Nightly News, 27 April 2011.

41. NPR's "Morning Edition" News, 27 April 2011.

42. "Afghan Prison Attack Stirs Tensions with Pakistan," *Christian Science Monitor,* 16 June 2008.

43. NPR's "Morning Edition" News, 19 November 2010; ABC's Nightly News, 16 December 2010; "U.N. Maps Tell Security Story," *Time,* 10 January 2011, p. 15.

44. NPR's "Morning Edition" News, 17 May 2011.

45. Poole, *Dragon Days,* chapt. 7.

46. Bill Gertz, "China in Kyrgyzstan," *Washington Times,* 2 December 2010.

47. Ibid.

48. "As China Invests, Many Kazakhs Say: Not Too Fast," by David Greene, NPR's "Morning Edition" News, 7 June 2011.

Chapter 12: *Why All the Trouble in Thailand?*

1. Maj. Lawrence Spinetta (USAF), "Cutting China's 'String of Pearls'," *U.S. Naval Institute Proceedings,* October 2006, pp. 40-42.

2. "Country Profiles," BBC's News Online, s.v. "Thailand: Timeline."

3. Ibid., s.v. "Thailand."

4. "Profile: Thailand's Reds and Yellows," BBC's News Online, 20 April 2010.

5. Ibid.

6. Paul Battersby, "Politics and the Broader Politics of Thailand's International Relations in the 1990's: From Communism to Capitalism," from *Pacific Affairs,* vol. 71, no. 4, Winter 1998-1999, pp. 473-488, in *Wikipedia Encyclopedia,* s.v. "Communist Party in Thailand."

7. William R. Heaton, "China and Southeast Asian Communist Movements: The Decline of Dual Track Diplomacy," from *Asian Survey,* vol. 22, no. 8., August 1982, pp. 779-800, in *Wikipedia Encyclopedia,* s.v. "Communist Party in Thailand."

8. "The Rise and Fall of the Communist Party of Thailand," by Pierre Rousset, *International Journal of Socialist Renewal,* 9 September 2009.

9. "Background Note: Thailand," U.S. State Dept., 28 January 2011.

10. "Country Profiles," BBC's News Online, s.v. "Thailand: Timeline."

11. "PM Urges Public to Remain Calm Following Thaksin's Threat of Forming People's Army," *The Nation Online* (Thailand), 29 October 2010.

12. "Country Profiles," BBC's News Online, s.v. "Thailand: Timeline."

13. "The Rise and Fall of the Communist Party of Thailand," by Rousset.

14. NPR's "Morning Edition" News, 4 July 2011.

Chapter 13: *All This over Ocean Chokepoints?*

1. *CIA — The World Factbook* (www.cia.gov), s.v. "Thailand."

2. "The Afghan Endgame," by Barry et al, p. 45; Peters, *Seeds of Terror,* p. 129.

3. Sen, review of *Karachi,* by John; Peters, *Seeds of Terror,* p. 31; Lawrence Lifschultz, "Pakistan, the Empire of Heroin," in McCoy and Block, "War on Drugs," p. 320, Lifschultz, *Heroin Empire,* pp. 71-72, and *The Herald* (Pakistan) of 1985, all in *Seeds of Terror,* by Peters, p. 37.

4. "World: South Asia, Pakistan Army Seizes Power," BBC's News Online, 12 October 1999; *Wikipedia Encyclopedia,* s.v. "Military Coups in Pakistan."

5. John, *Coming Blowback,* pp. 39, 184; "Pakistani Government in Turmoil . . . ," by Shah.

6. *South Asia Intelligence Review* database (satp.org) and *Wikipedia Encyclopedia,* s.v. "Tehreek-e-Nafaz-e-Shariat-e-Mohammadi."

7. "Pakistani Government in Turmoil . . . ," by Shah; "Assassination Intensifies the Crisis," p. 14.

8. Poole, *Expeditionary Eagles,* p. 111; Australian Govt. Nat. Security Website (www.ag.gov.au), s.v. "Lashkar e-Jhangvi."

9. "Pakistan Releases Top Terrorist Leader," by Roggio.

10. *South Asia Intelligence Review* database (satp.org), s.v. "Harkat-ul-Jihad-al-Islami"; Poole, *Expeditionary Eagles,* p. 33; Issam Ahmed, "Pakistan's Old Jihadis Pose New Threat," pp. 8, 9; Mir, *Talibanisation of Pakistan,* p. 57.

11. John L. Esposito, *Unholy War: Terror in the Name of Islam* (London: Oxford Univ. Press, 2002). pp. 15-17; Khaled Ahmed, *Pakistan: Behind the Ideological Mask* (Lahore: Vanguard, 2004), pp. 223, 226.

12. *Pakistan Country Study,* Areas Handbook Series (Washington, D.C.: Library of Congress, 2003); Tini Tran, AP, "Tape Targets Clerics," *Jacksonville Daily News* (NC), 25 November 2004, pp. 1A, 4A.

13. "Unpacking 'Punjabi Taliban'."

14. "GHQ Attack Mastermind Apprehended in Bahawalpur"; *South Asia Intelligence Review* database (satp.org), s.v. "Sipah-e-Sahaba Pakistan."

15. "Pakistan Releases Top Terrorist Leader," by Roggio; "The Marriott Blast," by B. Rahman, South Asia Analysis Group (India), *International Terrorism Monitor,"* Paper No. 449, 22 September 2008.

16. "GHQ Attack Mastermind Apprehended in Bahawalpur"; *South Asia Intelligence Review* database (satp.org), s.v. "Sipah-e-Sahaba Pakistan."

17. *South Asia Intelligence Review* database (satp.org), s.v. "Harkat-ul-Jihad-al-Islami."

18. "Pakistan Releases Top Terrorist Leader," by Roggio.

19. "Karachi Terror Attack: Siege On after 13 Hours; 12 Killed, 2 Planes Destroyed," NDTV Online (Mumbai), 23 May 2011.

20. "Pakistani Islamists Sign Deal With China," by Bokhari.

21. "China's Discreet Hold on Pakistan's Northern Borderlands," by Harrison.

22. "Smoking Al Qaeda Out of Karachi," by B. Raman; "Dawood Gang Provided Logistics to Lashkar Militants," from Press Trust of India, and "Dawood's Drug Net Financed 26/11: Russian Intelligence," as both retrieved from NDTV Online (Mumbai) on 18 December 2008; *Wikipedia Encyclopedia,* s.v. "Dawood Ibrahim"; Craig Whitlock and Karen DeYoung, "Attributes Suggest Outside Help," *Washington Post,* 28 November 2008, p. 1.

23. Poole, *Expeditionary Eagles,* chapt. 10.

24. "Profile: Pakistan's Military Intelligence Agency," by David Chazan, BBC's News Online, 9 January 2002; "Pakistan Trims Top ISI Chairs," p. 3; "A Godfather's Lethal Mix of Business and Politics"; "Dawood's ISI Links Could Trouble Musharraf," by John; John, *Coming Blowback,* p. 187.

25. John, *Coming Blowback,* p. 222.

26. Hunwick, "Africa and Islamic Revival," p. 8; "National Islamic Front," *Who's Who: Significant People and Organizations,* Sudan Update (West Yorkshire, England), from its website, www.sudanupdate.org; Poole, *Terrorist Trail,* pp. 8, 9.

27. Gunaratna, *Inside al-Qaeda,* p. 158; Poole, *Terrorist Trail,* p. 8.

28. "Blood for Oil," *Investor's Business Daily* (Los Angeles), 2 May 2005, as reprinted in *Sudan Tribune,* 3 May 2005 and 15 June 2006.

29. Chris Suellentrop, "Abdullah Azzam—The Godfather of Jihad," MSN News, n.d.; Esposito, *Unholy War,* pp. 7, 94, 95; *Encyclopedia* (encyclopedia.com), s.v. "Muslim Brotherhood."

30. Hunwick, "Africa and Islamic Revival"; *Britannica Encyclopedia* (Britannica.com), s.v. "Muslim Brotherhood."

31. Poole, *Homeland Siege,* intro. and appendix; Poole, *Tequila Junction,* part one.

32. Bradsher, "North Korean Ploy Masks Ships under Other Flags."

33. "Why Tunisia, Why Now," by Christen Chick, *Christian Science Monitor,* 31 January 2011, pp. 8, 9.

34. Poole, *Homeland Siege,* intro. and appendix.

35. "Chinese Hackers Seek U.S. Access," *USA Today,* 11 March 2007; John Wagley, "Foreign Hackers are Overwhelming U.S. Government Computers, Says Analyst," *Security Management,* 19 December 2008.

36. Poole, *Dragon Days,* pp. 92-97; *Wikipedia Encyclopedia,* s.v. "West Bengal" and "Kolkata."

Chapter 14: *How Eastern Powers Influence Things*

1. "China's Discreet Hold on Pakistan's Northern Borderlands," by Harrison; "China Puts 700,000 Troops on Alert in Sudan"; Bill Gertz, "Notes from the Pentagon," *Washington Times,* 5 March 2004; "China Winning Resources and Loyalties of Africa," *The Financial Times* (UK), 28 February 2006.

2. "Rolling Thunder (1965–8)," *American Military and Naval History Online,* 5 November 2010; *The United States Strategic Bombing Surveys,* reprinted by Air Univ. Press, Maxwell Air Force Base, October 1987; "Vietnam, Cambodia Bombing," zFacts, as retrieved from its website, zFacts.com, on 13 January 2011.

3. Memorandum for the record by H.J. Poole.

4. H. John Poole, *The Tiger's Way: A U.S. Private's Best Chance for Survival* (Emerald Isle, NC: Posterity Press, 2002), pp. 153, 154, and 161-167.

5. *Mao's Generals Remember Korea,* trans. and ed. Xiaobing Li, Allan R. Millett, and Bin Yu (Lawrence, KS: Univ. Press of Kansas, 2001), pp. 153-155.

6. "China's 'Comprehensive Warfare' Strategy Wears Down Enemy Using Non-Military Means."

7. Poole, *Tequila Junction,* part one.

Chapter 15: *A U.S. Version of the Chinese Model*

1. Terrence Maitland and Peter McInerney, *Vietnam Experience: A Contagion of War* (Boston, MA: Boston Publishing, 1968), p. 97.
2. Ibid.
3. Edward Doyle, Samuel Lipsman, and Stephen Weiss, *Vietnam Experience: Passing the Torch* (Boston, MA: Boston Publishing, 1981), picture caption, p. 45; *Mao Tse-tung: An Anthology of His Writings,* ed. Anne Fremantle (New York: Mentor, 1962), p. 69.
4. Edwin P. Hoyt, *The Marine Raiders* (New York: Pocket Books, 1989), p. 16.
5. Memorandum for the record by H.J. Poole.
6. *Handbook on the Chinese People's Liberation Army,* DDB-2680-32-84 (Washington, D.C.: Defense Intel. Agency, November 1984), p. 33.
7. Fareed Zakaria, "What America Has Lost," *Newsweek,* 13 September 2010, p. 18.
8. "From Makin to Bouganville: Marine Raiders in the Pacific War," by Maj. Jon T. Hoffman, *Marines in WWII Commemorative Series* (Washington, D.C.: Marine Corps Historical Ctr., 1995), p. 1.
9. Truong Chinh, *Primer for Revolt,* intro. Bernard B. Fall (New York: Praeger, 1963), pp. 114-117.
10. *McGraw-Hill Dictionary of Scientific and Technical Terms* (2003), s.v. "unconventional warfare."
11. Former member of the 3rd Raider Battalion, in conversation with author in October 2010.
12. "From Makin to Bouganville: Marine Raiders in the Pacific War."

Chapter 16: *How Best to Make a 4GW Difference*

1. Memorandum for the record by H.J. Poole.
2. General Patton, as quoted in *Hitler's Last Gamble,* by Trevor N. Dupuy, David L. Bongard, and Richard C. Anderson, Jr. (New York: HarperPerennial, 1994), pp. 498, 499.
3. Lt.Gen. Collins, *Common Sense Training*, p. 214.
4. Maj.Gen. Robert H. Scales, U.S. Army (Ret.), "Small-Unit Dominance: The Strategic Importance of Tactical Reform," *Armed Forces Journal,* October 2010, p. 14.
5. Ibid., p. 42.
6. Poole, *Tequila Junction,* appendix.
7. Adm. Mike Mullen, as quoted by NPR's "Morning Edition" News, 6 July 2010.

8. *Handbook on the Chinese Communist Army,* DA Pamphlet 30-51, (Washington, D.C.: Hdqts. Dept. of the Army, 7 December 1960), p. 55.

9. *The Pentagon Labyrinth: 10 Short Essays to Help You through It,* ed. Winslow T. Wheeler, Ctr. for Defense Info., December 2011.

10. Bruce I. Gudmundsson, *Stormtroop Tactics — Innovation in the German Army 1914-1918* (New York: Praeger, 1989), pp. 147-149; Poole, *The Tiger's Way,* chapts. 12 and 19.

11. "Toward an Adaptive Army," by Col. Robert B. Killebrew, *Army Magazine,* January 2002.

12. Poole, *The Tiger's Way,* pp. 168-172.

13. Poole, *Terrorist Trail,* pp. 34-38; Poole, *Dragon Days,* pp. 54, 55.

14. Shipunov and Filimonov, "Field Artillery to be Replaced with Shmel Infantry Flamethrower."

Chapter 17: *Opportunity-Based Offense*

1. Memorandum for the record by H.J. Poole.

2. Ibid.

3. Lanning and Cragg, *Inside the VC and the NVA,* pp. 206-208.

4. Ibid.

5. Ibid.

6. Ibid.

Chapter 18: *Opportunity-Based Defense*

1. *Handbook on the Chinese People's Liberation Army,* pp. 26, 38.

2. Nicholas Warr, *Phase Line Green: The Battle for Hue, 1968* (Annapolis, MD: Naval Inst. Press, 1997), pp. 155-160.

3. Ibid.

4. Eric Hammel, *Fire in the Streets: The Battle for Hue, Tet 1968* (Pacifica, CA: Pacifica Press, 1991), pp. 304, 305.

5. "5th Marine Division Intelligence Report of 24 March 1945," as quoted in *Iwo Jima: Amphibious Epic,* by Lt. Col. Whitman S. Bartley (Washington, D.C.: Hist. Branch, HQMC, 1954), p. 190.

6. Memorandum for the record by H.J. Poole.

7. "Operation Allenbrook," as retrieved from the following url: http://www.allenaustin.net/oab.htm.

8. Poole, *Tactics of the Crescent Moon,* chapt. 1.

9. Poole, *Phantom Soldier,* chapt. 6.

10. *Sun Bin's Art of War: World's Greatest Military Treatise*, trans. Sui Yun (Singapore: Chung Printing, 1999), p. 190.
11. Poole, *Phantom Soldier*, chapt. 9.
12. *Sun Bin's Art of War*, p. 189.

Chapter 19: *Rifleman Tactics*

1. Number of infantrymen versus total number of enlisted personnel, as retrieved on 11 March 2011 from the U.S. Army's Recruiting Website, GoArmy.com, at the followng url: http://www.goarmy.com/careers-and-jobs/browse-career-and-job-categories/combat/infantryman-11b.html, and from the DoD publication "Active Duty Military Personnel by Rank/Grade September 30, 2009."
2. *Handbook on Japanese Military Forces*, TM-E 30-480 (Washington, D.C.: U.S. War Dept., 1944), reprint (Baton Rouge, LA: LSU Press, 1991), p. 394.
3. *Handbook on the Chinese Armed Forces*, pp. 5-21, 5-30.
4. *Global Security* (globalsecurity.org), s.v. "PLA Uniforms and Insignia."
5. *Mao Tse-tung: An Anthology of His Writings,* ed. Anne Fremantle (New York: Mentor, 1962), pp. 132, 133, 139; *Handbook on the Chinese Armed Forces*, p. 1-7; *Handbook on the Chinese People's Liberation Army,* pp. 5, 6.
6. Maitland and McInerney, *Vietnam Experience,* p. 97.
7. Phillip B. Davidson, *Vietnam at War—The History: 1946-1975* (New York: Oxford Univ. Press, 1988), p. 64.
8. *Mao Tse-tung,* ed. Fremantle, p. 69.
9. Ibid., pp. 5, 6.
10. Joseph S. Bermudez, Jr., *North Korean Special Forces* (Annapolis, MD: Naval Inst. Press, 1998), p. 219.
11. "Some Interesting Facts about Korea: The Forgotten War," *DAV Magazine,* May/June 2000, p. 28.
12. Attributed to U.S. Army Gen. J. "Black Jack" Pershing in WWI.
13. Memorandum for the record by H.J. Poole.
14. Col. Merritt A. Edson, as quoted in *Fighting on Guadalcanal,* FMFRP 12-110 (Washington, D.C.: U.S.A. War Office, 1942), pp. 14-19.
15. ABC's Nightly News, 10 March 2011.
16. *Handbook on the Chinese Armed Forces*, p. 5-19; *Handbook on the Chinese People's Liberation Army,* p. 15.
17. *Handbook on the Chinese Armed Forces*, p. 5-28; *Handbook on the Chinese People's Liberation Army,* p. 17.
18. Maj.Gen. Edwin Simmons USMC (Ret.), in "An Entirely New War."

Chapter 20: *Acquiring Enough Individual Skill*

1. Bill D. Ross, *Iwo Jima: Legacy of Valor* (New York: Vintage, 1986), p. 163; Lt.Col. Whitman S. Bartley, *Iwo Jima: Amphibious Epic* (Washington, D.C.: Hist. Branch, HQMC, 1954), p. 111.
2. Maj.Gen. Edwin Simmons USMC (Ret.), in "An Entirely New War."
3. Lynn Montross and Capt. Nicholas A. Canzona, *The Chosin Reservoir Campaign,* U.S. Marine Operations in Korea 1950-1953, vol. III (Washington, D.C.: Hist. Branch, HQMC, 1957), pp. 161-178.
4. Memorandum for the record by H.J. Poole; Poole, *The Tiger's Way,* chapt. 7; Nguyen Van Mo, 40th Sapper Battalion, as quoted in *Portrait of the Enemy,* by David Chanoff and Doan Van Toai (New York: Random House, 1986), pp. 161, 162.
5. Navaho Codetalker, in "Japanese Codetalkers," *In Search of History,* History Channel, 30 March 1999.
6. Marine infantryman, as quoted in *Iwo Jima,* by Ross, p. 135.
7. Col. Merritt A. Edson, as quoted in "Fighting on Guadalcanal," *FMFRP 12-110* (Washington, D.C.: U.S.A. War Office, 1942), p. 14.
8. *Night Movements*, trans. and preface by C. Burnett (Tokyo: Imperial Japanese Army, 1913), reprint (Port Townsend, WA: Loompanics Unlimited, n.d.).
9. Ibid., pp. 37-133.
10. Ibid., p. 29.
11. Ibid., p. 39.
12. Arthur Zich and the editors of Time-Life Books, *The Rising Sun: World War II* (Alexandria, VA: Time-Life Books, 1977), p. 35.
13. Ibid., p. 30.
14. *Night Movements,* p. 33.
15. Ibid., p. 51.
16. "How the Japanese Army Fights," by Lt.Col. Paul W. Thompson, Lt.Col. Harold Doud, Lt.Col. John Scofield, and the editorial staff of "The Infantry Journal," *FMFRP 12-22* (New York: Penguin Books, 1942; reprint Washington, D.C.: HQMC, 1989), p. 51.
17. *Mao Tse-tung,* ed. Anne Fremantle; *Handbook on the Chinese Communist Army,* p. 54.
18. Poole, *Phantom Soldier,* chapt. 7.
19. *Handbook on the Chinese Armed Forces,* p. 5-25.
20. *Mao's Generals Remember Korea,* pp. 70, 71.
21. Bermudez, *North Korean Special Forces,* p. 222.
22. Ibid.
23. Ibid., p. 219.

24. James F. Dunnigan and Albert A. Nofi, *Dirty Little Secrets of the Vietnam War* (New York: Thomas Dunne Books, 1999), p. 279.

25. Ibid., pp. 276-279.

26. Lanning and Cragg, *Inside the VC and the NVA,* p. 56.

27. Ibid.

28. Ibid., p. 55.

29. Ibid.

30. Poole, *The Tiger's Way,* chapt. 3.

31. Memorandum for the record by H.J. Poole.

32. Poole, *The Tiger's Way,* pp. 12, 74, 75, 98, 310.

33. *Handbook on the Chinese Armed Forces,* pp. 5-21, 5-30; *Mao Tse-tung,* ed. Anne Fremantle.

34. Menges, *China: The Gathering Threat,* p. 328; *Wikipedia Encyclopedia,* s.v. "People's Liberation Army"; *Chinese Defense Today* (www.sinodefence.com), s.v. "Home Ground Forces Order of Battle."

35. NPR's "Morning Edition" News, 23 February 2009; "Wushu & Sanda," *Fight Quest,* Discovery Channel, 28 December 2008.

36. Col. Wesley L. Fox, *Marine Rifleman: Forty-Three Years in the Corps* (Dulles, VA: Brassey's, 2002), pp. 237, 238.

Chapter 21: *Policeman Tactics*

1. "DoD Cooperation with Civilian Law Enforcement Officials," DoD Directive 5525.5, 15 January 1986, Administrative Reissuance Incorporating Change 1, 20 December 1989.

2. "Doomed SWAT Sergeants Didn't Expect an AK-47," by Phillip Matier and Andrew Ross, *San Francisco Chronicle,* 23 March 2009.

3. "Killer of 4 Officers Wanted to Avoid Prison," by Demian Bulwa and Jaxon Van Derbeken, *San Francisco Chronicle,* 23 March 2009; "Woman Says She Pointed Police to Oakland Killer," by Demian Bulwa, *San Francisco Chronicle,* 24 March 2009.

4. "Independent Board of Inquiry into the Oakland Police Department: March 21, 2009 Incident," by James K. Stewart, Senior Fellow, CNA, Inst. for Public Research, December 2009, electronic file designator, opdreport.pdf.

5. Ibid.

6. Poole, *Homeland Siege,* chapt. 9.

7. Ross, *Iwo Jima,* p. 13.

8. Ibid., p. 294.

9. H.J. Poole, *The Last Hundred Yards: The NCO's Contribution to Warfare* (Emerald Isle, NC: Posterity Press, 1997), chapt. 20; Poole, *Dragon Days,* chapt. 15.

10. Poole, *Dragon Days,* chapt. 16, fig. 16.2.

11. Poole, *The Tiger's Way,* chapt. 7.

12. Ibid., chapt. 17.

13. Poole, *The Tiger's Way,* chapts. 6 and 7; Poole, *Dragon Days,* chapt. 15; *Night Movements*, trans. and preface by Burnett.

14. Poole, *The Last Hundred Yards,* figures 12.3 through 12.5.

15. Poole, *The Tiger's Way,* p. 356.

Chapter 22: *Conclusion*

1. Brigadier Mohammad Yousaf and Maj. Mark Adkin, *Bear Trap: Afghanistan's Untold Story* (South Yorkshire, UK: Leo Cooper, n.d.).

2. "Luke 1:68-79," New Testament, *Christian Bible.*

3. *South Asia Intelligence Review* database (satp.org), s.v. "Strategy and Tactics of the Indian Revolution (Maoist)."

4. "Colombian Army Adaption to FARC Insurgency," by Thomas Marks, p. 16; "Betancourt, 3 US Hostages Freed From FARC Rebels," from AP, 2 July 2008; "An Unacknowledged War," by Toby Westerman, *Canada Free Press,* 27 August 2009; "Colombia: FARC Linked to Peruvian Guerrillas," by Brett Borkan, *Colombia Reports,* 8 March 2010; *Wikipedia Encyclopedia,* s.v. "Socio-Economic Structure of the FARC-EP" and "Jacobo Arenas" (as retrieved in early 2008); Sara Miller Llana, "El Salvador Joins Latin Leftward Tilt," *Christian Science Monitor,* 17 March 2009, pp. 1, 11; Brookes, "Venezuelan Vagaries," pp. 12, 13; "Four Spies for the U.S. Have Been Caught by Venezuelan Security," World News in Brief, *Christian Science Monitor,* 21 August 2006, p. 7.

5. Poole, *Tequila Junction,* p. 253, chapts. 1-8.

6. "Chavez Eyes China, Russia, More on 'Strategic'-Interest Tour."

7. "Leftist Wins Election," The World, *Time,* 20 June 2011.

8. "Global Economic Warfare," from its website, http://globaleconomicwarfare.com.

9. Poole, *Tequila Junction,* part one.

10. "China's 'Comprehensive Warfare' Strategy Wears Down Enemy Using Non-Military Means."

11. Global Security (globalsecurity.org), s.v. "Project Bojinka"; "Path to 9/11"; "Philippines: U.S. Missed 9/11 Clues Years Ago."

12. *Unrestricted Warfare,* by Liang and Xiangsui, pp. 54, 144, 145, 158.

13. "The Spy Factory"; Gunaratna, *Inside al-Qaeda,* p. 196.
14. Poole, *Dragon Days,* pp. 42-44; Nat. Commission on Terrorist Attacks upon the U.S., chapt. 5 of its report, footnotes 59-61; "The Emir," *Unmasking Terror,* ed. Heffelfinger, pp. 402, 403.
15. "Profile: Al-Qaeda 'Kingpin' "; Erika Kinetz, "U.S. Congress Warms to Cambodia," *Christian Science Monitor,* 14 March 2007, p. 4.
16. *Unrestricted Warfare,* by Liang and Xiangsui, p. 146.
17. NPR's "Morning Edition" News, 23 February 2009; "Wushu & Sanda," *Fight Quest,* Discovery Channel, 28 December 2008.

Glossary

ABC	American Broadcasting Company	U.S. TV network
AIAI	*Al-Itihadd al-Islamiya*	*Al-Qaeda*-affiliated forerunner of *al-Shabaab* in Somalia
AK-47	Small-arms designator	Communist Bloc assault rifle
AQAP	*Al-Qaeda* in the Arabian Peninsula	Yemen-based branch of *al-Qaeda*
ASEAN	Assoc. of Southeast Asian Nations	Alliance of countries in Orient
BBC	British Broadcasting Company	U.K. radio and TV network
B.C.	Before Christ	Before the year zero
CCCCLTD	China Communications Construction Company Limited	Possible business extension of the PLA
CCP	Chinese Communist Party	Ruling party of the PRC
CD	Compact Disc	Repository for computer files
CEIEC	China National Electronics Import and Export Corporation	Known business extension of the PLA
CHEC	China Harbor Engineering Company	Possible business extension of the PLA
CIA	Central Intelligence Agency	U.S. spy organization
CNN	Cable News Network	U.S. TV channel
COSCO	China Ocean Shipping Company	Known business extension of the PLA

CP	Command Post	Place from which unit commander operates
CPT	Communist Party of Thailand	Second largest Communist movement in Southeast Asia in the early 1970's
CRBC	China Road and Bridge Corporation	Possible business extension of the PLA
CRCC	China Railway Construction Corporation	Probable business extension of the PLA
CRSSG	China Railway Shisiju Group Corporation	Probable business extension of the PLA
CSCEC	China State Construction Engineering Corporation	Probable business extension of the PLA
D.C.	District of Colombia	Site of U.S. capital
D-Day	Debarkation Day	Day that Allies invade some place
DEA	Drug Enforcement Administration	U.S. narcotics-monitoring bureau
DIA	Defense Intelligence Agency	U.S. enemy information bureau
DMZ	Demilitarized Zone	No-mans land between North and South Vietnam
DNI	Director of National Intelligence	Coordinator of all U.S. collection of enemy information
DoD	Department of Defense	Civilian headquarters of all U.S. military services
DRC	Democratic Republic of the Congo	War-wracked nation in Central Africa
DTO	Drug Trafficking Organization	Illicit-narcotics ring
E&E	Escape and Evasion	Art of eluding a pursuer

EPR	Popular Revolutionary Army	Marxist guerrillas in Mexico
EU	European Union	European partnership of nations
EZLN	Zapatista National Liberation Army	Populist guerrilla movement in Mexico
FAE	Fuel Air Explosive	Flame munition that sucks up all surrounding oxygen
FARC	*Fuerzas Armadas Revolutionarias de Colombia*	Maoist rebels from Colombia
FATA	Federally Administered Tribal Areas	Pakistani area at border with Afghanistan
FBI	Federal Bureau of Investigation	U.S. crime-monitoring agency
FCL	Final Coordination Line	Imaginary line behind which maneuver force forms to assault daytime objective
FIA	Federal Investigative Agency	Pakistan's crime bureau
4GW	Fourth-Generation Warfare	War waged in four arenas at once—religious/psychological, economic, political, and martial
GI	Government Issue	Colloquial term for U.S. military service member
GM	General Motors	U.S. car company
Hezb	*Hezb-ul-Mujahideen*	*JI*'s military wing, founded by Hekmatyar in Azad Kashmir
HQMC	Headquarters Marine Corps	Various staff sections through which U.S. Commandant manages the organization
HUJI	*Harakat ul-Jihad-i-Islami*	Deobandi affiliate of *JUI/F*
HUM	*Harakat ul-Mujahideen*	*JUI/F*'s military wing

ICU	Union of Islamic Courts	*Al-Qaeda*-linked forerunner of *al-Shabaab* in Somalia
IDF	Israeli Defense Forces	Military services of Israel
IED	Improvised Explosive Devise	Remotely detonated mine
IIF	International Islamic Front	Osama bin Laden's alliance of Pakistani religious party militias
IJT	*Islami Jamiat-i-Talaba*	Student wing of *JI*
IMU	Islamic Movement of Uzbekistan	Close *al-Qaeda* affiliate that helps to run Afghanistan's northern drug conduit
IRGC	Iranian Revolutionary Guard Corps	Protectors of the Iranian Revolution
ISI	Interservices Intelligence	Pakistan's spy agency
JEM	*Jaish-e-Mohammed*	Militant faction, an offshoot of the merger between *HUM* and *HUJI*
JI	*Jamaat i-Islami*	Anti-Western Pakistani religious political party
JuD	*Jamaat-ul-Dawa*	Pakistani militant faction, previously called *MDI*
JUI/F	*Jamiat Ulema-i-Islam* Fazlur Rehman faction	Legal Pakistani religious political party, primary supporter of Afghan Taliban
LeJ	*Lashkar-e-Jhangvi*	*SSP's* military wing
LET	*Lashkar e-Toiba*	*JuD's* military wing
MCC	China Metallurgical Group Corporation	Possible business extension of the PLA
MDI	*Markaz-ud-Dawa-wal-Irshad*	Pakistani militant faction, forerunner of *JuD*

MDMA	3,4-methylenedioxy-methamphetamine	Drug known on the street as "ecstasy"
MG	Machinegun	Fully automatic small arm
MILES	Multiple Integrated Laser Engagement System	Individually worn device for simulated casualty assessment
MMA	*Mutahida Majlis Amal*	Pakistani religious party alliance with *JI* and *JUI/F*
MoH	Medal of Honor	America's highest award for bravery
MOIS	Ministry of Intelligence and Security	Iranian spy agency
MQM	*Muttahida Qaumi Movement*	Pro-military Pakistani political party
NAFTA	North American Free Trade Agreement	Economic pact between nations
NATO	North Atlantic Treaty Organization	Western military alliance
NCO	Noncommissioned Officer	Military pay grades E-4 and E-5
NDIC	National Drug Intelligence Center	U.S. bureau that gathers information on drug runners
NEFA	Northeast Frontier Agency	India's Assam region
NIC	National Intelligence Council	Panel that assists the DNI
9/11	September 11, 2001	Day planes hit U.S. buildings in New York and D.C.
NLC	National Logistics Cell	Pakistani-army-run trucking company that carried drugs during Soviet-Afghan War
NPR	National Public Radio	U.S. educational radio network

NVA	North Vietnamese Army	U.S. foe in Vietnam
NWFP	Northwest Frontier Province	Pakistani province
PBS	Public Broadcasting System	U.S. educational TV network
PDRY	People's Democratic Republic of Yemen	Former Yemeni Marxist State
PLA	People's Liberation Army	Parent of Chinese armed forces
PLA	People's Liberation Army	Name chosen by the Maoist guerrillas in Assam, India
PLAT	People's Liberation Army of Thailand	Military wing of the CPT
PLD	Probable Line of Deployment	Imaginary line behind which maneuver force forms to assault nighttime objective
PPP	Pakistan People's Party	Pakistani political entity
PPP	People Power Party	Thai political entity
PRC	People's Republic of China	Mainland Communist China
PT	Physical (Fitness) Training	Group exercising in military
S-2	Staff designator	Military headquarters section that gathers enemy intelligence
SAIC	Shanghai Automotive Industry Corporation	Chinese business
SEAL	Sea, Air, and Land	U.S. Navy commando who specializes in overseas raids
2GW	Second-Generation Warfare	Focus is on destroying enemy strongpoints
SIM	*Shura Ittehad-ul-Mujahideen*	Alliance between Baitullah Mehsud, Maulavi Nazir, and Hafiz Gul Bahadur to aid Mullah Omar & bin Laden

SKS	Small-arms designator	Communist Bloc rifle
SLA	Southern Lebanese Army	Israeli-affiliated militia in Southern Lebanon
SNCO	Staff Noncommissioned Officer	Military pay grades E-6 and above
SSP	*Sipah-e-Sahaba*	Pakistani militant faction
SWAT	Special-Weapons Assault Team	Paramilitary police squad
TAOR	Tactical Area of Responsibility	A unit's assigned sector
TBA	Tri-Border Area	Corner of Argentina, Paraguay, and Brazil
TFG	Transitional Federal Government	Somalia's legitimate regime
TFP	Transitional Federal Parliament	Somalia's governing body
3GW	Third-Generation Warfare	Focus is on bypassing enemy's strongpoints so as to more easily destroy his strategic assets
TNSM	*Tehreek-e-Nafaz-e-Shariat-e-Mohammadi*	Radical offshoot of *JI*
TTP	*Tehrik-i-Taliban Pakistan*	Pakistani Taliban
TV	Television	Electronic media device
UAE	United Arab Emirates	Middle Eastern nation
UDD	United Front for Democracy against Dictatorship	Thai political party
U.K.	United Kingdom	Great Britain
U.N.	United Nations	Alliance of countries
UNIMED	United Medical	Hong Kong pharmaceutical company with subsidiary in Mexico City

UNODC	United Nations Office on Drugs and Crime	U.N. office that monitors all smuggling and crime
UPS	United Parcel Service	American package delivery company
U.S.	United States	America
UW	Unconventional Warfare	For infantrymen, E&E and fighting like a guerrilla
VC	Viet Cong	NVA-advised local guerrillas during Vietnam War
WWI	World War I	First global conflict
WWII	World War II	Second global conflict
WWIII	World War III	Third global conflict

Bibliography

U.S. Government Publications, Databases, and News Releases

"Active Duty Military Personnel by Rank/Grade September 30, 2009."
    From Department of Defense. Retrieved through *Wikipedia
    Encyclopedia,* s.v. "Infantry."
"Asian Organized Crime and Terrorist Activity in Canada, 1999-2002."
    By Neil S. Helfand. Federal Research Division. Library of
    Congress, July 2003.
"Background Note: Thailand." U.S. State Department, 28 January
    2011. As retrieved from the following url on 5 February 2011:
    http://www.state.gov/r/pa/ei/bgn/2814.htm.
Bartley, Lt.Col. Whitman S. *Iwo Jima: Amphibious Epic.* Washington,
    D.C.: Historical Branch, Headquarters Marine Corps, 1954.
Berry, Laverle and Glenn E. Curtis, John N. Gibbs, Rex A. Hudson,
    Tara Karacan, Nina Kollars, and Ramon Miro. "Nations Hospitable
    to Organized Crime and Terrorism." Federal Research Division.
    Library of Congress, October 2003.
"The Caucus Papers: A Conversation on China." By Congressman J.
    Randy Forbes. As retrieved from following url on 12 February 2011:
    http://forbes.house.gov/caucuspapers/.
CIA—The World Factbook. As updated every three months. From its
    website, www.cia.gov, during the period may 2010-August 2011.
Clinton, Hillary Rodham. U.S. Secretary of State. In interview
    with Chris Wallace. FOX's News Online, 30 January 2011.
    As retrieved on the same day from the following url:
    http://www.state.gov/secretary/rm/2011/01/155589.htm.
"Country Profile: Venezuela." Library of Congress. Federal Research
    Division, March 2005.
"DoD Cooperation with Civilian Law Enforcement Officials."
    Department of Defense Directive 5525.5, 15 January 1986.
    Administrative Reissuance Incorporating Change 1, 20 December
    1989. File named 5525_5.pdf.
"Drug Trafficking and North Korea: Issues for U.S. Policy."
    By Ralph F. Perl. Congressional Research Service Report
    RL32167. Last in a series of updates, 27 November 2006.

Fighting on Guadalcanal. FMFRP 12-110. Washington, D.C.: U.S.A. War Office, 1942.

"From Makin to Bouganville: Marine Raiders in the Pacific War." By Maj. Jon T. Hoffman. *Marines in WWII Commemorative Series.* Washington, D.C.: Marine Corps Historical Center, 1995.

Handbook on Japanese Military Forces. TM-E 30-480. Washington, D.C.: U.S. War Dept., 1944. Reprint, Baton Rouge, LA: LSU Press, 1991.

Handbook on the Chinese Armed Forces. DDI-2680-32-76. Washington, D.C.: Defense Intelligence Agency, July 1976.

Handbook on the Chinese Communist Army. DA Pamphlet 30-51. Washington, D.C.: Headquarters Department of the Army, 7 December 1960.

Handbook on the Chinese People's Liberation Army. DDB-2680-32-84. Washington, D.C.: Defense Intelligence Agency, November 1984.

How the Japanese Army Fights. By Lt.Col. Paul W. Thompson, Lt.Col. Harold Doud, Lt.Col. John Scofield, and the editorial staff of "The Infantry Journal." FMFRP 12-22. New York: Penguin Books, 1942. Reprint. Washington, D.C.: Headquarters Marine, Corps, 1989.

"Iran: U.S. Concerns and Policy Responses." By Kenneth Katzman. Congressional Research Service Report for Congress. Order Code RL32048, 26 October 2010.

Malik, Mohan. *Dragon on Terrorism: Assessing China's Tactical Gains and Strategic Losses Post-September 11.* Carlisle, PA: Strategic Studies Institute, U. S. Army War College, October 2002.

Montross, Lynn and Capt. Nicholas A. Canzona. *The Chosin Reservoir Campaign.* U.S. Marine Operations in Korea 1950-1953. Volume III. Washington, D.C.: Historical Branch, Headquarters Marine Corps, 1957.

National Commission on Terrorist Attacks upon the United States. Chapter 5 of its report. As retrieved at an uncertain date from the following url at a website that was frozen in 2004: http://www.9-11commission.gov/report/911Report_Ch5.htm. The record is now at National Archives and Records Administration and can be accessed through legislative.archives@nara.gov.

National Drug Threat Assessment (for) 2008. National Drug Intelligence Center, October 2007. As retrieved from the Drug Enforcement Administration website, www.usdoj.gov/dea, in October 2008.

National Drug Threat Assessment (for) 2009. National Drug Intelligence Center, December 2008. As retrieved from the following url: http://www.justice.gov/ndic/pubs31/31379/heroin.htm.

National Drug Threat Assessment (for) 2010. National Drug Intelligence Center, February 2010. As retrieved from the following url: http://www.justice.gov/ndic/pubs38/38661/heroin.htm.

Pakistan Country Study. Areas Handbook Series. Washington, D.C.: Library of Congress, 2003.

Pakistan Country Study. Area Handbook Series. Washington, D.C.: Library of Congress, 2004.

Pakistan: A Country Study. Edited by Peter R. Blood. Federal Research Division, Library of Congress, Area Handbook Series. Headquarters Department of the Army, DA Pam 550-48. Washington, D.C.: U.S. Government Printing Office, 1995.

Patterns of Global Terrorism, 2002 Report. Washington, D.C.: U.S. Department of State, April 2003.

The United States Strategic Bombing Surveys. Reprinted by Air University Press. Maxwell Air Force Base, October 1987.

U.S. Army's Recruiting Website, GoArmy.com.

U.S. Congressional Testimony. In "Iran Continues Support of Terrorism." *Voice of America,* 17 February 2005.

"U.S. Designates Dawood Ibrahim As Terrorist Supporter." U.S. Treasury Department Press Release, 16 October 2003.

U.S. Embassy in Mexico. Press Release 07. "Largest Cash Seizure in History Product of U.S.-Mexico Counter-Narcotics Cooperation." Statement by Ambassador Antonio O. Garza, 20 March 2007. As retrieved on 15 January 2011 from the following url: www.usembassy-mexico.gov/eng/releases/ep070320seizure.html.

Civilian Publications

Analytical Studies, Databases, and Websites

Ahmed, Khaled. *Pakistan: Behind the Ideological Mask.* Lahore: Vanguard, 2004.

Atwan, Abdel Bari. *The Secret History of Al-Qa'ida.* London: Abacus, an imprint of Little, Brown Book Group, 2006.

Australian Government. From its national security website, www.ag.gov.au.

Bermudez, Joseph S., Jr. *North Korean Special Forces.* Annapolis, MD: Naval Institute Press, 1998.

Britannica Encyclopedia. From its website, www.britannica.com.

China Communications Construction Company Limited (CCCCLTD). From its website, ccccltd.com.cn.

China Metallurgical Group Corporation (MCC). From its website, www.mcc.com.cn/.

China National Electronics Import and Export Corporation (CEIEC). From its website, ceiec.com.cn.

China Railway Construction Corporation (CRCC). From its website, crcc.com/cn.

China Railway Shisiju Group Corporation (CRSSG). From its website, crssg.com/english.

China Road and Bridge Corporation (CRBC). From its website, crbc.com/cn.

Chinese Posters. Hosted by the International Institute of Social History (Amsterdam). From its website, chineseposters.net.

China State Construction Engineering Corporation (CSCEC). From its website, app.cscec.com.cn.

Chinh, Truong. *Primer for Revolt*. Introduction by Bernard B. Fall. New York: Praeger, 1963.

Collins, Lt.Gen. Arthur S. Jr., U.S. Army (Retired). *Common Sense Training—A Working Philosophy for Leaders*. Novato, CA: Presidio Press, 1978.

Columbia Encyclopedia, Sixth Edition, 2008. As accessed through the following url: www.encyclopedia.com.

"Country Profiles." BBC's News Online. From its website, bbc.co.uk.

Davidson, Phillip B. *Vietnam at War—The History: 1946-1975*. New York: Oxford University Press, 1988.

Doyle, Edward and Samuel Lipsman, and Stephen Weiss. *Vietnam Experience: Passing the Torch*. Boston, MA: Boston Publishing, 1981.

Dunnigan, James F. and Albert A. Nofi. *Dirty Little Secrets of the Vietnam War*. New York: Thomas Dunne Books, 1999.

Encyclopedia. From its website, encyclopedia.com.

Encyclopedia Britannica Online. From its website, www.britannica.com.

Esposito, John L. *Unholy War: Terror in the Name of Islam*. London: Oxford University Press, 2002.

Federation of American Scientists. From their website, www.fas.org.

Fox, Col. Wesley L. *Marine Rifleman: Forty-Three Years in the Corps*. Dulles, VA: Brassey's, 2002.

Gertz, Bill. *The China Threat*. Washington, D.C.: Regnery Publishing, 2002.

"Global Economic Warfare." From its website, http://globaleconomicwarfare.com.

Global Security. From its website, globalsecurity.org.

Gudmundsson, Bruce I. *Stormtroop Tactics—Innovation in the German Army 1914-1918*. New York: Praeger, 1989.

Gunaratna, Rohan. *Inside al-Qaeda: Global Network of Terror*. Lahore: Vanguard, 2002.

Hammel, Eric. *Fire in the Streets: The Battle for Hue, Tet 1968*. Pacifica, CA: Pacifica Press, 1991.

Hitler's Last Gamble. By Trevor N. Dupuy, David L. Bongard, and Richard C. Anderson, Jr. New York: HarperPerennial, 1994.

Hoyt, Edwin P. *The Marine Raiders*. New York: Pocket Books, 1989.

Hutchison Whampoa. From its website, hutchison-whampoa.com.

Islami Davet Islamic Politics and Cultural Website (Turkey). As viewed on 26 November 2010 at http://www.islamidavet.com/english/.

Jalali Ali and Lester W. Grau. *Afghan Guerrilla Warfare: In the Words of the Mujahideen Fighters*. St. Paul, MN: MBI Publishing, 2001. First published as *The Other Side of the Mountain*. Quantico, VA: Marine Corps Combat Development Command, 1995.

John, Wilson. Observer Research Foundation. *Coming Blowback: How Pakistan Is Endangering the World*. New Delhi: Rupa & Co., 2009.

King, Gilbert. *The Most Dangerous Man in the World*. New York: Chamberlain Bros., a Penguin imprint, 2004.

Lanning, Michael Lee and Dan Cragg. *Inside the VC and the NVA: The Real Story of North Vietnam's Armed Forces*. New York: Ivy Books, 1992.

Maitland, Terrence and Peter McInerney. *Vietnam Experience: A Contagion of War*. Boston, MA: Boston Publishing, 1968.

Mannes, Aaron. *Profiles in Terror: Guide to Middle East Terror Organizations*. Lanham, MD: Rowman & Littlefield, 2004.

Mao Tse-tung: An Anthology of His Writings. Edited by Anne Fremantle. New York: Mentor, 1962.

Mao's Generals Remember Korea. Translated and edited by Xiaobing Li, Allan R. Millett, and Bin Yu. Lawrence, KS: University Press of Kansas, 2001.

McGraw-Hill Dictionary of Scientific and Technical Terms (2003). From its website, www.mhprofessional.com.

Memorial Institute for the Prevention of Terrorism (MIPT) database. An affiliate or member of the U.S. Dept. of Homeland Security. From its website, www.mipt.org.

Menges, Constantine. *China: The Gathering Threat*. Nashville, TN: Nelson Current, 2005.

Mir, Amir. *Talibanisation of Pakistan*. New Delhi: Pentagon Press, 2010.

Mir, Amir. *The True Face of Jihadis*. Lahore: Mashal Books, 2004.

Nationmaster Encyclopedia. From its website, www.nationmaster.com.

Night Movements. Translated and preface by C. Burnett. Tokyo: Imperial Japanese Army, 1913. Reprint. Port Townsend, WA: Loompanics Unlimited, n.d.

Nojumi, Neamatollah. *The Rise of the Taliban in Afghanistan: Mass Mobilization, Civil War, and the Future of the Region*. New York: Palgrave, 2002.

Pearl, Mariane. *A Mighty Heart: The Inside Story of the Al Qaeda Kidnapping of Danny Pearl*. New York: Scribner, 2003.

The Pentagon Labyrinth: 10 Short Essays to Help You through It.
Edited by Winslow T. Wheeler. Center for Defense Information,
December 2011.

Peters, Gretchen. *Seeds of Terror: How Heroin Is Bankrolling the
Taliban and al-Qaeda.* New York: Thomas Dunne Books, 2009.

Pintak, Lawrence. *Seeds of Hate: How America's Flawed Middle East
Policy Ignited the Jihad.* London: Pluto Press, 2003.

Poole, H. John. *Dragon Days: Time for "Unconventional"
Tactics.* Emerald Isle, NC: Posterity Press, 2007.

Poole, H. John. *Expeditionary Eagles: Outmaneuvering the Taliban.*
Emerald Isle, NC: Posterity Press, 2010.

Poole, H. John. *Homeland Siege: Tactics for Police and Military.*
Emerald Isle, NC: Posterity Press, 2009.

Poole, H. John. *The Last Hundred Yards: The NCO's Contribution to
Warfare.* Emerald Isle, NC: Posterity Press, 1997.

Poole, H. John. *Militant Tricks: Battlefield Ruses of the Islamic
Insurgent.* Emerald Isle, NC: Posterity Press, 2005.

Poole, H. John. *One More Bridge to Cross: Lowering the Cost of War.*
Emerald Isle, NC: Posterity Press, 1999.

Poole, H. John. *Phantom Soldier: The Enemy's Answer to U.S.
Firepower.* Emerald Isle, NC: Posterity Press, 2001.

Poole, H. John. *Tactics of the Crescent Moon: Militant Muslim Combat
Methods.* Emerald Isle, NC: Posterity Press, 2004.

Poole, H. John. *Terrorist Trail: Backtracking the Foreign Fighter.*
Emerald Isle, NC: Posterity Press, 2006.

Poole, H. John. *Tequila Junction: 4th-Generation Counterinsurgency.*
Emerald Isle, NC: Posterity Press, 2008.

Poole, H. John. *The Tiger's Way: A U.S. Private's Best Chance
of Survival.* Emerald Isle, NC: Posterity Press, 2003.

Ross, Bill D. *Iwo Jima: Legacy of Valor.* New York: Vintage, 1986.

Scales, Maj.Gen. Robert H., U.S. Army (Retired). *Firepower in
Limited War.* Washington, D.C.: National Defense University
Press, 1990.

Silent Soldier. By Brigadier Yousaf. South Yorkshire, UK: Leo
Cooper, n.d.

South Asia Intelligence Review. South Asia Terrorist Portal database.
Institute for Conflict Management (New Delhi). From its website,
www.satp.org.

Sudan Update (West Yorkshire, England). From its website,
www.sudanupdate.org.

Sun Bin's Art of War: World's Greatest Military Treatise. Translated
by Sui Yun. Singapore: Chung Printing, 1999.

Tehran's War of Terror and Its Nuclear Delivery Capability. By
Stephen E. Hughes. Victoria, Canada: Trafford Publishing, 2007.

Trip Atlas. From its website, tripatlas.com.

Unmasking Terror: A Global Review of Terrorist Activities. Volumes I, II, and III. The first two edited by Christopher Heffelfinger, and the third by Jonathan Hutzley. Washington, D.C: Jamestown Foundation, 2005 through 2007.

Unrestricted Warfare. By Qiao Liang and Wang Xiangsui. Beijing: PLA Literature and Arts Publishing House, February 1999. FBIS translation over the internet.

Van Creveld, Martin. *The Sword and the Olive: A Critical History of the Israeli Defense Force.* New York: PublicAffairs, Perseus Books, 1998.

Warr, Nicholas. *Phase Line Green: The Battle for Hue, 1968.* Annapolis, MD: Naval Institute Press, 1997.

Wikipedia Encyclopedia. From its website, www.wikipedia.org.

World Drug Report 2009. U.N. Office on Drugs and Crime. As retrieved from its website, www.unodc.org, in November 2009.

World Drug Report 2010. U.N. Office on Drugs and Crime. As retrieved from its website, www.unodc.org, on 25 June 2010.

Yousaf, Brigadier Mohammad and Maj. Mark Adkin. *Bear Trap: Afghanistan's Untold Story.* South Yorkshire, UK: Leo Cooper, n.d.

Zich, Arthur and the editors of Time-Life Books. *The Rising Sun: World War II.* Alexandria, VA: Time-Life Books, 1977.

Videotapes, Movies, DVDs, TV Programs, Slide Shows, and Illustrations

"Ambush in Mogadishu." Written, produced, and directed by William Cran. PBS's *Frontline.* In conjunction with WGBH, Boston, 2002. Videotape.

Energy Information Administration Map. From "A Natural-Gas Gang." *Time,* 16 April 2007.

"An Entirely New War." *Korea—the Unknown War.* London: Thames TV in association with WGBH Boston, 1990. NC Public TV, n.d.

"Japanese Codetalkers." *In Search of History.* History Channel, 30 March 1999.

"The Spy Factory." PBS's *Nova.* NC Public TV, 3 July 2010.

"Varja Sky over Tibet." By John Bush. PBS's *Journey into Buddhism.* NC Public TV, 27 January 2011.

"Wushu & Sanda." *Fight Quest.* Discovery Channel, 28 December 2008.

Letters, E-Mail, and Verbal Conversations

Company commander of 3rd Battalion, 7th Marines. In conversation with author during training evolution of 15, 16 January 2005.

Grand Floridian hotel waitress (recent Lebanese immigrant). In conversation with author on 20 December 2008.

Caracas art store owner. In conversation with author on 16 August 2008.

Former member of the 3rd Raider Battalion. In conversation with author in October 2010.

Longtime owner of Khartoum hotel. In conversation with author on 31 May 2006.

Texas police officer. In conversation with author on 16 May 2011.

U.S. Army indigenous police trainer. In conversation with author in early January 2011.

U.S. special operator. In conversation with author on 2 January 2011.

Newspaper, Magazine, Radio, and Website Articles

Aboul-Enein, Lt.Cmdr. Youssef H. "The Hezbollah Model: Using Terror and Creating a Quasi-State in Lebanon." _Marine Corps Gazette,_ June 2003.

"The Afghan Endgame." By John Barry, Sami Yousafzai, and Ron Moreau. _Newsweek,_ 12 July 2010.

"Afghan Military Officer Kills 8 U.S. Troops." New Briefs/Wire Reports (AP). _Jacksonville Daily News_ (NC), 28 April 2011.

"Afghan Pipeline Raises Security Questions." By Travis Lupick. _Global Research,_ 21 July 2008.

"Afghan Policeman Kills Six U.S. Troops." From Associated Press. _Jacksonville Daily News_ (NC), 30 November 2010.

"Afghan President Hamid Karzai Readily Admitted He Accepts Bags of Money." News in Brief. _Christian Science Monitor,_ 8 November 2010.

"Afghan Prison Attack Stirs Tensions with Pakistan." _Christian Science Monitor,_ 16 June 2008.

"Afghan Rebels Using Iranian Arms: Canadian Defense Minister." From Agence France-Presse, 26 December 2007.

"Afghan Soldier Fires on German Troops, Killing 3." From Associated Press. _Jacksonville Daily News_ (NC), 19 February 2011.

"Afghanistan's President: Partner Or Obstacle." By Soraya Sarhaddi Nelson. NPR's "Morning Edition" News, 24 March 2010.

Ahmed, Issam. "Pakistan's Old Jihadis Pose New Threat." _Christian Science Monitor,_ 6 December 2009.

"All Travelers to Bhutan Must Arrive . . . ." World News in Brief. _Christian Science Monitor,_ 21 March 2008.

"Alleged Drug Trafficker Arrested in Maryland." _Washington Times,_ 24 July 2007.

Al-Obeidi, Abdul Hussein. Associated Press. "Holy City Najaf Fighting
    Worst Since Saddam Fell." *Jacksonville Daily News* (NC),
    7 August 2004.
"Al-Qaeda Blows Up Gas Pipeline in Yemen." *Hindustan Times*
    (India), 15 September 2010.
"Al Qaeda Deploys Paramilitary 'Shadow Army'." By Bill Roggio. *Long
    War Journal,* 10 February 2009.
"Al Qaida Now Controls Somalia." *Geostrategy-Direct.* Middle East
    Report, 30 June 2006.
"Al-Qaeda on Pakistan: Dr. Ayman al-Zawahiri's Morning and the
    Lamp." Jamestown Foundation. *Terrorism Monitor.* Volume 8,
    issue 11, 19 March 2010.
"Al Qaeda Yemen Wing Claims Parcel Plot, UPS Crash."
    From Reuters Online, 6 November 2010.
"Al-Qaeda's Influence in Yemen." By Jeremy Bowen. BBC's News
    Online, 5 January 2010.
"Al Shabaab Takes Aim." The World. *Time,* 6 September 2009.
Amiuzadeh (Deputy Minister of External Affairs of Asia-Oceania of the
    Islamic Republic of Iran). "Special Address to the Federation of
    Indian Chambers of Commerce and Industry." New Delhi, 22 July
    2003.
"Analysis: Somalia's Powerbrokers." BBC's News Online,
    8 January 2002. As retrieved from its website on 13 May
    2010.
"APNewsBreak: Nigeria Links Iran to Arms Shipment." By Bashir
    Adigun and Jon Gambrell. *Yahoo News*, 11 November
    2010.
"Are India's Maoist Rebels Winning the War." BBC's News
    Online, 28 May 2010.
Arkady Shipunov and Gennady Filimonov. "Field Artillery to be
    Replaced with Shmel Infantry Flamethrower." *Military Parade*
    (Moscow). Issue 29, September 1998. As retrieved from the
    following url in 2003: www.milparade.com/security/29.
Arnoldy, Ben. "South Asia." World (in Summary).
    Christian Science Monitor, 27 December 2010.
"As China Invests, Many Kazakhs Say: Not Too Fast." By David
    Greene. NPR's "Morning Edition" News, 7 June 2011.
"Assassination Intensifies the Crisis." The World.
    Newsweek, 17 January 2011.
"Attack Kills 3 Coalition Troops in Afghanistan." News Briefs Wire
    Reports (AP). *Jacksonville Daily News* (NC), 6 December 2010.
"Averting Blame in China." By Isaac Stone Fish.
    Newsweek, 6 December 2010.
Baker, Aryn. "Pakistan's Army Flexes Its Muscles." *Time,* 18 October
    2010.

"Bahrain Protests Joined by Arab Anger in Libya." News Briefs/Wire Reports (AP). *Jacksonville Daily News* (NC), 17 February 2011.

Baldauf, Scott. "How Al Qaeda Seeks to Buy Chinese Arms." *Christian Science Monitor,* 23 August 2002.

Baldauf, Scott and Ali Mohamed. "Cash Lures Somali 'Holy' Warriors." *Christian Science Monitor,* 19 April 2010.

"The Battle That Helped Change the Course of the 'Israeli' Occupation." *Daily Star* (Lebanon), 6 September 2000.

Batty, Robin and David Hoffman. "Afghanistan: Crisis of Impunity." *Human Rights Watch.* Volume 13, number 3(c), July 2001.

"Beijing's Afghan Gamble." By Robert D. Kaplan. *New York Times,* 7 October 2009.

"Betancourt, 3 US Hostages Freed From FARC Rebels." From Associated Press, 2 July 2008. As retrieved from the following url: newser.com/story/31495/betancourt-3-us-hostages-freed-from-farc-rebels.html.

"The Black-Turbaned Brigade: The Rise of TNSM in Pakistan." By Hassan Abbas. Jamestown Foundation. *Terrorism Monitor.* Volume 4, issue 23, 30 November 2006.

"Blair's Resignation Follows Rocky Ride as DNI." CNN Online, 21 May 2010.

Blanford, Nicholas. "Hizbullah Reelects Its Leader." *Christian Science Monitor,* 19 August 2004.

Blanford, Nicholas. "Hizbullah's Resilience Built on Years of Homework." *Christian Science Monitor,* 11 August 2006.

Blandford, Nicholas. "Lebanon Defuses Crisis." *Christian Science Monitor,* 22 May 2008.

Blanford, Nicholas and Daniel McGrory and Stephen Farrell. "Tactics That Have Kept the Middle East's Most Powerful Army at Bay." *The Times* (UK), 10 August 2006.

"Blood for Oil." *Investor's Business Daily* (Los Angeles), 2 May 2005. As reprinted in *Sudan Tribune,* 3 May 2005 and 15 June 2006.

Bradsher, Keith. "North Korean Ploy Masks Ships under Other Flags." *New York Times,* 20 October 2006.

Brookes, Peter. "Venezuelan Vagaries." *Armed Forces Journal,* July 2007.

Burke, Jason. "Waiting for a Last Battle with the Taliban." *The Observer* (UK), 27 June 1999.

"Bush Leaves Opening for Hezbollah Move to Political Mainstream." National Briefs Wire Reports (AP). *Jacksonville Daily News* (NC), 16 March 2005.

Butters, Andrew Lee. "Welcome to Hizballahstan." *Newsweek,* 26 May 2008.

"Cadillac Sponsors Communist Propaganda Film." *China Auto Web—A Guide to China's Auto Industry,* 2 September 2010. As retrieved from its website, chinaautoweb.com, on 22 September 2010.

"Changes in War Against Latin America's Illicit Trafficking." By David A. Fulghum. *Aviation Week,* 27 April 2010.

"Chanting, 'We Don't Want Islamic Courts . . . '." World News in Brief. *Christian Science Monitor,* 7 June 2006.

"Chavez Eyes China, Russia, More on 'Strategic'-Interest Tour." From Agence France-Presse, 20 September 2008.

"China and Angola Strengthen Bilateral Relationship." By Loro Horta. *Power and Interest News Report,* 23 June 2006.

"China Corrects Diplomatic Faux Pas, but Maintains Presence in Gilgit-Baltistan." By B. Raman. Chennai Centre for China Studies. C3S Paper No.586, 5 September 2010. As retrieved on 14 September 2010 from the following url: http://www.c3sindia.org/military/1625.

"China in Angola: An Emerging Energy Partnership." By Paul Hare. Jamestown Foundation. *China Brief.* Volume 6, issue 22, 8 November 2006.

"China Puts 700,000 Troops on Alert in Sudan." Newsmax (West Palm Beach, FL), 27 August 2000. As retrieved from its website, newsmax.com, in 2006.

"China Railway Construction Corp. Plans $3.4B IPO." By Vivian Wai-yin Kwok. *Forbes Magazine,* 4 January 2008.

"China Railway Construction Seeks End-Feb HK IPO-Source." From Reuters Online, 15 January 2008.

"China Winning Resources and Loyalties of Africa." *The Financial Times* (UK), 28 February 2006.

"China's 'Comprehensive Warfare' Strategy Wears Down Enemy Using Non-Military Means." *Geostrategy-Direct,* 2 August 2006.

"China's Discreet Hold on Pakistan's Northern Borderlands." By Selig Harrison. *New York Times,* 26 August 2010.

"China's Global Reach." *Christian Science Monitor,* 30 January 2007.

"China's Kashmir Gambit: Stakes in India-Pakistan Dispute." *Rupee News* (India), 7 September 2010. As retrieved from its website, rupeenews.com, on 14 September 2010.

China's Rising Power in Africa. Part 3. "China, Congo Trade for What the Other Wants." By Gwen Thompkins. NPR, 30 July 2008.

"China's Young Officers and the 1930's Syndrome." By Ambrose Evans-Pritchard. *The Telegraph Online* (UK), 7 September 2010. As received through G2-forward.org from the following url: http://blogs.telegraph.co.uk/finance/ambroseevanspritchard/100007519/china's-young-officers-and-the-1930s-syndrome/.

"Chinese Company Gets EU Afghan Road Contract." *Dawn* (Pakistan), 2 December 2003.

"Chinese Company to Reconstruct Afghan Road." *People's Daily* (China), 28 August 2006.

"Chinese Gunned Down in Afghanistan." Cable News Network, 10 June 2004.

"Chinese Hackers Seek U.S. Access." *USA Today,* 11 March 2007.

"Chinese Military to Make Billions through Capitalism." *Geostrategy-Direct,* 16 January 2008.

"Chinese Navy Sends New Escort Ships to Somali Waters." *China Defense Mashup.* As reprinted from Xinhua on 1 April 2009 from this url: http://www.china-defense-mashup.com/?p=3174.

Chopra, Anuj. "Maoist Rebels Spread across Rural India." *Christian Science Monitor,* 22 August 2006.

"Civilians Flee From Battle In Southern Yemen." By Soraya Sarhaddi Nelson and Steve Inskeep. NPR's "Morning Edition" News, 24 September 2010.

"Coalition Partner Rejoins Pakistani Government." Voice of America News. 7 January 2011.

Cody, Edward and Molly Moore. "Analysts Attribute Hezbollah's Resilience to Zeal, Secrecy and Iranian Funding." *Washington Post,* 14 August 2006.

Collins, Joseph J. "The Way Ahead in Afghanistan." *Armed Forces Journal,* July/August 2010.

"Colombia: FARC Linked to Peruvian Guerrillas." By Brett Borkan. *Colombia Reports,* 8 March 2010. As retrieved from its website, ColombiaReports.com, on 13 September 2010.

"Colombian Army Adaption to FARC Insurgency." By Thomas Marks. PUB18.pdf. Stat<i>e</i>gic Studies Institute, January 2002.

Cordesman, Anthony H. (Strategy Chair). "Iran's Developing Military Capabilities." Working draft. Washington, D.C.: Center for Strategic and International Studies, 14 December 2004.

Cordesman, Anthony H. (Strategy Chair). "Iran's Revolutionary Guards, the Al Quds Force, and Other Intelligence and Paramilitary Forces." Working draft. Washington, D.C.: Center for Strategic and International Studies, 16 August 2007.

"Crackdown on Taliban Shifts U.S.-Pakistan Ties." By Julie McCarthy. NPR's "Morning Edition" News, 10 March 2010.

Crilly, Rob. "Foreign Intervention in Somalia." *Christian Science Monitor,* 21 June 2006.

Crilly, Rob. "Islamist-Warlord Clashes Hinder Somalia's New Government." *Christian Science Monitor,* 5 June 2006.

Crilly, Rob. "Somalia on the Edge of Full-Scale War." *Christian Science Monitor,* 25 July 2006.

"Dawood Gang Provided Logistics to Lashkar Militants." From Press Trust of India. As retrieved from the NDTV website (Mumbai), 18 December 2008.

"Dawood Ibrahim Had Played an Important Role in the Smuggling of Nuclear Weapons." By S. Balakrishnan. *Times of India,* 4 August 2004.

"Dawood's Drug Net Financed 26/11: Russian Intelligence." As retrieved from the NDTV website (Mumbai), 18 December 2008.

"Dawood's ISI Links Could Trouble Musharraf." By Wilson John. Observer Research Foundation (New Delhi). *Strategic Trends.* Volume I, issue 5, 4 November 2003.

Dehganpisheh, Babak. "A War's Hidden Hands." *Newsweek,* 6 September 2004.

Delany, Max. "West Trains Army to Fight in Somalia." *Christian Science Monitor,* 21 June 2010.

"Divine Calendars Testify of Abraham, Isaac, and Jacob." By John P. Pratt. *Meridian Magazine,* 11 September 2003. As retrieved on 9 September 2010 from the following url: www.johnpratt.com/items/docs/lds/meridian/2003/abraham.html#3.

"Do I Look Dangerous to You." By Frederic Dannen. Part I. Partners in Crime series. *The New Republic,* 14 & 21 July 1997.

"Doomed SWAT Sergeants Didn't Expect an AK-47." By Phillip Matier and Andrew Ross. *San Francisco Chronicle,* 23 March 2009. From its website.

"Drug Policy Changes Under New Director," NPR's News Online, 3 November 2009.

"Drug Seizures in West Africa Prompt Fears of Terrorist Links." By Jamie Doward. *Guardian Observer Online* (www.guardian.co.uk), 29 November 2009. As retrieved from the following url: www.guardian.co.uk/world/2009/nov/29/drugs-cocaine-africa-al-qaida

"Ecuador Offers Concession of Manta Air Base to China, Declines to Renew Contract with U.S." By Vittorio Hernandez. AHN News (Ecuador), 26 November 2007.

"Eliminating Terrorist Sanctuaries: The Case of Iraq, Iran, Somalia and Sudan." Center for Defense Information (Washington, D.C.), 10 December 2001.

Eshel. Lt.Col. David, Israeli Defense Forces (Retired). "Counterguerrilla Warfare in South Lebanon." *Marine Corps Gazette,* July 1997.

"Ethiopian Troops Lend Aid to Somali Allies." World Briefs Wire Reports (AP). *Jacksonville Daily News* (NC), 21 July 2006.

"Everyone Wants Cut in Afghan Drug Trade." From McClatchy News Service. *Jacksonville Daily News* (NC), 10 May 2009.

369

"Explosive Powder Found on Chinese Ship." FOX's News Online, 8 November 2006.

"Exporting the Revolution: Iran's al-Quds Force." Red Cell Intelligence Group. Course Announcement, n.d. As retrieved from following url: www.redcellig.com/.../exporting-the-revolution-irans-al-quds-force.php.

"FBI Informant Says Agents Missed Chance to Stop 9/11 Ringleader Mohammed Atta." By Brian Ross and Vic Walter. ABC's News Online, 10 September 2009.

Ford, Peter. "A Suspect Emerges As Key Link in Terror Chain." *Christian Science Monitor,* 23 January 2004.

"Foreign Journalists Beaten during Communist Party Crackdown." *Newsweek,* 14 March 2011.

"A Former Maoist Guerrilla Was Sworn in Monday As Nepal's First Prime Minister." World News in Brief. *Christian Science Monitor,* 19 August 2008.

"Former Members of Radical Somali Group Give Details of Their Group." Voice of America, 6 January 2007. As retrieved two days later from url: http://www.voanews.com/english/2007-01-06-voa25.cfm. In *Wikipedia Encyclopedia,* s.v. "Hassan Dahir Aweys."

"Four NATO Trucks Torched in Quetta." From ANI. Thaindian News Online, 16 July 2010.

"Four Spies for the U.S. Have Been Caught by Venezuelan Security." World News in Brief. *Christian Science Monitor,* 21 August 2006.

"Future of U.S. Base in Kyrgyzstan in Question." By Paul Reynolds. BBC's News Online, 9 April 2010.

Gall, Carlotta. "Afghan-Iranian Road Opens." *New York Times,* 28 January 2005.

Gardner, David. "'Israel': Hizbollah Sharpens Up Its Tactics." *London Financial Times,* 1997.

Garrastazu, Antonio, and Jerry Haar. "International Terrorism: The Western Hemisphere Connection." Organization of American States. *America's Forum North-South Center Update,* 2001.

Gertz, Bill. "China in Kyrgyzstan." *Washington Times,* 2 December 2010.

Gertz, Bill. "Chinese Military Trains in West." *Washington Times,* 15 March 2006.

Gertz, Bill. "Notes from the Pentagon." *Washington Times,* 5 March 2004.

Gertz, Bill. " 'White Man' Training Al Qaida Terrorists in Wilderness Camp near Kenya." *Geostrategy-Direct,* week of 14 December 2004.

Ghattas, Sam. Associated Press. "Nine Israeli Soldiers Killed in Fighting in South Lebanon." *Jacksonville Daily News* (NC), 27 July 2006.

"GHQ Attack Mastermind Apprehended in Bahawalpur." From ANI. Thaindian News Online, 28 October 2009. Retrieved from this url: http://www.thaindian.com/newsportal/south-asia/ghq-attack-master mind-apprehended-in-bahawalpur_100266623.html.

Girardet, Edward. "Clashes Worsen Somalia Food Crisis As Drought Sets In." *Christian Science Monitor,* 19 April 2006.

Glendinning, Lee. "The Secret World of Palestinian Tunnels." *Times Online* (UK), 27 June 2006.

"Global Double Crossing." By Charles R. Smith. *Newsmax* (West Palm Beach, FL), 27 February 2003. As retrieved from its website, newsmax.com, on 23 September 2010.

"A Godfather's Lethal Mix of Business and Politics." *U.S. News & World Report Online,* 5 December 2005.

"Governance Crisis." By Mohammad Amir Rana. Five-part series about Punjabi Taliban. *Friday Times* (Lahore), 7 July - 11 August 2010.

"Govt Blames LeT for Parliament Attack, Asks Pak to Restrain Terrorist Outfits." From Rediff News (India), 14 December 2001. As retrieved from its website, rediff.com, on 15 August 2010.

"Guarding Troubled Waters." By Sarah A. Topol. News in Brief. *Christian Science Monitor,* 19 June 2010.

"Guinea Bissau: Hezbollah, Al Qaida and the Lebanese Connection." By Marco Vernaschi. Pulitzercenter.org, 19 June 2009.

"Gunmen Torch NATO Trucks in Rawalpindi." *Dawn* (Pakistan), 9 June 2010.

"Gunmen Torch 14 NATO Oil Tankers in Pakistan." News Briefs Wire Reports (AP). *Jacksonville Daily News* (NC), 16 January 2011,

"Half-Hearted Security Operations in Punjab Do Little to Restrain Taliban Attacks." By Arif Jamal. Jamestown Foundation. *Terrorism Monitor.* Volume 8, issue 31, 5 August 2010.

Hassan, Harun. "Somalia Twists in the Wind." From harowo.com, 13 April 2006. Through G2-forward.org.

Hendawi, Hamza. "Israel Hits Beirut; Hezbollah Rockets Israel." From Associated Press, 3 August 2006.

"Hezbollah Chooses Lebanon's Next Prime Minister," By Anthony Shadid. *New York Times Online,* 24 January 2011.

"Hezbollah Fighters Said to Be in Iraq." *World Net Daily,* 21 June 2004. As retrieved in 2006 from www.intelmessages.org.

"Hezbollah Leader Vows Not to Give Up Weapons." From Associated Press. *Jacksonville Daily News* (NC), 23 September 2006.

"Hezbollah Uses Mexican Drug Routes into U.S." *Washington Times,* 27 March 2009.

Hill, Ginny. "Cold War Roots of Yemen Conflict." BBC's News Online, 17 September 2009.

"Hizbullah Offers to Pay Up to Five Times More for Suicide Attacks." *Geostrategy-Direct,* week of 22 February 2005.

371

"Hizbullah Suspected of Joining Sunni Insurgents." *Iraqi News,* 17 February 2005. As retrieved in 2005 from its website, www.iraqinews.com.

"Hizbullah Using Tunnels, Bunkers to Frustrate Israelis' Advance." *World Tribune* (Springfield, VA), 7 August 2006.

Hong Kong Taxation: Law and Practice, 2010-2011. By Garry Laird and Ayesha Macpherson. N.p.: Chinese University Press, 1 October 2010. One page excerpt. As retrieved on 21 January 2011 from the following url: http://www.barnesandnoble.com/sitemap/Books/Books_H_944.html.

"Hooked: Seattle High School Battles Heroin Addiction," ABC's News Online, retrieved in October 2010 from the following url: http://abcnews.go.com/WN/seattle-high-school-battles-heroin-addiction/story?id=11917881&page=2.

"How Big a Threat Is N. Korea." By Kristen Chick. *Christian Science Monitor,* 24 May 2009.

"How Mexico Fares in Drug War." By Sara Miller Llana. *Christian Science Monitor,* 17 January 2011.

"How Pakistan's ISI Funds Its Proxy War." By Syed Nooruzzaman. *The Tribune* (India), 28 November 1999.

Hughes, Stephen E. *Warring on Terrorism: A Comprehensive Dispatch Briefing.* Part I (internet piece), 2005.

"Hundreds of Soldiers from Neighboring Ethiopia Crossed into Somalia." World News in Brief. *Christian Science Monitor,* 19 June 2006.

"Hunting for Dawood Ibrahim." By B. Raman. South Asia Analysis Group (India). Paper No. 1952, 16 September 2006. Same as *International Terrorism Monitor,* Paper No. 122, n.d.

Hunwick, John. "Africa and Islamic Revival: Historical and Contemporary Perspectives." Extracted verbatim from MSA News by University of Georgia.

Ignatius, David. "Hezbollah's Success." *Washington Post,* 23 September 2003.

"Independent Board of Inquiry into the Oakland Police Department: March 21, 2009 Incident." By James K. Stewart, Senior Fellow. CNA, Institute for Public Research, December 2009. Electronic file designator, opdreport.pdf.

"India Wants Him, Pak Uses Jaish Chief to Defuse Mosque Tension." By Pranab Dhal Samanta. *India Express* (Delhi), 7 July 2009.

"In Iraq, a U.S. Enemy Returns," By Jane Arraf. *Christian Science Monitor,* 24 January 2011.

"Inside the Muslim Brotherhood," By Christopher Dickey and Babak Dehghanpisheh. *Newsweek,* 14 February 2011.

"Insurgents Take Control of Yemeni City." By Abigail Fielding-Smith. *Financial Times,* 24 March 2011. From its website.

"Iran Responsible for 1983 Marine Barracks Bombing, Judge Rules."
CNN Online, 30 May 2003.

"Iran Sends 6 Warships to International Waters in 'Saber Rattling'
Move." FOX's News Online, 25 May 2009. As retrieved from url:
http://www.foxnews.com/story/0,2933,521730,00.html.

"Iranian Proxies: An Intricate and Active Web." By
Scott Stewart. *STRATFOR Weekly*, 3 February 2010.

"Iran's Global Terrorist Reach." By Dr. Walid Phares. *The
Australian Conservative*, 12 July 2010. As retrieved from its
website, http://australianconservative.com, on 26 November
2010.

"Iran's Improved Fajr-5 Rockets Can Be Fired Remotely."
Geostrategy-Direct, 31 May 2006.

"Iraq's New Government." Editorial. *Washington Post Online,*
13 November 2010.

"Islamic Extremism in India (Page 2)." International Institute for
Strategic Studies (London). Volume 15, issue 3, April 2009. As
retrieved from its website, iiss.org, on 15 August 2010.

"Islamists Training in Somalia." *ERRI Daily Intelligence Report.*
Volume 11, number 363. Emergency Net News, 31 December 2005.
From Bill Gertz. Through *Geostrategy-Direct.*

"Israel Intercepts Dual-Use Military Shipment from China to Gaza."
World Tribune, 4 May 2006.

"ISW in Brief: Trouble Ahead in Afghanistan's East?" By Jeffrey A.
Dressler. Institute for the Study of War (Washington, D.C.).
Works by Our Authors, 17 March 2011.

Jaber, Hala. "Hezbollah: We've Planned This for 6 Years." *The Sunday
Times* (London), 30 July 2006.

"Jaish-e-Mohammed (JEM) Backgrounder." South Asia Analysis Group
(India). Paper No. 3320, 10 March 2001.

Jaish e-Mohammed profile. *Global Security News & Reports.*
Overseas Security Advisor Council. From its website,
www.ds-osac.org.

"Jamaat-e-Islami Moves Pak Senate on Jamaat-ud-Daawa Ban." From
ANI. *Malaysia Sun,* 14 December 2008.

"Jamaat-e-Islami: The Fountainhead of Religious Extremism." By
Yasser Latif Hamdani. *Daily Times* (Pakistan), 20 May 2010.

Johnsen, Gregory D. "Yemen Accuses Iran of Meddling in Its Internal
Affairs." Jamestown Foundation. *Terrorism Focus.* Volume 4,
issue 2, 20 February 2007. As retrieved from its website,
jamestown.org, on 8 May 2010.

"Karachi Terror Attack: Siege On after 13 Hours; 12 Killed, 2 Planes
Destroyed." NDTV Online (Mumbai), 23 May 2011.

"Karzai Attends Starting Ceremony of Road Project." Pakistani
News Service, 28 August 2006.

"Karzai Denounces U.S.-Russian Drug Raid in Afghanistan." *Los Angeles Times*. As reprinted in *Jacksonville Daily News* (NC), 31 October 2010.

"Karzai's Exit Strategy." By Dan Green. *Armed Forces Journal*, September 2010.

Khan, Rana Sanaullah (Punjab Law Minister). In "Dozen Dead in Suicide Bombing." Videotaped news story. From Associated Press, 8 March 2010. As viewed at Youtube on 5 February 2011, at the following url: www. youtube.com/watch?v=zniGlAAvINo.

"Killer of 4 Officers Wanted to Avoid Prison." By Demian Bulwa and Jaxon Van Derbeken. *San Francisco Chronicle*, 23 March 2009. From its website.

Kinetz, Erika. "U.S. Congress Warms to Cambodia." *Christian Science Monitor*, 14 March 2007.

Lafranchi, Howard. "Anti-Iran Sentiment Hardening Fast." *Christian Science Monitor*, 22 July 2002.

"Lashkar-e-Jhangvi & Al Qaeda." By B. Raman. South Asia Analysis Group (India). Paper No. 2526, 31 December 2007. Same as *International Terrorism Monitor*, Paper No. 337, n.d.

"Lashkar-e-Jhangvi, Sipah-e-Sahaba Working Like 'Paid Killers' for Taliban: Malik." From ANI. Thaindian News Online, 3 July 2010.

"Lebanese Find Troubles Fertile Ground for Cannabis." By Tom Perry. Reuters Online, 26 September 2007.

"Lebanon Government Collapsed." News in Brief. *Christian Science Monitor*, 24 January 2011.

"Leftist Wins Election." The World. *Time*, 20 June 2011.

Llana, Sara Miller. "El Salvador Joins Latin Leftward Tilt." *Christian Science Monitor*, 17 March 2009.

Llana, Sara Miller. "Nicaragua Plans a Big Dig to Rival Panama Canal." *Christian Science Monitor*, 1 December 2006.

Lubold, Gordon. "Mullen's Charm Offensive." *Christian Science Monitor*, 17 January 2010.

Luhnow, David and Jose de Cordoba. "The Perilous State of Mexico." *Wall Street Journal*, 21 February 2009.

"Maoists Attack." The World. *Time*, 19 April 2010.

"Markets Closed, Traffic Thin: 135 Arrested in Lahore." By Intikhab Hanif and Ahmad Fraz Khan. *Dawn Newspaper Group Online* (Karachi), 10 November 2001.

Marks, Thomas A. "A Model Counterinsurgency: Uribe's Colombia (2002-2006)." *Military Review*, March-April 2007.

"The Marriott Blast." By B. Rahman. South Asia Analysis Group (India). *International Terrorism Monitor*." Paper No. 449, 22 September 2008.

"A Means of Maintaining Social Order." By Fredric Dannen. Partners in Crime series. Parts II. *The New Republic*, 14 & 21 July 1997.

Melman, Yossi. "Ambush of Naval Squad 'No Accident'."
Ha'aretz (Tel Aviv), 13 August 1998.

"Mexicali Called Hub for Smuggling Chinese into the United States."
Geostrategy-Direct, 22 February 2005.

"Mexico's Sinaloa Gang Grows Empire, Defies Crackdown." By
Anahi Rama Anahi Rama. Reuters Online, 19 January
2011.

Meyers, Lt.Col Patrick and Patrick Poole. "Hezbollah, Illegal
Immigration, and the Next 9/11." *Front Page Magazine,* 28 April
2006.

"Middle East: Strait Shooting." *STRATFOR Weekly,* 8 June 2011.

"Militant or Peace Broker? A Profile of the Swat Valley's Maulana
Sufi Muhammad." By Imtiaz Ali. Jamestown Foundation.
Terrorism Monitor. Volume 7, issue 7, 26 March 2009.

"Militants Hit NATO Tankers Again." World Briefs Wire
Reports (AP). *Jacksonville Daily News* (NC), 4 October 2010.

"Militia Hunt Al-Qaeda in Somalia." From Agence France-Presse,
5 May 2006.

"Modernizing the People's Liberation Army of China." By Carin Zissis.
Backgrounder. Council on Foreign Relations (New York),
5 December 2006.

"More NATO Tankers Attacked in Pakistan." Press TV Online
(Iran), 11 November 2010.

"More Than Troops, Chinese Projects in PoK Worry India." By Pranab
Dhal Samanta. *Indian Express* (Delhi), 5 September 2010.
Reprinted by *Yahoo News,* 5 September 2010. As retrieved from
both websites, news.yahoo.com and indianexpress.com, on
14 September 2010.

Murphy, Dan. "The Other Karzai Boss." *Christian Science Monitor,*
19 July 2010.

"Muslim Brotherhood Declares War on America." By Barry Rubin.
Global Research in International Affairs (GLORIA) Center (Israel),
7 October 2010. From G2-Forward.org.

"Mystery Surrounds Alleged Hezbollah Links to Drug Arrests in
Curacao." By Chris Zambelis. Jamestown Foundation. *Terrorism
Monitor.* Volume 7, issue 18, 25 June 2009.

"NATO Airstrike on Afghanistan Fuel Truck Kills 40." *Telegraph*
(UK), 4 September 2009. As retrieved from its website,
telegraph.uk.co, on 4 October 2010.

"NATO Oil Tankers Destroyed by Militants in Pakistan." From IANS.
Thaindian News Online, 29 August 2010.

"NATO Tankers Torched in Afghanistan." Press TV Online
(Iran), 14 November 2010.

"NATO Tankers Torched in Pakistan." BBC's News Online, 1 October
2010.

"NATO Tankers Torched in Pakistan, but Alternative Routes to Afghanistan Limited." By Ben Arnoldy. *Christian Science Monitor,* 1 October 2010.

Nessman, Ravi. Associated Press. "Israelis Step Up Offensive." *Jacksonville Daily News* (NC), 10 August 2006.

"New Pirate Raids Expose International Efforts to Secure Trade Routes." From Agence France-Presse, 12 December 2008. As retrieved from the *Hellenic Shipping News* website on 13 May 2010.

"No De-Facto Control of Gilgit Baltistan to China." Zee News (India), 1 September 2010.

"North Korea Launched an Artillery Barrage . . . ." News in Brief. *Christian Science Monitor,* 6 December 2010.

"North Koreans Assisted Hezbollah with Tunnel Construction." Jamestown Foundation. *Terrorism Focus.* Volume III, issue 30, August 2006.

"Operation Allenbrook." As retrieved from the following url: http://www.allenaustin.net/oab.htm.

"Organized Crime, Intelligence and Terror: The D-Company's Role in the Mumbai Attacks." By Tom Burghardt. *Global Research,* 13 December 2008.

"Osama bin Laden Is Dead." CBS's Online News, 1 May 2011.

"Pak Ceded Control of Gilgit to China." By Chidanand Rajghatta. *Times of India,* 10 September 2010.

"Pakistan Is Handing Over De-Facto Control of the Strategic Gilgit-Baltistan Region. Rediff News (India), 28 August 2010. As retrieved from its website, rediff.com, on 14 September 2010.

"Pakistan Releases Top Terrorist Leader." By Bill Roggio. *Long War Journal,* 4 January 2011.

"Pakistan Trims Top ISI Chairs." From PTI Islamabad. *The Economic Times* (Chennai), 13 August 2009.

"Pakistani Commandos Break Siege on Army Headquarters." By Bill Roggio. *Long War Journal,* 10 October 2009.

"Pakistani Government in Turmoil after Coalition Party Quits over Fuel and Taxes." By Saeed Shah. *Guardian Online* (UK), 2 January 2011.

"Pakistani Islamists Sign Deal With China." By Farhan Bokhari. CBS's News Online. World Watch, 18 February 2009.

"Pakistani Military Hits Taliban in Orakzai." By Bill Roggio. *Long War Journal,* 17 November 2009.

"Pakistani Taliban Widen Jihad with Strikes on Fellow Muslims." By Arif Jamal. Jamestown Foundation. *Terrorism Monitor.* Volume 8, issue 28, 16 July 2010.

"Pakistan's 'New Zone of Militancy'." BBC's News Online, 12 October 2009.

"Pak's 'Friendly Attitude' towards JuD Bound to Raise Eyebrows: Pak Editorial." From ANI. Thaindian News Online, 7 July 2010.

"Path to 9/11." ABC's News Online, 10-11 September 2006.

Peraino, Kevin. "Somalia Strkes Out." *Newsweek,* 26 July 2010.

Peraino, Kevin and Babak Dehghanpisheh and Christopher Dickey. "Eye for an Eye." *Newsweek,* 14 August 2006.

Perlez, Jane. "Attackers Hit Mosques of Islamic Sect in Pakistan." *New York Times,* 29 May 2010.

Peter, Tom A. "An Afghan Insurgent Tries Politics." *Christian Science Monitor,* 28 February 2011.

Peterson, Scott. "In a War It Cannot Win, Israel Tries New Tactics." *Christian Science Monitor,* 9/20 October 1997.

Peterson, Scott. "Shadows of Tehran over Iraq." *Christian Science Monitor,* 19 April 2004.

Peterson, Scott. "Unresolved: Disarming Hizbullah." *Christian Science Monitor,* 15 August 2006.

"Philippines: U.S. Missed 9/11 Clues Years Ago." By Maria Ressa. CNN Online, 26 July 2003.

"PM Urges Public to Remain Calm Following Thaksin's Threat of Forming People's Army." *The Nation Online* (Thailand), 29 October 2010.

Powell, Bill and Adam Zagorin. "The Sopranos State." *Time,* 23 July 2007.

"Profile: Al-Qaeda in the Arabian Peninsula." BBC's News Online, 3 January 2010.

"Profile: Al-Qaeda 'Kingpin'." BBC's News Online, 28 September 2006.

"Profile: Pakistan's Military Intelligence Agency." By David Chazan. BBC's News Online, 9 January 2002.

"Profile: Thailand's Reds and Yellows." BBC's News Online, 20 April 2010.

Raman, B. "The New Trojan Horse of Al Qaeda." South Asia Analysis (India). *International Terrorism Monitor.* Paper No. 301, 10 November 2007.

Ramesh, Randeep. "Inside India's Hidden War." *Guardian Online* (UK), 9 May 2006.

"Rioting Spreads across Tunisia; Unrest Also Reported in Algeria." By Alexandra Sandels. *Los Angeles Times Online,* 8 January 2011.

"The Rise and Fall of the Communist Party of Thailand." By Pierre Rousset. *International Journal of Socialist Renewal,* 9 September 2009. As retrieved in December 2010 from the following url: http://links.org.au/node/1247.

Rodriguez, Alex. "Pakistan Reopens Checkpoint." *Wilmington Star News* (NC), 11 October 2010.

"Rogues' Gallery." By Bobby Ghosh. *Time,* 2 May 2011.

Romero, Simon. "Files Released by Colombia Point to Venezuelan Bid to Arm Rebels." *New York Times,* 30 March 2008.

Ross, Brian and Richard Esposito, Matthew Cole, Luis Martinez, and Kirit Radia. "Obama Ordered U.S. Military Strike on Yemen Terrorists." ABC's News Online. As retrieved from the url:. http://abcnews.go.com/Blotter/cruise-missiles-strike-yemen/story?id=9375236&page=1.

Rubin, Michael. "Ansar al-Sunna: Iraq's New Terrorist Threat." *Middle East Intelligence Bulletin.* Volume 6, number 5, May 2004.

"Russia's Georgia Invasion May Be About Oil." By Rachel Martin. ABC's News Online, 16 August 2008.

"Sacks of Cash." By Sami Yousafzai and Ron Moreau. *Newsweek,* 8 November 2010.

"SAIC-GM-Wuling (SGMW)." *China Auto Web—A Guide to China's Auto Industry,* n.d. As retrieved from its website, chinaautoweb.com, on 22 September 2010.

Santoli, Al. "The Panama Canal in Transition: Threats to U.S. Security and China's Growing Role in Latin America." American Foreign Policy Council Investigative Report, 23 June 1999.

Scales, Maj.Gen. Robert H., U.S. Army (Retired). "Infantry and National Priorities." *Armed Forces Journal,* December 2007.

Segal, Naomi. Jewish Telegraphic Agency. "IDF Absolved of Blame in Deaths of Naval Commandos in Lebanon." *San Francisco Jewish Community Publication,* 31 October 1997.

Sen, Chnakya. Review of *Karachi: A Terror Capital in the Making.* By Wilson John. *Asia Times Online,* 17 January 2004.

"Shiite Radicals Join with Sunni Insurgents in Ramadi." *DEBKAfile,* 7 April 2004.

"Shiites March throughout Middle East." From Associated Press. *Jacksonville Daily News* (NC), 22 May 2004.

"Show Me the Money." *Time,* 8 November 2010.

Slavin, Barbara. "Iran Helped Overthrow the Taliban, Candidate Says." *USA Today,* 10 June 2005.

Smith, Charles R. "U.S. Bombs Chinese Network in Afghanistan, PRC Sold Taliban Advanced Air Defense System." *Newsmax* (West Palm Beach, FL), 20 October 2001. As retrieved from its website, newsmax.com, in 2001.

"Smoking Al Qaeda Out of Karachi." By B. Raman. South Asia Analysis Group. Paper No. 519, 14 September 2002.

"Smuggled Chinese Travel Circuitously." By Irene Jay Liu. NPR's "Morning Edition" News, 20 November 2007.

"Somali Pirates a Growing Threat to Shipping." By Daniel Wallis. Reuters Online, 29 August 2008. As retrieved from its website, reuters.com, on 13 May 2010.

"Somali Troops, Militia Take Two Towns from Rebels." From Reuters Online, 28 March 2011.

"Some Interesting Facts about Korea: The Forgotten War." *DAV Magazine,* May/June 2000.

"South Korea Says North Torpedoed Ship." By Jack Kim and Ross Colvin. Reuters Online, 20 Mary 2010.

"South Waziristan's Maulvi Nazir: The New Face of the Taliban." By Hassan Abbas. The Jamestown Foundation. *Terrorism Monitor.* Volume 5, issue 9, 14 May 2007.

"Special Report: Iran and the Saudi's Countermove on Bahrain." By George Freidman. *STRATFOR Weekly,* 14 March 2011.

Spinetta, Maj. Lawrence (USAF). "Cutting China's 'String of Pearls'." *U.S. Naval Institute Proceedings,* October 2006.

Stack, Liam. "Fifth NATO Tanker Attacked in Six Days since Pakistan Sealed Border Post." *Christian Science Monitor,* 5 October 2010.

Suellentrop, Chris. "Abdullah Azzam—The Godfather of Jihad." MSN News, n.d. As retrieved from its website, slate.msn.com.

"Suicide Bomber Kills Peacekeeper, Civilian in Afghan Capital." World Briefs Wire Reports (AP). *Jacksonville Daily News* (NC), 28 January 2004.

"Syrian Reactor Detailed." By Pamela Hess and Deb Riechmann. Associated Press. *Jacksonville Daily News* (NC), 25 April 2008.

"Taliban Attacks, Establishes Control over Emerald Mine in NWFP." From ANI. *News Track India,* 2 April 2009.

"Taliban Claim Pakistan Army Raid." BBC's News Online, 12 October 2009.

"Taliban's Presence in Pak Punjab Officially Accepted." From ANI. Thaindian News Online, 17 May 2010.

Tarabay, Jamie. Associated Press. "U.S. Chopper Downed amid Fierce Fighting in Iraq." AOL News, 5 August 2004.

"10 Trucks Torched in Issa Nagri." By Roy Jawad Hussain. *Pakistan Criminal Records,* 4 August 2010. As retrieved from this url: pakistancriminalrecords.com/2010/08/04/karachi-10-trucks-torched-in-issa-nagri/.

"Terror Hoax Uncovers Border Threat." By David Hancock. CBS's News Online, 7 February 2005.

Theyson, Art. "New Warfront Opens in Iraq Three Months before Handover." *DEBKAfile* (Israel), 5 April 2004.

Thomlinson, Chris. Associated Press. "U.S. Backing Somali Militants against Islamic Extremists." *Jacksonville Daily News* (NC), 10 April 2006.

Thomlinson, Chris. "Video Shows Arabs Fighting in Somalia." From Associated Press, 5 July 2006.

"Three Guilty in 2003 Mumbai Bombings Trial." By Salil Panchal. Agence France-Presse, 27 July 2009.

Timperlake, Ed. "Clues How Chinese Missile Ended Up in Hezbollah's Arsenal." As posted on 26 July 2006 at G2-forward.org.

Toosi, Nahal. Associated Press. "Troubled Pakistan Faces Ruling Coalition Collapse." *Jacksonville Daily News* (NC), 4 January 2011.

"Top Iranian Defector on Iran's Collaboration with Iraq, North Korea, Al-Qa'ida, and Hizbullah." Middle East Media Research Institute. Special Dispatch No. 473, 21 February 2003.

"Toward an Adaptive Army." By Col. Robert B. Killebrew. *Army Magazine,* January 2002.

Tran, Tini. Associated Press. "Tape Targets Clerics." *Jacksonville Daily News* (NC), 25 November 2004.

"Trio Sign Up for Turkmen Gas." *Upstream* (International Oil and Natural Gas Newspaper, Norway), 25 April 2008.

Two Fuel Tankers for NATO Attacked in Pakistan." By Nasir Habib. CNN Online, 1 November 2010.

Tyson, Ann Scott. "Sadr's Militia Regrouping, Rearming." *Christian Science Monitor,* 15 July 2004.

"An Unacknowledged War." By Toby Westerman. *Canada Free Press,* 27 August 2009.

"U.N. Maps Tell Security Story." *Time,* 10 January 2011.

"U.N. Somalia Envoy Accuses Islamist of Coup Attempt." From Agence France-Presse, 14 May 2009.

"U.S. Drone Strike Kills Rebels in Pakistan." From Agence France-Press. *Sydney Morning Herald* (Australia), 5 October 2010. As found at the following url in late 2010: news.smh.com.au/breaking-news-world/us-drone-strike-kills-rebels-in-pakistan-20101005-164m6.html.

"U.S. Fighter Jets Attack Yemeni Fighters." Press TV Online (Iran), 14 December 2009. As retrieved from the following url: www.presstv.com/detail.aspx?id=113687&sectionid=351020206.

"U.S. Launches New Somalia Raids." *Guardian Online* (UK), 9 January 2007. As retrieved from its website, guardian.co.uk, on 8 May 2010.

"U.S. Navy Provoked South China Sea Incident, China Says." By Mark Mcdonald. *New York Times Online,* 10 March 2009.

"U.S. Resists Role for Iraq Cleric." By Sam Dagher. *Wall Street Journal Online,* 6 October 2010.

"U.S. Secret War against *al-Qaeda* in Yemen Idles." World Briefs Wire Reports (AP). *Jacksonville Daily News* (NC), 16 October 2010.

"U.S. Shifts to Seek Removal of Yemen's Leader, an Ally." By Laura Kasinof and David Sanger. *New York Times,* 3 April 2011.

"A Victory for Hizballah." *Time,* 7 February 2011.

"Vietnam, Cambodia Bombing." ZFacts. As retrieved from its website, zFacts.com, on 13 January 2011.

Wagley, John. "Foreign Hackers are Overwhelming U.S. Government Computers, Says Analyst." *Security Management,* 19 December 2008.

"Waziristan-Based Terror Group Takes Credit for Lahore Assault." By Bill Roggio. *Long War Journal,* 30 March 2009.

Weir, Fred. "Big Powers Jockey for Oil in Central Asia." *Christian Science Monitor,* 28 March 2007.

"White House Czar Calls for End to 'War on Drugs'." By Gary Fields. *Wall Street Journal Online,* 14 May 2009.

Whitlock, Craig and Karen DeYoung. "Attributes Suggest Outside Help." *Washington Post,* 28 November 2008.

"Why Did Armored Corps Fail in Lebanon." By Hanan Greenberg. Israeli News, 30 August 2006. As retrieved from the following url: http://www.ynetnews.com/articles/0,7340,L-3297431,00.html.

"Why Tunisia, Why Now?" By Christen Chick. *Christian Science Monitor,* 31 January 2011.

"Why West Africa Cannot Break Its Drug Habit." By Rose Skelton. BBC's News Online, 21 June 2010.

"Will Arab World's Freedom Wave Reach Iran or China?" By John Hughes. *Christian Science Monitor,* 21 March 2011.

Wilson, G.I. "Iraq: Fourth Generation Warfare (4GW) Swamp." *Military.com,* 18 June 2004.

"Woman Says She Pointed Police to Oakland Killer." By Demian Bulwa. *San Francisco Chronicle,* 24 March 2009. From its website.

"World: South Asia, Pakistan Army Seizes Power." BBC's News Online, 12 October 1999.

Wright, Robin and Peter Baker. "Iraq, Jordan See Threat to Election from Iran." *Washington Post,* 8 December 2004.

"Yemen: A Hezbollah Withdrawal," *STRATFOR Weekly,* 10 February 2010. As retrieved from its website, stratfor.com, on 2 December 2010.

"Yemen, America's Uneasy Ally in War on Terror." CBS's "Sixty Minutes," 14 January 2011.

"Yemen Conflict Map." By Katherine Zimmerman, Jonathan Frist, Chris Harnisch. American Enterprise Institute for Public Policy Research (Washington, D.C.). *Critical Threats,* 21 January 2009. As retrieved from its website, CriticalThreats.org, in August 2010.

"Yemen Intercepts Iranian Ship with Arms." United Press
    International, 28 October 2009.
"Yemen Opposition Backs Power Transfer to Vice-President." BBC's
    News Online, 6 June 2011.
"Yemenis Rally against Government." By Cynthia Johnston and
    Mohammed Ghobari. Reuters Online, 27 March 2011.
"Yemen's War." *The Economist,* 19 November 2010.
Zakaria, Fareed. "What America Has Lost." *Newsweek,* 13 September
    2010.

About the Author

After 28 years of commissioned and noncommissioned infantry service, John Poole retired from the United States Marine Corps in April 1993. While on active duty, he studied small-unit tactics for nine years: (1) six months at the Basic School in Quantico (1966); (2) seven months as a rifle platoon commander in Vietnam (1966-67); (3) three months as a rifle company commander at Camp Pendleton (1967); (4) five months as a regimental headquarters company (and camp) commander in Vietnam (1968); (5) eight months as a rifle company commander in Vietnam (1968-69); (6) five and a half years as an instructor with the Advanced Infantry Training Company (AITC) at Camp Lejeune (1986-92); and (7) one year as the Staff Noncommissioned Officer in Charge of the 3rd Marine Division Combat Squad Leaders Course (CSLC) on Okinawa (1992-93).

While at AITC, he developed, taught, and refined courses on maneuver warfare, land navigation, fire support coordination, call for fire, adjust fire, close air support, M203 grenade launcher, movement to contact, daylight attack, night attack, infiltration, defense, offensive Military Operations in Urban Terrain (MOUT), defensive MOUT, Nuclear/Biological/Chemical (NBC) defense, and leadership. While at CSLC, he further refined the same periods of instruction and developed others on patrolling.

He has completed all of the correspondence school requirements for the Marine Corps Command and Staff College, Naval War College (1,000-hour curriculum), and Marine Corps Warfighting Skills Program. He is a graduate of the Camp Lejeune Instructional Management Course, the 2nd Marine Division Skill Leaders in Advanced Marksmanship (SLAM) Course, and the East-Coast School of Infantry Platoon Sergeants' Course.

In the 18 years since retirement, John Poole has researched the small-unit tactics of other nations and written eleven other books: (1) *The Last Hundred Yards,* a squad combat study based on the consensus opinions of 1,200 NCOs and casualty statistics of AITC and CSLC field trials; (2) *One More Bridge to Cross*, a treatise on enemy proficiency at short range and how to match it; (3) *Phantom Soldier,* an in-depth look at the highly deceptive Asian style of war; (4) *The Tiger's Way,* the fighting styles of Eastern fire teams and soldiers; (5) *Tactics of the Crescent Moon,* insurgent procedures in Palestine, Chechnya, Afghanistan, and Iraq; (6) *Militant Tricks,* an honest appraisal of the so-far-undefeated *jihadist* method; (7) *Terrorist Trail,* tracing the *jihadists* in Iraq back to their home countries; (8) *Dragon Days,* an unconventional warfare technique manual; (9) *Tequila Junction,* how to fight narco-guerrillas; (10) *Homeland Siege,* confronting the 4GW assault by a foreign power's organized-crime proxies; and (11) *Expeditionary Eagles,* outmaneuvering the Taliban.

As of September 2010, John Poole had conducted multiday training sessions (on 4GW squad tactics) at 40 (mostly Marine) battalions, nine Marine schools, and seven special-operations units from all four U.S. service branches. Since 2000, he has done research in Mainland China (twice), North Korea, Vietnam, Cambodia, Thailand, India (twice), Pakistan (twice), Iran, Lebanon, Turkey, Egypt, Sudan, Tanzania, Venezuela, and Sri Lanka. Over the course of his lifetime, he has visited scores of other nations on all five continents. He tried to visit Lahore in the late Spring of 2011. The Pakistani visa request was not honored.

Between early tours in the Marine Corps (from 1969 to 1971), John Poole worked as a criminal investigator for the Illinois Bureau of Investigation (IBI). After attending the State Police Academy for several months in Springfield, he was assigned to the IBI's Chicago office. There, he worked mostly on general criminal and drug cases.

Name Index